# Zulu Empire Decolonised

## The Epic Story of the Zulu from Pre-Colonial Times to the 21st Century

Foreword by His Majesty King Zwelithini kaBhekuzulu

The moral rights of the author have been asserted.
All rights reserved. No part of this publication may be reproduced, stored in, introduced into a retrieval system, or transmitted, in any form, or by any means (electronic, mechanical, photocopying, recording or otherwise) without the prior written permission of the publisher. Any person who does any unauthorised act in relation to this publication may be liable to criminal prosecution and civil claims for damages.

© Shalo Mbatha 2021

© Photographic copyright holders for the pictures are credited with each caption.

Published by iZigi Publishing
52 Toby Street
Westdene
Johannesburg 2092
South Africa

ISBN 978-0-620-89782-2

Interior layout: Reprographic Designs
Cover and interior crafted with love by the team at: www.myebook.online

# Zulu Empire Decolonised

The Epic Story of the Zulu from Pre-Colonial Times to the 21st Century

### His Majesty King Zwelithini kaBhekuzulu

His Majesty King Zwelithini kaBhekuzulu, *Wena weNdlovu!* You made me realise my purpose in life. How do I begin to thank you for your unwavering trust in me despite the fact that I am a mere commoner from Soweto? It was my absolute pleasure to present this historical account of your subjects, as a continuation of the defence of the Zulu nation by other means, just as my ancestors did in the days of old. You have transitioned into spirit. But I am comforted that you will continue watching over us from another realm. *Bayethe!*

### My son, Loyiso

*My son, my son,* here is an attempt to answer the poignant questions you posed to me about our history in 1998. The account of what happened is complicated and by far not complete. This is the continuation of our conversation with more answers to come. *Homz* my son, you are the first person to donate towards publishing this book. You have made a big sacrifice by going to live in Australia in 2008 so that you could provide extra support for your sister and I. God and our ancestors bless you to eternity. What would my life be without you affirming me? I'm truly blessed and glad to call you my son. We have come a long way and let us keep on talking *mntanami*.

### My daughter, Nandi

*Amantombazana, De Luxe,* your laughter and wicked sense of humour kept me going. I would call you every time I discovered jaw-dropping facts and you once commented, 'aMama, by the time you're done writing, there won't be a need for me to read the book. You describe events in the book so vividly that it feels like a running commentary. You make me wish I lived in the ancient Zulu era'.
Everyone said it couldn't be done, but here we are! Your endless fact-checking left me exhausted, but the efforts were worthwhile. I'm sure you've seen the power of humility, grit, and single-mindedness to accomplish a dream. Thank you for reminding me that this work is eternal.

### My grandson, Zuzu

I started this work long before you were born and I'm glad you came along and made me a living ancestor! I enjoy watching you grow and as promised, I will write a children's version for you. Remember to be proud of your heritage.

Love you always, *your Abuelita.*

# Contents

| | |
|---|---:|
| Acknowledgements | i |
| Foreword | iii |
| Chapter 1 Ancient Origins of the Nguni People | 1 |
| 2 The Zulu Kingdom | 23 |
| 3 The Birth of King Shaka kaSenzangakhona | 38 |
| 4 Emperor King Shaka Creates the Zulu Empire | 59 |
| 5 Imfecane and European Colonisation | 99 |
| 6 Emperor King Dingane kaSenzangakhona | 166 |
| 7 Emperor King Mpande kaSenzangakhona | 200 |
| 8 Emperor King Cetshwayo kaShaka | 225 |
| 9 Emperor King Dinuzulu kaCetshwayo | 279 |
| 10 The Poll Tax Revolt | 306 |
| 11 The African Insurrection | 333 |
| 12 Emperor King Maphumuzana kaDinuzulu | 340 |
| 13 Emperor King Bhekuzulu kaMaphumuzana | 349 |
| 14 Emperor King Zwelithini kaBhekuzulu | 355 |
| The Royal Zulu Lineage | 372 |
| Pre-Shakan Map of Zululand | 374 |
| Epilogue | 376 |
| Selected Bibliography | 377 |
| Glossary | 388 |
| About the Author | 392 |

# ACKNOWLEDGEMENTS

MY PARENTS ALEX AND Nomakhosi Khosi Mbatha you were both a singular pillar of strength in my life. Mawe (mother), you have been in heaven since March 2010. Deti (daddy), you also went to heaven in October 2020 and since you left, it is clear that you both are truly amadlozi amahle (guardian angels) as my life could not be better. May this book be presented - through you - to my forefather, Manyosi kaDlekezele. It would please me greatly to know that amaShandu (ancestors) such as Dikane would pass it on from the youngest to the eldest, until it reached our Creator.

I am eternally indebted to all those many incredible people I met in my quest for answers to questions posed by my son which I could not answer adequately. He wanted to know why we allowed ourselves - the indigenous people - to be subjugated by white colonisers. I wish I could mention each one of you, but it would not be possible in this space, but be rest assured that I keep a bit of each of you in me. However, to the late Dr BV Mthethwa, *Nyambose, Magaga onsibansiba*, I am forever grateful for your belief in me. I'm proud of you for writing the book about the Mthethwa nation, your great people. Once again, thank you for introducing me to the Zulu royal family. To the late Phelelani Thungo, Jijiji your professionalism was admirable. This is just the beginning. *Bhungane*, I'll never forget how you assured me in your soft, calm voice that I would succeed in my attempt to write a book about the Zulu people when we were in the newsroom of *The Star* newspaper.

To the late Reggie Khumalo *Mntungwa*, I have kept my promise, even though you have joined your ancestors. I wish that King Shaka enlists you in one of his elite regiments.

To the members of iMpophoma regiment, you still represent the undying Zulu ethic of yesteryear - respect, honour and purpose. Never change. Cebolenkosi kaMdembulukwane kaXamu Mbatha, Mthiya, gumbi lamagwala, your unwaivering support gave me confidence. Our ancestors, uDikane kaXamu *ongavinjelwa eya esizibeni* are delighted with your help.

His Majesty's Private Secretary, Nhlavuyelanga Sithole, *Jobe kaMatshana*, my ancestors enabled our paths to cross. Thank you for the patience as you tried to untangle my township thought processes. The Royal Laudatory Reciter *inyosi* Buzetsheni Mdletshe kaSombila, *Msindazwe*, you helped me navigate the royal family maze.

I would like to thank the late Senior Prince Reginald Mandlenkosi kaMagangezintaba kaDinuzulu, and say to you *Mageba, wena weMbube*, I am grateful that you read and approved the manuscript before you passed on. You said I should not give up, but continue researching the Zulu nation. I also received the gift you left for me in your last days, which I treasure dearly. I continue to sing the songs you taught me as we sat under the fig trees at your residence *KwaQambushilo*, especially during hard times. Prince Mbonisi, *wena weSilo*, your easy smile made me feel welcome in *KwelikaMthaniya* (the Zulu kingdom) and I felt warmly welcomed part to the royal family.

Queen Thandekile MaNdlovu *okaMpongo* thank you for your kindness and proving the necessity of the monarchy and ensuring its future. I will never forget how petrified I was when I was about to have an audience with the king for the first time. I remember how I unsuccessfully tried to hide my face behind the door. You held my hand and taught me all about the Zulu royal protocol. I miss your mouth-watering meals in your *residence* at Linduzulu Palace, as well as your warmth and everything royal about you. Queen Mother *Magwabini*, I'm blessed to have met you as the connection to the immediate past. I pray you still attend to your fields on Wednesdays without hurting your knees too much, and I won't forget how we laughed at life's mundane matters.

His Majesty King Zwelithini, *Wena wendlovu!* You made me realise my purpose in life. How do I begin to thank you for your unwavering support in me despite the fact that I am a mere commoner from Soweto?

It is my pleasure to present this historical account as a continuation of the defence of the Zulu nation by other means, just as my ancestors did in the days of old. *Bayethe!*

# FOREWORD

WRITING HISTORY IS A mammoth task. Writing a book about a people is even more complex. Many authors have written books about the Zulu people and some are doing so and hopefully some will continue doing so.

Shalo Mbatha has thrown in a gauntlet on the Zulu royal history and the Zulu people. She has taken it upon herself to reopen the dialogue on several key events to mention but one, the Battle of iNcome (Blood River). What happened there? What has hitherto been regarded as unquestionable and unshakeable historical fact has not only been challenged but also turned upside down. In doing so, she has not invented new facts but points to existing material. One would find it hard to accuse her of bias in placing material which has been there for decades in the public arena. Her style, her analytical mind and the structure of her work makes it attractive reading.

One must commend Mbatha for the work well done. No doubt, no history book is perfect. However, a work of this nature by a Zulu person has long been overdue. I say this because for many years written Zulu history has been narrated mainly by outsiders. This does not in any way suggest that the available work is not credible. All I say is that the Zulu voice has been missing in the narration of Zulu history. Mbatha has the advantage not only of speaking the language being a Zulu herself but also of understanding the unarticulated nuances and some hidden messages from those she has interviewed.

Zulu people are great storytellers, but their messages were lost through translation. Non-speakers of the language are disadvantaged in the process of their research. Mbatha has, in my opinion, benefitted from direct conversation with her sources. This would throw some light on certain events. The dialogue has now started. Younger Zulu generations and others who have interest in this subject are afforded an opportunity to participate in this ongoing conversation. Who are these people - amaZulu? Where do they come from and where are they going? In conclusion, I should say, to a great extent, history has been told through a male voice. Women have been spectators. To hear and read a female voice is also refreshing. The book could not have come at a better time. I am sure the readers will find it stimulating and worth the wait.

*Mthiya! Shandu kaNdaba,*
*Uyibekile induku ebandla.*
*Halala!*

**His Majesty King Zwelithini kaBhekuzulu**

# 1

# Ancient Origins of the Nguni People

INDIGENOUS PEOPLE OF SOUTHERN AFRICA have occupied this territory from time immemorial. The Nguni believed in one God who had two fertile wives. In their cosmology, living and non-living things were created by a single entity (God) known as *uNkulunkulu* (the greatest one) or *uMvelingqangi* (the one who lived first). God then sent the founders of all nations to Earth through the reeds in freshwater ponds. This group was called *abomdabu* (original people who came into the world through the reeds). Because of how brave they were, Africans appeared on Earth first and the other nations followed. When it came to the Nguni people, God made some Nguni ancestors to 'appear' in the ponds bordered by the White iMfolozi River in the south, the uMhlathuze River in the north, the eThaleni Mountain east of uMkhumbane River, and the area west of the Buffalo River on Africa's south-eastern seaboard. This area is made up of gentle valleys, deep gorges, spectacular cliffs, and meandering rivers. Looking to the west, one sees the majestic *uKhahlamba* (Drakensberg) mountain range, which undulates gently down into valleys and cascades down to the eastern seaboard to meet Southern Africa's warm seas.

Another group arrived in baskets from the cosmos and they were referred to as (those who came down in a grain basket). These two groups met, intermarried, and produced many families who grew and eventually became kingdoms. These people lived near each other and spoke languages that were mutually intelligible except for a variation in intonation and dialects such as isiZulu, isiXhosa, and isiSwati. The Nguni were further divided into large clusters known as amaLala, amaNtungwa, amaMbo, amaTekela, amaDebe, amaNgwane, abaThembu, amaMpondo, amaXhosa, amaSwati, and many others. It is estimated that around the 15th century, the Nguni people totalled a few million people scattered from the Indian Ocean on the eastern seaboard up to the Drakensberg mountain range in the north-west, and as far down as the tip of South Africa. Of all the groups in southern Africa, the Nguni kingdoms produced exceptional leaders, statesmen and stateswomen, military strategists, diplomats, philosophers and visionaries. A few of them stand out, such as King Zwide of the Ndwandwe kingdom, King Dingiswayo of the Mthethwa kingdom, King Matiwane of amaNgwane kingdom, King Macingwane of the Mchunu kingdom, King Mthimkhulu of the amaHlubi kingdom, King Ngoza kaMkhuphukeli of the Mthembu kingdom, King Phakathwayo of the Qwabe kingdom and King Mzilikazi of the Khumalo kingdom who later founded the amaNdebele nation in today's Zimbabwe.

King Soshangane kaZikode kaGasa kaManukuza of the junior Ndwandwe kingdom founded the kingdom of the Tsongas who are scattered in the northern part of South Africa, southern Zimbabwe, and southern Mozambique. King Zwangendaba kaZiguda Jele of the once-tiny Gumbi kingdom established over 16 kingdoms in central Africa as far as Malawi, Zambia, Kenya and Tanzania. King Sobhuza Somhlolo founded the Swazi kingdom. But the most extraordinary leader of all is King Shaka of the Zulu kingdom who founded the mighty Zulu empire. The lands of the Nguni kingdoms have long meandering rivers that rage and break their banks during the heavy summer rains, which fall between September and February. The rivers, together with mountains and hills create borders between valleys called *izigodi*, which have been a source of many conflicts. This is where one finds one of the world's most spectacular waterfalls, the *uThukela* (Tugela) Falls; the highest in Africa and the second highest in the world with a plunge of almost 950 metres.

The climate is pleasant, mild, and tropical along the coastal parts, but nippy in the highlands during winter. The land is well watered, with many mighty rivers such as uPhongolo, which is the most northerly river in the land of the Zulu, and the White iMfolozi, Black iMfolozi, Buffalo, uThukela, uMzimvubu, Mooi, uMzimkhulu, uMhlathuze, iNonoti, uMdlothi, uMkhomazi, uMthamvuna, uMthwalume and *iNcome* (Blood River) crisscrossing the land. The most historic and important river in the psyche of the Zulu, is uThukela. It is the largest and the longest river in the kingdom, originating from the highlands of the Drakensberg *(uKhahlamba)* mountain range in Mount-Aux-Sources and plunges through the uThukela Falls. UThukela meanders for 520 kilometres through the KwaZulu-Natal Midlands with a catchment area of slightly more than 29 000 square kilometres before flowing gently into the Indian Ocean.

There are also breathtaking and historical valleys at Ophathe, Valley of a Thousand Hills *(KwaDedangendlale)*, eBabanango, Black iMfolozi and uMhlathuze, and spectacular mountains, uKhahlamba, Ophisweni, eMahlabathini, iNhlazatshe, iZihlalo, oNgoye and oNdini areas. The mysterious and dark iNgome, iDlinza, iDukuduku, and iNkandla forests - a source of many idioms and myths - teems with wildlife including bucks, buffaloes, cheetahs, crocodiles, elephants, hippopotamuses, hyenas, leopards, lions, porcupines, wild dogs, wild pigs, zebras, and a large variety of bird species. The cosmos was used to tell time. The appearance of the planet Jupiter *(iNqonqoli, iNdonsa, iNdonsakusa or iNdonsabusuku)* meant it was around three o'clock in the morning and the star called *iNtshola* or *iQhubankomo*.

The star that appears at the end of autumn is named *iSandulela* and *iNkwenkwezi* and is seen in the southeast early in the mornings in July. The planet Mars is called *iNdonsa* and Orion's Belt is called *iMpambano*. The string of stars that are visible to the right side of the Orion's Belt during the southern summer is called *oNdwenjana* or *uNdwendweni*. The Milky Way is called *uMthala* and the Pleiades are called *isiLimela*. An example of one of the celestial stars that played a significant role in the life of the Zulu people was Aldebarana *(uCwazibe)* and the planet Saturn, which was referred to as *(inkayezi enkulu kakhulu)*. The Southern Cross was refered to as *(izinkanyezi eziyisiphambano ezulwini)*.

The planting season was always filled with high drama because before modernity, the elderly - especially women - in each homestead were responsible for keeping track of the months. The most reliable phenomenon that heralded the sowing season was the sudden and spectacular blossoming of the *umdukwa* or *umdubu* (bushwillow) trees around the oNgoye Mountains and Nkandla Forest. The low-lying areas used *inhliziyonkulu* (wild pear) trees to determine the time to sow. There was a general understanding in the Zulu culture that the year could be either early or late. For instance, when the trees flowered late or when the first rains delayed, this was an indication of the lateness of the year and vice versa. Perhaps it was the leap-year phenomenon. This also assisted in keeping track of the seasons as well as the appearance of certain stars and planets such as Venus. Unlike the current 12-month calendar year, the Zulu observed a 13-month calendar year. The number of days in each month depended on the moon. The names of the months describe what was expected to happen during that month. However, the months do not fit neatly with the Gregorian calendar.

The first rains - called *imbozisamahlanga* (time to till the earth) - signified the beginning of the year. August is the first month and is called *uNcwaba*, which means lush. September is *uMandulo*, which means that people were to begin to *ukwendulelisa* (plough) their crops. October is *uMfumfu* (sprout) when most plants begin to bloom and the crops sprout. November is *uLwezi* as frogs and some small insects and grasshoppers *(ulwezi)* make the loudest mating calls.

December is *uZibandlela* (covered path) when the grass is thickest, and footpaths are covered by the overgrowth. January is *uMasingana* because when the sun is in the centre of the sky, people shade their eyes to see in the distance if their plants have ripened in the fields. This was the time women looked under rocks for early seeds and made special dishes. February is called *uNhlolanja*, a time when dogs are notorious for mating everywhere when the bitches are in heat. March is called *uNdasa* (abundance) when everyone enjoys fresh crops. The end of March is called *uNgululaziboya* (removal of corn silk from maize cobs). April is *uMbasa* (making of fires) because fires are kindled earlier in the evening due to the slight chill in the air.

May is *uNhlaba* (aloe vera - the verb *hlaba* means 'something that pierces') named after the aloe because the plant blooms in May. The significance is that May's winds are colder and figuratively 'cut' through the bones. June is *uNhlangulana* (shake off dust) because the trees begin to lose their leaves. Mid-June is called *uNtulini omncane* (mild dusty winds) because it is the prelude to the ferocious, chilly winter winds. July is called *uNtulikazi* because the winds are merciless and cover everything in fine dust. The following approximately four weeks are the 13th month and because nature and the weather are not clearly defined and somewhat vague, it is called *iNdida* (confusion). The Zulu identified five seaons; spring came after the full moon had appeared thirty times in the sky. It was called *intwasahlobo*, meaning the beginning of summer and late summer called *ihlobo* (summer). Autumn is called *inkwindla* and winter *ubusika*. It rains regularly from mid-September and crop planting is completed by the end of October.

The depth of the downpour was measured by digging into the soil either at the entrance of the household or at the tilled fields, which determined the exact time to plough. Weeding is done in November and December, while harvesting begins in February and lasts up until April. The animals were allowed to forage on what was left over in the fields. During the cold months - June and July - war was waged because wounds healed quickly, and the unforgiving harsh African sun was weak. These months were also the months for hunting game. Festivities were ideal at this time of year because food, especially meat, lasts longer in the cooler weather. This is when most weddings and traditional ceremonies were held, such as the coming-of-age ceremony *(umemulo)*, the symbolic ritual of bringing the spirits of the dead back home *(ukubuyisa)* and the cleansing ceremony after bereavement *(ihlambo)*. The chilly months made it possible to hold marathon singing, dancing, and stick-fighting competitions as well as youth matchmaking festivals *(ijadu)*. The most common *ijadu* song was:

| | |
|---|---|
| *Oh, hha, oh, akankomo* | *Oh, ha, oh, he has many cattle* |
| *Izibindindi ziyanikwana* | *that he gives away* |
| *Wena kamalume* | *you, my maternal uncle* |
| *Ngiyawuthatha esami ngomuso* | *I shall take mine tomorrow* |
| *Ngisho ngalokhuya* | *I am talking about those over there* |
| *Ongasakwaziyo* | *which you no longer remember* |
| *Usho ngalokhuya* | *you are referring to others* |
| *Kanti wena okwaziyo* | *what is it that you know* |
| *Ongasakwaziyo* | *that you no longer remember* |
| *Kanti wena okwaziyo* | *what is it that you know* |
| *Ongasakwaziyo* | *that you no longer remember* |

Whenever there was drought, people would plant food for wild animals and plead for divine intervention from God and the *uNomkhubulwane* ceremony would follow. This sacred ceremony was conducted high up on the mountain and rain would surely come, even before the people reached their home. The annual *umkhosi wokweshwama* (first fruits festival) was an agricultural ceremony that took place around December and January at the capital presided over by the king. Prior to this festival, the king would complete a series of cleansing rituals carried out by foreign traditional doctors from the north known as *amaHlengwa*. This was the time when new laws were promulgated, and the old ones were abrogated or repealed. Importantly, no executions took place during this period.

The festival - which coincided with the sitting of the national assembly - required that all adult males and nubile females attend. The army held spectacular dress parades in full military regalia. This was the only time the chain of command was relaxed, where soldiers and subjects alike were allowed to interact freely with senior officers and the king. They were allowed to cross-question the king with impunity and he was bound to reply. Some of his acts were denounced, thereby obliging him to defend and explain his intentions. The roll call of heroes and warriors was made public and they were issued with medals some made out of gold, brass, or copper. Usually, these were armbands (*izigxotha*) and a necklace made out of the intricate *umyezane* (willow tree) bark blocks strung on a rawhide lace - symbolising a snake's vertebrae. Each block represented the enemy killed in battle. After all the formalities were completed, it was a time for fun and entertainment, a fitting festive season that included dance and singing competitions from the different regions. This was a favourite festival that honoured the king:

| | |
|---|---|
| *Wamloyisa* | *you vilified him* |
| *Obani bayamzonda* | *where are those people who hate him* |
| *Vuma, vuma ngoba uyinkosi* | *admit it, admit it because he is the king* |

The royal wives and *umdlunkulu* were not allowed to sing with everyone hence they had their own first fruit festival song:

| | |
|---|---|
| *Weyiswa, wo, wo, wo* | you were treated badly wo, wo, wo |
| *Izizwe, wena nkosi* | by other nations, dear king |
| *Bakuncinshile* | they were mean to you |
| *Lala phansi* | lie down |
| *Inkube yendlala yimbi* | hunger from famine is very bad indeed |

Different areas within kingdoms were demarcated by a valley, a stream, a river, or even a dry riverbed and were governed by the *induna* (king's representative). Bigger rivers, valleys, and mountains demarcated regions or districts. It was also a sense of great pride to identify oneself with the river from which they drank. The common settlement pattern was that of dispersed households rather than villages. The houses were built in a circular pattern. An ordinary family lived in traditional beehive grass huts called *iqhugwane*. Families that lived within the same valley or sourced water from the same river did not generally intermarry because they regarded each other as family, even though they were not related. The division of labour was clear; the men hunted and collected the sticks and poles and built the grass hut structure while the women thatched and bound huts using skilfully braided split reeds and grass. In the general structure of a traditional grass hut was a central trunk that acted as the main support pillar of the hut. The doorways were made low so those that entered as well as potential foes were forced to stoop down or go on their knees before entering. Directly opposite the door was often a windbreaker wall.

**The Zulu Dwelling**

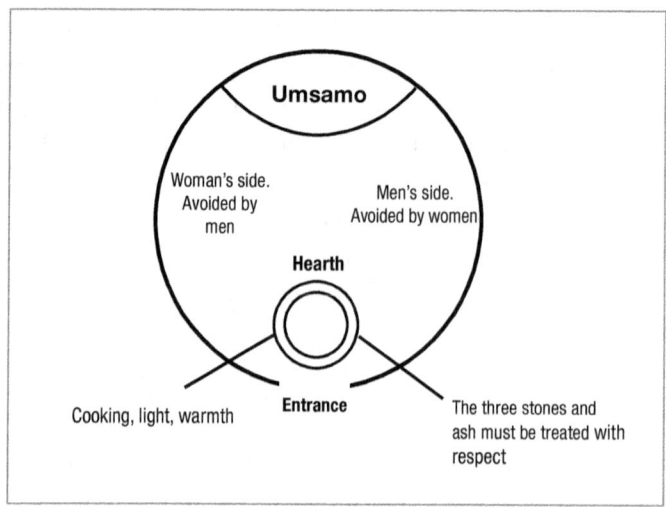

*Inside a typical Zulu hut. (Killie Campbell Africana Library)*

Ancient Origins of the Nguni People

*A typical beehive Zulu hut (iqhugwane) with a windbreaker wall. (Killie Campbell Africana Library)*

*Front row (left). A meat tray with a dishing spoon; a traditional beer sieve; headrest carved from a single block of wood; a grinding stone made out of granite. Second row (left). Grass woven baskets; clay pots; a covered watertight milk basket woven from palm; a war shield between throwing spears. (Killie Campbell Africana Library)*

Each homestead was surrounded by a perimeter comprising of either wood and prickly pears, or mimosa bushes, or stones depending, on the kingdom's custom. Each homestead had in the centre - or sometimes on the side - a cattle enclosure called *isibaya*. For the family living in the household, this was the heartbeat of the homestead. All the important religious and spiritual activities were held in that space. The social unit was self-sufficient and the household was centred on patrilineage but it also included relatives through a variety of kinship ties. The indigent, orphans, widows and the disabled were accepted and rewarded for their services and they usually attached themselves to a specific homestead. Like many ancient peoples, seasonal migration was a common feature of their lives. Otherwise, the homestead was a source of learning, worship, education, training, culture, rituals, and traditions, as well as a hospice and hospital. The man was the head of the homestead and had his own hut. His wives had their own huts positioned around their husband's and would take turns on different nights to visit him for overnight stays.

The Zulus believe in strict order and protocol. The senior wife's title was *uNdlunkulu* (same title used by queens) and her hut was on the right; the second wife occupied the hut on the left-hand side and her title was *iKhohlo*. The third wife's hut was on the right and her title was *iQadi*. The Zulu sense of identity is expressed by introducing oneself with the *igama* or *ibizo* (first name) followed by *isibongo* (surname). The *isibongo* could be the first name of one's father or any of their paternal ancestors. They always indicated whom their father was by adding 'ka' to the father's name, followed by their ancestor's name or *isithakazelo* (family praise names). For example, a female would identify herself as *nginguNonhlanhla kaMuziwakhe Myandu* (I am Nonhlanhla, daughter of Muziwakhe of the Myandu kingdom). This form of identification is critical among the Zulu because they are forever trying to find a sense of rapport or commonality with the next person. Some of the formidable bigger kingdoms had many smaller kingdoms under their dominion and had to acknowledge the sovereignty under which they lived. For instance, a male would identify himself as *nginguDlokwakhe kaBhekimpi wasemaMbatheni esigodini saseMakhanyakude phansi kwenkosi uSakhabesuka Mkhwanazi, ngiphuza uMkhuze phansi kwezintaba zoBombo* (I am Dlokwakhe, the son of Bhekimpi of the Mbatha kingdom, living in the valley of Mkhanyakude under King Sakhabesuka of the Mkhwanazi kingdom. I drink waters of uMkhuze River under the uBombo Mountains). Furthermore, children were often named after an occurrence, a dead relative, or what the parents wanted the child to become.

The traditional Zulu diet consisted of seasonal produce such as *amadumbe* (yams), *izindlubu* (black-eyed beans), pumpkin, maize, sweet potatoes, and honey.

Sorghum, grain, and millet were all called *amabele*. Beef and venison were only eaten on special occasions, whereas chicken and goat meat provided the staple protein diet. Pork was shunned. Traditionally, Zulu people ate two heavy meals a day. The first at about 11 o'clock in the morning when the cows came home to be milked, and the last meal was just before sunset with the whole family present. Eating after dark was rare. The milk left outside to curdle is called *amasi* and stored in special watertight calabashes made from dried-out pumpkin shell called *igula*. The strained *umlaza* (whey) made for a refreshing drink. Grain for everyday use was stored in baskets above ground. Granaries stored surplus grain in pits dug deep in the cattle enclosures. These pits were lined with clay that was fired to give it a brick-hard inner shell. The grain lasted for years and the pit opening was sealed with a large flat stone that was placed level with the ground of the cattle enclosure. A 15 centimetre-wide (or bigger) stone was placed on top to keep the pit tightly sealed because granaries collected dangerous levels of carbon monoxide. Special care had to be taken when opening them after heavy rains or when they were not completely full.

Fuel for torches was composed of a mixture of fat and cow dung, which provided outside light at night and the flame would not extinguish, even when it rained. Household lighting was provided by candle-like wax called *ubhaqa* and *isiphefu* made from cow dung mixed with sesame oil and pleasant fragrances. Every household had to maintain a perpetual flame or a smouldering fire on the hearth in the kitchen called *ixhiba*. Exceptions were made during the mourning period of a close family member or when mourning for royalty. Cooking fires in every household had to burn constantly, however small and were not to be started from scratch daily. Fires were kindled to life from scratch with a boring stick made of a hard stick, about 60 centimetres long, which was inserted into a small hole cut into a soft piece of wood measuring about ten by five by two centimetres. The hard wood was rapidly rubbed between the hands and the resulting friction made the soft wood glow; this would ignite the dry moss. Someone blowing on it helped the whole process along. The uqunqu (soft yet brittle) grass was the most ideal material to start a household fire.

Growing up in bygone days was a time of joyous wonder and bewilderment for the young ones. Their years were calculated by counting how many summers they had lived through, and actual birthdays were irrelevant. For instance, one would describe a particular phenomenon such as saying that they were born 'at the time chickens used to wear trousers or when it snowed'. Every stage of their growing lives was honoured with a ceremony. The first one, *ukukhunga* took place when the father gave the child a name at infancy, and also a gift of a particular type of beads.

The child was given a number of names throughout his or her lifetime. The first name was the mother's pet name. The father would then give the official name during the ceremony. Relatives, neighbours, and friends also gave names. Additional names were given when the child underwent the various rites of passage. Ceremonies were performed in groups, such as the second stage *ukuqhambusa* (ear piercing) ceremony, which signified that they now had a certain level of responsibility. The third stage for girls was when she reached puberty and the ceremony was called *ukujutshwa*. This allowed a girl to start having relationships with boys through the permission of an older girl *(iqhikiza)* who mentored younger girls; the fourth stage *umemulo* (coming of age) ceremony followed. The fifth stage was *ukukhehla* (readiness to become a wife). The final female rite of passage ceremony was called *ukukhwabula* which was a celebration upon reaching menopause. This ceremony made suitable women qualify to sit in the king's council, because according to King Shaka, they were no longer influenced by the fluctuations of unreliable hormonal emotions. For boys, the third stage began at about the age of seven years, which was when they began to herd cattle and their peers would give them names. The fourth stage was when boys reached puberty.

Elderly women who were past menopause, gave them lessons about the female anatomy and the importance of sexually satisfying a woman. This was a necessary skill because pleasing a string of future wives was vital in a society where polygamy brought prestige to a man. Upon entering a regiment, which was the fifth stage when they are around 15 years old, additional names followed. This was based on the boy's successes or failures on the romantic front and other masculine exploits. This name was called *igama lobunsizwa*. Both girls and boys played games such as *ingqathu* (skipping rope) and hide-and-seek under open skies after completing small chores. Girls were taught child rearing, weaving, cooking, looking after a home, the functioning of the male psyche and physique, and how to compete and survive in a polygamous marriage. Boys were taught about outdoor life and how to trap birds. They learnt about insects, plants and medicines, weather patterns, the cosmos, animal husbandry, general principles of warfare, and stick fighting, which was regarded as character building. One's temperament was observed as the fight is done with two sticks. The left held was in the middle to parry and the right held near its end to strike for self-defence, alertness, and self control. If you lost your temper and struck wildly, others would thrash you thoroughly.

When girls menstruated, they used sanitary pads made out of grass moulded into a boat-like shape and held together on either side of the hips. Only married women were allowed to use *isivatho* (tampons) made out of soft aromatic herbs called *ijoye* (soda apple tree) and from *umsuzwane* (lemon bush tree). During menstruation, women were expected to use sweet-smelling herbal fragrances mixed with hippopotamus fat as perfume. The girls were allowed to have up to four lovers at a time. They, however, were only allowed to enjoy *ukusoma* (non-penetrative sex) with one boy per month to avoid both pregnancy and confusion over the identity of a child's father in the case of a pregnancy. Once a girl had decided which man she wanted to marry, she would give him her most intimate possession - *ucu* (a string of white enthronement beads) that had been tied around her waist since childhood or make one for him as a sign of her eternal love. *Ucu* served the purpose of reminding the girl that *intombi iqoma kanye* (a girl was meant to remain married to the man she had given *ucu* to for life). Sadly, today *ucu* is erroneously referred to as a Zulu love letter. However, girls could only indulge in non-penetrative sex after they were given permission to do so by their *iqhikiza*. Even then, the permission was granted to girls that showed maturity that they would be able to control themselves in the heat of passion, and not allow the boy to go all the way.

Non-penetrative sex was one of the ways young people were taught iron-fist discipline, particularly during intimacy. Furthermore, for absolute enjoyment, the girl had to lie down on her right side throughout. Boys were told to respect and revere the girl's hymen because it was considered the gateway to heaven. To ensure that girls remained virgins before marriage, a designated woman inspected girls by inserting a small reed into the vagina to check if the hymen was intact. If the girl was a virgin, the reed was expected to bounce. If it did not, it brought great shame and disgrace not only to the girl but also to her family and her peers *(ontanga yakhe)* because they had collective responsibility over each other's behaviour. On the occasion the girl fell pregnant, many families would have preferred to conceal the scandal by quickly marrying the girl off. If that was not possible, the girl was taken to live with faraway relatives or married off to a much older man.

Young girls and teenagers also had an option of being flowers of the nation *(umdlunkulu)* and live in one of the king's palaces if they so wished. This brought prestige and prominence to the girl's family. They were objects of beauty to be admired by all, especially visiting dignitaries. Once of age, they were either married off to other kingdoms to avert future hostilities or sent to other kingdoms as ambassadors. Invariably, they would find a husband at the host nation. Sometimes the king would allow them to leave the palace and marry a man of their choice, but only after consulting their families. The king could also marry them or have children with them without making them his wives. If they bore children, they were also referred to as prince or princess, but they could never rule. An *umdlunkulu's* main purpose was to provide beauty, grace and femininity in a palace. Their dwelling area within *isigodlo* (the palace) was considered sacred. Any man caught lurking around or trespassing this part of the palace was put to death immediately.

Younger boys from wealthy families and the aristocracy lived at the king's palaces and looked after the royal herd. The older boys were encouraged to have as many lovers as possible as a sign of virility and to be considered a successful *isoka* (ladies' man). They travelled far and wide with only one thing in mind, to practice and improve their art of *ukweshela* (charm a female). The truth of the matter though, charming as they were, most of the time both the boys and girls had no real intention of having a long-term love affair with the other. This act was fulfilling the Zulu saying that *intombi ayidlulwa ngendlela* (you have to charm every girl you come across because ignoring her was an insult). This was regarded as a training ground to diffuse future polygamous tensions. Couples were matched based on particular skills needed in their respective kingdoms and all marriages were out of community of property. The husband had to provide his wife with a piece of land to grow food for herself and her children and breed her own livestock.

Wedding ceremonies were elaborate affairs with many stages that culminated with the bride and groom dancing together in public. This particular ritual marked the actual wedding day. The day before the wedding day, the female bridal party, comprised of her female peers arrived at the future groom's home after sunset and the bride hid among her companions. She would only show herself when she began to sing her family hymn *(ihubo)* and danced a slow sensual rhythmic hypnotic dance *(ukuqhobosha)*. She would slowly bend her knees while going down simultaneously moving her hips side to side. Her friends and the rest of the people would join her and sing in a low, impressive chant inviting her ancestors to her matrimonial proceedings. Her veil was strings of twisted fig leaves that hung down from her head to her chin, black finch plumes were stuck on her head and white cow tails were tied around her legs and arms. She carried a small ceremonial spear *(isinqidi)* pointed upwards as a sign of being a virgin. She arrived with a variety of personal property such as pots, mats, cooking utensils, hoes and presents for a number of her in-laws.

Most importantly, the bride came with one or more of *izinkomo zokwendisa* (cattle that were gifts for the bridegroom's cattle enclosure). During the wedding ceremony the cattle enclosure's gate was barred and could only be entered after the female bridal party had thrown a cooked piece of meat over it as an entrance fee. Thereafter, the father-in-law gave the female bridal party a goat for breakfast the following morning. Wedding procedures varied slightly from area to area but in essence the wedding process starts with *ukulobola* (the formalisation of marriage by presenting gifts such as cattle, goods or other property from the groom's family to the bride's family or guardian). The gifts given to the woman's family are called *ilobolo*. Similarly, the man's family received gifts from the bride's family called *umabo*, which usually occurs on the day after the wedding. From time immemorial the *ilobolo*, was accepted, regardless of the number of cattle or goats or whatever gift the bridegroom deemed fit - it was not set. The British, however, obligated that *ilobolo* could only be cattle, and set the minimum number of cattle at 15.

This led to the complicated and often-painful process where the male relatives of the bridegroom *(abakhongi)* were expected to negotiate with the future in-laws about the number of cattle the bride's family had to be given. The purpose of the negotiation was to accommodate the groom's family because not all families could afford the number of cattle requested by the bride's family. In some cases, wedding ceremonies were completed posthumously, where a close relative on the side of the deceased would stand in place of the late partner on the wedding day. This type of marriage however, is not to be consummated. It was, however, not expected that the *ilobolo* process would be completed during the initial negotiation stage. The rest of the wedding stages continued and the logic was to leave room for regular communication between the two families. For instance, years later, the bride's family would remind the in-laws about outstanding *ilobolo* cattle. This was also a way of enquiring about how the marriage was progressing. If the whole process was completed, the in-laws would be suspicious and think that the groom wanted to conclude the process in its entirety so that he didn't have to see his in-laws ever again. Hence, the saying: *"umfazi akaqedwa"* (the marriage process is never completed).

Divorce as it exists today was unheard of. If the marriage was considered irreparable, the woman could move back home provided her *ilobolo* would be returned to the bridegroom. Both parties were then free to remarry. But if there were no more cattle, she had to continue living at her husband's homestead. If there were any children, she would raise them and continue behaving like a wife without having to sleep with her husband. Furthermore, a married woman was allowed to leave her husband to marry another without acrimony by simply returning her husband's *ilobolo* cattle. If there were children, each child would be compensated for by the new husband in the form of cattle. This was known as *(ukukhipha umfazi endodeni yakhe)*.

In addition, post-menopausal women were allowed not to share a bed with their husband. They could return to their homes to grow old among their own people.

This act is not interpreted as divorce but as retiring from marriage. Hence, when the wife or wives grew older, they were in the forefront of acquiring younger wives for their husband as they prepared to retire from their married life and its nocturnal demands. More often than not, being the only wife was a foreign concept and today's idea of cheating was interpreted differently. The wife was allowed to have a lover, so long as she kept it secret, hence the word *ishende* (a married woman's secret lover). But if it was found out, her husband was blamed because she would not have it in her to 'cheat' if her husband satisfied her sexually. So, in essence, it was the husband's fault that she went astray. Even though a bride fully integrated into her new family, there were strict etiquette she observed to maintain her special status as the one who was going to procreate and continue the family bloodline. Some of the attributes that enhanced her unique status was to switch to a special language called *ukuhlonipha* (to respect) as a sign of humility and feminity.

If after a year passed, she was still not expecting a baby, her female in-laws would conspire with her to find someone else to make her pregnant. They did this to protect the husband's fragile ego, hence the Zulu saying that the mother is the only one who knows the identity of a child. For instance, when a baby cries a lot for no apparent reason, the mother calms the baby by loudly invoking the child's praise name linked to its father. But in the event that the child did not belong to the husband, the mother was encouraged to go to a private place to calm the baby down. The truth is that it was a code for her to invoke the 'real' ancestors of the child. The real ancestors would invariably calm the baby down.

Once a woman has given birth and the placenta had been removed and the baby washed, an old woman would make tiny incisions on the baby's body and apply powdered medicines into the incisions Then be exposed to the smoke made from whiskers of a leopard, a meteorite, the skin of a salamander, claws of lion etc. These are to make the child have similar qualities of the animals. But the meteorite powder was the most important ingredient which had to finely ground. It is was believed that it made the child smart, brave and courageous. Furthermore, when the baby was between eight and ten months old, it was put inside a hole waist-deep, between the huts when it was raining or under a tree that has been struck by lightning for a few minutes. This was to to make it one with nature and not to fear the rain.

As a sign of maturity, a man wore *isicoco* (a maturity head ring) that also distinguished a married man from a bachelor. It was worn with pride and as a badge of honour and dignity in society. It was made out of a plastic-like fungoid growth obtained from trees. The body of the ring was about 50-centimetres in length and cylindrical in shape. Its dimensions were about 12-centimetres in diameter when fitted end to end around the crown of the head. It was fixed around the head while the plastic was still malleable. After a short period of time, it would harden and shine when polished. Except for children, everyone worked every day because there was no concept of weekends. The only days off were days of heavy rain, death, royal ceremonies and traditional functions. Women did all the continuous, unending tasks such as cleaning, sweeping the yard, looking after infants and children, and cutting the grass for weaving into mats. They also made kitchen utensils, blankets, sleeping and sitting mats, and rugs from animal hides. They thatched huts, cooked, made feeding bottles for infants or the ill and the old. This was done by attaching a piece of soft leather to create a teat on the tip of a kids horn. Women worked in the fields, gathered firewood and collected water from the ponds, rivers or wells every day of their lives.

They were able to accumulate their own wealth, invest, barter and traded without interference of their husband or in-laws. Some women became extremely wealthy, like Nozidiya's white cattle called *inyonikayiphumuli* are still the backbone of the royal herd. The female dress code was determined by age and status. All toddlers walked around naked and young girls wore a few beads. Teenage girls and unmarried women wore slightly more beads to cover their private parts called *isigege*, but their buttocks remained bare and they walked around bare-breasted. Engaged women wore soft knee-length leather skirts made out of cattle or goat hide called *isidwaba*. The hide would come from their fathers' herd. Beads worn by the women depicted their stage in life and social status but not age because it was considered irrelevant. The colours of the beads that adorned their skirts were coded to show whether they were married, engaged or single. If they were single, their decoration would show that they were available to become a wife or that they were single but not yet ready to become a wife. *Isidwaba* is tied around the waist with a leather string called *umchilo* which is difficult and complicated to tie and undo. Hence, the Zulu saying '*insakavukela umchilo wesidwaba*' meaning that an issue is extremely tricky and complex.

They also had different types of hairstyles that depicted their status and stage in life. It was compulsory for engaged and married women to wear a headdress decorated with ornaments and intricate beadwork and a variety of colours called *isicholo*. Each kingdom was at liberty to design a style suitable to them. Some wore it at an angle, others wore it straight up, some were short or small and some were huge and colourful. These head-dresses were worn only after the *umkhehlo* ceremony as an indication that the woman was available to become a wife or was already engaged.

*A teenager carrying a beer calabash with a small stick inside to stop it from spilling over. (Killie Campbell Africana Library)*

*Dancing girls during a ceremony. (Killie Campbell Africana Library)*

## Ancient Origins of the Nguni People

*A married woman seated in front of a calabash serving traditional beer. (Barbara Tyrell).*

*A recently married woman (umalokazana) bending slightly forward as a sign of respect. She is wearing a black leather skirt (isidwaba); her headgear (isicholo) is decorated with beads. (Barbara Tyrell)*

*MaCebekhulu Mbatha is one of the wives of Foko, who is one of my grandfather's younger brothers. She proudly danglies her earlobes without iziqhaza taken in Eshayumoya, Kwahlazakazi in Nquthu on Christmas Day 2012. (Shalo Mbatha)*

*Engaged women covering their breasts with isibhodiya. (Killie Campbell Africana Library)*

*A young couple in their daily wear. She is wearing isigege and he is wearing izinjobo. (Killie Campbell Africana Library)*

Men erected huts, hunted, built and carved bigger household items such as headrests, small stools, bowls, spoons, spears and weapons of war. They built livestock pens, looked after the cattle and provided safety for the community. Toddlers and young boys also walked about naked and when they became teenagers, they wore a small strip of leather called *izinjobo* that left their buttocks bare. Grown men wore two pieces of leather aprons called *ibheshu*, one piece covered the front and the other covered their buttocks and was tied around the waist. Under it they put *umncedo* or *umcwado*, a canoe shaped-like contraption that was made to fit neatly around their genitalia. Its main purpose was modesty, in order to arrest an inappropriate erection at the sight of an attractive adult female. If the head of the family died the heir, usually the firstborn son, inherited his estate. As the heir, he also had to honour all the debts of the deceased, which led to all sorts of awkward situations.

Both genders could be involved in bartering and trading of various items that were made specifically for sale such as gourds, spears, hoes, shields, *izinhlendla* (harpoons) and sleeping mats. The accounting system and trade included the concept of *amasonda* (a bonus). It was the men's duty to start household fires from scratch, and, it was the women's duty to ensure that the fire does not burn out. The hearth near the centre of the hut was revered because when the congregated, they would sit according to their age around it with the men on the right-hand side and the women across on the left-hand side; when entering the hut. The man of the household would sit nearest to the door and the first wife would sit nearest to the door on the other side. Stocktaking of the royal herd took place every day and the cattle were divided according to the colour of their hides and the shapes of their horns. Having many cattle signified wealth. Everyone was allowed to amass as many cattle without fear of appropriation by the king. However, they were expected to donate to the imperial herd. This meant that they were indirectly donating to the community.

During national ceremonies or during times of food shortage or drought the imperial herd was slaughtered to feed all subjects commoner and nobleman alike. Inherited cattle were more valuable than those newly acquired, because the inherited cattle connected the past with the present. Some cattle were kept with different families as insurance, in the case of an outbreak of some cattle disease like rinderpest; and it was also done to assist poorer families, called *ukusisa*. In the event of a death of a visiting or 'stray' cow, the owner had to be shown its hide to prove that it had died of natural causes. Kings of bigger kingdoms, on average, had at least 5000 cattle in one herd. These were kept in the various palaces and looked after by at least 50 men. There was no private ownership of land because all land was owned by the people; held in custody by the king, who had the right to allocate it to his subjects or refugees. An important person in every king's court was *inyosi* or *imbongi* (the laudatory praise reciter), who was also the conservator of the history of each kingdom. He was allowed to criticise the king, with impunity, by using poetic language during his praise recitations. The king would listen to the *inyosi* carefully to hear what his subjects liked or disliked about him or what he did that was either good or bad in the eyes of his subjects.

Kingdoms were typically constituted by a group of related patrilineal families or, common descent groups, united by common ancestry who had attached themselves to a particular king. Each subject had the right to leave and join another kingdom. Larger kingdoms sometimes exercised limited control over smaller ones. The most democratic decision-making platform was *ibandla* (the king's council) that included post-menopausal women. Here, the king's advisers would tell him in no uncertain terms if he was out of order and they were allowed to differ with his opinion. In deciding to go to war, relevant post-menopausal women in the kingdom were consulted as equal partners and their opinion taken into meaningful consideration. The king's word was final but only after he consulted the council.

Each kingdom owned a sacred coil called *inkatha*, a cylindrical coil of interwoven grass measuring about 100-centimetres in diameter and encased in a python's skin tied together with *umtshiki* (palm fibre). It was kept in a secret place and was every kingdom's prized possession, as they believed that their ancestors bestowed it with power and protection. The preparation for war was an elaborate affair that involved an age-old tradition of young men chasing a big, unspotted black bull around its pen. This would be done for about an hour and then they would attack it with their fists. Using its horns as leverage they'd twist its neck and throw the beast to the ground, dead. The war doctors would then boil certain parts of the bull and mix them with herbs into a potion for the soldiers to drink. The rest of the animal's carcass was burnt to ashes; and then the ashes were buried. The soldiers would file past the war doctor who would then sprinkle them with the medicinal potion using an oxtail outside the cattle enclosure. Then they would vomit into a deeply dug pit before returning to the cattle enclosure where they had to catch and eat the roasted pieces of meat thrown into the air by the war doctor.

After every battle, the victorious army returned home with the spoils of war such as serfs, women, children, food, cattle and valuable items. Once they reached home, they first paraded the booty. The defeated enemy's cattle were given to the king and he would distribute them among the heroes of the battle as he saw fit. The married young women of the defeated kingdom - likely widowed by war - had to parade in front of the king and the army with the hope of being chosen as a wife. The king would have the first choice among the women; then the most heroic warriors would have an opportunity to choose from the women. The senior officers would follow and then the warrior infantry soldiers who fought in that war would have their turn to choose from the women. However, the king would be the first to choose the best women among the virgins and the rest would also be distributed amongst the heroes. The beautiful girls not chosen would become *umdlunkulu*. The men and women who did not go to war observed rituals at home, such as putting white ash on their faces, and, kept each soldier's *icansi* (sleeping mat) upright.

After a battle, soldiers were only allowed to take part in normal daily activities after they had carried out a ritual called *ukusula izembe* (to wipe the axe clean). This involved putting a piece of wild asparagus in the hair and having non-penetrative sex with the first obliging unmarried woman. The logic of this was based in a belief that after a battle the disease that urged them to kill still afflicted the soldiers. The only antidote for this was to participate in *ukusula izembe*. This was the only time a willing woman could have non-penetrative sex with a total stranger. Death and burial rituals were serious matters and were accompanied by other strict rituals. The departed were referred to as *amadlozi* or *amathongo* and were feared more than the living. Ancestors were regarded closest to God and therefore, were considered angels. Because of their proximity, they were able to plead directly to God, on behalf of their living relatives, to ward off bad luck and provide protection. The way to appease the departed and remain in their favour was to talk to them regularly by burning *impepho* (sage) at the place directly opposite the door called *emsamo* in the grandmother's hut, and, by slaughtering a goat or a cow. This custom continues to this day.

The grieving and mourning processes were from six months to a year and had many taboos. For an example, working in the fields during the mourning period was sacrilegious and certain foods such as *amasi* (curdled milk with whey) were also not to be eaten. The death of a king was a matter of great importance. Firstly, the death was kept a secret and his subjects would be told that the king *iyadunguzela* (is indisposed). The death was only announced once the successor was ready to take over the throne or once the contenders were neutralised by being sent to exile or killed. The king's body was put in an upright sitting position and bound by *umthwazi* (a glossy forest grapevine) a strong creeper plant, to keep him in place before rigour mortis set in. His eyes were kept wide open and the body was wrapped in an unspotted black bull's hide. He would be kept in his hut under constant guard and was seated in front of a fire that was not allowed to go out. There was no specified time frame to bury a king and his grave would be almost three-metres deep. From the floor of the grave a horizontal excavation extended about a metre sideways. The king's body servant *(insila yenkosi)* - in the United States of America, he'd be called a body-man - who was responsible for the king's personal hygiene, was willingly sacrificed shortly before the king was to be placed in the ground. He would be buried face-to-face with his king in the same grave, for eternity.

# 2

# The Zulu Kingdom

THE ANCESTORS OF TODAY'S Zulu nation originates from a place called KwaNobamba in the eMakhosini Valley near uLundi and KwaNongoma in the heart of the land of the Zulu people. Of the Nguni people, the Zulu have the most intriguing history. Initially, they were members of the amaLala group who speak with the *thefula* accent but later became amaNtungwa by adoption. It was a son of the Zulu kingdom that brought African military prowess to the attention of the world. The tiny Zulu kingdom transformed itself from an insignificant people to a power that reigned over a significant part of Southern Africa, right up to the shores of Lake Victoria in East Africa. It was the only kingdom to defeat a premier world power, the British, in the 19th century using spears and some modern weaponry. The Zulu kingdom regards King Luzumane, born in the 16th century circa 1550, as their first ancestor because information before him is sketchy and not much is known about him either. What is for certain is that he had a son called Malandela (crowned approximately in the 17th century) whose wife was Nozidiya kaGwabini Zungu. She was industrious and became wealthy through interbreeding her goats with those of a distant male relative and butler, named Mpungose kaPhahla of the Gwabini kingdom.

Queen Nozidiya's goats multiplied in great numbers. She also bought and bred pure white cattle known as *inyonikayiphumuli* (a bird that never rests), which grew steadily in number. Henceforth, cattle formed the backbone of wealth for the royal house of the Zulu, which remains true to this day. King Malandela and Queen Nozidiya had several children, most notably their two sons, Prince Qwabe and Prince Zulu. When their father, King Malandela died, Prince Qwabe not only demanded his father's estate as the firstborn but he also wanted his mother's estate even though she was still alive, accusing her of infidelity. Queen Nozidiya rejected this demand and they fell out. Prince Qwabe left their ancestral home KwaNobamba, together with a group of followers, and headed eastwards before settling near the sea below the oNgoye Mountains. This is how the Qwabe kingdom was formed. He died without ever going back to his place of birth. His younger brother Prince Zulu remained at KwaNobamba with the rest of the family and created a new kingdom which he named after himself, the Zulu kingdom. This is the tiny group that gave rise to the world-famous military strategist King Shaka who shaped it into the powerful Zulu empire.

That is how the two sons of King Malandela kaLuzumane separated. They regard themselves as fraternal kingdoms to this day, hence marriage between members of the two families remains taboo. King Zulu kaMalandela had several children. Some of the sons were Prince Ntombela, Prince Mpangazitha, Prince Gumede, Prince Phunga and Prince Mageba. Prince Phunga and Prince Mageba were twins, and they are always mentioned together in the roll call of Zulu kings. After the death of King Zulu his son Prince Phunga ascended to the throne. King Phunga's reign was brief and he died at his principal residence, eBulawini Palace near KwaNobamba Palace. Since he did not have any offspring, his younger twin brother, Prince Mageba, automatically took over as king of the Zulu kingdom. After King Mageba died his son, Prince Ndaba, became king. As far as the Zulu kingdom is concerned, their glory begins with King Ndaba. His principal residence was eMqekwini Palace near KwaNobamba. He stood tall and was a handsome figure who sang and danced better than any of his peers. He composed a song that he would *giya* to (a traditional military dance) and that became *ihubo lesizwe* (the Zulu national anthem). It is still sung in times of trials and tribulations to this day:

| | |
|---|---|
| *UNdaba, uyinkosi* | Ndaba is king |
| *Uyamemeza okaNdaba* | Ndaba's descendant is calling |
| *Wasibiza savuma* | he called us and we responded |
| *Uyinkosi yohlanga* | he is the king of humanity |
| *Ohho, O* | Ohho, O |
| *Hha, oye* | Hha, Oye |
| *Jijiji, ajiji* | Jijiji, ajiji |

King Ndaba was brave and fought many wars to gain respect and increase the size of his puny kingdom. He is the first one to create military regiments in his kingdom called amaGwadle and amaNkankane regiments. His descendants continued his legacy and made an impact on the future history of the Zulu kingdom. For instance, through the line of his son Prince Nkwelo, his direct descendants Prince Mudli and

Prince Mhlaba, fought in the 1906 Poll Tax Uprising. King Ndaba's youngest son Prince Jama, whose mother was Princess Sithuli kaNkombana Mbatha from the Mbatha kingdom, automatically became the crown prince because of his mother's high station. One of his children, Prince Xhoko, ran away from eMqekwini Palace after falling out with his father and built himself a palace named eMgazini. One of Prince Xhoko's sons, Ntshakweni, had a daughter called Mehlwana and a son called Ntopho. In his ripe old age, King Ndaba caused a royal scandal by allowing his great-granddaughter Mehlwana kaNtshakweni, to marry one of his grandsons, Prince Senzangakhona kaJama. In Western culture, they are considered first cousins once removed and, therefore in many cases, they could marry. However, in Zulu culture they are considered brother and sister, so their marriage was incestious. Such relationships were strongly forbidden to avoid inbreeding.

King Jama, one of King Ndaba's famous sons, was a short man notorious for being unusually cruel. With little regard he personally killed many of his subjects over minor issues. He was a notably intelligent but highly strung and temperamental individual prone to mood swings. In those days, Nguni culture dictated that a king must marry many wives to enhance the dignity and importance of his kingdom. King Jama's fierce independence saw him buck against the custom and remained married to only one wife for a long time, a scandal as far as his subjects and neighbouring kings were concerned. Despite constant nagging, threats and begging, King Jama refused to marry another wife just for the sake of custom.

Even his wife, Queen Sikhombazana Sibiya succumbed to the pressure, and reluctantly asked him to take another wife, but the king refused. Moreover, she had yet to conceive. She eventually gave birth to a son, Prince Phalo, who died in infancy. King Jama's subjects became concerned and began to emotionally blackmail him saying that he would go down in history as the king who had destroyed the Zulu kingdom. They told him that they feared that he didn't have an heir and they would be overrun by other powerful kingdoms and made serfs. King Jama continued to ignore them and doted on his fragile wife who was now resented by the kingdom for two reasons. They blamed her for failing to produce a son and they thought that she was the one stopping the king from taking more wives. It is only after a long and painful five years and eventually treatment by a Zulu traditional doctor from south of the oNgoye Mountains that the queen finally conceived. Everyone was ecstatic, and when she went into labour, the king insisted on being present during the birth.

The midwives objected and flatly refused because the Zulu were deeply steeped in superstition and mythology. His demand was not only taboo for an ordinary Zulu man, but to have a king present at the birth would be inauspicious and definitely bring misfortune upon the whole kingdom. King Jama reluctantly stayed away from the maternity hut. On a cold wintry morning in 1739 the queen gave birth. Instead of the customary sounds of jubilation from the hut, everyone spoke in hushed tones as though there was a death. The king's councillors were informed about the birth, and even though they were relieved by the news, none of them wanted to deliver the news to the king. Finally, it was left to the king's great-uncle, Prince Nkwelo and his sons, senior Princes Mudli and Mhlaba and some of his brothers, two advisers Mswelazonke Manqina, Mpungose Sibiya as well as Commander Nodela kaSondoda Mbatha, a member of Nkakane regiment to go and deliver the news.

'*Wena wendlovu*' (You the great elephant), they said without any enthusiasm as they entered the king's hut. 'Come in quickly and give me the news,' the king said, taking a swig of *utshwala* (a sorghum beer with an alcohol content of less than 5 per cent) from his *umancintshane* (small calabash). The delegation said nothing, and remained bowed crouching, sweating and staring at the floor. After the customary long silence, King Jama gave them more time, but they continued to say nothing. Instead, they began to shake from fear. He became irritable watching his brave kinsmen and advisers collapsing like weaklings.

'My brothers, what is the matter? I have never seen you like this before? Is Her Majesty fine?' Strangely, they concurred. 'If she is all right, then what is eating you?' Continuing 'Is the child alright?' the king asked, almost hysterical. Still, they did not answer. Instead, they wiped the flood of sweat from their furrowed brows. After what seemed like an eternity, Nodela finally stammered: 'The, the...,' but words failed the elderly man. For the first time, King Jama began to worry, but did not show it. Instead, he continued to harangue them. 'If you do not want to talk to me, you better leave then. But before you go, tell me is the child alive?' Yet more stammering followed. Then, finally, words tumbled out. 'Yes, *Bayede*... ...yes, but... ...you see...'. 'Since when do you stutter? I cannot believe my eyes. What kind of child is it? Is it a girl?' asked the king. 'No, *Bayede* it is not. It is much more complicated than that.' 'What could possibly be so complicated when both the mother and my son are doing all right?' the king beseeched, raising his voice in utter confusion.

'Well, you see, *Bayede* it is not actually a son or a daughter, it is ...' 'What do you mean it is not a daughter or a son? Are you out of your mind! What is wrong with all of you today, is it an animal?' infuriated King Jama tried to understand what had overcome them. '*Bayede* it is twins that you have.' Nodela blurted out, followed by immediate dead silence. The king took another swig, saying nothing, joined them staring at the blank floor. 'What's more,' they added, 'it is girl twins.' King Jama perspired profusely, and took deep breaths one after another, as though he had run a marathon, and asked to be left alone with his thoughts. The tired queen was equally devastated, inconsolable, and slipped into post-natal depression. She blamed herself for all the present and future woes that could possibly befall the Zulu kingdom.

The whole kingdom was invited to KwaNobamba, and it was left to a miserable looking Mswelazonke to announce the catastrophic news. Apprehension engulfed the assembled subjects because, as far as they were concerned, twins were inauspicious in the best of times. Since they were royalty, it was *umhlola* (a bad omen), and untold bad luck was going to be unleashed upon them all. Many myths surrounded multiple births, and people believed that twins were the original witches. The truth, is that in those days, mothers could not sustain two children simultaneously because adequate nutrition was not guaranteed whether or not they were breastfed. Therefore, it made sense to kill one child to increase the survival chance of the other one. It was usually the firstborn twin that was to be killed, and this process was called *ukugingiswa igabade* (choke with a lump of clay) or *ukwendiswa* (removed from the earth). After the assembly, many people did not sleep in their homesteads that night; they ran away to join other kingdoms. Those who chose to stay, waited to hear when one of the twins would be killed, but days became weeks and weeks became months. Still nothing happened. In early spring, three months later, the king called to see his twin daughters and their mother. This was another deviation from custom because, under normal circumstances, he should have really only met the surviving twin. When his subjects heard that both twins were still alive after three months, and both were invited to their father's hut, they swore that King Jama was already mad because of the existence of both twins. The optimistic subjects hoped that the king called to announce the death of the unfortunate twin.

On the given day, the king called to see the twins, the queen with twins in tow, members of the royal family such as Prince Mhlaba, Prince Nkwelo, Prince Mudli and dignitaries such as Mswelazonke, Mpungose, *imihlalandlini* (palace dwellers) all went to the king's great hut. They were hoping that he would *khunga* only one child. But King Jama took one of the twins, and looked at her tenderly. This one had a pretty face with dimples, and a burning gaze that reminded him of his own father, King Ndaba. It was the older twin, who stared back at her father without blinking or crying. He called her Mkabayi and presented her with black and white beads. To everyone's dismay, the king called for the other child who was placid and wide-eyed. She resembled her mother and not once did she look at her father. Without any provocation, she let out a loud sorrowful cry and refused to keep quiet even when her mother suckled her. King Jama called her Mmama and presented her with a pile of white beads. After giving back the children, the king merely stared at the floor and said nothing. No one said anything either as all the women shuffled out. His councillors wanted to know which child was to be killed, but he calmly informed them that neither child would be killed. There were loud gasps of disbelief and they all quickly filed out, bewildered.

The news reached the rest of the subjects and many more ran away from the Zulu kingdom, as bad luck would surely follow. After the birth of the twins, the royal couple tried unsuccessfully to have more children. When he continued to refuse to take another wife, his remaining subjects avoided KwaNobamba altogether, fearing the contamination of bad luck from the twins. Consequently, the twins grew up isolated, and became close to their doting parents who were particularly protective of them. The queen suffered poor health after their birth, and she blamed herself whenever there were natural misfortunes such as late rains, poor crops, loss of cattle or some other misfortune. When the twins were about eight years old, a typical summer storm broke out with thunder accompanied by lightning. This day turned out to be an extraordinary day for the twins. Princess Mmama was out playing around the palace while Princess Mkabayi was sitting by their ill mother in her hut. As the rain pounded heavily outside, Queen Sikhombazana Sibiya took her last breath as Princess Mkabayi watched helplessly. Princess Mkabayi never made a sound or cried. Instead, she calmly went to inform her father and swore that she would never allow herself to be helpless again.

Mayhem broke out because the queen had died without an heir. As far as the subjects were concerned, it was the end of the Zulu kingdom and the twins were disliked even more. Princess Mkabayi only managed to cry days after her mother's burial and even then, it was in the privacy of her father's hut. She blamed herself for her mother's death. The king's mood swings became more unpredictable. He aged rapidly and lost all interest in state matters. What hurt him the most were rumours that the girls were not real human beings, but witches. His subjects once again implored him to get married, but he said he would only consider what he called 'a drastic act' once the twins were older. This resulted in that the girls grew up in an extremely hostile environment.

Yet Princess Mmama remained sociable and lived under the shadow of her twin sister who was a loner and had a domineering personality. Princess Mkabayi never cried when hurt or beaten by other children and, for that reason she became the primary target for everyone's cruelty. This made her self-reliant and confident from an early age. She learnt to master the art of manipulation and reading situations. She developed an acerbic tongue, and through her disengaged father, she had a significant influence on the domestic matters at KwaNobamba palace. Before long, she was privy to the sensitive matters of the whole kingdom. A year after the queen's death, there was a severe drought. The king sent the imiDlenevu regiment led by his uncle, senior Prince Mudli to raid the weaker Mhlabangubo kingdom in *Buthonga* (the Thonga kingdom) in the north because they had plenty of food. These were non-Nguni who lived in their tiny area of present-day Mozambique. The expedition lasted for two months. Besides food, they returned with women, cattle and serfs as well as sweet seeds called *mswela*, which became a new delicacy in the Zulu kingdom. From the war booty, King Jama chose a big and curvy beauty with glowing skin called Nongati Muhali whose father was king of the Thonga kingdom who lived in the vicinity of today's Maputo in Mozambique. Everyone was horrified by the king's choice, and for once, the kingdom and the twins were united against him.

The king was expected to only marry virgins, but King Jama had deliberately chosen a woman who was visibly heavy with child. Again, it was left to Nodela and Zinsonge, Commanders of the Gwadlu regiment to confront the king about the possible disastrous consequences if Princess Nongati were carrying a boy child. But the king refused to get rid of his new acquisition, even though she could have been carrying a son of a Thonga man who could possibly make claim to the Zulu throne. Princess Nongati, on the other hand, was inconsolable. She made it clear that she was a married woman and wanted to go back to her Thonga husband Mhlaba, the father of the child she was carrying. She had no desire to become King Jama's wife. As a spoil of war, her feelings were irrelevant, and she was forced to remain at KwaNobamba.

Again, it was another disastrous day for the beleaguered Zulu kingdom when the announcement was made that queen Nongati had given birth to a boy she came carrying. Out of respect to their indifferent king, the kingdom dutifully took part in the royal celebrations that accompany the rituals to *khunga* Nongati's son. King Jama named the child *Sojiyisa* (to turn things around). He did this to spite his subjects for forcing him to take a wife against his will. As time passed, the twins grew up to be regal and attractive young princesses. But Mkabayi's beauty was legendary. She was a tall, light-brown beauty with breasts that *ekhuza impisi* (taut and firm) with a perfect and beautiful set of bright white teeth and a dimpled smile that captivated men's hearts. Despite her drop-dead good looks, she was sagacious, and had a clear vision of where she wanted to take her father's kingdom. Eligible bachelors came from far and wide, from as far north as north of the *Bulingatho* River (Zambezi) and from as far south as *the Flat Mountain* (Table Mountain) in today's Cape Town to ask for her hand in marriage. Notable suitors included Prince Mgwazeni kaDonda Khumalo from a prominent and vast kingdom and Prince Nontshiza Mchunu from the Mchunu kingdom. The most illustrious of her suitors was King Jobe kaKhayi of the powerful and feared Mthethwa kingdom.

King Jobe and his entourage undertook a week's journey just to reach KwaNobamba on the hope of winning Princess Mkabayi's heart. But the Princess wasn't interested. Her father had to force her to show some semblance of respect to the honoured visitors. She reluctantly welcomed the Mthethwa entourage with her cousin Princess Nontombi and her favourite aunt Princess Thozi (Mudli's sister) who was her *iqhikiza* as well. King Jobe, who was now very old, tried to endear himself to the desirable Princess, but she rejected his advances with contempt: '*Hawu, ungihlolelani kodwa ngempela. Uphele kanje, usuzokufa nokufa. Azikho yini izalukazi lapho uvela khona?*' (How dare you! You are very old and about to die. Aren't there any old women where you come from?). No one could believe their ears as no one ever spoke to the powerful king with such contempt - the protocol does not allow that for a visiting king. Moreover, no sane woman would ever turn down a chance of being one of the queens in the Mthethwa kingdom where wives lived a life of absolute luxury. Princess Mkabayi caused a serious diplomatic incident, and an incensed King Jobe left at first light the following morning, without the usual fanfare farewell. King Jama was equally infuriated with his daughter, and barely averted the crisis by quickly returning the visit to King Jobe at oYengweni Palace. He took a stupendous number of cattle and many fine young flowers of the nation as appeasement. King Jobe was flattered by the quality of the gifts. By the end of the visit, the two kings negotiated a non-aggression agreement between the Mthethwa and the Zulu kingdoms.

Princess Mkabayi's foolhardiness and King Jama's stroke of diplomatic genius came in handy and had a major role on the relations between the two kingdoms some decades later. Years later, Princess Mkabayi fell madly in love with a sweet-talking heir to the Ngcolosi kingdom, Prince Lamula kaNgwabini kaBhengu kaShongololo kaDlabazane Ngcolosi. Lamula lived on the other side of Ndlalathi River, way beyond Ntunjambili Rock near Kranskop over 150 kilometers away from kwaNobamba. Whenever Prince Lamula came to see Princess Mkabayi, it took him at least two weeks to cover that distance by foot. In preparation for his matinee he would steam, wash, administer an enema and smeared himself with the best herbs of endearment he could lay his hands on. But all he ever heard from the Princess was that she needed more time to think about whether she would become his wife. Even though she was madly in love with the handsome prince, the princess was torn between getting married, and looking after her fast-ageing father.

King Jama, however, encouraged her to follow her heart, and assured her that he would be well taken care of by the extended royal family once Princess Mmama got married too. Even though she was still undecided, she began to make *ucu* as a symbol of her eternal love. After five years of crossing rivers, ascending mountains, scaling steep cliffs and fighting off wild animals, Prince Lamula was once again on his way hoping for a positive answer from Princess Mkabayi. He arrived at KwaNobamba early in the morning unexpected this time, and sat down under the usual huge fig tree, where he waited for hours. He was welcomed with cold *amahewu* (fermented traditional non-alcoholic corn drink) and food. As always when the princess saw him, her heart raced and beat hard against her chest. Without thinking, she hurriedly got up to give him her *ucu*. But as she made her way to hand it to him, the *ucu* slipped through her delicate fingers and broke into hundreds of pieces all over the shiny pressed cow-dung floor. Stunned, she stared at the scattered beads for a long time. To her, it was an omen. Keeping her head down, she slowly made her way to her prince who sat under the fig tree, but this time she refused to sit close to the love of her life.

After the customary pleasantries, the prince once again begged her to become his wife. As she sat nearby with her head still hanging low, Prince Lamula told her that he was asking for her hand for the last time. He no longer wanted to risk his life if she could not make up her mind. Princess Mkabayi was devastated, and with a heavy heart, she finally found the strength to stand up. She gently fluttered her eyelashes, slowly raised her head, and with a faraway look, gazed past her prince and looked at the hazy blue-green mountaintops on the horizon. As tears trickled down her flushed cheeks, straining her eyes as though she was seeing the future, she softly whispered, *'Zinhle izintaba zakwaZulu'* (the mountains of the Zulu kingdom are breathtaking). Still in her early twenties, she meant that she was not able to abandon the stunning valleys and mountains of the Zulu kingdom.

Princess Mkabayi informed her father and her twin sister that since their father had ruled against her being killed at birth, she would dedicate her whole life to watching over the Zulu kingdom. Princess Mmama was shattered when she found out that the people in the Zulu kingdom blamed her and her sister for their mother's death. Mmama's carefree attitude had made it possible for her to be fairly sheltered from much of the cruelty since childhood. Her curvy body, big round eyes and sensuous lips were hypnotising. She gracefully sashayed through her daily routines, and remained an unassuming, innocent soul. She too had many eligible suitors, but she chose to fall in love with her relative King Mbanjwa *Dunjwa* kaShandu of the Mbatha kingdom, which was incestuous. She gave him an *ucu* as a symbol of her undying love. Princess Mmama initially also swore to forgo marriage but after the death of her father, she married King Dunjwa and they had a daughter.

King Jama was rapidly ageing and expressed his wish that they both marry before he died. They refused, and he implored them until they struck a deal that they would only get married once they had found him an appropriate wife. Obviously, poor Nongati who by now had two children with King Jama still did not qualify to bear an heir. She had not even been allowed to dance the ceremonial royal dance in public, as a wife of the king was expected. King Jama never married her, hence she never qualified to be referred to as *uNdlunkulu* (queen). After the death of their mother, the twins had no mother figure but were lucky to have been liked by a striking beauty Mthaniya kaManyelela kaZingelwayo Sibiya, whose younger sister was Bacobekile. Mthaniya lived with her elderly parents in the nearby valley and the twins visited her almost daily. She spent her free time taking care of them by braiding their hair, playing games and teaching them all the things mothers teach their daughters. She advised them about personal hygiene, taught them how to cook and tried out new dishes with them. Under normal circumstances, girls who had no mothers were taught these things by a wide circle of female relatives and friends within a kingdom, but the twins weren't so lucky.

It was left to Mthaniya to teach them even the names of each finger. On the left hand, the thumb is called *umwane*, the pointing finger *untamo usomagidi*, the middle finger *usogidamasi*, the ringfinger is *maquthela* and the little finger *usozidinjana*. On the right hand, the thumb is *ugwegwelunqume*, the pointing finger *uzigwemagwegwe*, the middle finger *owakhozingwe*, the ring finger *owakociki* and the little finger *ucikicane*.

After careful consideration, the twins decided that there was no better candidate for their father to marry other than Mthaniya. They discussed her with their father and King Jama said he would make up his mind only after seeing her in person. The girls were overjoyed and now the next person to be convinced was Mthaniya herself. Shortly after that, as she was braiding Princess Mmama's hair, they broached the subject. She was taken aback and said nothing. She had never imagined herself catching the king's attention. Moreover, everyone knew about the king's unpredictable mood swings. After what felt like forever, she said: 'How can I, a mere commoner, marry your father, a whole king?' Princess Mkabayi quickly answered: 'It doesn't matter. You are the perfect candidate as a member of the Ntungwa group and that's all that counts. You know perfectly well that the kingdom will welcome you because we are desperate for an heir before our old father dies.'

'What about the current wife queen Nongati?' Mthaniya wanted to know. 'What about her? She is irrelevant in the grand plans of the Zulu kingdom. Her children are not even referred to as *umntwana* (Prince or Princess). Forget about her, please marry our father,' Princess Mkabayi pleaded. 'But the king does not even know me, let alone love me,' she said, sounding a bit out of breath. She could see that it was a serious discussion. But Princess Mkabayi reassured her: 'Do not worry about that, my father will fall in love with you the instant he lays his eyes on you and sees how pretty you are. We will find an opportune moment and walk past. He will be taken by you, trust me.'

Mthaniya promised to think about it but altumately agreed. Within weeks, the twins organised the walk-by. Their father sat under the big fig tree with his advisers where he would have the best view of his potential bride-to-be. When she appeared with his daughters, the king stared without thinking or blinking. He could not believe his luck, as she was more than what he had expected. She had the full curvy figure that Zulu men drool over, shapely legs, a narrow waist with a flat tummy. Her beads and her hips swayed from side to side in a slow rhythmic motion as she walked past. The king was captivated and for the girls everything was going according to plan. Before long, the king's betrothal was announced and Queen Mthaniya moved to KwaNobamba for three months as per the custom before she could sleep in the king's hut. As old as the king was, even he could not wait for the wedding night.

The kingdom contributed to the *ilobolo* and the wedding was a fitting splendid royal affair. Queen Mthaniya performed the royal *ukusina* (dance) on the palace grounds for all to see, because she was no spoil of war and held a spear upright to indicate that she was still a virgin. The whole kingdom fell in love with her. When it was announced that she was pregnant, great apprehension gripped the kingdom. The biggest question was whether she was going to be able to produce an heir or not. The whole kingdom metaphorically held its breath when she went into labour. The king asked to be left alone as he waited in his hut.

The twins were present during the birth and their biggest task was to report the gender of the child to their father. Hours later when his daughters entered his hut out of breath, he did not look up. '*Bayede*, we have come to report about the future of *isizwe sikaNdaba* (Ndaba's kingdom). It is our pleasure to tell you that *okaManyelela* (the daughter of Manyelela) has given birth to a son,' Princess Mkabayi said, relieved. '*Hawu ngempela, kwakuhle lokho bantabami*' (Oh really, that's great news my children). I am overwhelmed by what you have just told me. Your suggestion that I marry Mthaniya was great; we really did well. The child's name will be Senzangakhona (we did well).' King Jama shed a lone, short tear and thanked his ancestors for the good fortune.

The Zulu kingdom finally had an heir. Everyone was euphoric. Queen Mthaniya produced the Zulu heir Prince Senzangakhona in 1757. She was instantly elevated to the level of a goddess and saviour, a status she holds to this day. So much so, that the Zulu kingdom was named after her *KwelikaMthaniya* (the Land of Queen Mthaniya). She walked the grounds of KwaNobamba Palace with grace, great pride and with a permanent smile fixed on her face. Prince Senzangakhona grew up to be a tall and handsome and admired by his kingdom. He grew up in a warm, loving environment a far cry from what his elder sisters had experienced. He was given affectionate names such as *Mjokwana* (tall one), *Ntinti* (dandy) and *Menzi* (performer).

Queen Mthaniya had more sons, named Prince Zivalele and Prince Sithayi, and daughters named Princess Nobongoza, Princess Nonkombo and Princess Mawa. King Jama reminded his twin daughters about the marriage deal they had. However Princess Mkabayi told him that marriage had to wait, because they were still too busy inducting the new queen and helping raise the pride of the nation, her new young brother, the Crown Prince Senzangakhona. The old man happily lost the argument and was pleased about the heir and everyone in the kingdom was finally relieved about the fortunate turn of events.

The Zulu kingdom had always been embarrassed by the praise name Prince Qwabe (Prince Zulu's older brother) had conferred on them - *lufunelwenja* (dog's testicle), when he broke away from KwaNobamba. Understandably, they were always looking to replace that name. According to legend, King Jama liked his mother's people's praise name *Ndabezitha* (a feared legend amongst his enemies), as they were courageous warriors. He then devised a plan to take it from them. He, therefore, dared Shandu, (who was the king of the Mbatha kingdom as well as his mother's relative), to a spear-throwing contest. King Shandu was a short and egotistical man, with an acute case of the short man syndrome. The deal was that if King Jama who was much taller, threw the spear further than King Shandu, he would appropriate the praise name *Ndabezitha* and further compensate him with a cow. As expected, King Shandu with his shorter arms lost, and King Jama indeed compensated the pained Mbatha king with a cow. Hence the Zulu saying: *igama lomuntu inkomo* (using someone's name costs a cow). That is how the royal family ended up being referred to as *Ndabezitha*. However, King Shandu had not consulted the Mbatha kingdom about this deal. They therefore refused to let go of their praise name and did not recognise that agreement. They continue to use the name *Ndabezitha* as their praise name to this day.

Another version of how the Zulu and Mbatha surnames came to share the praise name *Ndabezitha* is that King Shaka told his close friend Manyosi, the great-grandson of Shandu Mbatha that he wanted to use *Ndabezitha* as the praise name for his family. Apparently Manyosi agreed, yet he had no authority to agree without consulting the Mbatha king. All the Mbathas living under him Manyosi and Dikane then joined Shaka. However, when King Mangcengeza kaKhali kaShandu of the Mbatha kingdom who lived at eZivundleni Palace, eMsinga heard what Manyosi had done, he was furious. Moreover, Mancengeza was an ally of Zwide and Ngoza who were Shaka's enemies. Predictably, Shaka attacked the Mbathas that lived under Mangcengeza and Dunjwa and they fled south. They ended up settling amongst the amaMpondo people in the Mzimkhulu area and in some parts of *today's Western Cape*. That battle is illustrated in Shaka's laudatory praises:

*...Izwiwe uDunjwa waseluYengweni*   it was heard by Dunjwa of oYengweni

*Yezizwa uMagcengeza wakwaKhali*   it was heard by Magcengeza, the son of Khali

Manyosi the outstanding fighter was a fair-skinned mountain of a man and a legendary glutton. He walked about on any given day and was followed by people carrying large chunks of meat and calabashes of traditional beer, which he consumed with much gusto. His greatest claim to fame was to eat a whole goat by himself and consume more than 20 litres of beer in one go, a feat of which he was very proud of. Hence his personal praises are uManyosi owadla imbuzi nezimpondo zayo (Manyosi who ate a whole goat including its horns). Whatever the truth behind the sharing of the laudatory praise name Ndabezitha, it remains a source of banter between the Mbatha and Zulu surnames to this day. Parts of the Mbatha lauadatory praise are:

Shandu                    Shandu
Gumbi lamagwala           a refuge for cowards
Ndabezitha                a legend among the enemies

Jama kaNdaba kaMageba kaZulu kaMalandela kaLuzumane was already an old man when he got married to *okaManyelela*. He died peacefully in his sleep a happy man, because he had left the kingdom an heir under the eagle eye of his most brilliant daughter, Princess Mkabayi. King Jama's legacy was that he challenged commonly King held beliefs about royalty and polygamy. A year after King Jama's death, a death-cleansing ceremony was done, and life returned to normal and people slowly began to forget about the past turbulent times. Peace, tranquillity, and prosperity reigned in the Zulu kingdom, but not for Princess Mkabayi. Ever since her father's death, she worried about who was going to be made the regent because the crown Prince Senzangakhona was still too young to rule. She observed how some of her male relatives, such as Prince Mudli and Prince Mhlaba, were positioning themselves for the role. She did not trust any of them. She had to act swiftly and decisively.

Without consulting anyone, Princess Mkabayi called an *imbizo* (a national gathering). This surprised even her closest supporters because a female, even though royal, had never called a national gathering before. Moreover, no one knew the agenda. After three days, most people assembled at KwaNobamba parade ground. Princess Mkabayi allowed the usual praising of the ancestors, emotional singing and the spectacular dancing to go on for some time. She then slowly and majestically rose up and the people, in silence stood still as though in a trance and stared at her. After a spellbinding pause, she brazenly announced: '*Bantu bakababa besekusele isikhwehlela kuphela eNgonyameni uma ingicela ukuba ngivikele isizwe sikaPhunga noMageba. Ngakhoke ngizocela umntwana uMudli ukuba angilekelele.*' (My father's people, the king requested me with his last breath to rule the kingdom. I will, therefore, request Prince Mudli to assist me).

Everyone was horrified because no female had ever ruled over any Nguni kingdom. Up to that point, everybody assumed that the regent was going to be either Prince Mudli or Prince Mhlaba. She had anticipated the people's negative reaction and capitalised on her uncle's (Prince Mudli) vanity by making him her deputy to quash any possibility of a successful revolt. The gamble paid off because the military council concurred with her. Without entertaining further discussion, she led in the singing of the national anthem and everyone joined in before dispersing. Prince Mudli went back to his homestead KwaNodunga stunned and digested the sudden turn of unexpected events that almost left him in charge. He nevertheless, thanked his ancestors and eagerly waited for sunrise. By the time King Jama died, Nongati's son Sojiyisa had been living in his own homestead *eKuvukeni* and had several wives. He named his firstborn son Maphitha, *Nomdidwa* to his friends. The Zulu royal family treated Sojiyisa and his siblings such as Tokoto with utter contempt. King Jama regretted the negative attitude towards the innocent boys. After all, he did not choose his parents. Regent Princess Mkabayi did not even speak to him altogether. Sojiyisa built himself another homestead at KwaMandlakazi and people living under him grew steadily, and began to address him as *Bayede,* a title reserved for a reigning monarch only.

It slowly became clear that the kingdom was gradually divided between Sojiyisa and the Crown Prince Senzangakhona. Princess Mkabayi could not allow anything to threaten the Zulu kingdom, whether perceived or not, so she planned to crush Sojiyisa and his followers. She personally planned the military strategy for battle against Sojiyisa. She instructed her soldiers to kill Sojiyisa and all his followers, burn the houses to the ground and destroy everything in their wake, including their dogs. Princess Mkabayi leading in the front, attacked at dawn, under the cover of the thick morning mist. The password to attack was: '*Baphakathi*' (they are inside). Sojiyisa and his followers knew about the planned attack and tried to set up a defence and fortified their position. But they stood no chance against the ferocious daughter of King Jama.

Although Sojiyisa died in the battle, his two sons Maphitha and Tokotoko survived. They were hunted down and captured by a platoon led by crown Prince Senzangakhona. Princess Mkabayi left their fate to her brother who saved their lives and accommodated them at KwaNobamba because there was nothing left at KwaMandlakazi. This made Maphitha and Tokotoko loyal to the Zulu royal family because Senzangakhona had saved their lives. After the successful battle, Princess Mkabayi's fame grew far and wide. Not only had no female among the Nguni people ever ruled over a kingdom, but also no female had led men in battle from the front and won.

# 3

# The Birth of King Shaka kaSenzangakhona

WHEN THE CROWN PRINCE Senzangakhona was a young man, Bhebhe *Mbengi* kaMhlongo was the king of the eLangeni kingdom at eNgugeni in uMhlathuze Valley. One of King Bhebhe's wives was Mfunda kaKhondlo of the Qwabe kingdom. Prince Mgabhi and Princess Nandi were two of their children. Both Bhebhe and Mfunda died when Nandi was young and her older brother Mgabhi raised her together with his own three sons Princes Makhedama, Songweni and Mthandeka at his Bozeni Palace. Prince Nandi was a tall, dark-skinned beauty with long bowed legs that made her hips swagger when she walked, a rhythm that mesmerised men. Her character, however, left a lot to be desired because she was argumentative, lazy, loud and rude. Before Mgabhi died he had also married two of the Ndwandwe king's daughters. He lays buried near Goedertouw Dam which overlooks eNtumeni where the uMlovu River meanders south of St Mary's Hospital at KwaMagwaza near Melmoth. In 1938, Rev Axel *Mankwanyaza* Berglund, a Norwegian missionary built a church and named it after him, King Mgabhi Church. The same uMlovu River is mentioned in Shaka's lauadatory praises:

*Uteku lwabafazi bakwaNomgabhi*     the joke of the women from Nomgabhi
*Ababetekula behlezi eMlovini*     they sat near uMlovu River and joked
*Bethi uShaka akayikubusa*     and said Shaka would never rule
*Kayikuba nkosi*     that he would never be king

It was common practice for young men to search far and wide to find suitable pastures for their livestock. Often, they would leave home for weeks or months at a time. They roamed in the open valleys and spent their days fooling around with young women. One of the courting rituals involved the young men throwing their spears into a pile in front of the girls and each girl would then choose the spear of the thrower they fancied. These liaisons were temporary and were called *amahlaya endlela* (road entertainment) and the couples engaged in non-penetrative sex. When Prince Senzangakhona and his friends including Ntshingwayo kaMahole Khoza, who eventually became the commander-in-chief of the iSandlwana War, arrived with their livestock in uMhlathuze Valley, they did not know that that trip would change the history of Southern Africa.

One of Princess Nandi's relatives from the Ngobese kingdom, who was on his way to Qungebe in the north, told the eLangeni girls about the presence of young men from the Zulu kingdom, including its handsome crown prince, Senzangakhona. Nandi and her three assistants wore their finery and daubed themselves with perfume made from sweet-smelling bark, flowers, roots and hippopotamus fat. They went to look for the visitors, bringing them food and sorghum beer. Since Nandi was a princess, she was the first one to choose a spear and it was obvious whose spear she chose. Nandi and Senzangakhona spent the rest of the day getting to know each other under the shrubs and the girls only left at sunset. They came back the following day and continued to indulge in non-penetrative sex under the bushes. The girls were all virgins and the boys were all uncircumcised. After a few weeks of passion, Crown Prince Senzangakhona and his friends left and forgot about the eLangeni girls as they went to find greener pastures. Three months later, Nandi's relatives watched with revulsion as her body changed. She denied that she was pregnant and when they lay her down, spread her legs and checked her virginity with a reed straw, they found her hymen intact.

She was still a virgin, but her stomach kept on growing. Shocked and confused, they asked her with whom did she last 'did nothing'. When she told them, it was Crown Prince Senzangakhona kaJama, her family was outraged. Nandi was still puzzled not only by her own 'inexplicable' pregnancy, but she also failed to comprehend the reasons for the intensity of the resentment. She wasn't aware that the venom towards her was because her and Senzangakhona's relationship was considered incestious. Nandi's mother was the daughter of Mfunda kaKhondlo kaKhuzwayo kaQwabe kaMalandela. Senzangakhona's father was Jama kaNdaba kaMageba kaZulu kaMalandela. Therefore, their great-great-grandfathers Qwabe and Zulu were brothers and shared both a mother and father (Queen Nozidiya and King Malandela). Unfortunately, neither of the two was aware of their bloodlines.

This was the beginning of Princess Nandi's suffering. When her relatives reported the matter to the Zulu royal family, senior Prince Mudli simply denied it ever happened and brazenly claimed that the two had never met before. According to Zulu custom, being intimate with anyone vaguely related to you is incestious and unfortunately the 'relatives' pool is extremely wide. That is why a Zulu male first establishes a woman's surname and her mother's surname before he can court her. If any sexual relations took place - deliberately or not - both families had to slaughter a goat to ask for forgiveness from the ancestors. The underlying factor against such unions was to avoid inbreeding. Crown Prince Senzangakhona hardly recalled meeting Princess Nandi because he met so many willing girls wherever he went. However, he was adamant that he did not once penetrate any of them. The more the Mhlongo kingdom pestered senior Prince Mudli about a quick wedding to avoid a scandal, the more the Zulu royal family wanted nothing to do with Nandi. Mudli even offered them an antidote for her condition because as far as he was concerned, Nandi was merely suffering from a stomach ailment caused by an intestinal beetle called *ishaka*. This beetle was infamous for bloating the stomachs of its victims. As Princess Nandi's stomach ballooned, her peers avoided and taunted her by singing songs that described the disgrace she had caused.

Princess Nandi's family hardly spoke to her because of the shame to them, she was now less than a dog. They even began to call her names that suggested she was 'loose' as she was still too young to have indulged in non-penetrative sex anyway. According to the Nguni belief system, the thighs of a girl below the age of 16 were not fully developed for sexual relations. Hence, young men did not find such thighs an object of desire because non-penetrative sex depended on the quality of the thighs. Her laudatory praises illustrate her shameful behaviour:

| | |
|---|---|
| *Uxebe lwaseMhlathuze* | the seducer from uMhlathuze Valley |
| *Amathanga kawalingani* | whose thighs do not rub against each other |
| *Ahlangana ngokubona indoda* | they only do when there is a man |

She was thrown out of her brother's homestead and told to go and give birth at KwaNobamba as no self-respecting Mhlongo midwife wanted to be tainted by incestuous blood. When she went into labour, she tried to hide it from the eagle eyes of the elderly women. But they caught her wincing as the birth pangs cut through her body. Devoid of any feelings, the old women hounded her out of the house and made sure that she took her few earthly possessions with her. She hurried away to KwaNobamba. But on the way, the compulsion to push overwhelmed her and she staggered towards the nearest tree. Holding her breath, she grabbed the tree's lowest branch and prayed for more time. She did not make it to Senzangakhona's home and gave birth alone under a euphorbia tree. Weak, she staggered home carrying her nameless baby boy in her hands. It was 1787.

The Zulu still refer to children born out of wedlock as *ingane yesihlahla* (a child born under a tree) a demeaning and unkind depiction. That tree is still known as King Shaka's Tree. To spite the Zulu royal family, Nandi's people sent a delegation to tell Mudli that miraculously the beetle in Nandi's stomach had mutated into a human being, *uShaka*. Insiders in the Zulu royal household wanted to get rid of the colossal embarrassment and decided to kill both baby Prince Shaka and his mother Princess Nandi. They then invited Nandi to come and live at the KwaNogqogqa homestead attached to KwaNobamba. Even Senzangakhona wanted to see his firstborn son dead. Part of his laudatory praises confirms it:

| | |
|---|---|
| *USenzangakhona eshabashabeka* | *Senzangakhona was incensed* |
| *Wagawula izingoge zokumginqa* | *he cut down logs to kill him* |

One of Senzangakhona's *izinceku* (personal aides) tipped Nandi off and she escaped to her mother's people, the powerful Qwabe kingdom, with her son Prince Shaka. When the assassins were sent to find her at KwaNogqogqa homestead and pretended to be bearing gifts for the newborn, they were told that Nandi was so embarrassed by her behaviour that she had killed herself and Prince Shaka. Relieved, the assassins returned to KwaNobamba. It was only months later that they discovered that they had been lied to. Mudli did not give up and pretended to have had a change of heart; he begged Nandi to come back but she refused. Unfortunately for Nandi, her relatives could only take so much of her unruly behaviour and ended up chasing her away. She had no alternative but to return clandestinely to her people at eNgugeni and keep a low profile with a fast-growing Shaka. Queen Mother Mthaniya found out about her grandson's existence during the wedding of her son Crown Prince Senzangakhona to his first wife, Mkabi *Nohindi* kaSodubo. Infuriated, she ordered the reluctant senior Prince Mudli to find out where Nandi was living and bring her first grandson to her as soon as possible. Mudli smuggled Shaka in and out of Queen Mother Mthaniya's hut because Shaka and his mother were, supposedly, 'dead'. But Mthaniya's nosy neighbour Mfemfe, used to overhear her speak in low tones using baby language late into the night. This puzzled him since he knew of no small child living with the Queen Mother.

Whenever he tried to enter her hut during her baby-talk time, Queen Mother Mthaniya would claim she was busy taking a herbal bath and could not be disturbed. But she would then continue with the baby talk. Mfemfe became convinced that

Queen Mother Mthaniya was a witch who could be heard talking to her monkey and told anyone who cared to listen. The rumour spread, and the royal family was under pressure to do something about it. The family secretly hoped the gossip would go away because they knew the truth, but it persisted. In order not to show any favouritism when dealing with witchcraft, a large crowd raided Queen Mother Mthaniya's hut in the middle of the night, but neither a monkey nor a real child was found. Mudli had made sure the child had been sent away to his mother, eNgugeni the night before.

After the raid, Queen Mother Mthaniya named her homestead *eMangeni* Palace (Palace of Lies) to remind people that she had been wrongly accused. The cat and mouse game between her and the palace guards continued for a while. When she couldn't handle it any longer, she begged her son Senzangakhona to allow Nandi to live at KwaNobamba so that she could have easy access to her only grandson, but he refused. Queen Mother Mthaniya need not have worried. Before long Nandi's relatives threw her out, since Mthaniya doted on her grandson Shaka, they came to live at KwaNobamba. The day Princess Nandi left eNgugeni, she was accompanied only by a handful of young boys as her relatives and her peers could not be seen to be supporting her. This was a big disgrace in the eyes of her family and friends throughout the Mhlongo kingdom. The disgrace was exacerbated because she was a princess from the Mhlongo kingdom and neither the *ilobolo* process with Senzangakhona's family took place nor did her own family seek *inhlawulo* (a penalty for making her pregnant before marriage). Her praise names highlight this disgrace:

| | |
|---|---|
| *Obengabafana baseNgugeni* | she was with the boys from eNgugeni |
| *Abeza beluhayizana* | they arrived in a small group |

The symbolic umbilical cord of the Zulu kingdom is in *eMakhosini* (Valley of the Kings) between iSikhume Mountain and the iMpembeni River whose waters constantly smoke as it thunders into the uMnyengezi pool that flows past King Dinuzulu's grave. The uMnyengezi pool never dries up, even in the severest droughts. It is here that the Zulu kings would usually bath before appearing an audience infront of their subjects. Most of the Zulu kings are buried in the eMakhosini Valley. But for those buried elsewhere, trees were planted in their memory. The tree planted in King Shaka's memory is near his father's grave on *Heelgoed* Farm. King Cetshwayo's tree is near King Ndaba's grave and King Dingane's tree is near King Mageba's grave. This is where KwaNobamba is and for many years it was a centre of contentment for the Zulu extended royal family. But it was not so for Princess Nandi and her young son, Shaka.

After a few months of living at KwaNobamba, she was addressed as Queen and moved to esiKlebeni Palace where she joined two of Senzangakhona's wives, Queens Mkabi and Fudukazi. Mkabi took kindly to Nandi because they were related on their maternal side. Even so, there was no ceremony welcoming Queen Nandi to the palace. She was often involved in running battles with everybody at the palace and extremely protective over Shaka because no one liked him as a product of incest. In a blind rage, Nandi assaulted one of the king's senior advisers in front of everyone after he had taunted Shaka. This was too much for the dignity of the palace, and once again they were chased away. Reluctantly, they returned to her people at eLangeni kingdom. But by this time, she had a second child with Senzangakhona, Princess Nomcoba.

When Crown Prince Senzangakhona built himself the esiKlebeni Palace, Maphitha (whose pregnant grandmother had been attained as a spoil of war by King Jama) also left KwaNobamba and built himself a homestead he called *eNkungwini* (a misty place). This name did not sit well with Princess Mkabayi who thought that Maphitha planned to avenge what had happened on that fateful misty morning when she led the army and killed most of his family including his father Sojiyisa. She kept a beady eye on him and remained suspicious of him until her death many years later. Princess Mkabayi only gave up her position as the ruler of the Zulu kingdom after Crown Prince Senzangakhona was coroneted as the king, after he had married his second wife. Princess Mkabayi surprised her detractors because they thought she was a power-hungry despot. Again, her subjects had misjudged her.

King Senzangakhona was spoilt and had little time for matters of state and continued relying on both Princess Mkabayi and Prince Mudli, even though he had been crowned as the king of the Zulu kingdom. He spent long hours grooming himself in the presence wo of his courtiers, who kept him entertained with long, enrapturing tales. King Senzangakhona was physically flawless, tall and dark and had milk-white teeth and exceptionally handsome, vain, a paragon of masculinity. He had inherited the physical attributes of his grandfather, King Ndaba. He could not help marrying the many women who swooned before him. Princess Mkabayi was slightly disappointed with him but she was comforted in knowing he was investing in the survival of the *House of Zulu* through the many offspring. King Senzangakhona's laudatory praises allude to his magnificent physical attributes:

| | |
|---|---|
| *Obemzimba muhle nangendlala enkulu* | *he was perfect even during the famine* |
| *Obebuso bungenandawo yokusolwa* | *with a flawless face* |
| *Obemehlo engenandawo yokusolwa* | *with arresting eyes* |
| *Obemlomo ongenandawo yokusolwa* | *with appetising lips* |
| *Obezandla zingenandawo yokusolwa* | *with hands were without scars* |
| *Obenyawo zingenandawo yokusolwa* | *with unblemished feet* |
| *Obezitho zingenandawo yokusolwa* | *with faultless legs* |
| *Obesiphundu singenandawo yokusolwa* | *with a shapely head* |

King Senzangakhona's esiKlebeni Palace was built on the summit of the ridge on the southern bank of Mkhumbane River and was designed to accommodate his ever-growing number of young women. It had 338 huts, 18 of them housed about 40 *imidlunkulu*. He later built Zindela Palace that accommodated his *imidlunkulu* only. He married Mkabi *Nohindi* kaSodubo Nzuza in 1784 and their son died in infancy. Then followed a daughter Princess Nozinhlanga *Ndikidi*, who was named after the uMzinhlanga River, a tributary of the iMpembeni River. Princess Nozinhlanga, at the age of 45, became the principal wife of Shaka's best friend, King Mlandela (*Myandeya*) kaSomkhele of the Mthethwa kingdom in 1829. She did not bear Mlandela any children. She ended up slitting her throat in full public view when, in 1879, the British attacked the Zulu empire because she could not bear to witness the attempt to destroy the Zulu nation.

Queen Fudukazi Cele was the next wife and they did not have children. Queen Nandi was the third woman to join the other two wives, but King Senzangakhona never married her at that time. She eventually gave birth to Prince Shaka (Senzangakhona's first son and was followed by a sister, Princess Nomcoba). It was more than a century later that Nandi's dignity was salvaged posthumously when her marriage process was finalised in 1985 by the current monarch, His Majesty King Zwelithini. This time relatives, aristocrats, regiments, *imidlunkulu*, members of the public and well-wishers as well as 3000 cows, hundreds of other livestock and many gifts were given to the Mhlongo kingdom who reciprocated with the customary *umabo*. His Majesty King Zwelithini also asked for forgiveness from the Mhlongo kingdom for having ill-treated Queen Nandi and her son, King Shaka.

The fourth wife Queen Langazana kaGubeshe Sibiya was mild-mannered and huge, their son was Magwaza *Nongqobo*. Shaka eventually made her the commander of several regiments. She also had the significant task of being the royal keeper of the nation's most precious item *inkatha* which was kept at esiKlebeni Palace. Queen Mzondwase Zungu was the fifth wife and the mother of Mhlangana - one of

Shaka's murderers. The sixth wife was Dingane's mother, Queen Mpikase kaMlilela Maqungebe. She also lived at KwaKhangelamankengane (*KwaKhangela*). The seventh wife was Queen Magulana kaNtshongolo kaNene Mngadi and their only daughter Sikhakha married Dikane kaHlakanyana kaMatshana kaNkomo kaShandu of the Mbatha royal kingdom. The eighth wife was Queen Bhibhi kaSompisi Ntuli, her father was Prince Shaka's specialist *amasi* chef and her older brother was Ndlela, the great warrior. They had a son Prince Sigujana and a daughter Princess Nomqotho. She became one of the many wives of the king of the Mthethwa, Mlandela, and they had three boys, Ndlebezomlilo, Somcuba and Sokwetshatha. Queen Bhibhi was well liked and remained prominent in the Zulu royal house, even during King Dingane's reign, so much so that there is a Zulu saying: '*You must have something special like Bhibhi whose star ascends whatever king is in power.*' She was killed for no apparent reason by Mqundane kaNobongoza Zulu on King Mpande's instructions.

The ninth wife was a short, dark-brown beauty Queen Songiya kaNgotsha Hlabisa. She had a quiet disposition and was never known to have raised her voice at anyone. She had a great sense of humour and enjoyed being flattered by her praise names. Her people had originally joined the Zulu kingdom during King Ndaba's reign. Their children were Princess Ntikili, Prince Mpande, Princess Nomzimba, Princess Nozicuba and Prince Nzibe. Ntikili was a respected poet and she married King Malanda kaVelani of the Mkhwanazi kingdom and one their children was Somkele. The tenth wife was Queen Sondaba *Mangcengceza* kaPhungashe Buthelezi. The eleventh wife was Queen Ncaka kaMancinci Gubashe their son was Kholekile. The twelfth wife was Queen Nozibuko kaNxumalo Ndwandwe and the thirteenth wife was Kishwase. His marriage to his fourteenth wife Queen Mehlwana kaNtshakweni kaXhoko kaNdaba was also considered to be incestuous as Ndaba was also King Senzangakhona's great-grandfather. His fifteenth wife was Mjanisi and his sixteenth wife Queen Zishungu kaMudli kaNkwelo kaNdaba was also incestuous as they shared the same great-grandfather Ndaba.

King Senzangakhona is said to have had at least 40 wives and a countless number of children such as Prince Gowujana who died in 1835; Princess Nozilwana died in 1840; Prince Gqugqu was brutally murderd by Mpande for no apparent reason in 1843; Princess Ziwelile married King Jobe Sithole; Princess Nomanqe married King Mlandela Mthethwa; Princess Mantongela married King Njakayisuke Buthelezi; Princess Zayi married one of Shaka's closest friends Nhlaka Mdlalose; Princess Maqukazi married a member of the royal family of the Mthethwa kingdom; Princess

Mthembazi married Masiphula from the Mgazini kingdom. Other children were Princess Noziqubu, a drop-dead beauty; Princess Nomchoba and Princess Nomaklwa was tall and stunning just like her father; Prince Sigwebana; Princess Mfihlo; Prince Ngqojana; Prince Ndunge; Prince Magwaza.

It is because of the huge number of Senzangakhona's male children that Princess Mkabayi decided on who the heir would be, even though Senzangakhona was still alive. She justified her action by claiming that there could be a fierce fight over the throne and that it could even split the kingdom. She chose Bhakuza because his mother Sondaba was Senzangakhona's favourite wife. At this time, in the history of the Nguni people, it was common practice to avoid loss of life at all costs during a battle. Winning was based on the number of women and livestock that had been taken from the other side. It was a spectator sport where each kingdom's strongest men would be the ones to start with fist fights. King Senzangakhona never declared war on any king during his reign. Instead the stronger kings from the Buthelezi, Qwabe, Mchunu and Ndwandwe kingdoms regularly harassed him. He was made ransom many times because the Zulu nation was extremely vulnerable. But he was popular because of his generosity of welcoming homeless wanderers and offered them asylum which increased the size of the Zulu kingdom.

The last ransom paid to King Phungashe was 60 cows, which was astronomical in those days and nearly bankrupted the Zulu nation. This colossal embarrassment made King Senzangakhona change tact and he resorted to marrying many wives as insurance against being attacked. He rapidly increased the number of wives after marrying a Buthelezi girl Mangcengceza as his tenth wife. He also began to use medicines to protect himself and luckily for him, two Basotho war doctors from Maboko in the north were visiting his kingdom. They gave him lucky-charms and as part of payment, King Senzangakhona gave them large tracts of land on either bank of the iMfule River near Eshowe and sure enough, he was not harassed or kidnapped again. These visitors were honoured and allowed to form the Nzuza kingdom and adopted Zulu names and surnames *Mqalane* and *Mngadi*. Their lineage survived for years unbroken from the time of one of their sons King Shandu (no relation of the Mbatha's), who bore Majiya who bore Ngwenya who died of malaria in 1915. After the death of Ngwenya, Mnyameni's son became regent until Sisila was old enough to rule and crowned king of the Nzuza kingdom in 1926.

*Inkosi Matubatuba Mkhwanazi. He is the descendant of Princess Sobejile kaMpande and King Mlandana kaVelana of the Mkhwanazi kingdom. The small coastal town of Mtubatuba is named after him. (Killie Campbell Africana Library)*

*Inkosi Manyala of the Mahlayizeni section of the Biyela kingdom died at the age 72 years old in 1952. His descendants can be found in the area. (Killie Campbell Africana Library)*

## The Birth of King Shaka kaSenzangakhona

The 1802 *umdlathule* (eat and say nothing) drought led to a great famine that caused havoc in the Zulu kingdom. At this time, Queen Nandi lived with her family with her relatives at eLangeni in the Mhlongo kingdom. She had three children by now Shaka, Nomcoba and a son Ngwadi, who was fathered by Gendeyana Qwabe. Ngwadi was also a product of incest as Nandi's mother's great great-grandfather was also a Qwabe. Nandi's family was tired of her uncontrollable temper and as well as her lewd behaviour. They intended to throw her out to live with Gendeyana in Mpaphala near the source of the aMatigulu River. But Queen Nandi was not interested in living with Gendeyana because he was a commoner. Luckily, Prince Shaka's unheard-of bravery bought them some time at eLangeni. A black mamba, the world's fourth most venomous snake had killed many people and livestock in the area. Prince Shaka thought of a highly risky but most ingenious way of getting rid of it, after it also killed the Mhlongo king's favourite bull. He noted that when the mamba struck, it first stood on its tail.

So, one fine morning, he asked his mother to come watch as he was going to kill the snake. Bewildered, people gathered to watch a kamikaze Prince Shaka balancing a clay pot on the top of his head, calmly walk past the hole. Suddenly, the hissing snake sprung from the hole and stood on its tail as usual, fangs exposed. Shaka did not flinch and continued walking. Like a lightning bolt, it aimed for the top of Shaka's head. Just as quickly, it dropped dead because it had struck its tiny head in hot porridge inside the clay pot on Shaka's head. Nothing like this had ever been seen before, let alone such fearlessness of a 13-year-old. Shaka made a name for himself. Unfortunately, months later when a dog killed a sheep under his watch, Nandi and Shaka and her other children were finally chased away.

Princess Mkabayi and Queen Mother Mthaniya were devastated when they heard that Nandi and her children had nowhere to live. After roaming in the wilderness for a long time, they were finally forced to live with Gendeyana. Unfortunately for Prince Shaka, his bravery was unwelcomed here, and he was sent to live under King Macingwane at iNgonyama Palace in eNkandla. Queen Nandi could not stand living away from his son, so she went to join him. When King Senzangakhona heard that Prince Shaka was living with Macingwane, the king promised Macingwane three of his sisters, Mawa, Mmama and the highly-prized Princess Mkabayi as wives if Macingwane agreed to kill Prince Shaka. Macingwane refused and instead, he asked Nandi and her brood to leave. They were homeless once again as no one wanted to accommodate someone who had committed incest repeatedly, especially when there was little food available. They wandered from place to place and often slept under the stars with a real threat from wild animals. Despite the ridicule, pain, degradation, torment, hunger and assassination attempts Queen Nandi never gave up hope of achieving greater things with her brave son Prince Shaka one day.

She even tried her luck at ekuPheyeni homestead at *kwesikaMthethwa* (Mthethwa kingdom) where her *ubabekazi* (father's sister) was married to Mbiya kaShangane Mthethwa. Mbiya became Shaka's first and only father figure and he learnt ancient wisdom from the old man. This move by Queen Nandi was one of the most significant actions that influenced modern history in Southern Africa because of the big influence the Mthethwa kingdom had on the formation of the Zulu empire. They were received by the king's *inyosi* Ngomane kaMqomboli Mdletshe at his homestead Oheni. Ngomane had a distinct birthmark on the side of his torso and 11 fingers, a genetic oddity that distinguishes his descendants to this day. Queen Nandi and her children lived with Ngomane until they recovered from the ravages of a hard life. They were then moved to the KwaQoqintandane Valley, where they joined refugees from all over the place and were given land. This is where they built their first homestead Gqagqa near Nselenyana River where for the first time ever, they were content. Jobe, the Mthethwa king was extremely popular with his subjects and he was the first Nguni king to see no value in circumcision and banned it. Instead, he allowed *ukugweda* (partial circumcision) where the foreskin is not removed but the tissue under the penis glans is cut to allow the foreskin to move back and forth easily. He was ahead of his time and a visionary who sought to modernise his kingdom and encouraged trade beyond his territory. He dreamt of a single empire from Table Mountain in the south to Mount Kilimanjaro in the north, which was as far as his known world stretched. The capital of the Mthethwa kingdom was oYengweni Palace where King Ntemba kaMhlana kaSokwetshatha kaMyandeya Mthethwa resided until his death on the 17th of December 2017 at the ripe old age of 94 years.

OYengweni palace is situated between iNsele and iMfolozi Rivers which run between the iSangonyana and Dondotha areas on the north coast of the Zulu kingdom. The earliest known Mthethwa ancestor is King Xaba who bore Prince Madango, whose wife was Queen Makasa kaGumede who bore Prince Khayi, who bore Prince Jobe who later became the king of the Mthethwa kingdom. Some of Jobe's sons were Prince Mawewe, Prince Godongwana, Prince Tana and Prince Myaka. As a rule, the Nguni placed a high premium on virginity so when Khayi found out that one of the women he married was already pregnant by her lover from the Seme Kingdom he called his homestead eNhlambeni (insult) Palace. However, as expected from a self-respecting king, he raised the child Shangane as his own. Jobe lived until he was very old, and his subjects often speculated about who was going to succeed him. His sons Godongwana, Tana and Mawewe also spoke about the same issue. But Jobe's spies told him that his sons were plotting to kill him. Jobe then tried to kill them first but only managed to kill Prince Tana and Prince Mawewe but Prince Godongwana managed to escape with a harpoon spear still stuck in his back. He collapsed in the nearby forest. His sister nursed him back to full health. Godongwana fled south and lived in exile.

Prince Myaka, who was not implicated, lived a long eventful life and became friends with Nathaniel Isaacs, the first Jew to become a Zulu subject in October 1825. Myaka's homestead had 100 huts and was between the uThukela and aMatigulu Rivers. Prince Godongwana's mother was Princess Mabamba kaMzimase of the Mbokazi kingdom. He was born at ebeLungwini Palace near the iMvamazi River that overlooks aMawunzi forest on the south bank of the White iMfolozi River. Prince Godongwana put as much distance as possible between himself and his father and roamed around until he found refuge under King Bhungane of the amaHlubi kingdom and lived at Ngqwashu homestead in the highlands of the Drakensberg Mountains. Prince Godongwana excelled in everything he did.

Before long he caught King Bhungane's attention who imparted valuable secrets to him. One day King Bhungane dared Prince Godongwana to prove the potency of the sacred medicines he shared with him. Then Prince Godongwana's body was smeared with 'supernatural' herbs. He was told to go into the forest and milk the first nursing wild animal he came across. Prince Godongwana brazenly marched into the forest and lo and behold, the first animal he came across was a nursing lioness. Suddenly, he wasn't so sure, but the crowd urged him on. When he approached the lioness, instead of ferociously protecting its cubs, it continued lying down and merely purred. He slowly leaned over and stroked the spellbound lioness that enjoyed the stroking. He then gently milked her, plucked a few hairs and took two of her cubs home. The lioness merely looked on, yawned and let him go. After this act of bravery, Godongwana became legend and promoted to becoming the king's representative.

A few years later, a white man arrived at KwaMagoloza Palace, south of uMzinyathi River in the Hlubi kingdom. He was on horseback and was accompanied by Nomashingila kaBango, Ntshuku kaGawula, Bhovungana kaMahlase and several servants. It is believed that the white man was Dr Alexander Cowan because according to the diaries of the Scottish missionary Rev Robert Moffat, Cowan travelled through

*Bechuanaland* (Botswana) around 1809 and was on a mission to plot a route to the east coast through the land of the Hlubi people. The white man had, among other things, a firearm which was something many Hlubi people had never seen before. This white man lived with them for about three months and he taught Prince Godongwana the mechanics of firearms. In return Prince Godongwana showed him the easy way to the coast via the Qwabe kingdom. It was during the reign of King Khondlo of the Qwabe kingdom, who did not trust whites. He ordered the white man's death two days after their arrival.

This was because, prior to the arrival of this particular white man, King Khondlo's encounter with shipwrecked whites was a violent one. They used to shoot his subjects without provocation, and they had an insatiable appetite for tusks. As far as Khondlo was concerned, whites were strange sea animals who crossed the ocean in large *isiququmadevu* strange steaming shells (ships). They fed on elephant tusks that were to be placed at the shore and in return, the whites left beads gathered from the bottom of the sea and left them on the shore for the locals. That is why whites were not permitted to roam freely in the land of his forefathers. Prince Godongwana inherited the firearm, the horse and the white man's servants. One of the descendants of these servants, Nomxamama Soshaya ended up in high office as one of King Shaka's senior assistant. Prince Godongwana only returned home after his father's death. He arrived at oYengweni Palace around 1809 in style. He was on a horse, galloped at full speed and brandished the firearm. The spectacle worked because the people were impressed and ran alongside the horse singing his laudatory praises. He declared himself the king of the Mthethwa kingdom on arrival and changed his name from Godongwana to *Dingiswayo*. Having been a homeless wanderer, King Dingiswayo was welcoming to wandering strangers and became renowned as a truly tolerant king.

Travelling had broadened his mind and introduced innovations in his kingdom such as the mass manufacturing of common items such as beads, pottery, fur, baskets and shields, which differed in shape and size. For instance, he introduced *igqoka* (the small courting shield), *igabelomunye* (the smallest courting shield), *ihlubelo* (the hunting shield) which was supposed to bring good luck, *isihlangu* (the fighting shield) and *umbumbuluzo* (the sturdiest shield). The *umbumbuluzo* shield was broad and often used as the king's umbrella which was about a metre in diameter. It was regarded as the protector of the king on the throne. It was therefore highly revered and anointed with special herbs before a war. To demonstrate confidence in his shield, a warrior would parry with lightning in an open field during the spectacular summer thunderstorms for sheer entertainment but most importantly, to impress the fairer sex.

It was believed that the shield had medical efficacy as well as an emblem of power and authority. It was recognised as the coat of arms or flag because it was not allowed to be left at the battle thearter. In order to honour warriors that died in battle, the army would lower their shields in a silent tribute as in lowering the flag and each fallen warrior was covered with his shield. King Dingiswayo encouraged trade with different nationalities from near and far-flung places. He sent hawkers and merchants beyond Delagoa Bay (Maputo) in Mozambique to trade with the locals and passing trade ships as well. Hence relics from China, South America and Europe can still be found all over Southern Africa. He grew his sphere of influence by persuading the agreeable but ruthlessly conquering the stubborn and subjugated the weak. But diplomacy was his preferred art of negotiation. That is how all the kingdoms on both sides of the White iMfolozi River ended up under the Mthethwa Commonwealth.

**Prince Shaka's Life in the Mthethwa Kingdom**

When Nandi arrived in the land of the Mthethwa, Shaka was *ibhungu*, a tall, strapping 16-year-old with great muscle tone. No one tormented them about their past because they were part of a group of refugees, outcasts and deserters. Upon finding out that Nandi was living peacefully there, Senzangakhona became afraid of what he could do to him because of the way he had treated them. Ever the diplomat, he sent gifts to Dingiswayo such as *ikhathazo* (a fever prophylactic) to strengthen diplomatic ties. The two ended up being so close that Dingiswayo gave Senzangakhona a pet name *Qegwa*. The close relationship between the two kingdoms remains to this day. Shaka assimilated into the Mthethwa way of life and even spoke with a trace of the *ukuthefula* dialect of the amaLala group to which the Mthethwa people belong. For example, '*loku*' is '*yoku*', '*Mlandela*' is '*Myandeya*' and '*Balethe*' is '*Bayethe*'. The Zulu described it as speaking with a 'flat tongue'.

Life was finally good for Shaka and he thrived. His creative side blossomed, and he composed many wedding songs, death songs, battle songs and even love songs. He invented new dances and his mischievous sense of humour was a true source of joy for his friends. Shaka was enlisted in the Special Forces unit, iZichwe regiment based at eMangweni barracks around 1809. After the first commander, Thayiza Mthethwa was married, Buza took the reigns as commander. Shaka showed unparalleled bravery in mock battles and had the ability to make decisive tactical decisions in the heat of the moment. One of the elements of warfare in those days was that the losing party could retreat or when facing defeat, all they needed to say was *maluju* (surrender) and the victors would let them go. But Shaka saw no point in this type of warfare and wanted the enemy to be annihilated. He shared his thoughts with Ngomane, but the old man admitted that it was too radical. What upset Shaka the most was that he had lost one of his closest Mthethwa friends from wounds following what he termed 'sham battles'.

IZichwe regiment was venerated for its bravery, its agility (as expected of any special forces unit) and for having the best songs and dance moves. Shaka's extraordinary talent shone for the following six years and he was rewarded repeatedly for his military prowess and astonishing intellect. They herded Dingiswayo's cattle in a forest full of wild animals and they swam in the nearby iNcwabi River to dare the crocodiles. Shaka particularly loved this river. Hence the reigning monarch King Zwelithini performed an important posthumous ritual of symbolically fetching Shaka's soul from the river to let it roam freely at eMakhosini Valley. Shaka's favourite part of the river remains under special care of Mthethwa kings.

Shaka more than his peers, had no fear. For example, he devised a trick to kill a leopard single-handedly. He mounted two pillars and a crossbar at the hut's entrance and lured the leopard. It chased him, and he stood behind the pillars with his spear ready. He knew that the leopard would leap over the bar to pounce on him and thus, both its legs would be airborne, and its chest would be exposed. Indeed, the leopard leapt at the sight of easy prey. Shaka stabbed it in the heart in a split second and it dropped dead. His regiment watched, dumbfounded. After this spectacular killing, Mbiya and Ngomane felt compelled to introduce the young Shaka to Dingiswayo. After listening to Shaka's sad and painful history, Dingiswayo was moved and gave him the praise name *Nodumehlezi* (legendendary even when seated). He promoted him to lead his *iviyo* (platoon) and presented him with 12 cows for bravery. This was Shaka's first estate and Nandi was proud.

Dingiswayo's standard war arsenal for his army included *unhlekwane, isijula and isiphapha* spears whereas *inhlendla* the harpoon shaped spear was usually carried by the royalty as well as *isihlangu* whose top end was up to the owner's mouth. IZichwe's uniform were white oxtails on the wrists, ankles and around the head, a leather apron, made out of strips of pure white fur, tied on the waist covering the front and the back, black widow-bird plumes as the headdress and *izimbadada* (ox-hide sandals). It was during this period of happiness that Shaka developed a close cameradery with two fellow refugees, Nqoboka Sokhulu and a mountain of a man, Mgobhozi *ovela entabeni* (of the mountain) Msane. He also started noticing the opposite sex in the form of his sister's friend, Phampatha Majola. They were soon a couple. Shaka's harsh upbringing made him humble and sensitive, regrettably his affectionate and tender traits are often overlooked in history. He excelled in all aspects of warfare and introduced new fighting methods. He discarded the ox-hide sandals and demonstrated the added advantage of running barefoot. He also demonstrated how to hook the enemy's shield aside on the left side and stab the exposed left torso, aiming for the heart for swift death, all at lightning speed. He created a revolutionary spear and had the prototype custom-made by the best blacksmith Mabhodla kaMbuyazi Mbonambi, who also lived in the Mthethwa kingdom. Shaka named this spear *iklwa*, after the sound it made when pulled from a victim's body. The *iklwa* demanded a fight at close quarters to intimidate the enemy, physically and psychologically. With his *iklwa* and his first shield, he called it *unomkhwayimba*. Shaka was getting closer to his dreams of conquering Southern Africa.

In 1810, Dingiswayo heard that the Zulu heir Bhakuza was visiting his grandfather Phungashe at eMthandeni Palace in the Buthelezi kingdom. Harbouring ambitions for the Zulu kingdom, Dingiswayo saw an opportunity to realise his plans such as placing Shaka to the Zulu throne. He then ordered Shaka to lead his regiment iZichwe as well as uYengondlovu regiments to attack Phungashe. The now 23-year-old Shaka was barefooted and carried his *unomkhwayimba* and *iklwa* while the others carried long spears. The Buthelezi ran away and hid in the White iMfolozi River valley. Their pitiful 600 soldiers stood in front of their cattle and their women and children were behind the cattle. Dingswayo told them to surrender, but the Buthelezi women taunted the Mthethwa army and hurled insults at them including calling Shaka's first commander Buza, a dog. This was the last straw for Shaka. He rushed the Buthelezi army in lightening speed and when he was about thirty metres away, a Buthelezi brave threw the first spear. It bounced off Shaka's shield and it was rapidly followed by another. Seconds later, Shaka was face-to-face with him and hooked the left side of his shield around the left edge, and it exposed his left armpit. Then Shaka pierced it with such great force that it went right through his chest. Everyone was astounded at Shaka's speed and skill and looked at him anew. The Mthethwa overwhelmed the now utterly disorientated Buthelezi army. They tried to fight back but ended up hiding among their cattle and among the women. Fleetingly, it was all over.

Prior to the attack, Dingiswayo had instructed Shaka to find Bhakuza and make sure that he kills him personally. But Shaka did not stop there, he also made sure that Bhakuza's mother Queen Sondaba was also killed. Now that Shaka had proved himself, brimming with his newly-found prestige, he decided to sort out a local menace, a giant called Lembe kaSomadela Ndwandwe. Lembe was King Zwide's relative and lived alone on the Siyembeni cliffs at the confluence of the Black and White iMfolozi Rivers. After smoking a large quantity of *igudu* (marijuana), he would rush down in a superhuman stupor, killing and maiming men and animals alike with his huge axes. Hence, the cliffs became a no-go area. Sometimes he would keep the cattle for himself and the terrified cattle herders were forced to take their cattle to graze a long way around the cliff instead of going over where the pastures were best. Shaka led his platoon to Lembe's hideout and studied his tactics as he terrorised the locals all day.

Using the sun to his advantage, Shaka led a charge up the cliff three times, with the sun's glare in the giant's eyes. But each time Lembe rushed at them in a murderous rage and they would all retreat and everyone told Shaka that the giant could not be defeated. Shaka ignored their pleas to give up and with a glint in his eye, he asked for a volunteer to go on a suicide mission with him up the hill. Only a young boy Ngomane, raised his hand and Shaka whispered his plan to him. Then Shaka ascended the hill slowly with the boy following at a safe distance. When Lembe noticed Shaka armed only with his *iklwa*, became enraged and hurled insults, axes and spears. Shaka easily dodged them and only a few grazed his arms. Undeterred, Shaka continued to advance. Only after throwing his last spear and axe did Lembe notice that there were none lying around.

Shaka had instructed the little boy Ngomane to make a neat heap behind him. Oozing with testosterone, Shaka told Lembe that if he wanted his arsenal, he had to go through him first. Lembe realised that he had been outsmarted and charged screaming: 'You dog, who you do think you are, attacking me with one short spear? You want to stab me at close quarters like a dog?' Shaka stood still in front of the pile of spears and axes and waited for Lembe who came for him with his bare hands. In one powerful thrust of his *iklwa* Shaka stabbed Lembe through the heart. The giant fell to the ground with a loud thud. Shaka then walked away whistling, calm as ever. Everyone watching the spectacle was speechless. Shaka's *ilembe* laudatory praise refer to the metaphorical axe (his sharp wit). While *uNomakhwelo* refers to him whistling after killing Lembe:

| *Ilembe eleqa amanye amalembe* | the axe that is sharper |
| *Ngokukhalipha* | than other axes |
| *UNomakhwelo, ingonyama* | Whistler, great lion |

He appropriated Lembe's livestock that was so large that their dust was described as having covered the sun. He presented Ngomane with ten cattle as a sign of appreciation and the rest he sent to the royal herd at oYengweni Palace. Shaka presented his friend Mgobhozi with Lembe's weapons but kept two of the teak and ivory handled axes for himself. He then ordered the burning of Lembe's homestead. They then marched back to oYengweni Palace at a leisurely pace. After celebrating Phungashe's defeat Dingiswayo called for one of his youngest advisers, Sisiyana kaSihayo Ngobese (whose family dispute was partly responsible for the iSandlwana war in 1879). They planned how to dispose of Senzangakhona now that Bhakuza was out of the way, so that Shaka could be king of the tiny Zulu kingdom. Shaka was the new war hero and soldiers raved about a '*Nodumehlezi*' that many people did not know. Phampatha was particularly distressed because she wondered who could have surpassed her lover, Shaka. Together with Nomcoba, they rushed to eMangweni barracks with food for Shaka, hoping to catch a glimpse of this new hero. They were pleasantly surprised when they heard along the way that *Nodumehlezi* was in fact Shaka. Phampatha made sure that she was the first female he 'happened' to meet on his return, in order that they could engage in the post battle or post-war non-penetrative sex ritual as well as to gently dress his superficial wounds afterwards. Fascinated with Shaka's genius, Dingiswayo summoned the platoon to tell the story about the killing of Lembe, blow-by-blow. Shaka gave a short, precise military report and Dingiswayo was impressed. Mgobhozi joined in and emphasised the physical movements of the encounter. Nqoboka not to be outdone imitated the shouts and deranged screams of Lembe. Everyone was entertained and Dingiswayo allowed Shaka to keep all the cattle from Lembe and added another 15 on top.

After a few days' rest, Shaka was summoned to Dingiswayo's private hut where he found him seated alone on a chair carved from a single block of wood. They shared roasted meat and beer from Dingiswayo's personal small calabash, a truly intimate gesture from the powerful king. They spoke late into the night and Dingiswayo shared his vision about the future and told Shaka to be mentally ready to take over the Zulu kingdom. Without hesitation, Shaka concurred. Shaka was renowned for his 'marathon' walks from the banks of the uMhlathuze River in the north to KwaKhangela, about 200 kilometres south. He called it stretching his legs. Shaka spent hours relaxing along the beach and studied the movement of the waves. From here, he developed his famous 'pincer-movement' battle formation made up of 'ikhanda (head), isifuba (chest), amahlombe (shoulders) and izimpondo (horns). The pincer movement execution on the battlefield was that the war veterans would be in front constituting the head (ikhanda) and would engage the enemy in formation leaving enough space for one person to fit between them. Then after a few bloody intensive minutes, they would crouch on their haunches, and walk backwards, allowing the chest (isifuba), the inexperienced fighters to jump into the spaces left for them and engage the enemy.

This was a swift and seamless movement and the enemy would be surprised by the sudden vigour of soldiers because it was not easy to see this changeover in the heat of the battle. On either flank were the shoulders (amahlombe) whose role was to engage the enemy by trying to go behind the chest. The horns (izimpondo) were the fleetest and the youngest regiments who would envelop the enemy trying to flee at lightning speed. This wave-like movement was efficient because it saved the energy of the soldiers and they fought longer than their opponents. This battle formation is taught in many military academies worldwide to this day.

## The Pincer Battle Formation

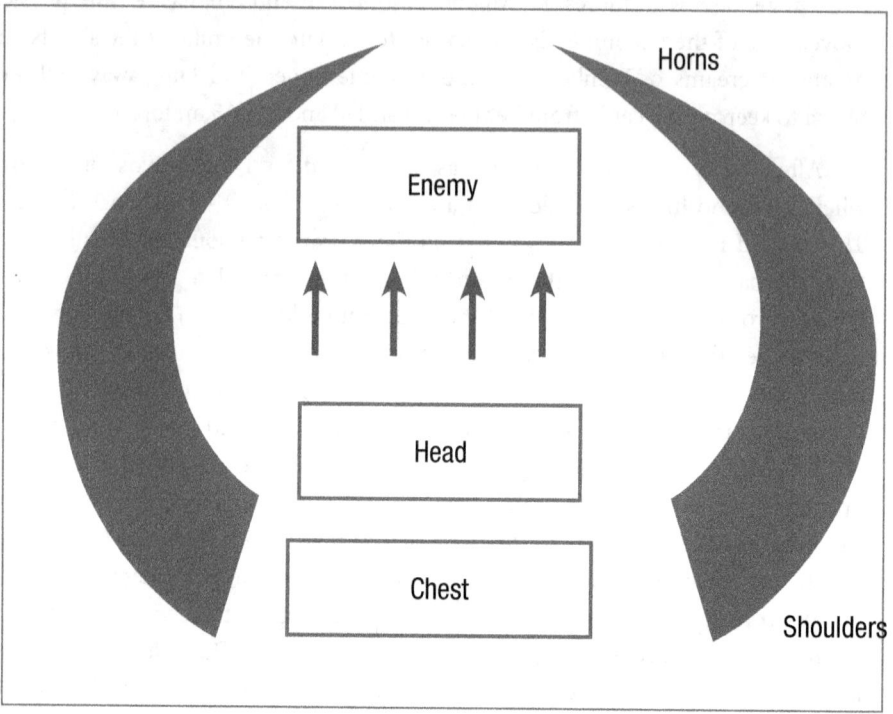

*The 'pincer-movement' battle formation was made up of 'ikhanda (head), isifuba (chest), amahlombe (shoulders) and izimpondo (horns). The pincer movement execution on the battlefield was that the war veterans would be in front constituting the head (ikhanda) and would engage the enemy in formation leaving enough space for one person to fit in between them. Then after a few bloody intensive minutes, they would crouch on their haunches, and walk backwards, allowing the chest (isifuba), the inexperienced fighters to jump into the spaces left for them and engage the enemy. This was a swift and seamless movement and the enemy would be surprised by the sudden vigour of soldiers because it was not easy to see this changeover in the heat of the battle. On either flank were the shoulders (amahlombe) whose role was to engage the enemy by trying to go behind the chest. The horns (izimpondo) were the fleetest and the youngest regiments who would envelop the enemy trying to flee at lightning speed.*

# 4

# Emperor King Shaka Creates the Zulu Empire

SHAKA MADE A GRAND appearance dressed in full battle regalia. He was 29 years old, tall and regal; his light-brown skin glistening as though licked by an angel in the midday sun. He wore stuffed otter hide around his head with plumes made from lourie feathers. At the front of his head, he had a high glossy blue-crane feather about 60 centimetres high. Around his shoulders and chest, he wore a seven-centimetre fringe of manufactured 'tails' of spotted genet and blue-grey monkey fur. From his waist down, he wore the male apron covered by similar 'tails' made from the same furs. Above his elbows, he had four cow tails concealing his gleaming arms and had the same below his knees. On his left hand he carried a snow-white shield with a single black spot in the centre and on his right hand he held *iklwa* and a polished assegai.

Shaka oozed irresistible high-grade raw testosterone. Both his ears were pierced like many of his contemporaries and wore *iziqhaza* (Zulu-style round earring ornaments) with pride. His chiselled face had a strong jaw and a chin bone set off by big brown eyes accompanied by stunning white teeth. Shaka had an easy smile, an endearing small gap in his buck teeth and spoke with a lisp. On hot days, a few sweat beads would gather on his button nose, and he would scrunch it up to allow the sweat to roll off. He had a natural presence and stood head and shoulders above his peers and looked a great deal like his great-grandfather, Ndaba. Unlike his father, who was jet black he was *thusi* (light-brown) as illustrated in his laudatory praises:

Ntonga yethusi kaMjokwane          Brass rod, the son of Mjokwane

The Mthethwa regiments jumped into formation in attention when Shaka appeared. Since they could only salute Dingiswayo, they instead did a rolling rumble as every soldier would beat their *iklwa* against their *ihawu* (shield) in rapid succession. This would culminate with them all synchronically beating their *ihawu* three times, then they would simutenously stamp their right foot, hiss and after ten silent counts, seemingly unexpectedly they would shout '*Sigidi!!*' this salute is called *ingomane*. The party began, and the brand-new Zulu monarch ordered the slaughter of many cattle. His old friends and family were happy to see him especially Queens Magulana, Mkabi and Langazana. After a few hours of celebrations, Shaka called his father's confidants and close friends aside and appointed them as his *ibandla* (king's council) and military high command. This included Sojiyisa (Maphitha's son), two Mdlalose brothers Mvundlane and Nhlaka one of whom married one of Shaka's paternal sisters, Zayi kaSezangakhona, his relatives Mbopha kaSithayi kaJama Zulu who became his principal aide and Nkunga kaSithayi kaJama Zulu (a member of isiPhezi regiment). Nkunga's claim to fame was his elaborate *umnaka* (copper rings) around his neck to impress women. Shaka found no real standing army in the Zulu kingdom so on the first day on the throne he declared a call-up of all the males who were fit and old enough to carry arms. He renamed and re-organised the regiments according to their age, war experience and circumcision status. Everyone was impressed with his decisiveness.

Every new king personally hand-picked the royal guard and it was composed of close friends, family and trusted confidants. Shaka called his royal guard uFasimba (haze) because he said they were so quick that the last thing the enemy would see before they died would be a haze. These agile 20-year-olds had ornamental incisions inside the calf of their legs and their level of fitness was equivalent to that of today's presidential guard or Special Forces. Shaka formed the uMbelebele division at KwaNobamba under the command of Mkabayi. Some of the regiments that made up the uMbelebele division were uNomdayana or iziNtenjane *ezakhala oNgoye*, amaPhela, iziNkwembu, iNzimane and amaNkwenkwe, iziZimazana, regiments. He also established amaWombe, a medical regiment based on the west bank of the uNolele River in the eMakhosini Valley. They were part of the iziMpohlo division under the command of Mkabi and the deputy was Langazana. Their uniform featured *iminaka* (copper neck rings) and white sticks. The division included the uGibabanye, uFojisa, iMfolozi, iNdabakawombe, iNtontela, iNqabayembube and uMgamule regiments. He reorganised uDibinhlangu (*uJubingqwanga*) and uDlambedlu regiments.

Shaka built KwaBulawayo Palace for himself close to the uMhodi River, but it was unimpressive. He built eMkhindini Palace for his mother not too far away near the iMfule River. After a few eventful weeks, Shaka was in full control of his tiny kingdom. The uFasimba regiment received its baptism-of-fire training from

Shaka. The iZichwe regiment was stationed nearby to ensure that their protégé was well settled. Having the Zulu kingdom as an ally was in Dingiswayo's interest because he needed a strong ally as his kingdom was surrounded by the powerful but hostile Ngcobo, Mchunu and Qwabe kingdoms on his eastern front and the equally contentious Ndwandwe and amaNgwane kingdoms on his western front. Now that he had organised the Zulu regiments to his liking, Shaka decided to deal with his childhood enemies. He called a national gathering that lasted for about a week. He sat on his 'throne' of rolled-up grass mats under a great mango tree and held a marathon trial that will be forever remembered in the Zulu psyche.

The uFasimba royal guard squatted behind him and the Queen Mother Nandi, who sat on a grass mat on his left, looked on with a satisfied smile. He sentenced those who hurt him and his mother the most to death. Of all the people he condemned that day, his great uncle Mudli stands out. He was frog marched from his Ndabakadezibona homestead to KwaBulawayo and made to account for his actions in front of the assembly. Mudli did not bother to mitigate or justify his actions. However, he requested to be stabbed through the heart as a soldier. He then stoically recited laudatory praises of the Zulu kings when he was stabbed. He continued even after he fell and only stopped after his last gasp of air. The mass weeping began because Mudli was loved and revered as an elder and custodian of Zulu affairs. Some who were found guilty were set on fire and chased upwind, the remaining transgressors were impaled. Shaka taunted them for the last time and said *hlalani kahle* (sit well) playing on the Zulu words for departing *salani kahle* (stay well).

Shaka ordered all the orphans to the land of the Mthethwa where they were to be looked after by Dingiswayo. Shaka wanted to ensure that what happened to him as a child, the perpetual hunger, abuse and cruelty would not happen to any child ever again. He then erected an anti-child abuse monument *uMdlamathe* near Makhedama's eZuluwini homestead at Eshowe. There is no truth to the popular myth that Shaka was unusually cruel to the eLangeni people because many of them were his relatives through his mother. On the contrary, they were only too happy to be ruled by their *umshana* (nephew) whom they knew well. After the marathon public trial, the eLangeni people prepared to return home, when a phenomenon befitting the Old Testament took place.

A lion came near their temporary shelters and roared. Everyone ran into an unfinished cattle enclosure nearby and the men armed themselves and sang eLangeni songs, invoking their ancestors. For the Zulu, unusual acts of nature are sacred and are said to be ancestors communicating. The lion did not attack them instead it crouched behind the cattle enclosure and roared. The cattle scurried out followed by the people. The people with their cattle tried to make their way back to their kingdom and lion trailed them slowly for the whole day. They were so concerned that some of the men walked backwards, facing the lion. At sunset, the lion went ahead of them, turned back to face them and roared. In the dark wilderness, they huddled together hungry and prayed for divine intervention as they were scared to slaughter a cow, lest the lion attacked them. As though it understood their predicament, the lion killed one cow and went to crouch at a safe distance and watched the people skin and eat the cow. The lion did the same thing every night until they reached their ancestral lands in uMhlathuze Valley where their descendants are found to this day. The lion only ate the ox it killed the day they arrived in uMhlathuze Valley and then disappeared without ever harming anyone.

Shaka visited at least one military base daily in an area of about 250 square kilometres. From his central position he could reach the area's border within the hour. Two months after his coronation, he called all his regiments for general military training and manoeuvers. He demonstrated the merits of his *iklwa* and the advantages of not wearing sandals. The blacksmith Mabhodla became a very wealthy man as Shaka instructed him to teach his secret spear-making skills to a few selected apprentices. The blacksmiths worked overtime and soon each of Shaka's soldiers used *iklwa* including all members of the oldest and most conformist regiments. But when he realised that each of his soldiers were not keen to discard their sandals, after begging them for a month he took it to the next level. He instructed the uFasimba regiment to collect the three-pronged devil thorns, about ten millimetres-long with one prong always facing upwards. He then assembled all soldiers to the parade ground at the capital KwaBulawayo and made them watch as he did the military dance. He stamped on the sharp thorns as he sang his favourite war song. Then they were ordered to follow suit and those who could not, were killed with their own *iklwa* instantly.

When Shaka was satisfied that they had learnt a lesson, he dismissed them, and the older soldiers sat down, exhausted and bleeding and wondered what was to come next. The younger soldiers made fun of them and they were soon at each other's throats. Mgobhozi loved a good fight and, instead of stopping them, he urged them on. Africa's greatest military son Shaka, had begun shaping the mighty Zulu military machine from this ragtag band of miserable souls. They ended up humiliating an undefeated world power the British, at iSandlwana 63 years later. After bringing some semblance of order among his subjects, Shaka visited his favourite aunt Mkabayi, even though their relationship had been strained since the killing of Mudli. Shaka arrived at KwaNobamba on a calm, early-summer's noon with motionless masses of neighbourly white clouds hanging as though suspended from a remote blue ceiling. When Mkabayi noticed her nephew's legion of attendants, she was baffled. Moreover, he had come to see her unannounced.

She however, pretended not to be bothered. After the customary lengthy greeting and comments about the weather, Shaka casually announced his reason for the visit: '*Wena kaPhunga noMageba*, I have nothing serious to report to you except that living by the coast in the land of the Mthethwa as a young boy has made me accustomed to mild temperatures. I intend moving closer to the sea and build myself yet another palace because I truly miss the coast, especially the sea breeze. But most importantly, I want to extend the southern border. I therefore humbly request you daughter of Jama, to keep an eye on the esiKlebeni and KwaNobamba palaces in my absence.' Taken aback by this great vote of confidence, Mkabayi sighed and quickly said: '*Bayethe, wena weNdlovu* as it is always a great pleasure to see you, I will oblige. But I am sad that you will be moving so far from here. But be rest assured, I will look after our ancestral homes and they will be in good hands. I am happy that you are extending and increasing the Zulu footprint.'

Without wasting too much time, Shaka thanked his aunt and was soon on his way. Mkabayi stood up and watched Shaka leave and stood still as she strained her eyes in the simmering heat and watched the towering frame of her nephew striding confidently into the future. Even though Shaka was a ruthless disciplinarian, behind that facade masked a sensitive soul and a highly emotional charmer. Many leaders tend to hide their weaknesses and pretend to be stronger than they really are, but not Shaka. He accepted vulnerability, a quality that allowed him to connect with his subjects - especially the military. There are many accounts written by those who knew him personally like Henry Francis Fynn, one of the many white Zulu subjects. He attested to have found Shaka imperturbable and centred with inner equilibrium that could only be described as spiritual. Shaka's strict daily routine was to wake up long before sunrise. His official duties began at about ten in the morning after his aide (*insila yenkosi*) Jeqe kaSikhunyana kaButhelezi and his assistants Nozitshela and Mbopha had made all the necessary royal preparations for the day.

As soon as the main laudatory praise reciter *inyosi* Mashongwe was aware that Shaka was up, he would recite all the Zulu kings' laudatory praises starting with Luzumane up to Shaka. The laudatory praises included Mkabayi who remains the only female to be mentioned amongst kings. The laudatory praise reciter was at liberty to add new information in the king's laudatory praises, no matter how insignificant or unpleasant it was. The king listened carefully because he picked up the mood in the kingdom and what his subjects were saying, a tradition that continues to this day.

Sometimes for grooming, Shaka took a bath in the nude at the uMhodi River near KwaBulawayo Palace in the presence of adult men and women who had come to seek an audience with him. The sight of his magnificent body made men envious and women swoon with admiration and longing. Water was brought in gourds by young men in outstretched arms above their heads and handed to the king. The gourds were not allowed to touch their heads. Shaka soaped himself with a paste of ground millet, fragrant fat from a black gourd or ash from the *imbidla* (forest silver oak) found at the coast. He would hold a conversation throughout the washing ceremony and his personal shaver Manokotsha would hold the basket of cosmetics as Shaka rubbed his wonderful body with red ochre followed by a scented butter that made his skin glow.

Still naked, he would go to his dressing room, under the shade of a large mango tree and put on an *umncendo*, a type of underwear made from reed and worn on the male organ. It is still worn to this day as part of traditional attire. His official dressers were from the Qwabe kingdom. Members from this family continue to serve as the royal dressers. He would emerge adorned with intricate and fancy beadwork, armlets, furry tails, leg-lets, silky white cow tails and on his head, lourie plumes. He would sit on huge, rolled grass mats shielded from the harsh sunrays by a royal umbrella, a large white ox-shield held up high by a young man.

Cattle symbolised existence to the Zulu, hence there are 100 names describing cattle from the shape and length of their horns, the colour, markings, body shape, weight, different stages of growth divided by gender and whether it has borne offspring or not. Shaka usually started the stocktaking by praising and talking to his favourite pure-white bull *uDududu* which he had appropriated from the Madlokovu kingdom at iMfule near eMthonjaneni. They were the original custodians of the all-white *inyonikayiphumuli* cattle. The descendants of *uDududu* can still be found in today's royal herd. Shaka liked having his herd assembled in uniform colours and markings. In that way, an intruder would be spotted easily. The cattle were paraded in single colours first, followed by the mixed colours and lastly the *inyonikayiphumuli* cattle. Most cows had praise names and if there was something wrong with it would be tended to but if it was too sick, it would be killed immediately. Shaka did stocktaking daily and always inspected the royal herd with admiration. According to Fynn's diaries, he personally counted more than 50 000 cattle in one day.

Even though the troops (or soldiers) lived a disciplined life of respect and honour, they had fun. They spent hours in the hot outdoors chasing rabbits and wild pigs, hunting, stick fighting, playing outdoor games, *beqomisa* (wooing girls), herding cattle and swimming. It was a time of wondrous pleasure. Young men were at liberty to choose when to be circumcised, when to wear the uniform of the regiment they chose to join, what war songs to memorise and when to be part of a dance retinue. It was in regiments that young men matured and showed off their individual talent. They chose the women they wanted to marry and a wedding date. They were only conscripted into regiments when necessary and demobilised after each battle, unless they were required to look after the king's farms. In other words, there was no standing army on active duty. The capital offences were incest, rape and espionage.

The most valued skill was working with iron ore. Nations usually specialised in one skill for an example, the Mbonambi, Nzama, Ndwandwe and Shezi nations were first-class mass producers of spears, swords, harpoons, hoes, knives and other metal objects. The second most admired skill was in the medical field because all medical practitioners were specialists. There were no general practitioners. The Buthelezi were skilled paediatricians and were also allowed to treat royal children, which was a great honour. The Zulu clan specialised in pharmacology and their *ikhathazo* (a prophylactic against fever) was effective, as fever was a deadly disease in those days. There was freedom of trade and people could barter between themselves even with other families but trading with people beyond their boundaries was strictly reserved for each king.

The idyllic lifestyle changed radically when Shaka became king of the Zulu kingdom because he believed in total war and by any means necessary. At the same time, he had no problem in promoting people based on merit. It did not matter where they came from or what circumstances had brought them into the Zulu fold. He welcomed refugees and mercenaries fleeing from factional fights or family feuds as well as runaways. Some of the famous refugees who reached high leadership positions in the Zulu kingdom were Mdlaka kaNcindi Mgazini (who came with a younger brother Masiphula), Nqoboka Sokhulu, whose brother wanted to kill him, Nzobo *Dambuza* kaSobhadli Ntombela (amaWombe regiment) and Ndlela kaSompisi kaGuqa kaMsalela Ntuli. His children and descendants also became prominent such as Gwashaza, Ngwane, Godide and Mavumengwana. In addion to introducing the pincer movement, he also created false formations, medical regiments and *udibi* (cadets) regiments for boys and girls who were between the ages of 12 and 15. Each *udibi* was responsible for about five soldiers and carried their water, weapons, medicines, cowhide blankets and *ukhothe* (war rations) comprising *izinkobe* (cooked dry corn) and dry smoked meat. The *udibi* regiment had to keep a distance of five kilometres from the main body of the army and remain alert to the needs of their soldiers. New army recruits were given one month to harden their feet without sandals. He abolished circumcision in the Zulu kingdom because he needed his soldiers combat-ready at all times. Marriages became orderly state-organised affairs.

As far as Shaka was concerned, marriage was more than 'taking a wife', as a married man would leave his father's homestead and start another production community. By controlling marriage in the kingdom through the military system, the king controlled the rate and direction of the fundamental social processes of production and reproduction within the kingdom. Furthermore, he believed that if women delayed marriage, it reduced their fertility span which affected the rate of population increase. Whereas if men were subjected to delays, it did not affect the population increase as much. This in turn impacted the intensity with which the environment was exploited. Shaka's purpose for war was direct and unambiguous - to terrorise his neighbours into submission, create an empire that was disciplined and centrally governed by him. The single-mindedness of Shaka's imperial ambitions and war strategies was aimed at uniting and arming Africans against colonisers and to make them ready against any onslaught.

Shaka and Dingiswayo had long conversations about the imminent threat of foreign invaders and colonisers. Dingiswayo had told Shaka about his encounters with white people along the coast when he was in exile and that many more were making their way to Africa. Their aim, among other things, was to seize all the lands they could lay their hands on, change the traditional ways of the people, make them dress like white people, speak the white man's language and adopt the white man's culture. More significantly, to make them despise their own ancestors and force them to believe in the God of Abraham. However, over the years the tactic of subjugating the Africans changed. Now the former colonisers are teaching and learning African languages such as isiZulu, even in their own countries.

During Shaka's reign, the king's council implemented a human settlement programme. After subjugating a kingdom, some people could continue living in their ancestral lands while others were moved and given land in the underpopulated parts of the Zulu kingdom or to reinforce borders. Another revolutionary feat Shaka pulled off was to make his female relatives commanders of the *amakhanda* (military bases) all over; a kingdom decision that was unheard of before and rare since. His rationale was that besides the trust born through blood, a post-menopausal woman thinks objectively like a man because she is no longer at the mercy of hormones that wreak havoc with her mood swings. She is also less ruled by her ego.

Once Shaka decided to attack a kingdom as part of his empire-building wars, the targeted nation had the option of either being annihilated or accepting Shaka as their sovereign. They would become a Zulu protectorate and advocate the Zulu rule of law. Once defeated, a kingdom's allegiance was to the Zulu empire first before their filial affiliation. Each defeated kingdom maintained their *inkosi* (king) and Shaka elevated himself to emperor. However, he chose the name *iSilo* as a title to mean emperor, whereas ordinarily *isilo* means a beast. Hence, all Zulu kings after him, were addressed as *iSilo* (emperor). After a few months of intense and relentless warfare, Shaka managed to acquire about two thousand soldiers from the neighbouring kingdoms he had conquered and from the kingdoms that merely surrendered. More mercenaries, fortune seekers, desperados, refugees, wanderers, thrill seekers and runaways swelled his popular and ever-growing empire. The newly defeated kingdoms paid taxes to the Zulu capital and surrendered their sons to be regimented within the imperial army, except for firstborn sons or if their only child was a male. The royal guard, uFasimba, now numbered about 800 men bolstered by young men from the Qungebeni, Gazini, Sibiya and the eLangeni kingdoms. They were all eager to fight under the energetic young king whose compassion, especially towards soldiers was quickly surpassing his ruthlessness.

Naturally, the same kingdoms offered their best-looking women as *imidlunkulu* to KwaBulawayo Palace. Shaka also established new types of military bases occupied by men with different surnames to cement social cohesion and patriotism, which was a first in the land of the Nguni people. There was one regiment that he did not change, the fierce abaQulusi regiment stationed at eHlobane under the command of his close friend Nhlaka. These extremely fit men were from the area called ebaQulusini, even though they had different surnames. The abaQulusi regiment was never drafted into or amalgamated with other regiments or assigned to be part of any division. Instead, it fought as a special force directly under Shaka. This tradition continued under successive Zulu emperors and for this reason it was also considered a royal force. The abaQulusi were the most daring fighters and one of their legacies is that they were the last regiment to fight the British during the iSandlwana War. Old as they were during the 1906 Poll Tax Uprising, they fought with admirable bravery and sang their abaQulusi war songs that reminded them the past.

Shaka's men loved him despite the gruelling training and his insistence on iron-fist discipline. He promoted the deserving on merit and encouraged everyone to excel, irrespective of their past. Cowardice was the worst crime in Shaka's eyes, hence he insisted that all soldiers return with their *iklwa* from battle. Those who could not produce it or had stab wounds on the back, were summarily executed. The loss of a soldier's *iklwa* meant that he had run away which was cowardice, unless he had a credible witness to state the opposite. Wars were mainly waged in winter and the attack posture was a stooped position with legs slightly apart, and they would attack the enemy at lightning speed. He allowed no one to hold his *iklwa* in the javelin position. It had to point upwards and the blade had to be above the hand and the shaft below for effective stabbing. He built the national armoury in a hut, on top of 12-metre long poles with ladders. Lomana, a small but brave Khoi man guarded the entrance. He was present when Dingane ambushed Piet Retief in 1838 and retired near KwaNobamba where some of his descendants can still be found. Shaka had learnt to show compassion when people least expected it from Dingiswayo. This endeared him to the most outlandish of his subjects. He instilled a culture of self-sacrifice, restraint, fearlessness, constancy of work and effort, civic duty, submission to authority, respect for superiors and extreme discipline. He introduced new systems of governance and the new recruits shared their skills and customs for the benefit of the empire. He incorporated into law whatever was progressive and useful, and everyone learnt songs from each other's kingdoms as well as the dances and effective fighting methods.

He treated the subjugated people with dignity and fairness, and they became extremely loyal to him. He also decreed high standards of hygiene because he believed that the first line of defence against diseases was cleanliness. He was known to be fussy about his food and did not like the way food was prepared by his relatives at KwaNobamba, so he imported a better chef from the Mthethwa clan. He also looked for a specialist to prepare his *amasi* (curdled milk with whey) and found him in the person of Sompisi kaGuqa kaMsalela Ntuli, who prepared the best *amasi* he had ever tasted. Shaka's genius lay in his meticulous personal attention to detail and for the most critical battles, he personally reconnoitred the ground and the disposition of the enemy. He verified all intelligence reports by procuring corroborating evidence.

Ever since Shaka made all his soldiers dance the war-dance on thorns bare foot, he had been spoiling for a fight to test his soldiers. His target was the Buthelezi kingdom as he wanted to finish what he had started when he was still in Dingiswayo's army. Then he sent a provocative message to Phungashe, demanding an apology for the embarrassment he had caused the Zulu nation over the years by kidnapping his father numerous times. Inevitably, the elderly king was incensed and called Shaka 'an upstart dog'. That was a sure sign of a war declaration and as usual, the festival-like war preparation by the Buthelezi kingdom got under way. Until Shaka burst onto the political scene, wars were comparatively a mere game in contrast to what was to come. Young women would be the first to arrive at the battle theatre and start the hostilities by hurling insults at the enemy. The Buthelezi women brewed even more beer than usual because they were confident the cheeky, young king was no different from his father whom they had often humiliated. As usual, Phungashe went to the battle theatre but sat at a safe distance from the action and drank even more beer under a tree.

The battle formation of the Zulu army was that Shaka led from the front while the uMbelebele and isiKlebe divisions formed the bulk of and 'the head' and 'the chest' and uFasimba regiment was in the centre of 'the chest' behind the head. Whereas 'the horns' attached on either side of uFasimba constituted the iziMpohlo Division. This was the first time that the *iklwa* was utilised as the official fighting weapon without other types of spears. Unfortunately for Phungashe, Shaka knew the enemy's strengths and weaknesses down to the last man and ensured his men were densely formed with the instruction to hold their shields by their sides at the 'carry'. He roared the first instruction to the 'head and chest' section of his army to take their proper fighting formation. When this was done, the second command was the 'show shields' to hold them broadside on. The psychological effect was that the opposing forces suddenly seemed to have doubled. The whole centre then advanced in measured strides to engage the enemy. Mgobhozi was in the front line of uFasimba and Shaka stood right behind them. When they advanced within 50 meters his men, like a singular pre-programmed machine, performed *ingomane* ritual and charged. By this time Shaka was immediately in front of uMbelebele division and once the enemy was engaged, he thundered a command for the horns to deploy.

The stunned Buthelezi first line was vapourised amid a chorus of *'ngadla'* (I have struck). Mgobhozi outperformed everyone with his physical dexterity. He effortlessly hooked his shield with one hand to expose the nipple on the left breast of his enemy and with the other stab them and kept encouraging his men, *'gwazani, madoda gwazani'* (stab, men stab). The Buthelezi were left with only one option, to flee. But Shaka's swift, barefooted men easily ran circles around them. The terrified Buthelezi women could not believe their eyes when they realised that they were not only losing, but the age-old custom of dropping down the spear as a sign of surrender did not apply. The Buthelezi men, humiliated, ran away and hid among the women because custom dictated that anyone who took cover under their women's leather skirts was an utter disgrace. This act was openly admitting defeat but the war-mad Zulu soldiers slaughtered the women as well. Every wounded enemy soldier was killed with a stab through the heart. Then they cut open their abdomens horizontally to let the spirit escape.

Phungashe and some attendants escaped through a densely-covered stream towards the White iMfolozi River while other attendants drew their pursuers away from their king until they too were captured and all were killed. Shaka's men went to Phungashe's capital eMthandeni and killed many people including old people, women and children who would ordinarily be left unscathed. After removing the cattle, they burnt the capital to the ground. Phungashe abandoned his kingdom for good and sought refuge in the Ndwandwe kingdom. The shocked Buthelezi survivors narrated in minute detail how Senzangakhona's son led the army from the front and fought like a wildfire. Poor Phungashe was later beheaded by Zwide's mother who hung his skull in her collection in the *Gallery of Death* hut. Hence, Shaka's laudatory praises:

| | |
|---|---|
| *UDlungwana lukaNdaba* | *Ferocious one of Ndaba* |
| *UDlungwana loMbelebele* | *Ferocious one of uMbelebele Division* |
| *Oludlunge emanxulumeni* | *who raged in the large homesteads* |
| *Kwaze kwasa amanxuluma* | *until the homesteads* |
| *Esebikelana* | *were turned upside down* |

After the war, Shaka and the military high command revisited the new stratagem of total war without sandals and the killing of enemy women. They agreed that the soldiers would permanently discard their *izimbadada* but killing enemy women was a waste. Mgobhozi not wanting to miss such an attractive opportunity, offered to marry as many Buthelezi widows as possible. Furthermore, Mgobhozi could adorn an *isicoco* (a maturity head ring) as a reward for his bravery during the battle. His quest to build a homestead and marry 20 women at the same time was stuff of legends. To fulfil this 'unenviable' task, Shaka became the surrogate *'father'*,

Nandi became the surrogate *'mother'*, Nomcoba and Phampatha became the surrogate *'sisters'* and uFasimba became his surrogate *'brothers'*. When it came to the matters of the heart, the brave Mgobhozi became soft and coy. He allowed each woman to make him promise that they would be the principal wife, every Zulu maiden's dream. Mgobhozi was expected to consummate the marriage with each one of them on the wedding day. According to Zulu culture, the bridegroom is fined a goat for every night the marriage is not consummated. So, it goes without saying, Mgobhozi was facing bankruptcy and his ludicrousness became a public joke throughout the whole kingdom. Amused, Shaka rescued his friend and paid the fines but never let him forget it. Shaka used to make fun of him and ask him how it felt like to be put in a pot and the lid held down by 20 pairs of hands. The wedding festivities lasted all day and ended with the new brides dancing slow voluptuous movements with their hips and thighs. Old women joined in for old time's sake and they all sang the old wedding song that is still sung to this day:

| | |
|---|---|
| Niboyigcina, niboyigcina lengane | be kind, be kind to this young woman |
| Niboyigcina, niboyigcina lentandane | be kind, be kind to the innocent soul |
| Kusasa nizothi uyeba | as tomorrow you will accuse her of being a thief |
| Nithi uyathakatha | you will accuse her of being a witch |
| Nithi udla amaqanda | you will say the |
| Umakoti | bride has unlawfully eaten eggs |

After Mgobhozi's hilarious wedding, life went back to normal and the rigorous disciplined lifestyle of the army continued. Shortly thereafter, a heart-breaking message reached Shaka that his adoptive father Mbiya, was gravely ill and sinking fast. Shaka handpicked 200 members of uFasimba and broke into a steady jog for the 120-kilometre journey to oYengweni Palace. They arrived 24 hours later and without showing any sign of fatigue, Shaka went directly to Mbiya's hut. Dingiswayo joined them and three reminisced about the days gone by and they discussed Shaka's bright future. The old man died in his sleep and both Shaka and Dingiswayo were deeply saddened.

Shaka informed Dingiswayo that he was going to attack one of the most-cruel kings in the land of the Nguni people, King Matiwane of the amaNgwane kingdom as part of the death-cleansing ceremony for Mbiya. The battle theatre was going to be at Ntabankulu at the mound where all the silver jewellery was collected from all over the Zulu empire and buried because Shaka thought that it transmitted smallpox. On a windless day in July 1817, Dingiswayo joined his forces with Shaka and they crossed the White iMfolozi River west of the iNhlazatshe Mountain to destroy the human bile-drinking Matiwane who had an inferiority complex. Matiwane realised that he was going to be defeated so he asked his neighbour King Mthimkhulu of the amaHlubi kingdom to hide his cattle amongst his in the rugged mountains of Ngcuba (Utrecht). Matiwane then deprived the two kings a war by meekly submitting to the Mthethwa sovereignty, moreover he knew that his cattle were safe. But Mthimkhulu did the unthinkable and brazenly refused to give back Matiwane's cattle because he was close to Dingiswayo. In anger, Matiwane managed to obtain some of Mthimkhulu's hair and made plans to bewitch him. But out of nowhere, the ferocious Ndwandwe soldiers swept down on hapless Matiwane and the amaNgwane kingdom and burnt their homes and looted their women and cattle. Now, amaNgwane had neither cattle nor homes and the stunned Matiwane fled immediately. He went berserk and caused havoc as he blazed through innocent people's homesteads in the northern, central and western areas east of today's Ladysmith. He even destroyed the Bhele clan which was related to Mthimkhulu. Matiwane managed to annihilate Mthimkhulu and settled in the area known as Bergville today. The two blood enemies, amaHlubi and amaNgwane fought their last battle over five days in 1825 at Mabolela where they maimed and butchered each other. After four years of sheer mayhem, Shaka sent Mdlaka to stop the madness but Matiwane ran to Qwaqwa where he lost all his cattle. A closer look at what led to the great internal bloody displacement called (*imfecane or uzwekufa*) will show that it in fact, was not caused by Shaka, but he only intervened to bring order.

Shaka did not ever attack people for no apparent reason. Instead, he wanted to create a stable, prosperous and united Zulu empire where peace, serenity and the respect of law reigned supreme. Mpangazitha became the king of amaHlubi after his brother Mthimkhulu died and continued with the havoc as he moved westwards towards the Drakensberg Mountains. He poured into Lesotho, killing everything in his path, and taking the unsuspecting Basotho by surprise. But they fought back courageously under the command of the queen regent Manthatisi of the Batlokwa kingdom whose son, Sekhonyela, was still too young to rule. After successfully repelling Mpangazitha, the petite Manthatisi attacked and defeated about thirty nations around today's Free State area, all the way up to present day Botswana and the land around the Vaal River and was only stopped in Aliwal North as she was heading for the Cape Colony. She left leaving devastation, death and misery in her wake. She also savagely fought off the Ndwandwe, the amaHlubi and amaNgwane armies. Her famous battle along the Caledon River against Moshoeshoe at Butha Buthe where she ran out of weapons and resorted to using kitchen utensils made her a legend in the battle called the *War of the Pots*.

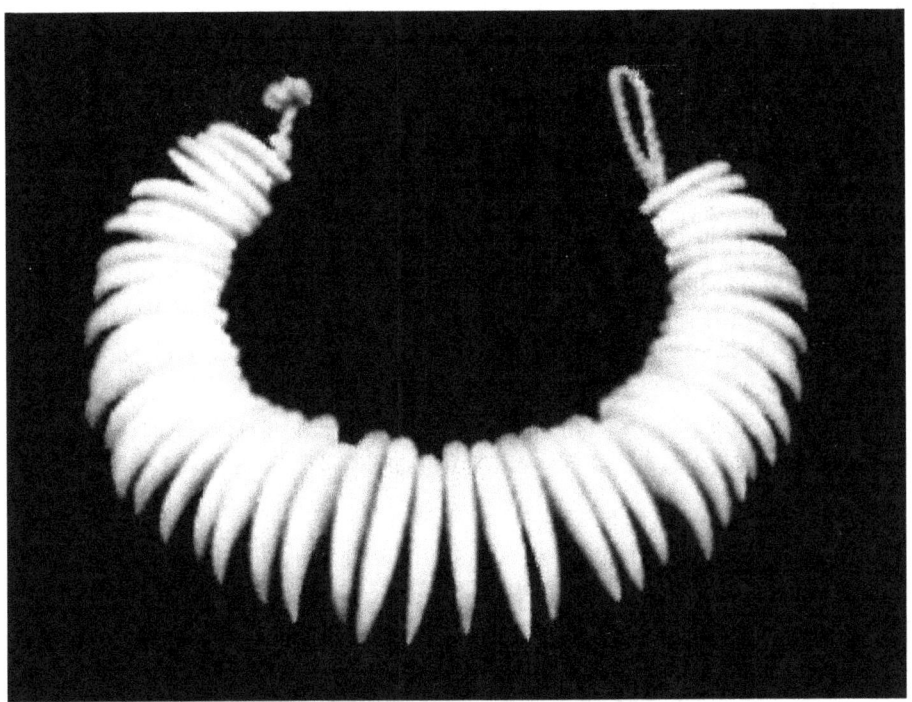

*The royal necklace made out of lion's claws. It is similar to the one Sir Garnet Wolseley, Commander of British Imperial Forces in Natal had ripped off from King Cetshwayo's neck and sent the priceless necklace to his wife Louisa, in England. He instructed her to remove each claw from the necklace and have it inscribed Cetshwayo 28 August 1879 and give to their female friends as a gift. Something extraordinary had happened before this brazen act. The defeated British Imperial Force showed absolute respect to the victorious Zulu king who was now, by forming a 100 metre guard of honour for him to walk through. Major Marter led the procession with a trumpeter, an orderly and a group of officers stood to attention all with drawn swords. They were followed by a company of Dragoon Guards with their accoutrements flashing in the sun and Captains Gibbins and Godsden marched the king. (KwaZulu Cultural Museum)*

## The Ndwandwe Wars

The ancestral land of the large Ndwandwe kingdom lies north-east of the Black iMfolozi River. During Shaka's time, King Zwide kaLanga Ndwandwe reigned supreme. Zwide was conceited and dedicated his life to becoming the leader of all the Nguni people, by any means necessary. He was unhappy that the Mthethwa kingdom was bigger and stronger than his and so ambitious was he that he resorted to witchcraft to make his dream come true. His mother, Ntombazi, holds the record of being the quintessential witch of all time amongst the Nguni people. Despite his might and access to the most potent witchcraft, Zwide lost all battles against Dingiswayo, who was the greatest king in the land of the Nguni people. After Zwide had attacked Matiwane, who was under the Mthethwa sovereignty, Dingiswayo demanded an explanation. When Zwide realised that Dingiswayo was yet again coming after him, he sent his prettiest sister Ntombazana as ambassador to the Mthethwa capital.

She was accompanied by her several attractive female relatives. It was common practice to exchange female relations with other kingdoms as ambassadors. As a result, they would marry into the host royal family and chances of war would be greatly reduced. Zwide's trick worked and Dingiswayo was seduced by Ntombazana and she became one of his wives. Ntombazana's main mission however, was to procure Dingiswayo's semen and take it home. She pulled it off and delivered the semen that she had carried inside her to her mother, Ntombazi. While waiting for the witchcraft to take effect, Zwide kept on sending Dingiswayo gifts to allay any suspicions and to avoid explaining why Ntombazana was not coming back. When Zwide was confident that the witchcraft had taken effect, he killed one of his paternal brothers Malusi who was married to Dingiswayo's favourite sister Nomathuli.

This was to provoke Dingiswayo and he was obviously, enraged. Leading from the front, he mobilised the iNyelezi division to crush Zwide. Dingiswayo's army marched to the Ndwandwe kingdom and camped near KwaDlovunga where Ntombazi lived. He then sent word to Shaka to join him after a week. Indeed, Dingiswayo appeared to have been under a very powerful spell because after a few days, he did the unthinkable - he went straight to the palace accompanied by only eight female bodyguards and kept the rest of the regiments at a distance. Seeing the Mthethwa king walk in, Ntombazi was beside herself with glee. She even slaughtered an ox for Dingiswayo and pretended it was a welcome gesture for the great king. He relaxed and enjoyed the entertainment of song and dance. It seemed as though he forgot he was at war with the Ndwandwe because he was taken aback when Zwide's hit squad forced its way into his hut. But his eight bodyguards put up a fierce fight and blocked the door when the hit squad laid siege. The Amazons hatched an escape plan for Dingiswayo, but he refused and gently told them that they had to accept that he was not going to live forever. After five days without water and food, the Mthethwa retinue finally gave in.

Dingiswayo majestically marched to his death at iSigwegwe Hill above KwaMinyamanzi Palace. And since he was a soldier, he was speared under the left armpit and died. The greatest Mthethwa monarch, King Godongwana Dingiswayo kaJobe kaKhayi kaMadango of the Mthethwa kingdom, fell stone dead without a whimper. The Amazons were unharmed and ordered to return to oYengweni but they refused to leave. Instead, they formed a tight circle over Dingiswayo's body and sang the Mthethwa death song in low, sorrowful tones. Then they simultaneously pulled out small spears they had concealed and plunged them into their hearts and collapsed over the body of the man they all swore to protect and loved.

Zwide subsequently beheaded Dingiswayo and his head joined other heads displayed in Ntombazi's macabre gallery. She carefully scraped Dingiswayo's *isicoco* for its dirt and dismembered the rest of his body. She then slowly removed the fat from his skin and forcefully gave it to Sobhadli Ntombela, one of Dingiswayo's advisers and ordered him to throw it to the pigs. Sobhadli, for fear of retribution, informed Shaka who had it respectfully disposed. The rest of his body was given a morbid royal burial by Ntombazi who slaughtered cattle to accompany Dingiswayo to the next life. It was King Donda of the Khumalo kingdom who covertly sent a message to Shaka before he reached KwaDlovunga about the 'capturing' and the cutting up of Dingiswayo. When Shaka got the news, he cried bitterly and openly, tears streaming down his stern face. He vowed to avenge and recover Dingiswayo's head and quietly lamented *lafa elihle kakhulu* (this is the end of an era) and went back to KwaNobamba. When the news about Dingiswayo horrific end reached oYengweni, his *imidlunkulu* and wives jumped to the top of the huts and pulled the thatch off wailing loudly and they pleaded to be put to death as well.

Dingiswayo's life had been different from his peers. He was well travelled and had met and traded with non-Nguni people such as the Chinese, Indians, Europeans and Arabs. He was a diplomat and ahead of his time as he sought peaceful solutions and preferred mutually beneficial agreements over wars. After Dingiswayo's death, the Mthethwa nation assembled on the parade ground at oYengweni Palace and the laudatory praise reciter. Ngomane addressed them standing next to Mondise, the

Mthethwa heir. He told them that the Mthethwa kingdom was going to be under the Zulu sovereignty but those who wanted to go and be subjects of other kingdoms were free to do so. The overwhelming majority chose to join the Zulu empire. The Sokhulu kingdom also decided to join the Zulu empire at this time. The great King Dingiswayo's laudatory praises illustrate his colourful character:

| | |
|---|---|
| Umafa avuke njengedabane | He who dies and resurrects like a day flower |
| USombangeya kaNdaba | the argumentative son of Ndaba |
| Bamhlaba ngenjongolo | who was stabbed with a sharp object |
| USobangwa | Disputed one |
| Bambangela amanxeba | they caused his wounds |
| Ukuluphala | not to heal |
| UMadlekezele yoYengo | Strong beast of Oyengweni Palace |

Zwide was informed about Shaka's imminent revenge attack for killing Dingiswayo. He approached the Qwabe and Mthembu kingdoms and proposed an alliance against Shaka. Zwide was very confident about his success against Shaka and promised them vast tracts of the land of the Zulu empire. Shaka had also approached the Qwabe and Mthembu kingdoms to join him against Zwide. The two kingdoms chose Zwide's side and mobilised their forces to destroy Shaka and help themselves to his lands. After killing Dingiswayo, Ntombazi's appetite for heads became insatiable. She ordered Zwide to kill Donda for telling on him, Zwide went beyond that he attacked Donda's brothers, Bheje and Mashobana. Bheje managed to escape to the dense Ngome forest where he hid in the caves undetected in his fort called *inqaba kaBheje* (Bheje's Fort). But Mashobana was killed. Mashobana's son Mzilikazi, was taken to live with his grandfather Zwide at KwaDlovunga Palace. But Mzilikazi ran away from his grandfather and went to live under Shaka's tutelage at KwaBulawayo.

Donda and Mashobana's skulls were also suspended in Ntombazi's hut. The brutal and gratuitous murders by Zwide caused great alarm among the Nguni kingdoms as it had never been heard of before. After terrorising everyone within reach Zwide felt ready for the ultimate prize, the Mthethwa sovereignty now that Dingiswayo was no more. It was only the young Zulu upstart Shaka, with a dodgy background and with no illustrious war history, that stood in Zwide's way to glory and absolute power. Nguni custom dictates that an heir did not only inherit the estate but also inherited the debts. In this case, Zwide reminded Shaka that his father Senzangakhona had died before making good on his promise of handing over his three sisters Princesses Mkabayi, Mmama and Mawa after helping him fight Phungashe. Therefore, Shaka had to handover his aunts immediately. Shaka dismissed Zwide with contempt and called him an 'old dried-out hide'. When word arrived to Zwide, as far as he was concerned, that was a declaration of war. His over confidence and hatred for Shaka made him make weak battle plans, whereas Shaka's battle plans were meticulous.

Shaka moved the uFasimba military base (*ikhanda*) from KwaBulawayo to Dlangubo near Empangeni where its ruins can be found to this day. The pre-war tension was tangible amongst Shaka's men and to relieve the pressure Shaka created a competition. He hammered a spear with a long staff deep into the ground and challenged anyone to pull it out with one hand. The reward was that that person would be bestowed with one of his praise names, *Nodumehlezi*. Many did not bother to try because the spear was too deep in the ground. But to everyone's surprise Shaka's personal floor polisher, Nomgqomfiya kaNogandaya Ncwane, stopped polishing the floors with cow dung. He stood up, wiped his hands clean and casually walked towards the spear and with little effort, yanked it out from the ground with one hand. Stunned by such physical might, the onlookers gave Nomgqomfiya a huge applause. Shaka was delighted to share his praise names with this Samson, a broad-shouldered two-metre tall mountain of a man. He became known as *Zulu* instead of *Nodumehlezi* because according to the Zulu culture, no commoner can use an emperor's name. Hence there are so few people called Shaka to this day.

The two had first met in Mpaphala, in the Qwabe kingdom when they were younger. Nomgqomfiya had joined Shaka's army together with his two friends, Sithunga and Magutshwa Qwabe, who were brothers renowned for their bravery. Shaka had been particularly grateful that the three friends had chosen to join him instead of joining Zwide. One of Nomgqomfiya's feats was to defeat a notorious bully Nkomo, Shandu's grandson of the Mbatha kingdom, in a famed hand-to-hand fight. Shaka specifically created uMgumanqa regiment (a part of uMbelebele division) so that the three friends could be its founder members. Prince Mpande later joined the regiment. The *ikhanda* was north of the White iMfolozi River near eMahlabathini. The uMgumanqa regiment was under the command of a thickset man Shaka nicknamed *uMabhekuzana* because when he walked, he waddled like a duck. In one of the empire-building wars, Nomgqomfiya almost single-handedly massacred the Ndawonde kingdom because they had attacked the amaChube kingdom.

The amaChube people were related to Shaka and they were also the royal copperware manufacturers and produced all royal copper ornaments and jewellery. Nomgqomfiya later built himself a homestead *eNtshaseni* and his friend Sithunga managed it. But after Shaka's death, Nomgqomfiya escaped Dingane's deranged purges by fleeing to the south of uThukela River. Shaka also offered a large reward to any soldier who would kill most of the Ndwandwe and offered a stupendous number of cattle. He said that the cattle would be so many that when a stick was placed across their backs it would not fall as they moved. Dengezimashumi kaKhuzwayo Mdlalose responded by jumping up with his shield held high, out dancing everyone and shouting: *'Uyababaza, uyababaza?'* (are you impressed, are you impressed?)

Everything being equal, Shaka stood no chance against the Zwide and his forces because the numbers favoured the Ndwandwe kingdom. Therefore, every male in the Zulu realm, including those below the military age and the retired were mobilised under *ukhukhulelangoqo* (national call-up) drive. The new recruits were knocked into shape by the indefatigable Mgobhozi and the new Mthethwa monarch Mondise swelled Shaka's army with the regiments from eMnini, eZiyodleya, oHheni, eManineni, eNhlabeni, eziChweni, eNyakeni, eNingizimu, eNtambanana, eNhlangano, eNyakatho, eBalungwini and eSifazaneni. Through sheer genius, Shaka managed to persuade the Ndwandwe head of the secret service, Noluju Mthembu *aka* Nzuza Nqayi, to spy for him. Mdlaka was second-in-command to Shaka and Nqoboka commanded the Sokhulu, Sibiya and Dlamini regiments and his deputy was Ndlela kaSompisi who was ordinarily the commander of iNtontela regiment. He was handsome, sported a small beard, light-brown in complexion and almost two-metres tall, yet he was still slighty shorter than Shaka. His homestead was at eziBungwini near eMacala Hill. He was famous for the battle scars which were all over his body, including his face. He once stayed at the battle theatre for several days, alone and finished off those who were wounded. But he ran out of food and ended up eating his *ilunga* (war shield) which was black with two white markings in the centre.

Mkabayi became intrigued by her nephew's audacity to take on someone whose regiments were six times larger than his. As she sat contemplating the future, she was startled by Shaka who burst into her private quarters with Ndlela in tow, again unannounced. Her blood froze. The two standing before her ought to have been blood enemies because Ngwadi had drowned Ndlela's uncle, Sigujana, not too long ago. But they seemed at ease with one another and they were discussing the forthcoming war strategy. After heartfelt greetings, Shaka officially shared his battle plan and Ndlela heard for the first time that the battle theatre was going to be at Gqokli Hill, above White Imfolozi River. He requested Mkabayi to burn *impepho* (sage, the royal herb) and to implore the Zulu ancestors to protect them during the war. He also appointed her commander of the rear guard that protected the cattle, women, children, the elderly and the infirm. When Shaka noticed that his aunt's apprehension, he reassured her by promising to defeat Zwide within two days.

That assurance did not have the desired effect because her body language and the sighs clearly expressed the Zulu forms of uneasiness. To allay her fears, Shaka gave her permission to watch the war from the lofty heights of eMthonjaneni Mountains. Mkabayi was thankful for the privilege and expressed gratitude that Shaka had personally come to share his plans and also reassure her. As far she could recall, this was a first because even though kings shared their battle plans with the nation's senior women, they rarely did so in person. Shaka also went to esiKlebeni and the KwaNobamba Palaces and discussed with the senior women and the royal women. Mkabayi noticed that Shaka's body language exuded confidence as he left. He was very much like her grandfather, Ndaba, and was for the first time confident that the future of the Zulu empire was in good hands. She began preparations to send her charge to the Nkandla forest and took all the maize from the granaries and all available food with them and spilt water from the gourds and went into the dense Nkandla forest. It had been a year since Dingiswayo had been beheaded and the Mthethwa kingdom had completed their mandatory mourning period and Shaka's fortunes were about to change.

It was April 1818 and the Zulu kingdom had every reason to be afraid, extremely afraid. The women spellbound, watched in horror as hundreds of Ndwandwe regiments marched past one of King Zwide's palaces, eKuqhobekeni in the iNhlungwane Valley near the Black iMfolozi River. Zwide's heir, Prince Nomhlanjana who was about Shaka's age, led the army and some of his sons led the legendary amaNkayiya, uMgazi, isiKwishi, iziBoya and amaPhela regiments. The Ndwandwe people were respected expert spear makers, so war and the use of such weaponry came naturally to them. There is a Zulu saying that: 'The Ndwandwe are born with spears in their hands'. Shaka's main army camped at the summit of Gqokli Hill and the rest were out of sight of the enemy. They had brought enough rations, water and firewood to last them for two days as per Shaka's anticipation. Since Mkabayi had removed all the food and water in the vicinity, Shaka was confident that there was no way the Ndwandwe army could survive for more than two days. Shaka did not want to risk an open war with the powerful Ndwandwe and knew that his advantage lay in striking hard when the Ndwandwe were fewer as they would be forced to go look for food and water in the areas surrounding the White iMfolozi and the uMkhumbane rivers, which were further away. His strategy was to retreat to iNkandla forest if his strategy failed. Moreover, he could rely on his cousin, King Zokufa kaDlaba kaNcube of the Shezi kingdom (they were related through their mothers) as well as on his close friend, King Zihlandlo kaGcwabe of the Mkhize kingdom, as they both lived inside the forest.

As usual, the war began before sunrise and the armies clashed inside and around the flooded White iMfolozi River. Nqoboka, Ndlela and Njikiza kaCuba Ngcolosi guarded one of the crossing points and killed many Ndwandwe soldiers who tried to cross the river. Njikiza towered over the other soldiers like a biblical Goliath with majestically bulging muscles. He was stubborn, arrogant, powerful. He used to wrestle leopards to death in the forest for fun. He used his oversized club to such good effect that he was given more praise names and called *uNohlolamazibuko* (watcher of the ford). On the first day Nomhlanjana retreated early from the battle theatre because they had lost many men and others had left in search of water. But overall, it was a good day for the Zulu army because they suffered fewer casualties. The Zulu military high command which included Mgobhozi, Mdlaka, Nzobo and Ngomane reviewed the day's events and went to sleep satisfied and exhausted. They slept on grass mats and covered themselves with warm animal hides and with fires around them.

At dawn, Nqoboka went to report to Shaka and found him long awake and in deep contemplation, all while the familiar snoring came from Mgobhozi's corner which made Shaka smile. The sight of the tired Zulu army sleeping in formation was a sight to behold. They even seemed to breathe in unison, these were Shaka's soldiers at their best. In the morning, the Zulu soldiers leisurely enjoyed grilled meat breakfast and once refreshed, they were raring to go. As Shaka was briefing his generals and lieutenants on his diversion tactics, which was to tempt the Ndwandwe into the following the Zulu cattle that over the eMthonjaneni Heights about 10 km south of the battle theatre, his lover Phampatha arrived. She begged Shaka to allow her to confuse and weaken the Ndwandwe regiments. She wanted to disguise herself as a married woman and then disrobe in front of the Ndwandwe soldiers and seductively walk slowly towards them, pointing at them with her right hand. Being superstitious, the Ndwandwe would have refused to fight after seeing the body of a naked 'married' woman, which was a sign of bad luck. Shaka was touched by the appealing gesture but turned her down and sent her home. Shaka gave final orders and cautioned them about the Ndwandwe's simulated flight and how to counter it. Finally, they were ready for the fight that would determine Shaka's future among the Nguni people and his place in history.

The Ndwandwe received reinforcements overnight and just before sunrise, they poured across the iNhlungwane River in their thousands at two points. Half hungry and thirsty from the overnight march, Shaka's ruse worked as they rushed to Gqokli Hill in pursuit of fleeing Zulu cattle. Nomhlanjana sent numerous Ndwandwe soldiers to retrieve them. Those not sent after the cattle came face-to-face with the Zulu army on the summit of Gqokli Hill. The time was now about nine in the morning. Shaka and his men - who had been lying in wait since daybreak - suddenly rose in unison, like one man. They performed the *ingomane* ritual and the hill vibrated and Shaka roared the attack command and they charged. Mgobhozi's instruction was to take a regiment and not engage in battle but guard the food and water supplies at the centre of the summit with their lives. Nzobo led from the southern front, Nqoboka from the eastern front and Ngomane from the western front and the battle ensued. The *udibi* were so excited by the battle that they got into mischief by participating in the war without being given authority and they used the fallen Ndwandwe spears to stab the outclassed and overwhelmed Ndwandwe regiments. Nzobo's southern flank came under heavy attack, but his men fought back with superhuman effort that could have only been inspired by a king like Shaka. They sliced through six or seven lines of the Ndwandwe soldiers and turned back and continued to attack their rear. They only stopped fighting when they were stabbed many times over and were bleeding profusely. This unprecedented bravery is the source of the adage that *'you must not only stab a Zulu to death, but you must also push him over to make sure that the corpse falls over'*.

During the furious battle, the principal wife of Lubongo, Ndwandwe, who was hiding in one of the Ndwandwe caves, went into labour. Unfortunately, it was a breach delivery and there were no midwives nearby because they were in hiding far away. She was then carried to the nearest Zulu camp in hope of assistance. This was the source of the repulsive fallacy that Shaka used to regularly cut open pregnant women's stomachs open to see how the baby lay inside the womb, started. Another version of this story was that Shaka cut the pregnant woman open because it was Zwide's child and Shaka wanted Zwide's blood to counter Ntombazi's evil magic. These rumours could not be further from the truth because when Shaka was informed about the predicament, he instructed a gynaecologist and obstetrician from the amaWombe regiment (the Zulu army's medical regiment) to perform a caesarean section. Both the mother and child survived, and their descendants can be found around Nongoma to this day.

The sound of clashing shields, the resonating sound of spears and the smell of fresh blood throughout the day, made Mgobhozi beg Shaka for a long time to join the bloodletting. But Shaka would not hear of it. Mgobhozi accused Shaka of wanting him to be remembered for dying in his sleep like an old woman. Shaka finally relented and allowed him to join the fray, but with strict instructions to personally find and kill Zwide's sons. Because Mgobhozi was reckless with his life, Njikiza and

Nkayishana kaKhuzwayo Mdlalose were to keep an eye on him. Without wasting any time Mgobhozi jumped into the fray and outperformed himself. He managed to single-handedly kill five Ndwandwe princes, Nomhlanjana, Mphepha, Sixoloba, Dayingubo and Nombengula but one of their brothers Sikhunyana escaped. Long before sunset, Zwide's pride and legendary amaPhela regiment fell, which was a gargantuan catastrophe for the Ndwandwe who began to lose focus and heart. Fountains of blood spurted from both the Ndwandwe and the Zulu soldiers and they tried to stop the bleeding by stuffing grass, leaves or hair into their wounds and continue fighting. Their eyes turned red and blood oozed from their mouths, noses and ears but each side kept on stabbing until they fell over. Shaka chose the fleetest platoon to outrun the deserting Ndwandwe soldiers and covertly set Zwide's capital, palaces and all homesteads under his domain they came across on fire.

The Ndwandwe soldiers who had run away from the battle could not believe their eyes when they saw Zulu soldiers burning their homes. To them this could have only meant one thing, that the Zulu army possessed 'special magic' that could make them be in more than one place at a time. As far as they were concerned, Shaka had sent all able-bodied Zulu men to the battle theatre. The morale of the Ndwandwe soldiers evaporated when they realised that their commander and the Ndwandwe heir Nomhlanjana, had been killed. Hence some of them never returned from looking for water and others plainly deserted. Some of the Ndwandwe regiments continued fighting with much vigour. Mgobhozi was stabbed from behind and had fallen face down motionless, even though Njikiza crushed Ndwandwe skulls that got too close to Mgobhozi. As a result, Njikiza went into a furore and frenetically crushed even more skulls.

The main Ndwandwe army had not given up hope yet and continued to bring the fight to the Zulu forces. The collapse of the iziMpohlo division was catastrophic because it meant Shaka was in danger of being killed. He fought gallantly but with the Zulu forces spread out thinly, it was necessary that he retreated to KwaBulawayo. He was accompanied by a few of his elite royal guards, with the Ndwandwe in hot pursuit. Shaka took his last stand in his private hut surrounded by uFasimba regiment and the outcome of what would follow was going to shape the history of Southern Africa. Outnumbered, a legendary strong man Manyosi, stood at the door of the hut as Shaka contemplated his destiny. Volley after volley of Ndwandwe spears rained down on Manyosi for over an hour and he fended them off with his shield and also fought them back in hand-to-hand combat, killing many of them and maiming the rest. He was only stopped when a marksman threw a spear from a distance and injured Manyosi in the chest. After the battle Shaka thanked Manyosi with huge tracts of land at Othini on Machanca Highlands where he died of old age in 1873.

As Manyosi was fighting off the Ndwandwe, Shaka made good his escape and went back to the battle front, even more motivated. He rejoined his forces, and this spurred them to fight more ferociously and to the Ndwandwe soldiers, it seemed as though they were deranged. The Zulu soldiers implemented more of his ingenious tactics, which finally saw the tide turn to their favour. Shaka only exhaled when the last of the Ndwandwe army retreated into the sunset. The Zulu military high command could not believe their luck as they watched the once invincible Ndwandwe army flee. It was during the debriefing assembly after sunset that it was confirmed that Mgobhozi was missing. In unison, the soldiers lamented sorrowfully: '*Bambulele uMgobhozi ovela entabeni* (they have killed uMgobhozi who comes from the mountain).' Some of the men could not eat their supper and cried openly.

They noticed that Njikiza was also missing and dispatched a small search-and-rescue mission back to the battle theatre. Njikiza was found in deep sorrow standing over a mound of corpses where Mgobhozi fell. He then recounted the last few minutes with his hero but as they spoke, loud snoring was heard beneath the corpses and Shaka's stony face relaxed for a moment. Listening carefully, Shaka heard the same snoring the previous night next to his soldiers. Filled with hope, he ordered the men to find out who it was. After being fished out from beneath the corpses, Mgobhozi cracked a lazy smile that allowed the hidden charm which captivated all those around him especially women, escape. He nonchalantly asked why people around him looked so morose. They all erupted in laughter and they prided themselves in their unbelievable achievement. This battle uncovered many heroes such as Gcogcomo Ngathini, Mvudlana kaMenziwa Biyela, two Khuzwayo brothers, Nkayishana and Ndengezi but *Ndengezimashumi* to his peers.

Shaka and everyone agreed, Ndengezi was the best fighter. True to his word, Shaka gave him 100 cattle but Ndengezi said it was not enough and demanded all Zwide's cattle. Shaka tried to reason with him and said other distinguished fighters had to be rewarded too, but Ndengezi would have none of it. He said that he either got what he wanted, or he would go into exile where his services would be better appreciated. Then Shaka called his bluff. Ndengezi went to his homestead, taking only a few cows. Yet, he had the audacity to return to where the army was still assembled and bid Shaka and everyone else farewell without flinching. He left his wives, children and extended family behind and Shaka, who was truly sad to see him go, wished him well. Ndengezi is said to have joined Soshangane far away in Mozambique. Sadly, his brother Nkayishana was killed years later by Mpande (when he was king) for no apparent reason.

Mkabayi watched the war from eMthonjaneni Heights and was in awe of her nephew's audacity and brilliance. She watched the amazing spectacle with Queen Mother Mthaniya and they both beamed with pride and they knew this was the beginning a bright future of the once despised kingdom. They recalled the difficult days when his obnoxious mother Nandi used to harass everyone in defence of her son. To celebrate his success, Shaka built the impressive eMpangisweni Palace in the Mthethwa kingdom. This is how the palace transformed into eMpangeni, a vibrant coastal town on the north coast near Eshowe and *Mandlanzini* (Richards Bay). Most of the Nguni kingdoms that were not members of the growing Zulu empire, such as the Mabaso, Ndlovu, Sikhakhane, Khumalo, Mamba, Khoza, Magulana, Ngubane and Mpungose now rushed to pay allegiance to the young warrior king. Shaka appointed his close friend Mlandela kaSomkhele as king of the Mthethwa kingdom and made Ngomane the prime minister of the Zulu empire. After this war, Shaka formed the first female regiment, the uMvuthwamini regiment. It comprised one thousand young, strong and beautiful women who were in their prime. They were named after a wild berry that ripens at midday. The women soldiers' uniform was the briefest attire, which ensured they could display their dainty ornamental scarring.

All the new Zulu recruits from the recently joined nations were drilled in the Zulu way of fighting such as the system of rapidly transmitting orders from the commander to the ranks. This also included the battle ritual of *ingomane* and the signal for executing an order. The soldiers also became exempt from being suspected of dabbling in witchcraft. This master stroke of making it illegal to suspect any soldier of witch craft, socially lifted the army above the reaches of the dubious divining profession. The soldiers also received a state pension of cattle on retirement, which had revolutionary repercussions. The daily 100-kilometre march, mostly jogging which culminated in battle manoeuvres, was the order of the day. In these marches, any soldier who fell out of line for no justifiable reason was killed instantly, with his own spear.

Having both male and female regiments as a standing army was a first among the Nguni people. What is more, Shaka kept a volunteer army because even though there was national conscription and every adult belonged to a regiment, no one was forced to go to war. Secret service officers were an elite unit comprising the brightest and sharpest minds. Shaka was debriefed by his secret service daily with reports from all over the empire. Superspy Noluju trained another great secret agent, Nongila Mabaso, who also served Dingane. Other notable spies were Bhocu kaNomabhuqabhuqa and Nomgqula kaNsizwana Dladla of the iNtontela regiment. The spies travelled as far as Lake Victoria and beyond in the north and went as far south as the Table Mountain and reached Namibia and Angola as well.

During an assembly or parade, whenever Shaka walked between his soldiers towards a podium, they would form a guard of honour whilst standing at attention. He would strike each shield on either side with his *iklwa* as he passed. When going to war, the army usually jogged toward the enemy's territory shortly after sunset and continue overnight. If the distance was far away, they would camp at strategic points but always in the enemy's territory. Often, Shaka was confident enough to inform his enemy of the day of the attack but left the actual time a surprise. His secret weapon was to choose a strategic time to attack and often, he would use nursing calves as an alarm clock. They bellowed for the first time around two o'clock in the morning and he would overwhelm the enemy suddenly with speed. He attacked at this time because sleep was at its deepest and ensured to attack upwind to avoid detection by the animals. His regiments adorned vivid colours and their steps were synchronised and deliberate which instilled mortal fear in his bewildered enemies.

Even though Shaka exclusively used *iklwa*, his regiments were also allowed to use an assortment of other weapons such as swords, arrows and spears in case their *iklwa* broke in action. Shaka took the business of war seriously and never went to war with poor intelligence. He knew the strength and skill of the enemy, which influenced his battle plan. It was only after thorough deliberations with the king's council and the military high command that the decision to go to war was taken. The council of women elders who were post-menopausal was also consulted and had the power to veto the war plans. The role of women throughout the kingdom during a war was to cover their faces with special herbs and wear leather skirts inside out. Grass mats and brooms and other household items were kept upright for the duration of war. Everyone else observed the restrain ritual in their daily activities. On the day of attack, Shaka would wake up earlier than usual and adorn his full battle regalia such as the *insimango* (blue monkey) tails and *uve* (flycatcher), *amagwalagwala* (lourie) as well as *indwe* (blue-crane) feathers on his head. The *indwe* feathers were procured by Fodo kaNombewu kaGansa Nhlangwini, who grew up between uThukela and uMzinyathi Rivers, where his descendants still live to this day. Shaka would walk around the capital and pause at the entrance of each assembly point and sing his favourite war song:

| | |
|---|---|
| UNdaba angadlizwe lonke | Ndaba can conquer all territories |
| Zonke inkomo zamadoda | and plunder the defeated men's cattle |
| Woya, ye | woya ye |
| Ayesaba amagwala | cowards are fearful |
| Ayasala | they stay behind |
| Ohh hhi hhi | ohh hhi hhi |
| Woya | woya |
| Khethani amagwala | isolated the cowards |
| Yiwo, ohho | there they are, hoho |
| Makhwelo | Dominant one |
| Woya | woya |
| Ohho | ohho |

Zwide did not rest after the humiliation at Gqokli Hill. He was convinced that the Zulu 'upstart' won by fluke and recruited well-known mercenaries Nqaba kaMbekane Msane and Zwangendaba kaJele Gumbi. He then appointed his relative, Soshangane kaZikode kaGasa kaManukuza Ndwandwe, as the commander-in-chief. When Shaka got wind that Zwide was planning a revenge attack, he also began preparing for the inevitable. Shaka sent Ncozana kaMoni to King Phakathwayo of the Qwabe kingdom to ask him for support. But Phakathwayo was not interested and said Shaka must go and ask for help from the Basothos, a non-Nguni group not known for being brave. This hostile response was a clear indication that he was against Shaka, so Shaka decided to sort him out before facing the formidable Zwide. He deluded Phakathwayo into responding to two false attacks and on the third attack, Zwide's only surviving decent regiment iziNkonde was annihilated.

Phakathwayo successfully ran away and hid at his Bhekunyawo Palace, where he was subsequently bitten by a snake. Eventually the Zulu tracked him down and Shaka decided not to kill him because they were related. Instead, he instructed Phakathwayo's brothers Nomo and Nqetho to take care of him overnight. However, in the morning his brothers claimed that he had died from the snakebite. But Shaka knew better because both brothers were vying for the throne, so he suspected that they had killed him during the night. But neither brother admitted to doing it, so as punishment Shaka sent them both to exile with nothing. Nqetho headed south and Nomo went to the land of the Mthethwa where his mother came from. That was the end of the sovereignty of the Qwabe kingdom because Shaka incorporated them into the junior House of Malandela, the Zulu empire.

The Qwabe were skilled fighters but even better swimmers. They formed the bulk of Shaka's engineers who built bridges from papyrus and, made *izihlenga* (reed canoes) that enabled soldiers to navigate and cross rivers rapidly. It pleased Shaka that the merger was achieved with little bloodshed and without destruction to property. One peculiar habit of the Qwabe nation was cremation, a ritual generally shunned by the Nguni people. When Phakathwayo's father Khondlo died, his body was cremated, and his ashes were swept into iNkwayinye River, a tributary of uMhlathuze River in an elaborate ceremony, which had been the old king's wish. After the defeat of the Qwabe kingdom, at least thirty other Nguni kingdoms joined the Zulu sovereignty. It included King Manzini of the Zungu kingdom together with his only regiment amaNketshane. Manzini had provided Shaka with intelligence about Zwide's war strategy.

In preparation for the imminent war, Shaka deployed the isiPhezi, uNteke, uMbonambi, uMgumanqa and uKhangela regiments to the east of iMatheku River. The mighty uDlangezwa regiment was moved closer to the sea between the mouths of the uMhlathuze and uMlalazi Rivers under the shadows of the oNgoye Mountains, not far from the current site of the University of Zululand. When Shaka was ready to go to war with Zwide, he secretly met with Noluju in person and they made final arrangements. Preparations for war included the removal of all food and water from within a large radius of the battle theatre while the women, children, cattle and the infirm were to be evacuated to remote caves in the eDlinza, eMhlathuze, oNgoye, eNgome, eNkandla and eDukuduku forests. Shaka's new war tactic was that only two people were to know the final battle plan and battle theatre. This battle tactic was used for many years later and by many Zulu leaders such as Sigananda kaZokufa kaNcube Shezi, Dingane, Mpande, Mgobhozi and Mzilikazi. This time it was only Shaka and Mdlaka who knew the final battle plan and battle theatre. This method of command continued even when Shaka no longer accompanied soldiers on faraway campaigns. This secrecy made it possible for Zulu enemies to be caught off guard as there was no leakage of information, and the army always achieved the element of surprise no matter how far away the military target was.

Shaka lured Zwide's army to the slopes of the uMhlathuze River in eNkandla forest where they found no army and no food. What enraged the Ndwandwe was that they had marched all day without any resistance. But what upset them more was that they had to spend their first night away from home on the bleak and frosty Melmoth highlands. Since they had to keep their exact position secret, they sat in the dark, freezing and made no fires. In the meanwhile, Shaka's army was having the last laugh as it terrorised the Ndwandwe with false attacks and blood-curdling war cries all night. As if that was not enough, the Zulu stole the Ndwandwe cattle they had brought as provisions. Shaka assembled his army deep inside the forest and their faces reflected eagerness in the glow of the flickering flames from the fires with their scintillating weapons next to them. Shaka sat against an ancient yellowwood tree and at his feet lay white shield speckled with black dots. A sense of foreboding was in the air. Close to Shaka sat Sigananda whose grandfather Mvakela was married to Shaka's maternal aunt. They had lived together at eLangeni. Mzilikazi was on Shaka's left and so was his two paternal brothers, Dingane who was 22 years old and a member of the amaWombe regiment and the 15-year-old Mpande who was also Shaka's *udibi*.

Shaka chose a guerrilla unit of about 50 men to go behind enemy lines. The plan was that they had to pretend to be a Ndwandwe and be the first to greet every person they came across by saying 'Ndwandwe'. If it was one of them, they would answer with '*qobolwayo*' (the real one) and the person who had greeted first would respond by also saying '*qobolwayo*'. If the person did not say so, they would be stabbed immediately. To further terrorise the Ndwandwe, Shaka's men had to hiss like snakes as they crept near the sleeping Ndwandwe, then suddenly stab them to cause great pandemonium. This tactic worked, as the Ndwandwe ended up killing one another in the mayhem and terrifying screams pierced the quiet night. Even Soshangane was disturbed by the 'supernatural' events that he could not explain to his now confounded soldiers. They gathered around his quarters and sat down facing outwards. Soshangane encouraged his men to sleep as he needed them fresh in the morning for the onslaught against Shaka.

The commander of the Zulu guerrilla unit Nomabanga kaNgidli was the last one to report to Shaka as he stayed back and stabbed the largest number of Ndwandwe men. Upon his return, he was given a standing ovation and Shaka bestowed him a new praise name, *inyoni eyalahleka phakathi kwamaphela* (the bird that gets lost in and around cockroaches). By daybreak the surviving Ndwandwe could not thank their ancestors enough for surviving the night, while some of them had deserted in the middle of the night and fled back to their homes. The Zulu faced the Ndwandwe east of iSungulwane Hill by mid-morning and both armies were in battle formations 500 metres apart. There were 10 000 highly trained and disciplined Zulu soldiers with great mobility compared with 16 000 Ndwandwe soldiers commanded by Zwangendaba. Shaka's iziNtenjana and uKhangela regiments as well as the younger regiments of the uMbelebele division stormed the Ndwandwe by spreading out along a 250-metre front, several lines deep and outflanked the Ndwandwe. This manoeuvre stunned Soshangane who quickly reorganised his men in front to prevent a catastrophe that would have come from behind. At one spear's throw way, in perfect unison, the Zulu did the *ingomane* and like a whirlwind, they were all over the awestruck enemy.

Despite Shaka having fewer soldiers than the Ndwandwe, the battle was completed within a few hours. The Ndwandwe were totally routed. Ndlela and Mdlaka were critically wounded and a deeply concerned Shaka instructed one of his praise singers, Ndlaludaka, to intercede and ask the Zulu ancestors to save the souls of his two friends, even if they were saved for just one more battle. Some of the surviving Ndwandwe soldiers joined Shaka while others fled into the wilderness. One of Shaka's paternal brothers, Huzula, was a brilliant military strategist and he suggested that the uMbonambi and isiPhezi regiments be dispatched at nightfall to secure Zwide and his evil mother Ntombazi who were both at ekuQhobekeni Palace. He said they had to reach the royal homestead before Ndwandwe fugitives could warn them of their defeat. Huzula said they must enter by deception and by the next nightfall, they had covered more than 110 kilometres. They entered the grounds of ekuQhobekeni Palace singing the Ndwandwe victory songs.

Excited, everyone came out to meet 'their' victorious sons, brothers and husbands. But suddenly 'their heroes' began to kill everyone including children - which was rare. As though they had sensed something was amiss, Zwide and his mother did not come out to meet the heroes. So, when the slaughter began only Ntombazi was caught. Zwide managed to evade the killers by hiding on a patch of dry land in the middle of a nearby riverbed. He walked by night through Vryheid and crossed the uPhongolo River and entered Swaziland with his two sons Madanga and Somaphunga, daughters Thandile (Nompethu), File, Nolwandle and others. They sought temporary refuge near Piggs Peak in Swaziland where Madanga and Thandile, File, Nolwandle remained. Zwide and Somaphunga fled further north-west to the land of King Thulare of the Bapedi kingdom near the iNkomati River. Thulare fought Zwide but was defeated and the unfortunate Bapedi people lived in fear under the rule of Zwide for years. Zwide put a good 320-kilometres between himself and his ekuQhobokeni Palace. His relative, Soshangane, managed to escape from the battle together with his cousins Sekhunyana, Nqaba and Zwangendaba along with some regiments and they all headed north. Nobody knew then that these men would change the history and destiny of a large tract of Southern Africa.

Zwangendaba meandered through Zimbabwe, Mozambique, Malawi, Kenya and Uganda. After 20 years of continuous war and about 1600 km from the Zulu kingdom, he was crowned king and finally settled in Western Tanzania where he built his *Maphupho* (dreams) Palace in Fipa where he later died. His descendants can still be found in the Songea and Mbongwe areas in Usumbwa, Tanzania as well as some of his palaces on the shores of Lake Victoria. Zwangendaba left a trail of about 16 kingdoms in his wake and one of his elite regiments *Thutha* conquered King Mirambo of the Unyamwenzi kingdom in Tanzania. Zulu soldiers who ended up in other countries such as Mozambique, Malawi, Kenya, Uganda and Rwanda named some of their homesteads and palaces after places that they left behind. For instance, Bhanganomo is called *Bhagamoyo* in Tanzania and *Burundi* is named after uLundi. Furthermore, the descendants of the Zulu regiments were called different names in these countries.

In Zambia's eastern province and in the south of the Democratic Republic of Congo they are called the *Ngoni*. In Malawi they are called the *Angoni*. Along the southern coast of Angola their descendants still speak a mixture of Zulu and local languages and are called the *Nguni*. In Uganda, they are called the *Chagga* (a misspelling of Shaka) and along the border of Tanzania and Kenya they speak a language called *Shaka*. Others still live around the slopes of Mount Kilimanjaro in the Ubetu, Reha and Kahe areas. In South Sudan, the capital city is called Juba, which means "in a dove" in isiZulu and one of their kingdoms is called the *Pojulu* kingdom which means 'from the Zulu' in Bari language and they claim their ancestry to the Zulu nation. Sikhunyana, Nqaba, Lubhedu and their followers crossed the Tubatse (*Steelpoort*) River and settled in the Bapedi kingdom. Nqaba also raided the peaceful Manyika people around Mutare and the Chimanimani Mountains in Eastern Zimbabwe. Some of his people can be found around the uMzilizwe River area to this day.

Some of Zwide's much younger sons Shimane, Nqabeni and Mlomo survived the slaughter and joined Shaka who enlisted them in the iziNyosi, the youngest and last regiment Shaka formed before he was murdered. Somaphunga returned to the Zulu kingdom after his father Zwide died. The benevolent Shaka allowed him to have his wives and cattle back but he did not allow him to return to the land of his forefathers, at iNhlungwane Valley. This decisive victory and utter crushing of the Ndwandwe kingdom had solidified Shaka's position as the emperor among the Nguni people without any doubt. This feat made everyone cower before him and no one thought of challenging him to war ever again. At last, Shaka's political and cultural footprint was larger than that created by his mentor Dingiswayo. Shaka now ruled from south of uMzimvubu River in the south to the uPhongolo River in the north, and from the Buffalo River in the west to the sea in the east an area of about 20 000 square kilometres. This area formed greater Zulu kingdom which fast became the heart of the Zulu empire.

Finally, Shaka felt convinced that he had power to standardise and rationalise all activity within his domain. After defeating Zwide, Shaka took a long leisurely walk towards the Ndwandwe territory which was devoid of any life and headed to ekuQhobekeni Palace where the 70-year-old Ntombazi was safely locked up inside her macabre thirty-skull gallery. Her trial began the following morning in full view of everyone. Shaka sat under a tree and led the prosecution. He was even-tempered with her because, instead of defending herself, she taunted Shaka about his birth and refused to co-operate. Shaka did not sentenced her to death, as she was a queen of an already defeated kingdom. Instead, he sentenced her to life inside a hut in the company of a special acquaintance.

A typical Zulu hut was in the shape of a beehive and covered with grass. It had no windows and became pitch black when the door was shut unless a fire burned inside. Ntombazi was led to her nefarious hut and she strutted slowly as though she was on parade and without blinking, she stared at the multitudes that had come to witness her trial. No one will ever know what went through her diabolical mind as she met her destiny. She knew that she needed more than a miracle to walk out alive from her gallery of horrors. Once her eyes had acclimatised to the darkness, she saw two bowls of water as well as two yellow glowing spots. She smelled something familiar with and she knew without a doubt that she was in the presence of a hyena. Instead of giving up she hoped against hope that something will happen to change her fate. That is when she started screaming at it and asked the guards to remove some grass on the roof for light. They obliged and there was an eerie silence in the hut as she thought of a cunning plan to outwit the beast.

At sunset, meat and traditional beer was lowered to her and she threw the meat at the hyena and it ate it hungrily, but the guards warned her against giving the animal her meat. She was worried about what could happen after dark. Her being ever resourceful, she decided that for the night, she would feed the hyena one of the skulls from the wall. She drank large amounts of the beer and when she became more intoxicated, the silence and darkness unnerved her. She started screaming obscenities at the hyena. False bravado made her laugh hysterically and the hyena's demonic laughter joined her and together they formed a symphony of the deranged. During the night, she tried to attack the animal with her bare hands, but it avoided her as it was still full. The following morning, sleep caught up with her as the Zulu idiomatic expression says *'ubuthongo yisiqhwaga'* (sleep is a bully). When she woke up, she was offered more food and beer and before long, she drunkenly chased the hyena around the hut. She then brought down her prized possessions, the skulls of all the kings she had killed and placed them near her for easy access to throw them at the hyena.

This continued for two days but as she slept on the third day, a blood curdling scream was followed by gushes of fresh blood streaming on the floor out of the hut. The hyena retreated into an imaginary corner with half of Ntombazi's foot. She requested the guards to ask Shaka for a bark bandage, a ball of spider's web and healing leaves. He agreed, but also gave her a spear for her courage, and she continued eating and drinking the beer and fell asleep despite the pain. She was woken up by another quick snap of her other calf. She was very weak at this point and all she could do was to sit leaning against the wall and watch in horror as the hyena licked the pool of blood with great urgency from her stumps. She knew the end was near as she was losing her sanity, she laughed dementedly and asked that the hut be burnt. As the guards set the hut on fire, she crawled to the centre of the hut on her stumps and looked up to the skulls for the last time. As the roaring flames engulfed her and the hyena, she fell face up and shouted *'Dingiswayo'*.

*A dwarf who would do reconnaissance for the Zulu army. (Killie Campbell Africana Library)*

*Men's hair style. (Killie Campbell Africana Library)*

After Ntombazi's death, Shaka organised a dramatic 100-kilometre march back to the Zulu capital which took three days, as they had 60 000 Ndwandwe cattle in tow. The cattle were arranged in their colours, followed by Shaka in the front with the military high command, then members of the king's council, aristocrats and the female regiment uMvuthwamini guarding the rear last. The young women looked stunning in the few beads that barely covered their private parts. They were followed by the war booty, the Ndwandwe women and children. When they approached KwaBulawayo, they were met by a five-kilometre-long guard of honour of shouting and ululating women. All the youngest *udibi* stood guard around the perimeter of the palace parade ground holding their black shields. The whole empire was ecstatic about the defeat of the powerful Ndwandwe kingdom. It was truly Shaka's finest hour.

After listening to a brief military report, he commended the army greatly and rewarded them with many cows, especially the officers and heroes of the battle. Shaka surprised everyone, even his worst enemies when he honoured both the living and his fallen soldiers, not excluding the Ndwandwe soldiers who were now members of the Zulu empire. The sky nearly opened as his men roared '*Bayethe*'. He gave a flat-rate reward to all regiments plus a bonus for soldiers who had performed outstanding acts of merit. Platoon leaders received double rewards while captains received twice as much. Regimental commanders received particularly generous rewards according to their levels of merit. Mdlaka, Ndlela, Mzilikazi and Mgobhozi each received about 500 cattle. After allotting the cattle accordingly, he granted 1000 outstanding fighters the right to wear the headring which allowed them to marry.

There was even more excitement when Shaka offered to provide *ilobolo* cows for their brides. These lucky men were to choose wives from the uMvuthwamini regiment. Shaka also released both the uMbelebele and iziMpohlo divisions to enjoy *ukusula izembe* with the uMvuthwamini regiment. The women were given six days off, while the iziMpohlo division was given the first three days to enjoy themselves and the uMbelebele division was to enjoy the last three days. A big party followed, hundreds of cows were slaughtered, and thousands of litres of traditional beer were consumed by all those who could make it to the capital. Everyone felt proud to be a member of the Zulu empire. Nqaba and Lubhedu became homesick after a few years of living in the Bapedi kingdom and they decided to go back to the land of their forefathers in the Zulu kingdom. They took ten beautiful Bapedi girls with them to present to Shaka as *imidlunkulu*. The day they arrived at KwaBulawayo they found Shaka teaching regiments new songs. When he saw them arrive, he composed a mocking song about Lubhedu, which is still sung to this day:

| | |
|---|---|
| *Hheshe, uLubhendu wakwaMasondo* | Oh yes, here is Lubhedu of the Masondo kingdom |
| *Siyambona namhlanje* | we finally see him today |

Shaka accepted the girls and allowed the returning men to settle and presented Nqaba with 100 cattle as a sign of appreciation for the *imidlunkulu*. This was also to assist him to start a new life. Suddenly, all the girls fell ill and had to return home but strangely, they only became ill after the two returnees had mysteriously disappeared with their cattle. Nqaba knew that before long he would have to personally answer to Shaka and his chances of survival were nil, so they never returned. As Soshangane was marauding in Mozambique in the foothills of the Lubhedu Mountains near the Mthembe River in 1823, he came across Captain William F Owen who was surveying the Delagoa Bay region. In his diaries, Capt Owen said that Soshangane was calling himself Manukuza after one of his ancestors and had named his newly found kingdom KwaGaza after his grandfather Gaza. He described Soshangane as well-built and wearing a headring with a single feather on the side of the head and across his nose hung a string of white beads. His earlobes were pierced with Zulu-style ear ornaments and on his arms and ankles he wore brass and copper bangles. The Gaza people found in Mozambique today are the direct descendants of Soshangane and his army who intermarried with the locals and broadened the local languages with Zulu lexicons. He found that Portuguese words were also widely used such as *garrafa* (bottle), *sabowa* (soap), *sumburero* (hut), *sapato* (shoe).

Soshangane initially lived in Chaimite in the Limpopo River Valley and he named his capital *Mandlakazi* after Sojiyisa's palace in the Zulu kingdom. This is where Shaka's army under the command of Ngomane found him. Soshangane forced everyone in his kingdom to learn isiZulu and named his new nation after himself, *aMaShangane*. He also forced his subjects to adopt the Nguni lifestyle such as marrying many wives, he, himself had at least 300 wives and his principal wife was the daughter of Lobengula kaMzilikazi Khumalo (the son of Mzilikazi who was now king in the south of today's Zimbabwe). Soshangane also established regiments such as the *iziNyoni ezimhlophe* and *aMavulandlela*. He drafted local young men from the Ronga, Ndzawu, Chopi, Vadzonga, Shona and Thonga nations into his regiments and they were taught to fight the Zulu way.

When Soshangane was satisfied that his new war machine was ready, he overran Portuguese settlements across Mozambique especially towns along the coast such as Inhambane, Sofala, Beira, Sena and Delagoa Bay. Hence for many years, Europeans were not allowed to dock anywhere in his area of influence. Moreover, these Europeans had the habit of kidnapping his 'new' subjects and sold them as slaves across the seas. At its peak, Soshangane's Gaza kingdom covered the Zambezi, iNkomati and Limpopo Rivers and parts of Zimbabwe and South Africa. In July 1836, a nine-wagon mercenary group, led by 59-year-old Johannes *'Lang Hans'* van Rensburg, camped near the Djindi River near the Limpopo River *en* route to trade in tusks in Delagoa Bay. There were nine white families made up of 49 people, an unspecified number of Malay, Khoi and black slaves. There were 30 horses, 450 cattle and 3000 goats and sheep. Soshangane did what he did best the night they arrived. He wiped them out, killing their trusted protector Malitel as well, and let only two white children survive. The children died of malaria a few years later. Soshangane kaZikode kaGaza kaManukuza Ndwandwe eventually died in 1856 and lies buried near his KwaMandlakazi Palace in Mozambique.

One of Soshangane's legendary grandsons, Mdungazwe kaMzila kaSoshangane Ndwandwe also known as *Ngungunyane, the Lion of Gaza* was a colourful character. Renowned as a great fighter, Ngungunyane became a general at a young age and seized control of the kingdom from one of his weaker brothers with the help of white mercenaries and left KwaMandlakazi Palace. He moved closer to the coast and built a new capital he called Manjakazi Palace, a variation in the pronunciation of his grandfather's capital KwaMandlakazi. Ngungunyane had many wives but his favourites were Vanya, Sibaeca and Soni who wore the *chifoco* (high cylindrical coiffure), which is similar to the Zulu *isicholo* coiffure. They adorned themselves with thirty gold bracelets on each arm. But the love of Ngungunyane's life was Vuiazi, a tall, fair-skinned beauty whose skin glistened like brass in the afternoon. Vuiazi had long, slender legs and it was a natural wonder how her slender waist hoisted two perfect little mountains of breasts. Her large, immaculate teeth lit up her face when she smiled, and her walk sent men into a trance. She was without a doubt, the most beautiful girl in the Gaza kingdom.

Even though Vuiazi bore Ngungunyane a son called Godide (named after Ndlela kaSompisi's son), she was never allowed to marry Ngungunyane because Vuiazi was in the habit of sharing her perfect body with any passing man as she so pleased. After fighting many heroic wars against colonisation, Ngungunyane was finally defeated and captured in December 1895. He went with his sons Godide, Malungo and Zixaxa and his seven wives Namatuco, Machachi, Patihina, Xisipe, Fuss, Muzamussi and Dabondi. Their entourage included several of their uncles such as Magejana and his three wives, a few generals, a chef and a dresser. On arrival in Portugal, Ngungunyane was first driven through town in a cage before being exhibited in the

Belem Botanical Garden in Lisbon. He was later shipped to Angra do Heroísmo Castle on the island of Terceira in one of the Azores Islands and died after 11 years of incarceration on the 23rd of December 1906.

A year after the defeat of and the victory euphoria long gone, Shaka remembered that Ngoza of the Mthembu kingdom had fought on Zwide's side and was still independent. He sent two brothers, Maphompo and Sigwegwe Mbatha as royal messengers, to propose an alliance with Ngoza. It was clear that Shaka was looking for an excuse to attack him, so he responded by giving the royal messengers a single reed and told them that they were to plant it in front of Shaka. A sign of extreme disrespect, which meant that even a single reed could stand up against the Zulu emperor. Since war was inevitable, Ngoza requested reinforcements from King Macingwane of the Mchunu nation. Macingwane was happy to oblige and deployed his iziNkwenkwezi and Nonyenye regiments and they clashed with Mdlaka along uMzinyathi River. On the other hand, Ndlela and Nzobo sent by Shaka, first took the Mthembu women, children and cattle as they were left unguarded at home and then they went to Hlazakazi Mountain and faced the rest of Ngoza's allied forces.

Shaka was commanding the war from the lofty eQhudeni Heights where he encountered King Jobe of the Sithole kingdom. After the customary greetings, Shaka realized that Jobe did not recognise who he was and introduced himself as *Jobana* (the diminutive of Jobe), making fun of the Sithole king. Observing the war, Jobe made unflattering remarks about 'the Zulu upstart' and was about to give Shaka intelligence about Ngoza when a Zulu messenger addressed Shaka by his correct title. In a towering rage Shaka stormed off without a further glance at Jobe and had the unsuspecting messenger killed for blowing his cover. The battle continued to rage on to an inevitable Zulu victory. After the battle and after Jobe recovered from the shock of having been so close to the 'Zulu upstart' and living to tell the tale, he went down on his knees and thanked his ancestors. The Sithole nation continues to venerate Shaka to this day and sing the following song in his honour to this day: '*Bayamqala okaNdaba.*' Jobe was especially gifted in working with leather and never ceased to provide Shaka with hides for his shields from his *amawaba* cattle (a distinctive breed with white spots on black flanks). He also presented the Zulu royal women with specially crafted leather skirts. Jobe lies buried in Mbilana near eQhudeni. Many fine Mbatha soldiers such as Nketo, Sigele and Mhlebi lost their lives during this battle. Ngoza was defeated but fled south with some allies, including members of the

Khuze and Mbatha nations. This war led to the second mass movement to the south and was accompanied by further atrocities. After the brutal battle, Shaka sorted out the dodgers, cowards and those who had lost their *iklwa* and had them summarily executed.

Shaka postponed pursuing the retreating Ngoza and his allies. Instead, he celebrated his victory by building a new palace at Nhlanabo near Eshowe and, also named it KwaBulawayo. It is situated on the southern slopes of the undulating uMhlathuze Valley and overlooks the uMandane and uMhlathuze rivers that meander between the Nyawutshane and Vungwini valleys, about eight kilometres from the northern border of the White iMfolozi River. It was, almost, in a straight line between the new capital and the river lying between the esiKlebeni and uMbelebele Palaces that were four kilometres and two kilometres, respectively from the boundary. The palace was like a huge flat plateau that was 27 kilometres from eMpangeni on the east side of what is now the eMpangeni Road.

A palisade surrounded the greater inner cattle enclosure of the palace with about 1500 huts within. The upper segment of the palace was further hedged around to form the king's private quarters and those of his female assistants. The huts along each flank were garrisoned by a few celibate soldiers. There were private exits in the king's sacred section, each manned by a guard. One of the entrances was the king's alone and the others were for his *imidlunkulu*. The king had a private entrance to the upper arch of the palisade which enclosed the cattle enclosure. This entrance was directly opposite the hut of the great council. A company of guards with several officers in attendance always guarded the large entrance. The toilets were outside under the scrub, separated for men and women, and strategically situated downstream of springs and rivulets where drinking water was drawn.

After building his new palace, Shaka built his mother the second palace with sweeping views also called eMkhindini. It was situated between the iMatheku and iMbuzane Rivers west of the eMpongo Hills a few kilometers away. Shaka also formed a royal regiment called iziYendane dedicated to his mother's every whim. The iziYendane royal guard comprised of debonair young men whose main purpose was to serve as female eye candy. Their dreadlocks, swayed from side to side with every step and were decorated with shells, beads and tiny feathers which hypnotised every woman. Shaka's sister Nomcoba, headed the first eMkhindini Palace after she left the eZigezeni Palace near the eMakhosini Valley. Shaka spread his 1200 *imidlunkulu* around his palaces in the empire but eMthandeni Palace, which was about 100-kilometres from KwaBulawayo was where his favourite hand-picked *imidlunkulu* lived. His favourite sexual partner was Mbuzikazi Cele who also lived there, appointed herself as the reigning queen of the palace. She often bullied everyone because she knew she was Shaka's favoured lover. He visited eMthandeni as often as he could but the physical thrill of Mbuzikazi did not dislodge Phampatha as the love of his life. As a result, Mbuzikazi would unleash her scorn towards everyone and equally everyone hated her, including other *imidlunkulu* and Mbopha (Shaka's senior assistant) who feared her. Phampatha on the other hand was loved by everyone because of her friendly disposition.

Shaka continued to consolidate his empire and for a change, he attended to internal non-military state affairs. He settled the nearly deserted land of the Ndwandwe with thrill seekers, adventurers, refugees, hunters and mercenaries from all over the world. He expanded his trade routes to the Zimbabwe and Mapungubwe kingdoms, to Limpopo, Angola, Namibia, Delagoa Bay and beyond. Shaka invited the whole empire to the capital to celebrate the defeat of Zwide and they came in their thousands and the festivities lasted for weeks. New members of the Zulu empire now outnumbered the once small Zulu nation. Shaka's ageing aunt Mkabayi left KwaNobamba with a large contingent of attendants and servants to attend the party at the capital. Along the way, she visited some of her old acquaintances who had known her father Jama, such as the Mpungose and Ntombela kings.

When she passed through the Mngadi kingdom, she was received with pomp and ceremony traditionally reserved for a visiting head of state. Shaka and his aunt were closest at this point and they trusted and depended on one another. When she arrived at the capital, several royal beasts were slaughtered for her. The army had grown in number, stature, prestige and were respected throughout the land of the Nguni people. This respect made Shaka even more ambitious and he set his sights further afield. Zulu subjects were so proud of their heritage and legacy that they informed the newcomers to the Zulu empire that they should refer to themselves as 'heavenly beings' because *Zulu* means 'heaven' in isiZulu. Therefore, they were now 'angels' living in 'heaven' (the Zulu empire) and Shaka was their 'Jesus Christ'. Furthermore, everyone else needed to pray hard if they want to enter heaven whereas as a Zulu, their place was a God-given right because heaven was home.

# 5

# Imfecane and European Colonisation

MACINGWANE was uneasy about being within striking distance of Shaka after the disastrous war on Ngoza's side. He fled overnight to the south with his people and unleashed unheard-of brutality on unsuspecting nations causing chaos everywhere he went. He even attacked Queen Machibisa of the Zondi kingdom around the uMsunduzi River where Pietermaritzburg stands today. Machibisa was a respected warrior and she successfully repelled Macingwane and his hordes. Like a whirlwind, Macingwane and his followers stormed the Ntamo kingdom living in uMkhomazi area, but they were repelled. On reaching the iGqunu forest near the iFafa River, Macingwane formed the uMungu regiment, which became the storm-troopers for the Mchunu nation. Their barbarism was considered unprecedented in Southern Africa as they amputated women's hands when they wanted their copper bracelets. They raped children, hanged the men in public and speared the cattle they could not take so that the survivors would not have meat or milk or hides to cover themselves.

This was the third large-scale emigration of misery and ruin spread between the uThukela and uMzimvubu Rivers. Shaka could not stand by idly when innocent people were suffering. He led his army and marched south in search of Macingwane and attacked his allies along the way. They passed through King Mshika *Maphinda* kaKhondlwane of the Mphephethwa kingdom and they lived in the foothills of the great Ophisweni Mountain. Shaka offered them protection against future attacks by Macingwane but Mshika refused. A typical characteristic of Mshika was that his facial incisions seemed to glow whenever he was angry, and his tiny kingdom was psychologically attached to the perpendicular Ophisweni Mountain. Mshika made it clear that he did not want to be part of the Zulu empire. They also practised cremation, something that made Shaka's stomach turn. He then fled with his people to the summit of the solitary circular piece of rock, with its sheer and almost smooth sides like the biblical Masada or Guge in the Tibetan Highlands. When Shaka attacked them, as expected they rushed to the summit and released their weapons of mass destruction - fast plummeting rocks.

Luckily, the retreat on the summit had a natural source of water and the only way to move anything up and down was on ladders whose access was hidden from outsiders. When they had taken everything up, they merely pulled the ladders up and jeered at the Zulu from the lofty heights of their fortress, feeling invincible. The situation both infuriated and fascinated Shaka. His generals saw no value in chasing such a small weak people. But it was not in Shaka's nature to walk away from challenges. So, after walking around the circular sheer escarpment a few times, like the prophet Jeremiah around the walls of biblical Jericho, Shaka suddenly became excited with inspiration. Without telling anyone the source of his joy, he ordered the immediate slaughter of some of their provision cattle but spared nursing cows and their calves as they acted as the alarm clock. The hides of the cattle were made into long durable ropes by cutting spiral patterns from the perimeter of the hide towards the centre. This made sections of rope measuring ten centimetres wide and 15 metres long. Stones and rocks were then tied to one end of the long rope and the soldiers practiced throwing them over the branches of the highest trees. This was easy to do because the hide was still raw and pliable. A few of them were ordered to climb up the ropes attached to the trees, each with his *iklwa* attached to the shield on his back. The results of this manoeuvre were hilarious. In testing the ropes strength and practicing the climbing technique, some soldiers at the top of the trees would throw rocks down to mimic the resistance to be expected during the real assault. Some rocks 'accidentally' landed on the heads of their climbing rivals. They were falling over and tripping each other. Everyone was in stitches and for a while, the new and young Zulu soldiers forgot they were on a life-and-death campaign.

A small unit was created and a tight column of five soldiers abreast with the shields of the inner files held over their heads, overlapping to provide cover. Those on the flanks held their shields on their exposed side. The leading lines held them in front of them to Shaka, this formation resembled the shape of a tortoise (*ufudu*). They practised the drill until they perfected the manoeuvres. The older *udibi* were instructed to show the soldiers how to climb trees with and without the leather ropes and how to pull those below them with lighter strings. Flattered to have been chosen for this task they finally had an opportunity to prove their worth to their king and they outperformed themselves. The source of Shaka's delight was that he had found a weak spot in Mshika's mountain defence. He then organised a few false attacks at different places around the mountain as a diversion. As expected, Mshika's people fell for it and hurled rocks with zeal. Meanwhile, the Zulu soldiers had begun to covertly ascend the mountain at dawn. Even the agile *udibi* made their way up with great difficulty and often used weighted strings over branches to move up. They were exposed where there were no more trees or bushes to cover them and the Mphephethwa saw them. Altogether each Zulu soldier crouched into the tortoise shape and pressed forward covered by their shields. This was the famous *ishongololo likaShaka* (Shaka's millipede) formation. The arsenal of spears, sticks, assegais, clubs, boulders and rocks rained down on them with free fall of almost 200-metres, but they kept on coming up in rhythmic steps.

This strategy was vintage Shaka, this is one of the many examples that illustrate his military brilliance and creativity. The shape of *ufudu* ensured that every missile rolled off but as they came closer to the summit, more and more feet began slipping. Every soldier's fallen shield was picked up and held up high to seal the gap on the 'roof' that was created. The Mphephethwa men, women and children were expert missile throwers as they had done frequently before successfully. Nothing and no one could have survived this missile assault except the Zulu ingenuity of the *ishongololo likaShaka*. By the time the army reached the summit, they had lost many men and they rammed through the Mphephethwa frontline on the summit and split them into two. The Zulu carnage began and the only place Mshika's people could run was to the 200-metre high precipice. They had to choose between the gaping death below and the blood-dripping Zulu spears behind them and they chose to dive rather than be speared by the Zulu. The screams, especially of airborne children touched even the most stony-hearted.

However, today stories are told about Shaka personally flinging men, women and children over the cliffs when in fact, the Mphephethwa refused to surrender and chose to die that way. Mshika, his son Myeka, and others survived by hiding in a cave. Shaka's ability of conquering the Mphephethwa 'Masada' brought him an even bigger prestige and proved that the Zulu army was indeed invincible. Mshika eventually came out of hiding and Shaka sent his close friend, King Zihlandlo of the Mkhize kingdom, to humiliate him for the last time and take what was left of his cattle, women and children. Mshika ended up dying of old age on the Ophisweni Highlands. After sorting out the Mphephethwa kingdom, Shaka defeated other kingdoms in the south. However, some like the Nxamalala and amaBomvu kingdoms welcomed him with great enthusiasm. Shaka returned to his capital and sent Mdlaka further south in hot pursuit of Macingwane.

Refugees from various conquered kingdoms had swelled Macingwane's numbers and he swept through the fertile plains of KwaCekwane (*Dronkvlei*) with devastating effect. He obliterated every kingdom he could find between the Ingwagwane and uMzimkhulu Rivers. He destroyed King Dibandlela of the Maphumulo kingdom and crushed the amaNtambo kingdom near today's Richmond. He also annihilated a few Xhosa kings such as King Maraule of the amaFunze kingdom, King Mkhaliphi of the Nyamnyini kingdom as well as the amaBhaca, the Mpevu, the Nqondo, the Nxasane and the amaWushe kingdoms. Mdlaka finally caught up with Macingwane and his followers near the thick forest of Ntsikeni Hill where they were hiding with their cattle. He used the old Zulu war ritual, *ingomane* to create an intimidating noise. The cattle stampeded out of hiding terrified and ran into the waiting arms of Mdlaka who waited for Macingwane to follow. They ended up fighting a ferocious battle on oPhatheni Hill where Macingwane was finally defeated.

But Macingwane together with one of his sons, Phakade and a few followers escaped. After living like wild animals in the forests and being hungry most of the time, they became tired and they decided to surrender. Before they surrendered, Macingwane made Phakade promise to hand over the royal Mchunu kingdom royal gourd, a copper bracelet and an axe to his heir Mfusi. He was living at KwaBulawayo under Shaka because Mfusi's mother was worried that he would be killed either by Macingwane, who had the tendency of killing his infant sons, such as Mayana and Ndezimbi, for no reason, or would be pretenders to the Mchunu throne. As far as she was concerned, Mfusi was safer growing up under Shaka's protection. Somewhere along the way back to surrender, the fair-skinned Macingwane simply vanished into thin air and to this day nobody knows what happened to him. Nomagaga became the new Mchunu leader and they surrendered to Mdlaka who sent them back to Shaka under heavy guard. Shaka pardoned them and sent them all to live at KwaMandlakazi under the watchful eye of Sojiyisa kaMaphitha.

The army continued with the sorties in the south before turning towards the Drakensberg Mountains to destroy Matiwane who had settled, under the snow-capped mountains of Bergville, with his followers. His fort was strategically built between the Little uThukela and Lambonja Rivers which left only one direction to attack. Their emergency exit route enabled them to go over the Drakensberg Mountains and into Lesotho through narrow, treacherous passes that were easily defendable. Shaka's secret service advised Mdlaka that they should attack from the extreme south, through the iNtabamhlophe and eMangweni Mountains. Again, Shaka's battle plan was promising. Matiwane, however, escaped into Lesotho with a few followers and continued to cause havoc. He later decided to return home and prayed that Shaka would spare his life. He travelled through the highlands of Thaba Bosiu in Lesotho - despite his barbaric acts against the Basotho a few years before.

King Moshoeshoe of the Basotho kingdom offered him a safe home in which to settle and grow old. But Matiwane, heartbroken and homesick, decided to journey on. Some of his followers remained behind and some of their descendants can still be found today. He finally reached the Zulu empire years later, with only one son and a handful of followers. Mdlaka returned home triumphantly with many women, children and cattle in tow. The new members of the Zulu empire, the amaNgwane nation were given land and cattle to start their lives anew either with new husbands or with their menfolk who decided to follow their women and children in defeat. The war-weary amaNgwane finally enjoyed a peaceful hiatus after more than 20 years of mayhem. After fighting with distinction, Shaka installed Mzilikazi kaMashobana Khumalo as the king of the Khumalo kingdom and promoted him to general in the Zulu Imperial army. Mzilikazi's first responsibility was to take charge of security in the southern entrance of the KwaBulawayo Palace. Shaka decided to expose Mzilikazi to a war in the north. This was Mzilikazi's first independent campaign to command where he was fully in charge.

Some of his sisters who remained behind were Ntanase and Nozinyanga, who later married Dingane when he was king. Mzilikazi's deputy was Somabhulane Dlodlo and the senior officers were Njikiza *Nhlolamazibuko* Ngcolosi, Thando and Takatso - a SeSotho speaker who was going to be the translator. Shaka gave him the following regiments - uDibinhlangu under Mdletshe Thembe; uMagoloza regiment under Mankanyana Thembe; amaTsheketshe regiment under Sifo Masuku; iNyamayendlovu regiment under Mkhokhi Masuku; iNgwengwe regiment under Mkhanyisi Masuku; aMagogo regiment under Maqekeni Sithole; amaBambeni regiment under Gagamela Ncube; iNhlambane regiment under Thambo Ndaweni; iGuqeni regiment under Mdletshe Ndaweni; iziMpangele under Mhlophe Ndaweni; oYengweni regiment under Mlotha Khumalo; uMzinyathi regiment under Majilijili Gwebu; iNyathi regiment under Ntabane Gwebu; iNsinda regiment under Shiyiwe Gwebu; iNtemba regiment under Mjojo Mlotshwa; uGodlwayo regiment under Thambisamahubo Mafa; iNqama regiment under Somhlolo Matema; iNtutha regiment under Mhabahaba Mkhwanazi; uMahlokohloko regiment under Mbabele Hlabangana; iNsingwa regiment under Somabhulane Dlodlo; iNqaba regiment under Mazwi Gumede; iNdinana regiment under Mfangilele Mashazi; iNxa regiment under Tshumane Khanye; isiPhezi regiment under Maqudela Sigola;

uMhlahlandlela regiment under Gwabalanda Mathe; uMabugudwane regiment under Mayenge Mthethwa; iNzwamazi regiment under Mphilwa Magutshwa as well as uThulilwezichwe and uMthuyasizwe regiments.

Mzilikazi's mission was to extend the empire's borders and cattle belonging to a King Ranisi (the Zulu called him Somnisi) a Mosotho who lived on the northern border, as he was starting to show signs of anarchy. Shaka presented Mzilikazi with a new battledress like his own, which comprised of a large glistening *iklwa*, a glossy white war shield which measured from his mouth to his toes with a single black spot in the centre. He also gave him his prized possessions, the well-crafted teak and ivory handle axe that once belonged to Lembe Ndwandwe. Mzilikazi left Shaka with a heavy heart but *ngesango elihle* (on good terms) holding his favourite weapon, the sword. After an elaborate farewell ceremony, Mzilikazi and his men made a sharp about-turn and in stunning formation, they took a deep breath, paused, raised their right foot and struck the ground in unison, hissed, fell silent to the count of ten, then saluted '*Sigidi*' for the last time.

They took off and jogged into history dazzling in their fine battle dress as they disappeared into the dust. From the type of speeches and gifts, it seems Shaka did not expect him to come back. Perhaps Mzilikazi needed his own *Lebensraum*. After all, other great generals and soldiers had struck out on their own and others had established 'miniature Zulu empires' in far-flung places in the heart of Africa. It was the beginning of a brighter future for the young ambitious Mzilikazi. He first went to see his family at his eNtubeni homestead inside the iNgome forest at eSikhwebezi Valley. He was extremely successful in his border extension and cattle-rustling mission. He took a great number of cattle from a cowardly Ranisi. Then Mzilikazi returned to eNtubeni with all his regiments intact and sent numerous rustled cattle to Shaka but kept some for himself. Shaka's secret service was superb and he instructed Mzilikazi to return all the cattle. In response, Mzilikazi cut off the plumes of the royal messengers which was a sign of extreme disrespect.

Shaka then sent the iziMphohlo division with instructions to bring Mzilikazi back alive, but one of his relatives Nzama Khumalo, tipped him off. He then hid in the caves and successfully repelled the iziMpohlo division, mainly by rolling rocks down from iNtumbane Hill. IziMpohlo returned to Shaka empty-handed and instead of punishing them, Shaka seemed privately pleased that they had not been successful. He made fun of them for having been defeated by a rookie general and let the matter rest. Unhappy with course of events, the military high command forced Shaka to act. After a year-long delay, Shaka eventually sent uMbelebele division but when they also failed to smoke Mzilikazi out, they laid a siege. When they were about to give up and go back to face Shaka's wrath, Nzeni Khumalo came to their rescue and showed them the secret access into Mzilikazi's fort and he was surprised from the rear. They fought a particularly violent battle and Mzilikazi managed to escape with several regiments such as iNsingwa, uThulilwezichwe, uMthuyasizwe and iziMpangele, a small number of *udibi* as well as fewer women and cattle. But many of his relatives were not so lucky, such as his sons Nhlanganiso, Nkayishana; his wives Nokufa, Gijima; his daughters Nothando, Nozinhlwathi, Nomabhunu, Nomanbhudle, Ngiyesaba, Nyakambi, Ntombayi; his commanders Dumaphansi, Dambuzamthabathe; his body guards Didiza, Mgigqilizana, Golela, Chachaza, Phuzukuyekela, Ndengezimashumi who had walked away from Shaka's army. This is where Dikane was gravely wounded as he was first stabbed above the right nipple, then a sword landed above his right eye, followed by another that went through his stomach and his intestines fell out. However, amaWombe medical regiment pushed the attackers back and stitched him with goat hide. Mzilikazi's treachery made Shaka decree that everyone in his domain were first *uZulu* or *umZulu* (member of the Zulu empire) before being members of their kingdom.

This decree brought pride to the 'People of Heaven' (*amaZulu*) but it brought both dread and admiration to those who were not yet members of the Zulu empire. Mzilikazi fled meandering to the north-west also causing chaos in his wake. His *modus operandi* was to seek 'asylum' from unsuspecting hosts because he was escaping from the 'cruel' Shaka. Everyone believed him because Shaka's ability to win battles was now well-known across the sub-continent. The unending African hospitality cost them their lives because Mzilikazi would attack them after adequate rest and assessing their military strength. Depending on the time of the year, he would also 'settle' down for a few months, plough and build a palace. But before his hosts knew it, he would kill as many of their men as possible, kidnap their women, children and their cattle, and flee further northwards with the new spoils of war and fresh food. The Nyoka kingdom that was under Zulu sovereignty, was one of Mzilikazi's early victims. The Nyoka put up a big fight and managed to imprison Mzilikazi for a while, before he broke loose, crushed them and fled taking all their cattle and women. The next victim was King Matokoto of the Baphuthing, a non-Nguni kingdom living at the border where Gauteng, Limpopo and Mpumalanga meet. Matokoto survived by camouflaging himself with white cloaks and hid among his white cattle. After years of living in a state of (*ukuhlala phezu kwamahawu*) combat readiness, Mzilikazi was relieved when he heard that Shaka had been killed. Moreover, Mzilikazi's followers knew that they owed their survival to their weapons hence they revered them more than food and water, which brought about the saying 'to guard something like *izikhali zamantungwa*'.

Mzilikazi began to build ekuPhumuleni Palace and gave refuge to his now destitute grandfather, old King Zwide. Despite that Zwide had killed both his parents, since 'my enemy's enemy is my friend', they were united when it came to Shaka and they got along like wildfire. They swore revenge against Shaka but never had enough courage to return to the south to challenge him. Mzilikazi thought his fugitive life was over, but he had celebrated too soon. The new king, Dingane sent uFojisa regiment to recover the cattle he never returned. So poor Mzilikazi was on the road again and was forced to flee from his unfinished ekuPhumuleni Palace but Zwide stayed behind. When uFojisa found Mzilikazi gone, they spared the wretched and poverty stricken Zwide to suffer his nightmare-filled life.

Mzilikazi built more palaces wherever he lived such as eMhlahlandlela located near the iNzwabuhlungu (Apies) River, eNkungwini, eNdinaneni, uMzinyanti, iNkenenkene and Ngodweni. He often returned to places he had pillaged before to steal more women, children and cattle. He was shocked when he returned to a few Batswana, Bakgatla and Bapedi villages he had pillaged before and discovered that they had resorted to living in tree villages. They built them about five metres above ground with six or seven horizontal suspension logs as bridges. These villages included open spaces where they could meet as a community. They lived far up in the trees not only to avoid wild animals but also to avoid Mzilikazi and his murderous Zulu renegades as well. Even the British missionary David Livingstone's father-in-law, Robert Moffat was astonished to find viable and functioning tree villages. But that was fine by him, so long as his mission was not disturbed to continue what he came to Africa for, to 'save' African souls living on stilts from eternal damnation.

After Mzilikazi successfully evaded the uFojisa regiment, Dingane sent uNomagoba Special Forces who were based at KwaHenqwa *ikhanda*, under the command of Siphingo. Mzilikazi knew it was time to run even further into deep Africa and sent one of the regiments he had created, amaKhandamnyama in advance under the command of Gundwane *Mkhaliphi* Ndiweni, whose deputy was his eldest son, Nkulumane kaMzilikazi. AmaKhandamnyama regiment entered today's Zimbabwe and went east of Matopo Hills and built Gibixhegu *ikhanda* and waited for Mzilikazi to arrive. But weeks turned into months without any sign of Mzilikazi and Nkulumane decided to go back and look for his father. Meanwhile Mzilikazi and his caravan had gone further westwards through the perilous Kalahari Desert.

While many of his followers died of starvation and thirst, they slowly soldiered on until they reached Makarikari Lake. They then trudged through the Sibanini pools and only rested at the confluence of the Gwai and Khami Rivers where King Zwanke (*Sawanga*) saw to their every need. When their strength had returned Mzilikazi on cue, returned to his heinous habit and killed him and fled with the women and cattle.

They eventually crossed the great Limpopo River under the guard of one of his regiments, amaKhandamhlophe, and entered the land of the gentle Shona people in Zimbabwe. Mzilikazi sent the secret service to look for his son in the north-west. They walked until they came across the awesome Victoria Falls without a sign of Nkulumane. When they returned to Mzilikazi, they confirmed the existence of the magnificent falls which they had heard about, when they were still living in the Zulu empire. However, by the time they found Nkulumane, he had been made king by commander Gundwane and the amaKhandamnyama regiment. Hence on his arrival in the vicinity, Mzilikazi did not go to Gibixhegu, instead he built a new palace on a flat-topped hill near today's Bulawayo. Like Shaka, he ordered a court martial of the officers who had appointed Nkulumane as the new king. They were all executed on the hill of his new settlement and it became known as *intaba yezinduna* (today it is called Thabas Induna, meaning the mountain for chiefs).

Mzilikazi decided not to kill Nkulumane because he had managed to keep his kingdom together when he was half starving in the Zambezi valley wilderness. Instead, he sent him to exile to the Zulu empire with numerous regiments. However, when he passed through the Bakwena kingdom, they asked him to assist in fighting a rival king. Always ready for a good fight, Nkulumane led the war and personally killed the enemy king and as a reward the Bakwena gave him land in Phokeng near Rustenburg. He settled, married many local wives and lived there until he died, and his grave can still be found there. Mzilikazi defeated all the kingdoms in the area with his favourite weapon – the sword, with which he ruled supreme in the battle theatre. He also built several palaces around Nyathi, and Matopo Hills and he named his capital Bulawayo as well, after Shaka's first palace. He incorporated the ragtag renegade Shona fighters into his ruthless killing machines. They were transformed into an efficient fighting force second only to Shaka's in size and achievements in Southern Africa.

At the zenith of his power, Mzilikazi had 31 regiments. He conquered every kingdom that lay between the *iGwa* (Vaal) River in the south and the *iBulingatho* (Zambezi) Rivers between Lake Ngami in Botswana and the eastern part of Mozambique, an area covering thousands of square kilometres. His followers comprised a diverse cross-section of people who spoke different languages and came from different kingdoms. Members of the Zulu empire formed the aristocracy and were called *abenzansi* (from the south). The second tier comprised members of the conquered Basotho, Khalanga and Batswana kingdoms who were collectively known as the *abenhla* (from the north). The remaining folk, the third social tier were called the *amahole* (the untouchables). Mzilikazi called his new nation *Mthwakazi* but for some unknown reason, they ended up being called *amaNdebele*. Their language is called *isiNdebele* and remains almost 100 per cent isiZulu.

Mzilikazi moved his capital from Bulawayo to Inyathi and finally to Mhlahlandlela where he died in 1868. He was buried in eNtumbane cave near the Matopo Hills and was succeeded by one of his many sons, Crown Prince Lobengula. A granite memorial stone was erected under a large shady tree at Mhlahlandlela Palace, where he used to hold court. The stone reads: '*uMzilikazi kaMashobana; inkosi yamaNdebele; intaba yadilika ngo-5 September 1868; zonke izizwe zithi; Matshobana; Hayete (Hail).*' (Mzilikazi kaMashobana; King of the Ndebele; Mountain that crumbled on the 5$^{th}$ of September 1868; All nations say: *Matshobana; Hail*). Today, Bulawayo (young Zimbabweans call it *Skies*) is Zimbabwe's second largest city. Many of the city's inhabitants can trace their ancestry directly to the Zulu empire more than a thousand kilometres away. These Zulu descendants still pay allegiance to the Zulu king, His Majesty, King Zwelithini kaBhekuzulu, because of their ancestry.

European Early Contact with Southern Africa

The interactions between peoples from different continents and places in ancient times are well documented. They traded and exchanged ideas for an example, they shared different agricultural techniques and technologies, even medicinal knowledge. However, this interaction did not always result in cordial relationships. Hence, the Khoi have a saying that 'all the problems of this world would have been far less, if people stayed where they came from.' According to the Greek philosopher, Herodotus, ancient Phoenicians were among the earliest civilisations that had sailed around the Cape of Good Hope. Similarly, for many centuries the coastal dwellers of the eastern seaboard interacted with seafarers and shipwreck survivors from several countries. These people fell into broad categories - some were of good character with noble intentions whereas the majority were travelling the world to pillage and conquer. Some were thieves, murderers, adventurers, hunters, thrill-seekers and soldiers of fortune.

The Portuguese adventurer, Bartholomew Diaz was one such character. After encountering inclement weather around the peninsula, he named it *Cabo das Tormentas* (Cape of Storms) and only managed to dock in Mossel Bay in 1487 about 1300 kilometres from Durban. He named the bay *Angra de São Brás* (Bay of Cowherds) because of the large number of cows. He sailed further north along the coast and named a river *Rio do Infante* (Fish River) because of the abundance of fish. He could not continue because of his mutinous crew. Ten years later in 1497, Diaz's contemporary, Vasco da Gama, left Portugal with four ships, a crew of 170 men with enough food to last three years. He piloted the *São Gabriel* and his brother Paulo piloted the *São Rafael*. The third ship, the *Berrio* (*São Miguel*) was piloted by Nicolao Coelho and the unnamed storage ship that was piloted by Gonçalo Nunes went missing.

Da Gama was notorious not only for being a thief and a slave trader but for also being notably sadistic and cruel. He recorded his coastal encounter with the Luthuli kingdom around Durban then called *eSibululungu*, but he renamed it *Terra Natalia* (Natal). He continued northwards and dropped anchor at St Lucia which the locals called *ichweba lasenhlengweni* (healing lagoon) and he renamed it *Rio de Medaos de Oure*. Today it is called iSimangaliso Wetlands Park. When Da Gama reached Delagoa Bay (Maputo) he disembarked from his ship decked in a long, white tunic and his head wrapped with a big white turban. He pretended to be a Muslim as Delagoa Bay was under Muslim rule. But once he was settled, he participated in slave trade and piracy, and also looted Arab merchant ships. Da Gama often travelled between India and Portugal to buy Indians to sell as slaves in Lisbon. In 1501, he sailed to India with 20 ships and 1500 men and looted every single Arab ship he encountered on the high seas. He often burnt his foes with hot oil, amputated their hands, ears and noses and kept those body parts as morbid trophies.

On one of his return trips to Lisbon, Da Gama encountered the *Miri*, a pilgrim ship that was carrying hundreds of wealthy Muslims. He robbed them of their gold, jewels, ivory and other riches before he burnt the pilgrims alive and watched with glee, at the horrific spectacle through his cabin porthole. Again, on one of his trips to India, he briefly stopped in Delagoa Bay where he brazenly kidnapped scores of locals to sell as slaves. Hence three years later, when another Portuguese trader Pedro da Nhanya who was on his way to India dropped anchor at Delagoa Bay to repair his ship, he was sent packing by flying spears from locals. Meanwhile, Diogo

Pereira on his way to India in 1536, sailing on a Kontiki-type craft recorded that he purchased fresh supplies from the Nguni people living along coast. Yet another Portuguese trader Captain Don Manuel de Sousa left India for Portugal via Sofala in Mozambique with his wife and children aboard the *São João* in February 1552.

But they were blown off course and crash-landed at the mouth of the uMthwavuna River near Port Edward in June 1552. Of the 500 people on board, 150 died, and 300 slaves of unknown origins and about 100 Portuguese survived. De Sousa insisted on continuing the journey to Sofala over land despite being advised not to walk through the African wilderness. They were attacked by both wild animals and people on the way and stripped of all their possessions. They ended up naked. The captain's wife, Dona Leonora who was also a Portuguese princess and a stunning beauty - could not handle the humiliation of wearing native clothes. Out of sheer frustration, she asked her husband to dig a waist-deep hole. She climbed down into the hole and refused to move any further, begging to die. The rest of the party pressed on and some of the survivors went mad along the way. The De Sousa family remained in place with some of their slaves, but one-by-one they began to die from tropical diseases and hunger. Only 25 reached Inhaca Bay (*KwaNyaka*) three months later, eight Portuguese and 17 slaves.

The news of this incident reached Portugal in 1575 and the Portuguese king commissioned navigator Manuel Perestrello to draw an accurate map of the south-eastern African coastline to help subsequent generations of navigators to avoid being shipwrecked. After a hiatus of shipwrecks, 14 years later the *Santo Thomé* sank close to Inhaca Island before arriving in Sofala. The survivors swam to the tiny island and some were ferried in canoes to the mainland, but two women liked it so much on the island that they only jumped onto a passing ship a year later. The *Santo Alberto* crashed at uMzimvubu River mouth on March 24, 1593 with 285 Portuguese and an unknown number of African slaves aboard. They too trudged nearly 1000 kilometres north by foot to their '*El Dorado*' Sofala where they believed they would find gold on the surface of the ground. Except for a few deaths along the way, they arrived at the halfway point, Delagoa Bay in a record time of 12 weeks and completed their trip. Meanwhile, around the Cape peninsula more Europeans, Arabs, Indians and Chinese either docked or shipwrecked. Few of them were interested in staying because they were sailing to other destinations. They were either nursed back to health or they traded with the Khoi, the Goringhaicona, the Chainoqua, the Goringhaiqua and other locals. They traded in fresh water, wine, blankets, medicines, food, and even in women.

A trading post was created on Robben Island and the ownership and control of it changed hands between the Portuguese, Dutch and ultimately the British. Sadly, relations between the natives and the visitors began to deteriorate because the visitors forcefully occupied land without permission from the kings and all the drunken brawls, rapes, theft and hangings of the natives grew. Most of the visitors who ended up being colonisers were undesirables from their own countries. What angered the locals the most was that some of their kings were lured aboard the ships and told they would be going on a pleasure cruise around the coast. Instead, they disappeared with them over the horizon, never to be seen again. King Xhore (Coree) is one such example, he was kidnapped aboard the *Hector* in 1613 by Captain Towerson. Xhore was taken to England and taught English against his will in the home of Sir Thomas Smythe in London. A year later, Xhore was unceremoniously dumped on the Cape peninsula beach wearing a bronze armour suit and bearing a bronze spear.

Similarly, King Autshumato of the Goringhaicona kingdom was sent to Batavia (Jakarta) and forced to learn Portuguese, French, Dutch and English. King Nommoa of the Goringhaiqua kingdom was luckier because he was not taken overseas. He was however, taught several European languages at different locations around the Cape. Ultimately the three kings were forced to interpret for their former kidnappers especially in their summer garden which was on Robben Island. In 1647 the ship *Haarlem* owned by the Dutch East India Company (whose acronym is VOC in Dutch) crashed on its way to India on the Cape Peninsula. The locals rescued the ship's survivors who fully recovered only after five months and then returned home. They told their company about the hospitality of the locals and suggested that they make the peninsula their pantry. The company agreed and decided to send a thief and gangbanger Jan van Riebeeck to Africa. He had been sentenced to serve a five-year sentence for stealing from the company in Tonkin (*Hanoi*), Vietnam. He eventually docked in Cape Town on a sunny autumn day on the 5th of April 1652, after the arduous currents around Robben Island prevented him from reaching the mainland for a whole three weeks.

By the time he arrived, Europeans named the peninsula the Cape of Good Hope and the European settlement called Table Bay was later called Cape Town. Van Riebeeck was tasked with establishing the pantry for passing Dutch ships. After his arrival, he planted a garden where the wild almond hedge in Kirstenbosch National Botanical Garden in Cape Town still thrives to this day. He arrived with his wife Maria, a son and 82 male and eight female prisoners. They were aboard three ships, the *Drommedaris*, the *Reijger* and the *Goede Hoop*. Another two Dutch ships, the *Walvisch* and the *Oliphant* sailed into Cape Town a few days later. More than 150 men aboard these ships died en route to the Cape. Van Riebeeck was welcomed ashore by King Autshumato of the Goringhaicona kingdom and introduced him to his niece Princess Krotoa, who could speak several European languages. She had learnt them by trading with passing ships and ended up working as Van Riebeeck's maid. When Van Riebeeck was not supervising the gardens or hunting down the Khoi and San for sport, he enjoyed stargazing through his telescope. He was the first European to report the comet *C/1652Y1* spotted from South Africa on the 17 of December 1652. He ended up serving ten years in the Cape before he was, allowed to, return to Jakarta where he ultimately died in 1677. The VOC ended its rule of the Cape of Good Hope after 150 years and it had turned into a British colony by then. Relations between the locals and the colonisers deteriorated and Robben Island was turned into a penal colony where the locals were jailed. The colonisers changed Autshumato's name to '*Herry de Strandloper*' and his niece's name Krotoa to '*Eva*'. They were part of the first Robben Island prisoners which included King Nommoa '*Doman*' of the Goringhaiqua kingdom because they amongst other things refused to spy against their own people as ordered by Van Riebeeck. This made Krotoa the first and last female prisoner on the notorious island.

Autshumato managed to escape from Robben Island which made him the first person to escape from the penal colony isle. Another Khoi leader David Stuurman was imprisoned on Robben Island, which according to his charge sheet, which listed his crime as 'suspicious conduct, and for living in a kraal near the boundaries of the colony'. Stuurman escaped from Robben Island twice and on his second escape, he was accompanied by thirty convicts together with the Xhosa prophet, Makana, who is believed to have drowned. He was eventually recaptured and became the first Khoi person to be exiled in Sydney, Australia another penal colony. He is said to have died in Sydney on the 22$^{nd}$ of February 1803 and was buried where Sydney's Central Railway Station stands today. Within 50 years of Vasco da Gama's shipwreck in Natal in 1497, hundreds of ships introduced various nationalities to the Cape peninsula. By 1657, some of these people had become colonisers and lived independently from the companies that had brought them to the Cape peninsula. There was intense interbreeding over the years and decades between the races such as the Xhosa, Khoi, San, Goringhaicona, Chainoqua, Goringhaiqua, Dutch, English, Portuguese, Chinese, Arabs, Indians, Indonesians, Malaysians, about 200 French Huguenots (who arrived in 1688 as refugees from the Revocation of the Edict of Nantes) and others.

Most of the people who came to the Cape peninsula were men hence, the only source of intimacy for them was the native women, which led to the birth of numerous mixed-race offspring during the late 17th century and they called themselves *coloured*. In the instances, where interbreeding was, largely limited, to Europeans most notably the Dutch, the French, the British and Portuguese they called themselves *Boer* and some of them had intimate relations with African women. To distinguish themselves from newly arrived Europeans as having been born in Africa, they called themselves Afrikaners. They developed their dialect into a distinctive language and 200 years later (in 1925), it was recognised as a separate language - Afrikaans. The language is made up several local languages and simplified Dutch sprinkled with French and German words. The Cape Colony Administration drove all the natives away from their land by force and gave it to white colonisers. The colonisers all received two pieces of land for free. The pieces of land were at least six thousand acres for summer crops and another six thousand acres for winter crops. They were also given numerous cattle, sheep and goats for free. The owners of that land have not been compensated to this day.

About 1000 kilometres away from the Cape, more ships were shipwrecked near Port Natal. For instance, the *Good Hope* a ship from England piloted by Captain John Adams ran aground around Port Natal in 1685. Adams some of his crew and a few shipbuilders from the Luthuli kingdom salvaged some broken pieces from the ship and built a smaller boat. Adams used this smaller vessel to sail to Madagascar, however, the ship's first mate John Kingston and four survivors decided to settle in Port Natal permanently. A year later, a Dutch ship the *Stavenisse* piloted by Captain Kniff was wrecked near Port Natal. He too used the services of the Luthuli shipbuilders to make a smaller craft from the wreckage of what was left of the *Good Hope* and sailed back to the Cape Colony. The first governor of the Cape Colony-Simon van der Stel-who was the first and last mixed-race governor of the Cape, bought the ship from Kniff and renamed it the *Centaur*. Three years later King Nkanyezi of the Luthuli kingdom sold a well-built seagoing ship the *Noord* to a Dutch adventurer Pieter Jan Timmerman. The following year the *Fidele* from England dropped three of her crew members in Port Natal and left. When they returned six years later, they found one of the crew members, Vaughan Goodwin, living with two African wives and their seven mixed-race children.

Whilst in the Cape, Van der Stel read a book called *A Cruising Voyage Round the World* by Woodes Rogers about Port Natal. It described the life of the natives in glorious detail. He was so impressed that he sent the *Noord* back to Port Natal to purchase Port Natal from Nkanyezi for 100 Dutch Guilders. News reached him that the purchase was successful, and it created so much excitement in the Cape that Van der Stel ordered Captain Gerbrantzer to sail the *Postlooper* to verify the purchase. However, Gerbrantzer found Nkanyezi long dead and his son denied having any knowledge about any sale of the land of his forefathers. That was the first recorded claim of 'purchase' of the land of the Nguni people. Scores of ships either sunk or crashed on the rugged coast between the Great Kei River and the uMthamvuna Rivers, hence it was called the *Wild Coast*. For instance, there are records of English vessels *Bonnybrook* crashing in 1715 followed by the *Grosvenor* which sank in 1782, near uMsikaba River mouth between Port St John's and Port Edward. Some of its crew, women and children lived to tell the tale and left inscriptions on a rock about their survival and the buried treasure nearby. Some of them hid in the thick bush to be found and were found starving to death by the natives. Some of their descendants can be found living around iNgquza Hill in emaMpondweni in the Eastern Cape to this day.

In the early 1800s, a few hundred kilometres north of the wild coast the area was bursting with newcomers. They were hunters, bandits, lowlifes, merchants, treasure seekers, arms dealers and slave traders who crashed into Port Natal hoping for a better life. At one time, some men from the Cele kingdom were out hunting, when they noticed a human-like figure eating bird's eggs at the beach. When they got closer, they realised that indeed it was a human. Most people living in the Zulu empire as they had never seen a non-Zulu person before. They noticed the unfamiliar long wavy toussled like strands that resembled a maize cob before going to report the unusual sighting to King Magaye kaDibandlela of the Cele kingdom at eMdlazi Palace. The bizarre figure put up a serious fight before being captured and brought before Magaye.

On closer inspection, they noticed tiny pink breasts - it was a girl. She was taken care of and when she could finally speak isiZulu, she told them about her shipwreck ordeal and about some survivors who later died. She lived as *umdlunkulu* at the king's palace and later married Mbukwe Mtwana from Ntabankulu. She bore two sons, Mxokwana and Mntengwane. Mntengwane later fathered a daughter Nqolisa. Decades later, white hunters discovered some writing on a seashore rock, near where the little white girl was found, which detailed a shipwreck and a girl survivor. They looked for her and found her living around Springvale High Flats. By then she was about 80 years old and could only speak isiZulu. Her descendants can still be found in the outskirts of Durban. The existence of an old white woman living like 'a Zulu' was confirmed by Duka Fynn, whose father was one of the whites who became Zulu subjects under Shaka and took part in his Zulu empire-building wars.

# Imfecane and European Colonisation

*Narina's beauty was legendary. She was a member of the Gonaqua people living in the Cape in the 1780s. Her ornaments are made up of cowrie shells and she is carrying a water tight basket. (1820 Settlers Museum)*

*This depiction of a young man living in the Cape was drawn by Francois Le Valliant around 1780. His bracelets are made from elephant tusks and necklaces are made from animal bones polished white. (1829 Settlers Museum)*

# Imfecane and European Colonisation

Henry Francis Fynn was a one of the white colonisers who became a Zulu subject. He was enlisted into the Zulu army and fought in some of Emperor Shaka's empire building wars and married over five Zulu wives. (Killie Campbell Africana Library)

Percy Fynn is a mixed race descendant of Henry Francis Fynn and a Zulu woman. Percy died in 1966 and the rest of the Fynn dynasty can be found around Port Shepstone, south of Durban. (Killie Campbell Africana Library)

In 1823 Shaka decided to concentrate on domestic affairs and established more female regiments such as iNzawu, iKhwani, uChenyane, iNgcotsha, iNkehlela and uMkhindi *'usiba lukaMatshekana'* (Matshekana's feather). He then turned his attention Ntombazi's despicable profession, witchcraft. Some claimed that they had a 'gift' and disguised it in the form of a ritual or custom or traditional healing. Shaka had no qualms with herbalists who healed people using traditional medicines. But he had a serious problem with people who played God and struck terror in everyone who did not possess their 'gift'. A 'close second' after the super-witch Ntombazi, was a woman called Nobela. She would even masquerade as a medium and her speciality was the psychic ability to 'see' or 'spiritually detect' evildoers. Then Shaka called everyone to a national gathering and summoned all types of mediums to the capital. He instructed them to 'spiritually detect' the person responsible for smearing blood which he found on the wall of his private hut. He further instructed them to work in teams. They tried to object to working in teams because they wanted to individually impress him the most, but Shaka insisted and they ended up agreeing.

This on its own, made Shaka's blood boil as per common knowledge, no medium has ever been able or even willing to work with another unless they were all genuine witches. By the end of the day, the teams had identified more than 50 petrified people as the wrongdoers. Out of the 22 teams, only Mfiswa Dladla's three sons, Mleku, Mbube and Mehlo as well as Nobhiyane Madondo correctly identified Shaka as the perpetrator. Shaka had pulled this stunt to expose their deceit and fraudulence. All were killed except for the Dladla boys and Nobhiyane. Thereafter, Shaka banned witchcraft outright in the entire empire. His reasoning was that if your people (ancestors) want to talk to you from beyond, they will do so directly. They will not send non-relatives to tell you intimate family matters. Herbalists could continue their work. After exposing the false 'traditional healers' he went after phony rainmakers and banned them as well. In the wake of this horrifying ordeal, Shaka undertook a long slow walk as part of his rest and recreation and went to a natural hot-springs resort in the Cele kingdom for some well-deserved rest. He took a few thousand troops with him and got to know them even better. Shaka was particularly fond of Magaye, and even referred to him as *umnawami* (younger brother). As a favour to Magaye, Shaka allowed the iNjanduna regiment from the Cele kingdom to remain in its own area around uMdloti, whereas other regiments were required to move towards the centre of the empire and join other regiments.

In the same year, the *Salisbury* was shipwrecked in Port Natal and on board were two interesting characters, Canadian-born James Saunders King and his English friend Lt Francis George Farewell. They had both served in the British Navy during the Napoleonic wars and now Africa's south-eastern coastline was their new hunting ground for fame and fortune. They spent a few weeks in Port Natal and then left for the Cape, but Farewell returned a year later with two chartered ships that also wrecked on the shores of Port Natal. The ships were the *Ann* which was piloted by Captain Robert Newton Dunn. The other ship was the *Julia* piloted by Henry Francis Fynn whose over 40 passengers included the following; Farewell and his wife Ann, who is the first white woman to settle in Port Natal; John Powell; Henry Ogle; Thomas Halstead; John Cane; Collins; Davids; De Bruin; J Hoffman; JS Hoffman; JP Hoffman; Lt John Saunders; Johnstone; Nel, Buxman and Pieterson.

After recovering from their ordeal, Farewell sent word through King Siyingela of the Mkhize kingdom whose kingdom was located around uThongathi (*Tongaat*) and requested an audience with Shaka to *khonza* (request to be the king's subject). The whites caused consternation as they walked to the capital. They passed through Sinqila kaMpimpi Ngati's homestead in uMhlali and the locals reported their sighting to Magaye who summoned them to his palace. On arrival, Fynn entered the palace on horseback and was instructed to disembark from the horse in the presence of Magaye, a command he obeyed. The people were terrified of the horse, especially the women who repeatedly chanted:

| | |
|---|---|
| *Ngqwabangqwaba, hamba la* | *evil spirit, go away from here* |
| *Ngqwabangqwaba, hamba la* | *evil spirit, go away from here* |

The newcomers were overwhelmed with Zulu hospitality and they were even given welcome gifts of cattle and ivory 'supposedly' from Shaka. But after a few days Fynn and his entourage were told to go back to Port Natal as Shaka could not meet them at that time. This was a Zulu way of saying: 'We do not know who you are. Stay right where you are, where we can see you so that we can study your ways before you can meet our king.' Two brothers, who were both ambassadors and secret service officers, Mhlophe Mthethwa, who was amiable and soft-spoken, and Mbikwane were instructed to befriend the strangers and watch their every move. He even built himself a homestead on the Berea ridge overlooking the white settlement. In the meantime, the whites had managed to salvage some dignity and had built Zulu-style windowless homesteads with individual huts made from wattle and clay featuring a single door and a thatched roof. They lived next to each other near today's Durban Town Hall and Gardens.

Fynn, Ogle and Farewell married over five Zulu wives each, even though Farewell had arrived with his white wife, Ann. They all practised the married Zulu sexual relations custom whereby the woman would go to her husband's hut only when called upon, even if it was to merely sleep over. As it were with Zulu men, they never had a reason to go to the huts of their wives. Fynn built a homestead that accommodated over 100 locals called *eSibumeme* and his senior servant was a San woman called Rachel. His other homesteads were called *eMpendwini* near iSiphingo and *eNsimbini* south of the uMzimkhulu River. His principal wife was Vundlase Zelemu and some of their children were Duka, Nomanga and Mashingana. One of the sons lies buried at eNsandlundlu Ridge near Durban after he was killed on Dingane's orders in 1828. After Shaka's death, Fynn ran away from the kingdom and left Vundlase in charge of his followers who had formed a regiment called *iziNkumbi* (locusts). Her deputy was a man called Juqula kaNqawe Mpemvini. This regiment comprised of Zulu, white and mixed-race refugees, murderers, lowlifes, thieves, hunters and other undesirables. They were referred to more as mercenaries than as a regiment because they were also hired to break the law or carry out atrocities.

After a year-long wait, Mbikwane took Fynn and his entourage which included Peterson, Frederick and others to meet Shaka. They used the coastal path covered by acacia and savannah trees. They slowly crossed the mouths of the uThukela and aMatigulu Rivers and went through the iNyezane plain on the northern side of the oBonjeni Ridge. They slept at the iNtontela *ikhanda* which was headed by Shaka's aunt, Mawa kaJama. Not only were they overwhelmed by the usual Nguni hospitality of meat, beer, song and dance but were also mesmerised by the mighty and imposing iNtontela regiment presented to them in full battle regalia. Fynn had brought Shaka woollen blankets, some brass and copper ornaments, pigeons, dogs, a pig and a full-dress military coat decorated with gold lace, all discarded by Shaka. In his diary Fynn described his journey through the Zulu kingdom and his first encounter with Shaka: 'Order and discipline was visible everywhere. All the abodes were maintained to the highest standard of cleanliness — the kraal and homesteads. Ashes or dirt could not be seen anywhere inside or outside their homes. On arriving within a mile of the king's residence, we were directed to wait under a large tree till the arrival of the messengers who were to call Mr. Farewell and myself and the rest of the party. At the time of our entering the gates of the inner kraal it was lined by about twelve thousand men in their war attire.

'We were then desired to gallop around the palace several times and, returning, bring the remainder of our party. When we came again we were directed to gallop four times more around the kraal, and then stand at a distance of twenty yards from a tree at the head of the cattle enclosure. Mbikwane, who had accompanied us, made a long speech to the king, who was so surrounded by his chiefs that we could not distinguish him. One of the chiefs spoke in reply to Mbikwane, to whom he stood opposite. His speech concluded he brought an elephant's tusk as a present to Mr. Farewell. Mbikwane again spoke, urging us frequently to exclaim "yebo" meaning "yes", but what we were assenting to we did not know. Shaka then sprang up from among the chiefs, striking the shield of the chiefs on either side of him. The whole body then ran to the lower end of the cattle enclosure, leaving us alone, with the exception of one man who had been in the crowd.'

Fynn was shocked when he eventually deciphered that the person standing at the back of the crowd was Farewell's former interpreter Jacob *'Jacot'* Msimbithi, a former Robben Island prisoner who could speak Portuguese, French, Dutch and English. The governor of the Cape had given Msimbithi to Capt Owen on condition that if Msimbithi behaved himself, he would be freed. However, after spending a year with Capt Owen, Msimbithi was further sold to Farewell and Thompson as a slave and they took him to the Cape with them to explore the east coast of Africa. As fate could have it, their ship failed to land in Port Natal and was blown to St Lucia where it wrecked. Four passengers and the whole crew drowned and Msimbithi, who was an excellent swimmer managed to save both Thompson and Farewell. Instead of thanking Msimbithi for saving their lives, Thompson blamed Msimbithi for the bad weather and gave him a severe beating and left him for dead. When Msimbithi recovered, he ran away into the hinterland and found refuge under Shaka. With Msimbithi's knowledge of several European languages and understanding of the European mentality, he became an asset to Shaka who made him the senior royal interpreter. Shaka called him *Hlambamanzi* (swimmer) and gave him a large piece of land near the uMdlothi River. As Fynn and Hlambamanzi glared at each other for a long time, a mixed-race Portuguese-speaking man presented himself to Shaka. Hlambamanzi and the Portuguese man began to narrate the behaviour of the Europeans to Shaka and they had nothing positive to say about English people. Also present during this interaction was Sigananda, who was only 14 years old at the time. He lived long enough to be the leader of the 1906 Poll Tax Uprising. He described his first encounter with whites as follows: 'Their eyes seemed to have fire. They may have lacked in other aspects such as their private parts, but they were brave to have travelled such long distances.'

Shaka sat on his throne of rolled mats under a fig tree and Phampatha, carrying beer on her head, knelt in front of Shaka and took a sip from the calabash. Then Shaka took a sip and handed it back to her to give Farewell who circulated it among the white visitors. Shaka told them about his empire, his wealth in the form of cattle and about his invincible army that brought terror to all his enemies. He boasted about law and order in the empire, where nothing was lost and not found and where the women and children were safe from molestation. The whites could only respond by agreeing with him by repeatedly saying '*Bayethe*'. Then Shaka enquired about the English monarch, King George IV, and about the size of his capital, the number of his wives, cattle and about his government and army. Shaka found it amusing that the British king only had one wife, but said it was probably because of his old age. He also said that King George should imitate him and have no wife at all. He offered them a royal banquet of 13 calabashes of beer, fresh lamb and beef, baskets of corn, sweet potatoes, groundnuts and honey but no green vegetables because it was winter. Shaka also invited them to his daily bath spectacle where they noted he was uncircumcised. In his diary, this is what Fynn had to say about the glory of the Zulu military parade:

'The glamour and extent of pomp and ceremony that followed is something that we had only seen in aristocratic Europe. Regiments passed, each with their distinct shields and plumes, the praise singer calling out their name and battle honours. Fifteen regiments swept past us and did mass war dances that made the earth shake. The cattle followed in herds of 5000 each, and each herd of uniform colour, sixty thousand in all. The best was reserved for last; finally the female regiments made their grand appearance, headed by one of their own officers and went to the centre of the arena.

'There were between eight-thousand and ten-thousand in each regiment and each held a tiny staff in their hands and joined in the dances, which lasted for about two hours. Then the royal ladies were followed by more than five-thousand imidlunkulu. The king joined in the dances with many of his aristocrats and each dance ended up with a short speech by him. Afterwards, Shaka enquired what we used our hides for and I told him that we used them to make shoes and other things that I could not easily describe. He told me that our forefathers had done us a disfavour by encouraging us to protect our feet, further they had missed the ultimate purpose of hides; to make the most beautiful item ever, the shield. Shaka was also of the opinion that our weapons were inferior to theirs. He claimed that if a shield were dipped in water prior to being shot at from a distance, it would be able to repel a bullet and that while reloading, a Zulu soldier would be able to engage at close quarters. Since we did not have shields, we would attempt to run away which would be futile because we would be hampered by our sandals.

'I suspect the interpreter added his own spin to things and I was also hesitant to strongly disagree with a king. He would make fun of all our ways and customs in the presence of his subjects, all in good humour but, once we were on our own, he would praise our superiority. Our justice system of putting people in jail is something he found horrific. His idea was that if the person was guilty, kill him. If he was under suspicion, free him as the arrest would be a warning for the future. This topic came about when he heard that our interpreter had been incarcerated on Robben Island. It was difficult for me to explain the concept of innocent until proven guilty, so once again I had to concede about our inadequacies. I must point out that there were things he did not agree with about our laws. Even though the Zulu people were polite and friendly when speaking to us, they called us *silguaner* (a beast) that came from the sea behind our back and it was followed by a non-flattering gesture.'

In the evening, Fynn fired an eight-gun salute and three rockets into the clear night sky with intention of impressing the Zulu. But they did not seem impressed because they had been exposed to European weaponry before through white traders from Delagoa Bay. After the festivities, Farewell and the entourage went back to the budding white community in Port Natal and reported about their face-to-face meeting with Shaka. Shaka gave them numerous gifts and Ambassador Mbikwane escorted them back to Port Natal but Fynn chose to remain at KwaBulawayo because he was taken by everything Zulu. In British society, Fynn was a nobody, whose English origins were vague before he gained reputation in the Zulu empire at the age of 15. He was known to have only one fear in his life, which was the demonic laughter of a hyena behind him at night. Fynn wasn't happy with the rising number of whites in Port Natal so he informed every white person he came across that he was not only a Zulu subject but that Shaka had also made him a 'white Zulu chief'. He further claimed that that was the reason Shaka had given him a large piece of land around Port Natal which was about 50km to the north, 20km to the south and 200km inland. This is yet another claim about land being offered to non-black subjects. Shaka was stabbed when Fynn was still at the capital and in his diary, he wrote that:

'Having spent the afternoon reading, I was induced to take another peep at the dancers. As it was dark when I came, the king ordered a number of people to hold up bundles of dried reeds, kept burning, to give light to the scene. I had not been there many minutes when I heard a shriek and the lights were immediately extinguished. Then followed a general bustle and cry, I immediately turned away to call Michael (one of Fynn's Hottentot servants). I immediately told him what I had heard, and sent him to prepare a lamp, and to bring some chamomile, the only medicine I had by me. Jacob (the interpreter) fell down in a fit, so that now I could ask no questions nor gain information as to where Shaka was. He had been stabbed with an assegai through the left arm, and the blade had passed through the ribs under the left breast. His own doctor, who appeared to have a good knowledge of wounds, gave him medicine to vomit, and afterwards repeated doses of purgative medicine, and continually washed the wound in decoctions of cooling roots.

'He also probed the wound to ascertain whether any poison had been used on the assegai. We then understood that six men had been wounded by the same assassins who had wounded Shaka. From the road they took, it was supposed that they had been sent by Zuedi, King of the Endwandwe, who was Shaka's only powerful enemy. Accordingly, two regiments were sent at once in search of the aggressors. In the meanwhile, the medicines which Mr Farewell had promised to send had been received. The king, however, was hopeless for four days. On the fifth day there were symptoms of improvement in the king's health and wounds, and the favourable indications were even more noticeable on the day following. At noon, the party sent out in the search of the malefactors returned, bringing with them the dead bodies of three men whom they had killed in the bush. The restoration of the king's health made some great changes. The tumult gradually ceased. A force of a thousand men was sent to attack the hostile tribe, and returned in a few days, having destroyed several cattle enclosures with eight hundred head of cattle. Mr Farewell, and Mrs Isaacs, her servant uNosiphongo and other whites came to visit Shaka after having received a letter from me stating particulars of the recent occurrence'.

Shaka spent many hours discussing all aspects of life with his new white subjects often with hilarious consequences. He discovered that they shared a belief in the one Creator, but the difference was that the Zulu Creator possessed two fruitful wives. Captain King had spent many months mapping the coastline around Port Natal and later went to England to show off his drawing achievement. This enabled him to convince King George to bestown on him the title of Honorary Lieutenant for the effort. When he returned, he shared his latest travels with Shaka who was fond of him. The new Lieutenant tried to convince Shaka that the earth was round but Shaka refused to believe him. Shaka asked him how the oceans remained on a round earth and questioned the mechanics of a revolving earth. Poor Lt King tried to explain to the best of his ability, but Shaka remained unconvinced and even asked for a demonstration of this phenomenon using a pumpkin as the earth and seeds as the people. Lt King placed seeds on the pumpkin and begun to spin it around, obviously the seeds flew all over the place. This demonstration made Lt King desperate he even tried to hold the pumpkin at a different angle, but to no avail. His spectators responded with raucous laughter. Shortly after Shaka's stabbing, Farewell drafted an incredulous title deed for land. He claimed to have bought the land from Shaka and showed it to all the whites who cared to read it. How could an illiterate Shaka been able to write or sign a document, moreover the notion of selling land was a foreign concept to the Zulu. The title deed read: '

I, Inguos (Nkosi, meaning Chief) Shaka, King of the Zulus and of the country of Natal, as well as the whole land of Natal to Delago Bay, which I inherited from my father, do hereby of my own free will, in consideration of diverse goods received, grant, make over and sell to FG Farewell and Company the entire and full possession, in perpetuity, of the Port or Harbour of Natal and the surrounding country herein described, viz. the whole of the neck of land or peninsula on the south-west entrance and all the country ten miles to the southern side of Port Natal as pointed out and extending along the sea coast to the northward and eastward as far as the river known by the native name Gumgelote, being about twenty-five miles of sea coast northeast of Port Natal, together with all the country inland as far as the nation called Gowagnewkos by the Zulu, extending about one-hundred miles backward from the seashore with all rights to the rivers, woods, mines and articles of all denominations contained in therein. In witness whereof I have placed my hand, being fully aware that the doing so is intended to bind me to all the articles and conditions of my own free will and consent to hereby before the said FG Farewell, whom I hereby acknowledge as a chief of the said country with full power and authority over such natives that like to remain there promising to supply me with cattle and corn as a reward of his kind attention to me in my illness from my wound.'

**Signed:** 8 August 1824

**Witnesses:** Mbikwane, Msika, Mhlophe and Hlambamanzi

*According to Henry Francis Fynn, this scribble was done by Emperor Shaka. (Killie Campbell Africana Library)*

As soon as the white Zulu subjects left, Shaka and his best friends Mdlaka and Nqoboka and Mbopha reminisced about the olden days. They strategised about how they could overcome whites in case of wars against them. Shaka said big fires would spook their horses and they would be forced into broken terrain where the whites would be forced to dismount and then be overcome by the Zulu numbers and Mgobhozi added - Zulu courage. Shaka took a decision that two regiments would go to England and learn the white man's art of war and weapons. But before they left, they should be trained in the kingdom by the white subjects. A few weeks later before arrangements were made for the training, news reached Shaka, who was seated with Fynn and Farewell, at the capital that Shaka's grandmother Mthaniya was gravely ill. Shaka was inconsoleable and sought all the medical help he could find for the old lady.

Fynn described Queen Mother Mthaniya's last hours in his diaries: 'Shaka requested me to attend to his grandmother, who was dangerously ill with dysentery and fever. I accordingly went to see her. As her age was about 80, I saw no hope of recovery, and candidly told the king my fears. He requested me to put a white shirt on her. I did so. He then began to cry bitterly. Jacob, the interpreter, told me of Shaka's great affection for his grandmother. When he happened to visit her, he frequently washed her eyes and ears, which were in a sad state because of her age. He also pared her nails and otherwise treated her as a father might his child. We could hardly believe that a man of an apparent unfeeling disposition could be possessed of such affection and consideration for others. Further observation, however, convinced us that this was indeed the case.'

The much-loved Queen Mother, Mthaniya kaZingelwayo Sibiya was revered, loved and regarded as the saviour of the Zulu kingdom for having given birth to the Zulu heir, Senzangakhona. Hence, the Zulu empire is still called *KwelikaMthaniya* to this day. She died in November 1825 somewhere between the age of 90 and 100 years old. She lies buried near Ndaba's grave alongside the iMpembeni River in the eMakhosini Valley. After her death, Shaka was concerned about the approaching years of his now 60-year-old mother who now had white thinning hair. Fynn, who was now fluent in isiZulu, told Shaka that the whites had dye that could restore the original colour of hair. But it seems Shaka must have understood that if something reverses hair colour, it could also reverse the ageing process and ordered Fynn to import it for her. Notwithstanding the fact that it was still the mourning period, Shaka, ever the comic, managed to bring a smile to everyone's face when he played a practical joke on one of his white subjects. Isaacs heard rumours about an animal that could only have been a unicorn and his life's greatest ambition was to own it. So, he set out to hunt it down as well as pay his condolences to Shaka on the 30th of November 1825.

Isaacs told Shaka that he was on a quest to attain his latest obsession and Shaka feigning concern asked: 'What is that you desire so much that keeps you sleepless at night?' Isaacs responded: 'I heard that Magaye has an *inyamazane eluphondo lunye* (a unicorn) and I am desperate to get it.' Shaka said: 'I will personally make sure that you lay your hands on it, even though it is further inland'. Isaacs could not thank Shaka enough and began to describe his fame and fortune in detail to an amused Shaka. Then he dispatched a fleet-footed platoon to Magaye and within no time, they trotted back with the creature. Instead of the expected excitement when Isaacs looked at his 'prized possession' there was nothing but embarrassment. 'Why do you look so miserable, because I have kept my promise? What is the problem?' Shaka asked, trying to suppress a mischievous smile. Isaacs sheepishly replied: 'It is only a billy-goat which has lost one of its horns. I thought it was a genuine unicorn *Bayethe!*' This provided the much-needed amusement.

During one of his trading expeditions in St Helena Island, Lt King came across Nathaniel Isaacs. He was a 17-year-old nephew of one of his slave-trader clients, Saul Solomons. Lt King and Isaacs became friends and during one of their binge-drinking nights in the bars of the island, they befriended an aimless, red-haired 15-year-old vagrant from England, St Helena Island. They sailed him with them on the *Mary* and arrived in Port Natal in October 1825 but the following day, the ship was wrecked by the waves. After sending a request to be Zulu subjects to Shaka, they then built another ship with some Zulu shipbuilders under the supervision of the ship's senior carpenter Hatton. They used salvaged material and some locally hewn wood, but as they waited for the local wood to season perfectly, Isaacs, Hatton and the ship's crew participated in Shaka's empire building wars for a few years. When the ship was finally completed, Isaacs named it *Chaka* but was told that it was tasteless in Zulu culture to name a ship after a king. He then changed it to the *Elizabeth and Susan*. The ship was slipped into the sea on March 10, 1828.

The whites at Port Natal sent Ross to Delagoa Bay which was about 650 kilometres away to buy them medicine. This was extreme cruelty as the poor boy had to brave disease-infested terrain, wild animals and indifferent locals, not to forget the murderous Zwangendaba, Nqaba and Soshangane who were lurking in the northern parts. Ross paid homage to Shaka on his way north and Shaka was impressed by the 15-year-old's courage who had only two Zulu guides. Moreover, another white man John Powell had attempted the same journey before and was never heard of again. Shaka gave him a shield and a spear and made him travel under the guidance and protection of fearless officer Langalibalele who could speak

English and Portuguese. The thirty soldiers who went with them were to trade ten pairs of tusks at the coast. Langalibalele used the stars to guide them to the north as he had undertaken this journey many times before. They survived many perils along the way and two months later arrived in Delagoa Bay. The Portuguese were initially suspicious of the Zulu entourage. They thought they were an advance spy team suggesting they were going to be attacked by Shaka's mighty army and refused to interact with them. However, the Portuguese later relented and gave them all the medicine they needed, free of charge and bought their tusks.

For some whites, life was too desolate in Port Natal and they went back to the Cape where there were more whites. It was mostly the white desperados who remained and made a life for themselves among the Zulu such as Fynn. According to Isaacs, after one of the hunting expeditions around the Kei River in the south, Fynn returned to Port Natal looking truly comical: 'He was barefoot with unsightly, long facial hair like a baboon, his eyes were pools of misadventure under a crownless straw hat, a loose tattered blanket hanging from his neck fastened by strips of hide and his one free hand was covering up his modesty, because there was very little left of the blanket.'

Shaka did not want to father any children, especially boys because they could kill him and take over the throne. First, he noticed that the highly temperamental Mbuzikazi had suddenly become coy and her physique had altered, and he was no fool. Indeed, against his deepest wishes, his favourite sexual partner had conceived. The information was secretly conveyed to Nandi who ensured that no one was told about it especially Phampatha and Shaka. But as expected, Shaka found out. Delighted, Nandi sent Mbuzikazi to live with Shaka's sister Nomcoba in eMkhindini Palace where she gave birth to a boy child Zibizendlela in 1825. She only allowed Zibizendlela to suckle a few times, lest her breasts betrayed her and used a wet nurse Nomagwebu as a decoy. Everyone at eMkhindini thought Zibizendlela was Nomagwebu's son. Unlike his father, Zibizendlela grew up surrounded by love from a doting grandmother, mother and aunt and all the residents of eMkhindini Palace.

Perhaps Shaka turned a blind eye to please his mother who had been nagging him for a grandchild and there was nothing in the world he would not do to please her. History has a way of repeating itself. Nandi did all she could to hide her grandson Zibizendlela the same way Queen Mother Mthaniya had hidden Shaka. Initially Nandi hid him inside a big earthen clay pot but as time passed, she became bolder by the day. When Shaka moved to KwaDukuza she seldom hid Zibizendlela. She called him *Nkunzana* (little bull) as she had called Shaka *Mlilwana* (little fire). Even though Nandi had other grandchildren from Ngwadi and Nomcoba did not have any children, *Nkunzana* was her favourite grandchild. When Zibizendlela learnt how to walk he was removed from eMkhindini together with his mother and his wet nurse. They went to live at KwaMhlabuyalingana under the King Tembe in the north-eastern part of the Zulu empire. Here, they forever kept a low profile, and Zibizendlela's descendants are known only by a few important members of the Zulu royal family. Nandi was deeply sad to see *Nkunzana* go and after a short period of time, she became melancholic. Her health declined sharply, and she ended up suffering from an incurable type of dysentery. She became delirious one night while Shaka was away hunting elephants with Fynn more than 100 kilometres away.

When he received the news, he literally ran the whole distance but by the time Shaka arrived at eMkhindini, she had slipped into a coma and in the middle of the night passed away. Shaka was inconsolable. Nandi had wished for nothing more in her tumultuous life than what she got before dying, respect. She had almost done it all, she had committed incest twice, was an unwed mother, a despised consort and she cohabited with a commoner. As the mother of Africa's greatest military strategist, she was awarded a befitting grandiose funeral, over 100 cattle were slaughtered. Her grave was dug close to where she had died and 1200 soldiers, including the iziYendane regiment, stood guard at her grave for a year. Today, she lies buried in the ruins of eMkhindini Palace, under a pile of vandalised rocks in Eshowe. The *iNdlovukazi* Nandi kaBhebhe Mhlongo of the eLangeni kingdom died on 10 October 1827.

The national mourning commenced with everyone having to remove all forms of personal adornment. More than 50 000 people converged at eMkhindini Palace. They yelled at the top of their voices, trying to outperform each other's grief. The Zulu Prime Minister Ngomane announced decrees that were to be observed during the mandatory year-long mourning period. He then, excessively, trying to impress the grieving Shaka banned any form of harvesting, planting, sexual pleasure, milking of cows and the suckling of calves with immediate effect. The consequence of anyone caught breaking any of these decrees was immediate death. Enemies accused each other of breaking one decree or the other, and for the first time in the young empire, chaos and anarchy surfaced. People began to die of starvation, while others ran away, mainly from Shaka and changed their identities before joining other kingdoms. After a few months Shaka went back to KwaDukuza and fell into a deep depression and became despondent, disinterested and disengaged. As he wallowed in his pain and depression, he became closer to Phampatha, who was now a colonel of the new, 3000-strong female regiment *iNkisimane*, based at KwaDukuza. Shaka blamed himself for not having done enough to keep his mother alive and became short-tempered. The only people he had time and affection for were Phampatha, Ngomane and Mdlaka.

The empire fell into a deepening state of atrophy and dysfunction. The Zulu were disciplined but never servile. They became restless and rebellious, weeds took over their fields, while their suffering increased. This once strong and healthy people began to waste away, so did their animals. It took one impassioned man, Gala kaNodade Biyela, to bring an end to the madness. He had known Shaka since the days of the *umdlathule* drought when they lived together at Mpaphala more than 20 years earlier. He decided to go and confront him as he did not believe Shaka was responsible for the lunacy. So, Gala woke up one morning, put on his best attire and told his family that he would not be half the man he thought he was if he did not confront Shaka. He took his favourite cow and journeyed across several rivers, valleys and mountains until he reached KwaDukuza. Risking death, Gala was granted an audience with the now highly stressed out Shaka. Without mincing his words, Gala reminded Shaka that his mother's death was not the end of the world. That death was inevitable, that is why there was no need to punish the living. He also told him that if he did not rescind the terrible orders, he would have no subjects because *inkosi yinkosi ngabantu* (a king is only a king because of his subjects). Shaka accepted the criticism and the mourning decrees were rescinded immediately. He thanked Gala and rewarded him with a few fat cattle. He also gave Gala's regiment permission to wear an *isicoco* which entitled them to marry. The empire revered Gala for his bravery and he basked in glory for the rest of his days.

*A side view of isicoco. A maturity head ring for men. (Killie Campbell Africana Library)*

*Indumezulu regiment was King Shaka's first Zulu Rifle Corps that used an assortment of modern European weaponry. The commander was a crack sniper, Jacob Hlambamanzi Msimbithi who was also the principal royal translator. He spoke Dutch, Portuguese, French, Dutch and English. (Killie Campbell Africana Library)*

A year before his mother's death, in July 1826, Sikhunyana kaZwide Ndwandwe tried to do what his father and extended family members failed to achieve. He decided to lead the Ndwandwe people back to their kingdom as they had been displaced by Shaka through brute force. He mobilised other kingdoms who had not been conquered by Shaka to join him. Shaka knew the power of the Ndwandwe army and ordered a national call up and all regiments reported at the capital after five days. Shaka also deployed the newly formed iNdumezulu regiment, which was the first Zulu Rifle Corps that used European weapons. It was under the command of Hlambamanzi, a crack sniper, and their excitement to see combat for the first time could not be contained. They used an assortment of weapons such as rockets and the following guns: The *ibala* (one-metre-long rifle), the *imbobiyana* (a long-barrelled rifle), the *iginanda*, *umhlabakude* or *igodla* (another long-barrelled rifle but not as long as the *ibala*), the *umakhalana* (a double-barrelled gun used exclusively by aristocrats), the *isinqwana* (a 50-centimetre rifle used for close-range fighting), the *ifili* (a long-range rifle, which used a small bullet and a small cap whose barrel was as long as the *umakhalana*).

Over the following years, more regiments were trained by the steady flow of hunters from Delagoa Bay and Port Natal on how to make, use and repair the European-made weapons. Shaka ordered the white subjects in Port Natal to bring their shields, *iklwa*, tents and white weapons to KwaBulawayo for inspection before they could be deployed to the battle theatre. The whites obeyed in numbers, eager to serve their Zulu king. Most of their European weapons, were, however, in dire need of repair and some their tents were torn or had gaping holes. Worse, some had no ammunition at all. Shaka flew into a rage because they had said that they had everything they needed for war. He made them step forward and severely admonished them in front of the rest of the regiments. Those whites whose weapons and gear were in order like Fynn, proudly marched to war with Shaka to the iNdololwane Battle in July 1826.

Sikhunyana assembled the Ndwandwe soldiers at the valley below the iNdololwane and iNcaka hills. Shaka assessed the Ndwandwe formation and strength before concluding that he needed volunteers to make a unit of *amadelakufa* (a suicide squad) to start the battle. Typical of Zulu valour and bravery, there was a fracas as almost everyone stepped forward to be considered for the ultimate mission. Not to be outdone by his 'boys', Mgobhozi somersaulted forward and rendered an awesome war dance. Shaka was not keen to let Mgobhozi be part of the *kamikaze* unit but on the other hand, to refuse him this honour would have made his friend lose face. Shaka's chosen *amadelakufa* were excited and could not wait for sunrise.

Those not chosen, were miserable. Late that night, the old coterie of Mgobhozi, Nqoboka and Shaka sat together as they always did. This time, however, the mood was different. Shaka tried to talk Mgobhozi out of the suicide mission but to no avail. Instead, Mgobhozi chose to go to sleep early so that he would be well rested in the morning, his last day on earth. Shaka watched his friend walk away and his heart broke when he recalled what they had been through together over the years. He, however, managed to steal a quick smile when he thought of Mgobhozi's wedding-day melodrama, when he could not consummate his marriage to 20 wives on his wedding day.

At the break of dawn, once again, Shaka deployed his pincer movement formation and led from the front of *ikhanda* (the head) his main division. Mgobhozi was behind Shaka in command of *isifuba* (the chest) the second division. Nzobo and Ndlela each commanded *izimpondo* (the horns) the divisions on either wing while Mdlaka commanded *amahlombe* (the shoulders) the lower division. Sigananda kaNcube Shezi and Njengabantu kaSobuza Ngubane were present as Shaka's personal *udibi*. Sigananda recounted the battle as follows:

'Mgobhozi, with a number of ardent volunteers of the suicide squad tore straight into the Ndwandwe ranks and left a pile of bodies where they had swept through. They only stopped in front of a gigantic boulder, surrounded, where they fought for their lives. The Ndwandwe veterans targeted Mgobhozi and ripped into him with virulent hatred as he was singularly responsible for the death of their princes during the Gqokli war. Equally, Mgobhozi and the volunteer unit fought gallantly, utilising the fighting tactics drilled into them by Shaka. Blood was oozing out of their bodies and often stuffed feathers and leaves in the gaping wounds as they fought on. When it became clear that the suicide squad was surrounded and outnumbered, the Zulu warriors shouted *'Sigidi'* and rushed at the Ndwandwe army. One particularly young brave Zulu warrior, Mashaya, chose to fight next to Mgobhozi and died gazing at his hero with blood shot eyes. Now left all alone against a boulder, with surprising nimbleness Mgobhozi tore into the murderous Ndwandwe soldiers until he too dropped dead. The Zulu were soon all over the Ndwandwe with equal ferocity and vengeance as they had witnessed their hero, Mgobhozi being stabbed to death. This began to turn the tide of the fight. The Ndwandwe were now fast retreating from the battlefield towards their women and children hoping that the Zulu would show them mercy. Shaka's intrepid regiments were in no mood for compassion or diplomacy. With remarkable swiftness, the Zulu slaughtered every Ndwandwe man, woman and child in their path. Sikhunyana escaped with a few followers as the Shaka and the Zulu army defeated the Ndwandwe nation for eternity.

In his diaries, Fynn also gave a first-hand account of the iNdololwane Battle: 'Shaka rushed up iNdololwane Hill from where he was watching the battle and led the army up the hill and divided each regiment into companies and stopped 50 meters from the enemy. Hlambamanzi was the first one to fire and his first two shots merely scared the Ndwandwe. But the fight ensued after the third shot while the enemy continued calling the Zulu cowardly dogs on the sidelines. They clashed for three minutes non-stop and then fell back. After their officers had assessed the losses, they engaged again, for twice the length of time and when they finally fell back, the enemy had more casualties. The Zulu then made a final rush and defeated the Ndwandwe regiments.'

After the success of iNdololwane Battle, Shaka sent two inexperienced regiments after Bheje who was still refusing to submit to him. Bheje easily repelled the rookie regiments. Then Shaka sent a few *imidlunkulu*, led by Noshuku kaNjongolo Zulu and Mcokamisa to the two rookie regiments who were to insult the soldiers with the worst possible insults and to call them cowards just before they went into battle. This tactic was to embarrass rookie regiments into action because it was the greatest shame to be called a coward by a member of the opposite sex. The consequences of cowardice were dire. Firstly, if you were married your wife or wives would leave you and that meant living without a female for life. Secondly, if you were not married, it meant you would never get married because nobody wanted to marry a coward. Not understanding the Zulu way of life, especially the strict military code of conduct of a Zulu soldier, two of Farewell's San servants Michael and John raped a young Zulu bride. Everyone wanted to skin them alive but Shaka decided not only to punish the culprits but meted common cause punishment to the people who came with them. So it happened that Shaka ordered Farewell, Lt King, Isaacs, Cane, Michael, John and their five Zulu and mixed-race friends to fight Bheje and stay in the battle theatre until they defeated him or die trying. Shaka also sent the uMbelebele division under the command of his aunt Mkabayi to escort them and make sure that they did not run away.

Mkabayi set up camp five kilometres away from the battle theatre and monitored the situation. The whites and their friends got to the battle theatre under the command of Isaacs and when they saw Mkabayi, they hoped she would attack first. When she realised that there was no action, she sent a royal messenger to remind them that if they did not carry out Shaka's instruction they would be killed immediately. Only then did Isaacs lead about 12 musketeers, who slowly and reluctantly advanced to the forest. They could only spot about 50 Khumalo fighters among the big rocks near the summit. Hlambamanzi, who had volunteered to be with Farewell's unit fired the first shot. Then the Khumalo sprang out of the rocks and jumped on Farewell's men and Bheje did not disappoint. In the ensuing battle, Myeka kaMshika Mphephethwa, who was living in the fort with Bheje after Shaka routed them, stabbed Isaacs with a harpoon in the back as he ran away. As the battle raged, Isaac asked Cane to take it out without causing further damage, but Cane failed. Then Isaacs asked one of his San friends to take it out but, he too failed. Eventually Isaacs had to humble himself and politely ask their Zulu friends to extricated it, which they did without causing further damage. Isaacs was so scared of dying that he asked one of the Zulu soldiers to piggyback him to safety, but they all laughed at him. After a few days of relentless fighting, Bheje finally proposed peace and offered some cattle and conceded to Shaka's sovereignty. Feeling unusually brave, one of the whites demanded 10 women as part of the peace offering to consolidate the relationship by natural ties. Bheje obliged and handed over the 10 women but he personally refused to come out of the forest. His tenacity of surviving in the forest for so long, is the basis of the Zulu idiom *uBheje useNgome* (Bheje is still in iNgome) meaning that things remain the same.

Shaka did not give his soldiers too much rest time after the iNdololwane Battle and commissioned a new capital KwaDukuza Palace south of the uThukela River in November 1826. It was built on high ground in the heartland of the Cele kingdom about 80 kilometres south of KwaBulawayo as the crow flies. It lay north of the uMvoti River and south of the iNonoti River. Its western boundary was the bank of the uMadundube River, while the Indian Ocean formed its eastern boundary. Shaka named it *KwaDukuza* because the thousands of huts were built in a maze, as a security feature. He was also attracted by the natural warm springs nearby and admired the pebbles found in the aMavivane River where his drinking water was drawn daily. He performed his ablutions in the iMbozamo waterfall north-east of today's Stanger. KwaDukuza had a small number of homesteads inside and outside its boundaries which housed the aristocrats, councillors, military officers and other folk. It also had several cattle enclosures for cattle and other livestock. The greater KwaDukuza area was used as the royal grazing ground where the uniformly coloured herds had apportioned areas. The colour grouping was an excellent tactic to spot any stray beast or intruder. Shaka's isiKlebe division, which had been stationed next to KwaBulawayo, and other military barracks nearby were broken up and sent to different parts of the empire. For instance, sections of the uDubinhlangu and iNtontela barracks which were based at eMthonjaneni Heights were moved to the oBonjeni Ridge under the command of one of Shaka's aunts, Mawa. The iNdabakawombe regiment was sent across the Black iMfolozi River and built a base to the west of eSigubudu River.

After building KwaDukuza, Shaka planned to go south and attack the amaMpondo who lived on either side of the uMzimvubu River near today's Port St

Johns. But before Shaka could depart, the shrewd Swazi monarch Sobhuza I, sent him two of his most beautiful *imidlunkulu* Mpandesi and Nonkulumo. That bought the wily Swazi peace of mind against being attacked by Shaka, even if only for a short while. In early 1828, Shaka deployed Mdlaka and Klwana kaKhobonyela Buthelezi (amaWombe regiment) to the north. Mdlaka had better results after attacking and they crossed the *uBhalule* (Olifants) River to crush the Bapedi and Basotho as well as King Falatse Ratsebe of the Baphuthing kingdom. He captured a respectable number of cattle as well as a young Baphuthing prince who had been orphaned. Shaka asked his aunt Mkabayi to adopt him and raise the little boy as her own, and she gladly did. Nearly 200 years later in October 2009, the Baphuthing nation requested His Majesty King Zwelithini to help them trace their ancestor's burial place.

However, Mdlaka and his men ran out of provisions, as they were turning back, they were suddenly confronted by hundreds of small but fearsome yellow-coloured men carrying smoking guns riding wild, prancing horses. These were the Griqua people, led by Barend Barends, who were out and enjoying an elephant-hunting expedition. They were equally surprised by the Zulu army and charged at them. Mdlaka remembered Shaka's advice when fighting men on horses and withdrew his regiments into broken terrain. The Griqua could not use their horses effectively and the Zulu suddenly had an advantage and charged at them at lightning swiftly. The perplexed Griquas fled as fast as their horses could gallop, never to be seen again. Mdlaka arrived at KwaDukuza three months later with a few head of cattle and he found Shaka in a smouldering mood. He was in no mood to hear any more bad news. Life was not what it used to be, moreover he was not used to failure. Barend Barends' clean getaway, besides his three casualties, was unthinkable. In reality, Shaka was still grieving the death of his best friends, Mgobhozi and Mbikwane who had recently died on the north side of the lower uMlalazi River.

Shaka needed an activity that would boost the morale of his subjects, so he decided on a radical diplomatic offensive. He instructed his top diplomat, Ambassador Sotobe kaMpangalala Sibiya to lead a delegation to establish diplomatic ties with King George in England. Sotobe went with his wives, including his favourite wife Ntombintombi, Mbozamboza Mqawe, Ncaphayi, Dliwayo, Swayimande (Manyosi's son), Ngwane Mafokose, Phikwane kaBizwayo, Hlambamanzi and some of his wives, aristocrats, assistants, Lt King, Farewell and his wife Ann, Isaacs as well as the finest six *imidlunkulu* as a present to the English king. Klaju kaNomdayi Luthuli used to travel regularly overseas as an interpreter on many English ships also joined the group. The delegation was protected by the highly trained Gingabanye regiment. Shaka gave them 86 elephant tusks to pay for the ship transport and gifts for King

George. The delegation left Port Natal on the 30th of April 1828 and arrived in Port Elizabeth five days later, on the 4th of May 1828. Alas, the English however, confiscated their boat. After waiting three months to proceed, the Zulu delegation realised that their journey was being sabotaged and tried to return home. Even though they were assured that they could continue with their journey, they were instead interrogated by Major Henry Cloete. He was an Anglicised Afrikaner who was despised by both the English and Afrikaners. He looked ridiculous in his laced scarlet uniform as he interrogated Sotobe. Isaacs recorded the interrogation between Cloete and Sotobe:

'Can Shaka write or make any characters to show his authority?'

'No. He cannot write or make characters.'

'How is he to be recognised as king and what distinguishes him as such?'

'By a bunch of red feathers and there is no one allowed to wear them but the king and two or three of his principal officials.'

'Did you come here at your own free will and consent?'

'We were sent by our king to show his friendly disposition towards the governor, the king and the white people and to acquire medicines and some such.'

'What authority do you have to show that you were sent by him?'

'We have nothing. We were sent with Lt King.'

'Don't you have a sign, token, feather, tiger's tail or tooth to show you were sent by Shaka?'

'We generally send cattle but the vessel could not take them and Shaka has sent ivory tusks.'

'Will you (Sotobe) go to Cape Town with me?'

'No, we have been here for too long, we wish to go back to our king.'

'What was your motive to come here if you do not intend to see the governor?'

'We hear Shaka is near the Cape Colony and we understand that the governor will protect the neighbouring clans and Shaka was not aware of that before we left our territory. We also hear that Lt King is going to meet him and we cannot leave him because we do not know of any other person. We look upon him as our guide. Mbozamboza should have long returned and then I should have gone to meet with the governor as Shaka wished.'

'Provided Mbozamboza returns from there, Sotobe will be able to go and see the governor,' Major Cloete said.

'As Lt King is absent we cannot say anything about it, we will not leave him as he was sent with us as a member of our mission.'

They went back to Port Natal on the *HMS Helicon* on 2 August 1828. Unknown to anyone, Lt King had been walking around with a letter in his back pocket the whole time, apparently dictated and signed by Shaka:

'I, Chaka, King of the Zulu, do in the presence of my principal chiefs now assembled, hereby appoint and direct my friend, James Saunders King, to take under his charge and protection Sotobi, one of my principal chiefs, whom I now create of the "Tugusa" cattle enclosure, Kati (probably another name of Pikwane), my body servant, Jacob my interpreter and suite. I desire him to convey them to King George dominions to represent that I send them on a friendly mission to King George and after offering him assurances of my friendship and esteem, to negotiate with his Britannic Majesty on my behalf with my chief Sotobi a treaty of friendly alliance between the two nations having given the said JS King and Sotobi full instruction and invested them with full power to act for me in every way as circumstances may seem to them most beneficial and expedient.

'I require my friend King to pay every attention to the comforts of my people entrusted to his care and solemnly enjoin him to return with them in safety to me and to report to me faithfully such accounts as they may receive from King George. I hereby grant him the said friend JS King in consideration of the confidence I repose in him of various services he has already rendered me, the presents he has made and above all obligations. I am under obligation to him for his attention to my mother in her last illness as well as having saved the lives of several of my principal people, the full and free possession of my country near the sea coast and Port Natal from Natal head to Stinkein River, including the extensive grazing flats and forests, with the islands in the harbour and Matabana nations together with the free and exclusive trade of all of all my dominions and I hereby also confirm all my former grants to him.' (Signed) Witness the above scrawl having been made by King Chaka as his signature. (Signed) NJ Isaacs. Sworn before H Hudson, Esq, Resident Magistrate Port Elizabeth 20 July 1828. By Nathanial Isaacs and John Jacobs the interpreter as a true document and signed in their presence. Quod Attestor (Signed) John Anthony Chabaud, Notary Public.

Ambassador Sotobe and his entourage arrived at KwaDukuza Palace in September

1828, angry at the whites. Lt King, who was an alcoholic, came back from the trip severely ill and Shaka sacrificed two bulls to appease his white ancestors, but it did not work. He died of liver sclerosis a few days later in his eSihlengeni homestead. Undeterred, Shaka sent another delegation, this time it was led by Dikane. This delegation included Nomadlambi, Mbozamboza and John Cane but Shaka recalled Cane shortly after they left KwaDukuza and replaced him with Isaacs. Once again, they were held hostage in a ship for three months but this time in Cape Town.

Cane was a tall Scotsman whose homestead, iSinyama, had been built by Farewell near today's Durban Botanic Gardens. It was surrounded by *umhluma* (mangroves) to keep out wild animals and his principal servant was Kofiyana kaMbengana. He had a wagon-making factory and managed to provide a comfortable lifestyle for his three Zulu and one white wife. His son, born to his white wife was also called John, and one of his mixed-race children was Lavutha Christian who built a homestead at eZintongeni. Lavutha was born in the wilderness of Mbizana when his mother had accompanied a buffalo-hunting party. Others were Charlie who ended up living in Phoenix near Durban, and a daughter Nanise who got married to Ndamane kaMkelo and they lived near Mabedlana Hills in uLundi. They did not have children of their own and Nanise ended up working as an interpreter for missionaries at Inanda School. She loved books and even presented one of Fynn's mixed-race sons Mashingana with a book about Zulu history.

Some of Cane's servants were Macala, Jadilili kaPudwa kaNgozi kaNyanise Mfeka, Ndandane kaMantiyane kaNgamelwa Maphumulo and Mdlaka kaMagoda Khanyweni. When Cane was killed during the Zulu civil war in 1860, his best friend Ogle conspired with Macala and burnt Cane's iSinyama homestead to ashes so that none of Cane's heirs could inherit anything. Ogle was renowned for his greed among the whites. He had one white wife, and one of his three Zulu wives was Princess Sibade kaMagaye of the Cele kingdom. Their homestead was in eZembeni and they had two sons, Shaka and Benjamin. The other wives lived at KwaBhekani and KwaThoyana homesteads. The particularly mean Henry Ogle died of old age in 1860 at uMkhomazi, south of Durban.

Shaka had sent Sotobe on a diplomatic mission, which was a smoke screen for his secret preparations to attack amaMpondo in the south for the *ihlambo* (the bereavement cleansing ritual) for his mother's death. King Faku of the amaMpondo kingdom was notorious for his brutality and had slaughtered many of Ngoza's followers who had sought refuge under him. Faku enjoyed cutting off the hands of the Mthembu women to remove their gold, copper, silver and brass ornaments. Shaka sent refugees, who had run away from Ngoza's atrocities, ahead as spies and they reported about Faku's strength and oddity of many whites living along uMzimvubu River. But Shaka was unfazed by their presence so close to his southern border. In May 1828, Shaka left his KwaDukuza with Ngomane in charge of state affairs. After a few days march they stopped south of the uMzimkhulu River and made a huge bonfire as part of the death-cleansing ceremony. Years later, a thick bush grew on that spot and that place is, to this day, known as the eZintongeni (place of sticks). For this campaign Shaka chose the uNobamba and iNdumezulu regiments as his royal guard, the umCekeceke, iNzawu, uNtshuku and iNkisimana female regiments saw active combat, and two whites, Fynn and Ogle. Fynn described the campaign as follows:

'I went to meet him (Shaka). I found him about forty miles from my place. He was resting there for the night, having left the whole of his forces about five miles in the rear. We went forward the following morning and in the afternoon we arrived at one of my cattle enclosures, where I had about one hundred miuds of Indian corn. On his asking, therefore, I gave him the whole of it for the use of his army. On the following day, we arrived at my residence (esiHluthakungu Hill) alongside the uMzimkhulu River. Knowing it to be custom for me as host to present the king with a bullock, I produced my herd and requested him to make himself welcome to as many as he thought fit. He selected seventeen and thereupon made the place his headquarters. By this time I knew the Zulu language, customs and mannerism, hence I was able to spend my time pleasantly with Shaka. He always demanded my attendance during his leisure moments. All this, moreover, gave me an opportunity of minutely ascertaining the basis on which he acted.'

When they arrived in the vicinity of today's Port Shepstone, on the north side of uMzimkhulu River, Shaka set up camp on a protruding rock on a hill. Nearly a 100 years later, the Natal government gave Ndongeni kaXoki Zulu (Ndaba's descendant) a farm there as a reward for having shown Dick King the way to Grahamstown. From the rock, Shaka and his military command processed the intelligence reports which were coming in thick and fast from the frontline and they adapted their war strategy accordingly. Today, this rock is called *Itshemahlamvu* (seed rock). Shaka divided the army into two divisions and Mdlaka led a division that included Ogle. They marched along the coast and slept overnight in the Ngcwanguba forest west of the uMthatha river. Manyundela kaMabuya of the eMkhindini regiment led the half that included Fynn. Their battle theatre was around the cool highlands of the Ingeli Mountains and in the forests of Mount Ayliff and Mount Frere. Manyundela fought pitched battles with amaMpondo and their allies which were smaller kingdoms such as amaBhaca (*bhaca* means to hide) and the amaMfengu (*mfenguza* means to wander aimlessly).

## Imfecane and European Colonisation

These smaller kingdoms were the product of the thousands of refugees who were wandering aimlessly around the forests in the Eastern Cape at the time of *imfecane*.

Shaka crossed the uMzimvubu and uMthatha rivers and camped between the Mphako and Mbashe rivers and waited to be attacked by the amaMpondo army. This area was under the rule of King Gambushe of the amaBomvana kingdom. But he never attacked Shaka, instead, the whole nation stayed out of sight for two weeks. Shaka's laudatory praises describe this encounter:

| *Inyathi ejame ngomkhonto* | the buffalo that waited with a spear |
| *Phezu koMzimvubu* | at uMzimvubu River |
| *AmaMpondo ayesaba* | the Mpondo people were too afraid |
| *Ukuyiyehlela* | to fight him |
| *Nani boGambushe* | you too Gambushe, |
| *Nani boFaku* | you too Faku |
| *Ningamhlabi, ukuba nimhlabile* | dare not stab him because if you do |
| *Koba senihlabe uPhunga* | you would have stabbed Phunga |
| *Nihlaba uMageba* | you would have stabbed Mageba |

Mdlaka, on the other hand laid a siege around the Ngcwanguba forest and as the days wore on, amaMpondo and their allies got hungry and started surrendering. Mdlaka pretended to leave for good and went further down to Maphozi and set up camp by the sea. The rest of amaMpondo soldiers came out of the forest thinking that they were in the clear, but it was an elaborate trap. The Zulu attacked them in lightning speed and they fought a savage battle. Faku did not bother to venture out and directed the war from the safety of the forest. Once amaMpondo lost, he went even deeper into the forest fearing that he would be killed now that he had been defeated. The Zulu army looted more than 30 000 cattle as well as thousands of other livestock and chose only beautiful women as spoils of war. They returned to Shaka's temporary headquarters, which he had set up at Mount Ayliff. They celebrated their victory with song and dance, moreover, the female regiments had demonstrated unheard-of bravery. However, the army's mood changed when Shaka was told that Manyundela had been killed in battle. The party stopped, and cowards were identified quickly and killed immediately. The Zulu warriors marched back home, grieving because Manyundela was as popular with the regiments as Mgobhozi had been.

Faku never left his fortress inside the forest fearing for his life but sent his last cattle as a sign of surrender. But Shaka refused to accept the cattle and sent a message to him that he had to come out of the forest so that the amaMpondo children, who were hiding with him, could have some milk. Again, Faku was too afraid to come out and sent his emissaries Myeki and Mbobo from the Jali kingdom, to surrender on his behalf. By the time they caught up with Shaka, to relay Faku's message, he was at eNyenyezi. Shaka's response was that Faku had to go to KwaDukuza and surrender in person instead of sending a messenger to *khonza* under a tree in the middle of nowhere. The Zulu found the uMzimkhulu River in flood and Fynn described the crossing of the river as follows:

'On our crossing the uMzimkhulu River, where the tide was high, many little boys would have been carried down with the stream. Shaka, foreseeing this plunged into the river, with only his headdress on and remained one and half hours in the water, giving boys to the care of the men, who otherwise would have left them to their fate and collecting calves, which were nearly drowned, ordered fires to be made to assist their recovery.'

Shaka arrived ahead of the rest of his army in KwaDukuza and immediately mobilised the whole empire for war in the north. The victorious returning regiments that had served in Pondoland were disappointed that they were denied the usual victory homecoming celebrations, especially *ukusula izembe*. But before the army departed, the uKhangela regiment was ordered to rout the Ntuli kingdom, which had become cannibals roaming the Port Natal beaches. Fynn and Isaacs requested permission to accompany the uKhangela but Shaka refused. The Ntuli cannibals were part of the bigger Bhele kingdom whose stronghold was at eLenge (*Kranskop*). The Bhele people were notorious for having tried to eat their king Mahlaphahlapha, his son Mgagathwa and grandson Bhalule during Senzangakhona's time. But they managed to escape with all their limbs intact, yet Mgagathwa and Bhalule continued this despicable behaviour. They roamed the greater area of the uThukela and uMzinyathi Rivers looking for people to eat. On the other hand, Mahlaphahlapha and some followers found refuge under Senzangakhona and joined the Zulu kingdom. They were, however, assigned the most degrading menial jobs and looked down upon. But that changed during Shaka's reign because he allowed all Zulu subjects to ascend the social order based purely on merit. Cannibalism was only eradicated completely in 1836.

Shaka's dispatch of his army to the treacherous north was the beginning of his end. By now there were enough people in the empire who were tired of his permanent state of war. This encouraged two of his paternal brothers Dingane and Mhlangana to plan his assassination. Dingane had long been harbouring an ambition to be the king. In an instant of unparalleled bravado, he broached the subject with his aunt, Mkabayi. He went to KwaDukuza Palace where Mkabayi was living and entered Mkabayi's main hut unannounced and sat down. This unbecoming behaviour surprised the old princess and she suspected that Dingane had something important to discuss with her urgently. He on the other hand, was unsure how Mkabayi would react to his desperate attempt to become king and if she would believe his lies about Shaka. He told Mkabayi that Shaka had personally killed his mother Nandi - which meant that she was also was in danger.

Mkabayi was stunned and said nothing for a while. She stared at her paternal brother's son without blinking. Dingane was a dashing man - he was fair skinned and solidly built with a distinctly melancholic streak. He had sparse hair and unusually short teeth. He seldom smiled or laughed and often grunted solemnly like a pig. He was well known for his pathological dislike of dirt and was obsessed with personal cleanliness, so much so that his food was prepared by male attendants only. As far as he was concerned, female chefs were not as hygienic as their male counterparts. He only drank water drawn from a special well in the eMthonjaneni Ridge, which is near the R66 road between Melmoth and uLundi. Today, this well is overgrown with reeds and weeds. Dingane was not really close to Mkabayi and because he was nervous, he rambled on in the *ukuthefula* accent in low tones. He lamented about the unrelenting destruction of the Zulu empire by the monster Shaka. Mkabayi let him speak without interrupting him and she began thinking. She realised that ever since Shaka had showed that he loved the Zulu empire more than anything on earth, she had gone into semi-retirement. She was extremely shocked by what she was hearing and slowly recalled the complaints she was told about Shaka when she was on her way to the KwaDukuza festivities. People had complained about the year-long mourning under absurd and cruel conditions which left them desolate and dejected.

She had also noticed that there was a lack of enthusiasm among the Zulu people, even among the aristocracy such as the Biyela, Ntombela, Mpungose, Mbatha, Zungu, Ntshangase, Mthethwa, Gwala, Sibiya, Mdletshe and others. For a moment, she regretted having stepped back from active duty because the councillors had assured her that Shaka was running the empire with great skill. She was not only proud of what Shaka had achieved for the once tiny Zulu kingdom within such a short period and but also admired his ability to build such an awesome empire. Then

Mkabayi's fiery eyes bored into Dingane quivering cheeks and asked: 'I am not sure if I understand you completely, my brother's son. What has Shaka done? Are you sure about him killing his own mother?'

Dingane quivered some more and replied: 'He has finished the nation. A kingdom is a kingdom because of its subjects but vultures have eaten our people. Where have you seen old men of Jama's age brought back from retirement to fight the amaMpondo in the south and one of the best decorated generals like Manyundela getting killed? Shaka also mobilised old men who were custodians of the Zulu history who are our grandfathers' contemporaries. The pillars of our nation are dying in far-off lands and being killed by pestilences that have never been seen here in our land. During the uBhalule campaign the regiments became so hungry that they ended up eating locusts and were pounded by the unforgiving harsh African sun. They died from drinking stagnant water. The people are tired of war. I was sent by the nation to talk to you in confidence. The nation wants to know how you can afford to bury your head in the sand when the empire is perishing.' Shaka had justified sending the army to war to her by saying that the Zulu known world had been conquered and the only way to expand was to go north.

Mkabayi regained some of her composure and asked: 'What is the nation complaining about?' Her voice suddenly became hoarse as she spoke. 'First, people want to know why they were expected to mourn for Shaka's mother when he killed her. He was…' In utter disbelief, Mkabayi interrupted Dingane: 'What did you just say, Dingane?' She even raised her voice and forgot that they were talking about the king. 'Who did you say killed my brother's wife?' Dingane responded in a pitched voice, as though he was trying to believe what he was saying: 'She was killed by Shaka,' Mkabayi asked in disbelief: 'Do you have proof of your allegations?' Dingane's voice was more stable now: 'We all know this, *iNdlovukazi* died by Shaka's spear because she was allegedly harbouring an *umdlunkulu*, Gxekayo kaKhobonyela Buthelezi who was pregnant with his child. Gxekayo went to seek refuge at eMkhindini Palace and lived with Nandi until she gave birth. Shaka caught Nandi red-handed playing with her grandchild and then he speared both to death.'

Mkabayi was stunned and asked him to leave her alone while she collected her thoughts. Dingane was happy because the news had the effect that he had hoped for. He left as quietly as he came. Mkabayi believed nothing would stop Shaka from killing them all if he could kill his own mother. On the other hand, it was not easy for her to fault Shaka because of what he had achieved. She asked herself quietly, if Shaka were to die, who would lead the empire because, as far as she knew, Shaka had no heirs. What was more perplexing was that she had never heard of the *umdlunkulu* called Gxekayo, as she had ways of finding out these things. She once again found herself where she was many years before when her father Jama was ageing fast without an heir. She remembered when she had to find a replacement for Sigujana after Shaka's maternal brother Ngwadi drowned him.

Mkabayi wondered who would rule her father's people now because the rest of the pretenders to the throne, such as Princes Dingane, Mhlangana, Mpande and Gqugqu inspired no confidence. Regrettable as it was, by the time Mkabayi went to sleep, she had decided that Shaka had to die. Even though part of her soul did not totally agree with the decision. She thought about it some more the following day and arrived at the same conclusion. When Dingane did not arrive during the day she became impatient and sent for him in the afternoon. He arrived at his aunt's hut with bloodshot eyes.

'Are you prepared to take over the reign from your brother?' Mkabayi asked Dingane, looking deeply into his eyes. Stammering, he replied: '*Mageba, wena owa...*' (Descendant of Mageba, the mighty one who…). 'Stop wasting my time by singing my praises and answer my question. Are you brave enough to be king of my father's people?' Mkabayi's eyes flared in anger. Dingane was taken aback. He wanted to become king bad enough, but he had not thought the process through properly. By now his aunt was pressuring him to respond to something so big, far too quickly. He needed time to ponder the idea in more detail. After all, Dingane was not the bravest of men. He began to fear his aunt because she had not needed much convincing and had not even verified his lies. Could he trust her in the long run? He wondered.

'You see Dingane,' Mkabayi continued, 'the ancestors have turned their backs against Shaka. We no longer have a king and, as a custodian of the nation, it is my sacred duty to present my people with another king. There are many of Senzangakhona's sons who would be willing to rule. But, before I pass it over to them, I need to know if you are brave enough to take over or not.' Unsure of himself, Dingane responded: 'If you assist me, I will be brave.' Mkabayi replied: 'I hear you, but I do not like your answer because I do not have time for people who lean on other people. I like independent people, even though it is a grave task to depose someone and need people to assist you, but you still need to be self-reliant. Another important question is whether or not you have mentioned your intentions to any of your brothers?'

Dingane, now lowering his tone, continued: 'I had discussions with Mhlangana about the life we now lead in the land of Malandela and he too, expressed great dissatisfaction. I am sure he would assist me in doing what I have to do.' Relieved, Mkabayi said: 'He is a brave one that one. Don't waste any more time, talk to him tonight.' Dingane began to sweat. Things were moving too fast for his comfort. He had no idea where to begin his discussion with Mhlangana about assassinating Shaka. What if he refused to be part of it and told Shaka? He trembled at the thought and Mkabayi noticed. Because of the stressful situation, Dingane's yellowish skin turned reddish. 'Why are you trembling? Is it the cold outside or it is because of your cowardice? I am now asking you for the third time if you are prepared to remove Shaka? Another thing I want to know from you, what have you planned to do about Shaka's *insila* and *inceku* Jeqe and Mbopha who are always around him?' Dingane was at a loss for words and regretted having discussed this issue with his aunt before he gave it enough thought. In all honesty, he had no clue how he was going to deal with the two fearless bodyguards. On the other hand, he had no fear of his paternal brothers, Gqugqu and Mhlangana. As though to jolt him out of his hesitation, Mkabayi bellowed: 'Why don't you take this *isidwaba* I am wearing, and you give me your *ibheshu*? You are an embarrassment.'

Even though she had decided that Shaka had to die, Mkabayi noted Dingane's indecisiveness to undertake such a significant gamble. But even with a weak Dingane to deal with for now, Shaka had to go by any means necessary. Dingane finally summoned enough courage to tell his aunt that he was ready to do whatever was necessary to dethrone Shaka. Mkabayi merely nodded and let him go to Mhlangana's residence. Mhlangana agreed to the plot half-heartedly and said he would only fully commit to the plot after discussing it with Mkabayi. Dingane did not have the courage to approach Mbopha and thought of asking Mkabayi to discuss it with him first. But he changed his mind and invited Mbopha to his hut. Shaka's efficient secret service tried its best to eavesdrop but could not clearly decipher what was being said in Dingane's hut. They only heard Mbopha say that he was tempted to report the matter to the king, but they did not know exactly what they were discussing.

It had been a long few days for Dingane. He seemed to have aged overnight and looked like an old man with hollow eyes and bent shoulders. After sunset on the third day, he crawled into his aunt's hut and she barked: 'I have been waiting for you for a long time. How far did you go with those whose names I cannot mention?' Dingane whimpered: 'They were both far too reluctant to take part in the plot, but they agreed to discuss the matter with you further.' With her eyes half closed, Mkabayi hissed: 'What did you promise them in return?' A now stuttering Dingane replied: 'I promised Mhlangana to be king and to give Mbopha half the kingdom.' Wincing Mkabayi retorted: 'Now that you made conflicting promises, I have to talk to them one by one, not together. Let Mhlangana come first, right away.'

Mhlangana feared only two things in his life, Shaka and Mkabayi even though Mkabayi was a woman. He dragged himself to Mkabayi's hut, numb with fear and found her agitated. Her face was dark and withdrawn. Her teeth twinkled eerily in the dark hut and she quickly made her point: 'Listen carefully and I am only sharing this with you because you are my brother's son. I am going to talk about the reigning king, your brother *iLembe* (Shaka). It is obvious that the ancestors have turned against him ever since he killed the hundreds of people after his mother died. If he is not stopped who knows, thousands more could die, including you. It is my responsibility to protect my father's people from Shaka. I have decided that he must die, and I will need your help to get rid of him. If you agree, your reward will be great. Remember that you too, are a prince. You deserve what Shaka is entitled to. Think about it and let me know.' She gazed at him attentively, deciphering his body language and trying to ascertain if he had grasped her concept. She got the desired effect. Mortified, Mhlangana left without uttering a word. He went to his hut and became so engrossed in thinking that he could not fall asleep for a long time.

The following evening was Mbopha's turn. He sat on the same mat Mhlangana had sat on the previous night and he too, was nervous. They were now more scared of Mkabayi than Shaka because the old matriarch was ruthless. They knew Shaka was already as good as dead. Moreover, what would become of them once *iLembe* was dead? Mbopha doubted that he would be given half the kingdom. How could they do that when there were many princes? He could not find one reason that would motivate Dingane and his aunt to make good on that promise. But he knew it was too late to turn back. Shaka's secret service found out about the plot and informed him but he was not overly concerned. Instead, he made the two conspiring paternal brothers command the *ukhukhulelangoqo* campaign in the north. He planned to have them killed by his trusted men on the way. But things were no longer what they used to be. Even before they reached KwaHlabisa, halfway to their destination both Dingane and Mhlangana feigned sickness and asked to return home. They were accompanied back by the iNkunziyezindlovu regiment.

One of Mdlaka's instructions was to kill Hlangabeza kaMabhedla Mtshali en route to the north because rather than mourning Nandi's death Hlangabeza deserted and went to live in the dense forest next to the White iMfolozi River where he drank cow's milk to his heart's content. When the army was near the forest, at nightfall

Mdlaka divided the army into two. One unit went behind the forest to block any escape route and the other unit went directly into the forest towards Hlangabeza's hideout and they attacked him simultaneously. All of Hlangabeza's followers were killed by the main army but he escaped by hiding in a shallow pond. However, he was seen by *udibi* when he came up for air and they killed him. The army's next stop was under the mighty Mount Ceza at Sithayi's homestead where Mbopha was born. This is where Mdlaka received orders to send back one of the main pillars of what made the Zulu win wars, *udibi*. Shaka ordered that all soldiers, including officers carry their own arsenal, food and baggage. This was the last straw for the already highly demotivated and tired army. But they complied, nevertheless.

They did not know that they were recalled for yet another one of Shaka's revolutionary ideas he had been harbouring since he became king. The youngsters were going to form a new regiment, iziNyosi and were going to learn how to read, write and speak English and other European languages. Shaka was not particularly interested in learning about English warfare strategies. Instead, he wanted *udibi* to learn how to manufacture and improve European weapons because, as far as he was concerned, they were inferior. He especially despised the muskets because they were useless when it was raining.

Before the army reached the perilous parts infested with mosquitoes and tropical calamities, skirting the Swazi border, they emerged in the land of the Bapedi where they camped on the banks of the Tubatse River. Thulare's son Sekwati, was now the king of the Bapedi kingdom. He welcomed them with great fanfare and ensured they were left in comfort and were well rest. Ngomane also took time to pay homage to the Rain Queen Modjadji of the Balobedu kingdom. After meeting her, the Zulu affectionately called her *Mabelemade* (long breasts) because of her unbelievably long breasts which she could throw over her shoulders. They crossed the Sabi (*iLusapha*) River and went to Lydenburg about 100 kilometers away. Two months later, they arrived within striking distance of Soshangane's KwaMandlakazi Palace. They found that Soshangane had created a big army out of the Zulu core he had run away with and his war arsenal was substantial. Soshangane ambushed them in their sleep on the first night and almost killed the whole outer-flank regiment. Mdlaka retaliated at dawn and chased him further north but did not capture him. They were forced to drink from poisoned wells during the hot pursuit. The unsuspecting Zulu army was also led to an area with a forest of the dazzling *umdlebe* (synadenium cupulare) trees and suffered its immediate deadly consequences. *Umdlebe* tree kills everything on contact because it creates a vacuum between the skin and its bark. Slowly, it sucks blood from any living organism that touches it. These deadly trees still exist in southern Mozambique and parts of KwaZulu-Natal.

Many of the fine Zulu soldiers who perished in this disastrous campaign include two of Senzangakhona's sons, Nzibe and Nomzimba (*they were Mpande's maternal brothers*). They died more from diseases such as dysentery, cholera, typhoid or malaria than from fatal battle wounds. The terrain, flora and fauna were nothing like what they were used to in the Zulu empire. As a good commander, Mdlaka knew when to retreat and they returned home along the coast to avoid the less hospitable interior with its cannibalistic trees. The soldiers were dropping dead one by one because of hunger and thirst. Ngomane had forbidden the eating of locusts and this order was known as the Ngomane Proclamation. But circumstances, forced them to disregard the proclamation with dire consequences. They did not only eat the locusts, but also carried them with them as provisions, which they later regretted. The locusts destroyed any potential food source along the way. They tried to dislodge the locusts by smoking them and making loud noises, but the locusts followed them home. They devastated every crop in the kingdom during 1829 and 1830 harvest. It seems, the locust pestilence was unknown before 1829 hence there was no effective remedy to the problem.

Even though the war was a big disaster, the slow retreat was an eventful affair. They encountered strange and wondrous things on the way. For instance, after crossing the uMkhuze and iMfolozi rivers at KwaMhlabuyalingana, they met a highly skilled magician, Sokhulu. He mesmerised them with amazing feats of entertainment, a welcome digression for the weary soldiers. They also witnessed a Zulu romantic tragedy near a hill at KwaNgwanase. Nomlingo kaMala was a drop-dead beauty admired by many men. Even Shaka's ace spear maker, Mabhodla kaMbuyazi Mbonambi found her irresistible. He had relocated to KwaMhlabuyalingana and changed his name to *Mhambi*, found her irresistible. He tried his best magic to win her heart, but it didn't work, despite that he was now much older.

Another contender for Nomlingo's attention was Bahu from the Mpukunyoni kingdom who was an expert giraffe trapper who offered her father 100 cows - a stupendous number of cattle at the time. There was also an elephant trapper who knew the secret ingredients to produce elephant poison cakes, a highly desired skill but he had no cattle. Nomlingo's father was excited and was about to take the 100 cattle but stopped because Nomlingo began sobbing because she could not decide whom to choose. So, her father decided that cattle would not be the only criterion for any man to marry his wonderful daughter. The potential husband had to excel in a series of exercises aimed at proving their physical prowess such as wrestling, throwing and running. On the set day, shortly before the cows came home to be milked, everyone was invited to come and see the spectacle. Nomlingo was asked to place a necklace, made of out charms sewn on crocodile skin, around the neck of the one she preferred. Suddenly, there were at least ten other contenders, including Mhambi, who were eager to impress their object of beauty.

There was tension as everyone waited to see who the lucky guy was. Nomlingo sauntered past the hopefuls, including a grinning Mfisi, who thought his cattle offer would do it for him. Instead she put it around Bahu's neck, and the die was cast. They then began wrestling with one another and Bahu threw all of them to the ground with ease. Then they started hurling spears at *insema* (a large soft spherical root) that regiments used for practice. But as they were aiming to hit the root, a duiker buck dashed across and there was a flurry of spears aimed at it instead and they all missed. Mfisi grazed it but Bahu steadily aimed at its lungs and brought it down. It was now time for the run, and they saw Nomlingo, on the summit of a hill looking stunning as ever, standing with her mother. They were a good 10 kilometres away from the contestants, and the first person to reach her would win the coveted prize.

Off they went, falling into ditches, dodging bushes, tripping on stones, up the hill they panted. Mfisi's white cow tails on his elbows could be seen glistening and Bahu's white ostrich plume fluttering in the breeze. They staggered, pushing on and they were neck-and-neck and Mfisi began to fall behind. With superhuman effort, Bahu reached her and held her hand smiling and collapsed. Blood oozed from his mouth and nose and Nomlingo became hysterical. His smile, etched with love, froze into eternity. Nomlingo's tears did not reach her cheeks. Instead, they were lodged in her eye sockets as she looked at the love of her life in disbelief and kept on rocking him until he died in her arms. The sun was at its zenith and crowds below watched in horror and remained helpless as the hill slowly faded from view because of the thickening haze caused by the heat and humidity at that time of the day.

By the time they reached the hill, a distraught and inconsolable Nomlingo, in a frenzy, started digging his grave with her bare hands. She allowed no one to help or touch his body, until she could not continue anymore as her hands were bleeding profusely. Finally, after she was assisted and Bahu gently laid inside the grave, she threw herself upon the mound, wailing and mourning far in to the night. Late that night her mother, who had been waiting out of sight, silently crept over and covered her daughter with a cow's mantle and left. But around midnight Nomlingo stopped moving. At dawn, her parents went to check on their daughter and her mother gently called her by her pet name, but there was only silence. Nomlingo had died of a broken heart and joined her lover in a place where no one grows old. Ever since that fateful day, a shimmering pall falls over the cone shaped *Love Memorial* that juts above the flatlands of the coast everyday. It can still be seen today, from five kilomettres away covering the sacred spot of where the lovers lie buried, embracing.

*The great warrior Manyosi Mbatha shielded King Shaka with his body during the 1818 Ndwandwe war. The granite tombstone reads: 'Inkosi Manyosi kaDlekezele Mbatha. Rest in Peace Hero. Born: 1765 - Died: 1873. Your descendants will honour you forever, Ndabezitha'*

*The royal delegation sent by Emperor Shaka to London to establish diplomatic ties with King George IV. But it was intercepted in Port Elizabeth and prevented from continuing with the journey. (Seated left) Ambassador Sotobe kaMpangalala Sibiya, Mbozamboza kaMqawe, Ncaphayi, Dliwayo, Swayimande (a son of Manyosi kaDlekekezele Mbatha). (Standing left) Ngwane kaMafokose, Phikwane kaBizwayo, Jacob Hlambamanzi Msimbithi, Klaju kaNomdayi Luthuli and some members of the crack unit Gingabanye regiment (Killie Campbell Africana Library)*

**Emperor King Shaka Murdered**

By 1828, Shaka had over 12 years built an empire on a foundation of submission to authority, terror, respect for the elders, obedience to the law, order and self-restraint, fearlessness and self-sacrifice, constant work and civic duty. He reinforced these principles so well that it became second nature among the Zulu. This continued even after the once-mighty empire had shrunk and almost floundered. Some elements of those virtues, such as submission to authority and honour and fearlessness, have survived to this day. There is scant evidence that the other virtues are still honoured. Shaka grew his once insignificant kingdom by conquering and annexing every clan in his wake and by casting his ambitions beyond where his eyes could see. He recognised that there were other civilisations elsewhere not better than the Zulu, only different. While all nations in his known world were in awe of him, his own paternal brothers and aunt were conspiring against him.

One fateful day, Mkabayi stepped out of her hut earlier than usual and took a long walk from KwaDukuza to the coast which is about seven kilometres away. Like her nephew Shaka, she loved and was fascinated by the ocean. She stood motionless watching the huge waves rise and break for a long time. Then she slowly rotated westwards and gazed at the mountain range at the horizon lost in thought. She was jolted out of her contemplation by the loud roar of a particularly large wave crashing in the sea and she sighed before stretching. Mkabayi cast her weary eyes southwards and finally gave the sea a long, deep look as though she would receive answers from it. She felt it was time for change in the mighty Zulu empire once more. The thought gave her goose bumps, and sent a tingle up her spine, despite a tiny voice of caution. She nodded silently and hummed a tuneless song to herself as she walked back hesitantly.

The two conspiring paternal brothers arrived at the palace during Mkabayi's absence and took the opportunity to instruct Jeqe to go and collect *amaselwa* (gourds) from KwaNdinisa near Delagoa Bay for the first fruit festival. Jeqe became suspicious of this instruction because the ceremony was still months away. But again, he decided to comply because he also needed to stretch his legs. Moreover, strange things had been happening of late and he decided to enjoy the solace of a lone adventure. Late in the evening, after Mkabayi returned the pretenders to the throne as well as Mbopha creeped into Mkabayi's enclosure undetected. However, they could not agree who would go into the hut first. Mhlangana and Mbopha tried to convince Dingane to lead:

'You should go in first and I will follow you. Moreover, you are close to her,' Mhlangana said with a strained voice. 'Wait a minute, how can I go in when there are guards everywhere. I think we should wait until we see someone we trust and then we can send them to Mkabayi,' retorted Dingane, equally scared. 'Unthinkable. I refuse to wait here indefinitely for someone we trust. As a matter of fact, do we trust anyone? Trust nobody Dingane. You must only trust a stone. If you are so scared of Mkabayi's security, I will go back right now on your crazy plan,' said a petrified Mhlangana. Dingane panicked. He realised he needed Mhlangana more than Mbopha to succeed, so he decided to go for broke. He thought he would be lucky because it was the middle of the night. Perhaps the guards would be fast asleep, and he tiptoed ahead but suddenly he heard: 'Wait, wait if you don't want to die, you witches,' said a voice in the dark. Dingane froze and a shiver went down his spine. He realised it was too late to run away because they would have been speared with broad-blade spears. To camouflage his fear, Dingane challenged the voice: 'Who are you? Do you know who I am? How dare you address me like a commoner?'

Dingane terrorised the poor guard into submission and the guard let them continue into Mkabayi's hut. Like snakes, they slid into Mkabayi's hut. The purpose of this visit was to finalise the plan. But after an uncomfortable long silence, they still could not bring themselves to rehearse the plan. Instead, they discussed unrelated issues, while Mkabayi sat there fuming and looking at the lily-livered cowards in her hut. It was way past midnight when they all finally drifted into restless sleep, without having discussed the execution of the plan. They agreed in the morning that Mbopha would give them the sign to execute. From then on, the conspirators said little amongst themselves and nervously waited for a sign from Mbopha to execute the plan. Outside the sky was grey with dark, low-hanging clouds. The air was unnaturally still, a sure sign of warm and heavy tropical rain on the way. The rain drizzled intermittently from mid-morning but did not once pelt down.

At sunset, the iziYendane regiment sauntered into the iNyakamubi homestead, a satellite residence at the edge of KwaDukuza Palace. They were returning from Pondoland where they had gone to procure Shaka's wardrobe of *indwe* (the royal bird) feathers, furs, ornaments and other royal paraphernalia. They had also brought Faku, his messengers Myeki, Mbobo and Mendu to finally *khonza* to Shaka properly in person. Mbopha informed Shaka about the arrival of the iziYendane regiment with merchandise as well as the presence of King Faku of the Mpondo kingdom and his emissaries Myeki, Mbobo and Mendu who had finally come to khonza properly. Shaka went to attend to them with a small royal retinue and the royal guard. But first he stopped to admire the royal herd in the iNyakamubi cattle enclosure. Mbopha quickly sneaked into Mkabayi's hut and told them to go and hide behind one of the walls of the cattle enclosure where Shaka was going to be seated.

Dingane and Mhlangana with their spears at the ready, moved stealthily not uttering a single word. They used only eye, hand and head gestures to communicate. They sweated and waited behind the cattle enclosure wall. They were afraid of Shaka more now, even though he was unarmed. Shaka was relaxed and joking with the herd boys and teased the iziYendane about their latest braids and sat down to inspect the new paraphernalia. Mbopha burst into the cattle enclosure, menacingly brandishing his knobkerrie and shouted at iziYendane for arriving at dusk. Shaka was dumbfounded by Mbopha's uncharacteristic fury, little did he know it was a sign to strike. The king's retinue remonstrated with the overzealous Mbopha and he looked sheepish and pretended to apologise. The assassins quickly jumped over the wall and stabbed Shaka from behind. The first spear missed his back but got his arm because his cloak deflected the blade. Shaka got up instantly and swung around only to be face-to-face with Mhlangana. Dingane did not waste any time and stabbed him directly in the chest. Shaka staggered forward and they continued stabbing him. Gasping, he asked: *'Hawu, ninyangibulala bafowethu na? Kodwa ngenzeni kini bantabakababa? Ngenzeni Dingane, ngenzeni Mhlangana? Hawu, niyangibulala bafowethu ningibulalela ubukhosi kodwa ngeke nilibuse. Ziyeza izinyoni izinkonjane zezulu. Jama, ngeke nilibuse liyobuswa izinyoni...* (Really, are you really killing me my brothers? But what have I done to you, my father's children? What have I done, Dingane, what have I done Mhlangana? Really, you are killing me for the throne, but you will never reign. Birds of the sky are coming. I swear by Jama you will not rule, it will be ruled by birds...).

They did not respond. Instead, they continued to stab Shaka repeatedly in the dark. He tried to defend himself with his hands, but excessive amounts of blood were pouring from the gaping wounds all over his body. He did not collapse and Mbopha then moved closer to him and for a fleeting moment Shaka hoped Mbopha, as his closest assistant was coming to his rescue. However, Mbopha had other ideas and delivered the final blow. Shaka's eyes lit up for the last time and asked: *'Hawu! Mbopha uyangibulala? Uyangibulala nawe Mbopha kaSithayi na? Hawu, ngikwethembe kanga...'* (Really! Mbopha are you killing me? Are you also killing me Mbopha kaSithayi? Really, not when I trusted you so...). But he did not finish the sentence as blood oozed from his nose and mouth. The king of the Zulu dropped dead, face down with a loud thud, as though he were an elephant. He rolled over and took his last breath on the 24th of September 1828. Lying face up he still retained a halo of majesty.

Emperor King Shaka *iLembe, uSigidi, uNodumehlezi kaMenzi, uDlungwana woMbelebele* kaSenzangakhona was between the age of 38 and 41. IziYendane ran away when the stabbing began, not knowing if they would be next. Ferocious thunder and intense lightning ignited the tenebrous sky over KwaDukuza. Within minutes, the gathering wind whirled out of control and rapidly transformed into a destructive tornado. Shaka's blood continued to flow freely in the cattle enclosure. Dingane, Mhlangana and Mbopha feared Shaka when he was alive. Now they were more frightened of him dead. He still commanded awe even as a corpse. After murdering Shaka, they all ran into Mkabayi's dark hut and stared at the floor, panting. The tornado worsened. People and livestock were blown away, and huts were ripped off within minutes as everyone ran indoors. Mkabayi's solo *ubhaqa* (a Zulu candle) was blown out by the strong wind which had provided eerie light. The hut was shaken to its foundation by the howling gusts of wind. They all sat together in the dark, quiet. Whenever lightning struck, the silhouette showed petrified and sweating killers, their hands still bloodstained.

After a while, Mkabayi slowly asked in a hoarse voice if the deed was done and they nodded. Not a word was uttered after that as they sat in silence, listening to the groaning gale outside. The force of the wind ripped deep into their souls as it carried everything in its wake. The silence, persisting fear and uncertainty caused them to argue about how to dispose of Shaka's corpse. Mhlangana said he should be buried. Mbopha, said he did not want to see his body ever again and suggested that it be left where it lay so that it could be devoured by hyenas overnight. Dingane said he was afraid that if wild animals ate the corpse, Shaka would become *idlozi elibi* (an evil ancestor) and bring a catastrophe upon the Zulu nation. Mkabayi was not particularly bothered with Shaka's body being left outside and eaten by wild animals. Surely, nothing could get worse now that he was dead.

They finally decided to leave Shaka's body where it was and tried to get some sleep. Everyone ran away from iNyakamubi and KwaDukuza to the nearest mountain and into the nearby iNonoti bushes when they heard that Shaka had been murdered. None of them ever imagined that anything or anybody would kill Shaka. They truly believed the sky would cave in and every imaginable catastrophe would befall the Zulu empire. Only one person did not run away, Phampatha. When people were scuttling, she looked for Shaka's body undeterred, despite the crashing lightning.

Ignoring flash after flash, Phampatha searched tirelessly through what seemed like little more than a gloomy and endless maze. She decided to check at iNyakamubi, and a blinding flash lit the sky when she discovered the lone and limp body of her best friend and the love of her life. She threw herself on his body and gently stroked his face in the driving rain. She tried to cry out, but no sound could escape from her mouth. Tears slowly welled in her eyes and suddenly a heart-rending cry from the bottom of her soul reverberated in the night.

She rocked him in her arms, deep in a trance looking without blinking at his glazed eyes. In slow motion, she vividly recalled the first day they met when she was only 11 years old. She remembered her initial pangs of joy, love and glory associated with a younger Shaka. A fresh bout of warm, torrential rain drenched them both and her own tears finally blinded her. After what seemed like eternity, the violent storm ceased. Phampatha hung on to Shaka tightly, protecting his corpse as she knew it would soon be dawn. After a last lingering farewell at dawn, she hid in one of the huts nearest to Shaka's body. She only crept out of iNyakamubi at sunrise after she had entertained the idea of killing herself on top of the body of her lover. She then ran away because she was convinced that whoever had killed Shaka would also come after her.

After the longest night of their lives, at sunrise Dingane, Mhlangana and Mbopha went to check on Shaka's remains and expected the worst. They were shocked to find Shaka's body intact. They noticed hyena footprints around the body but couldn't understand why the hyenas had come so close but did not eat the body. Who or what had protected Shaka's body? Did the hyenas know it was the king's body and could not eat it? Had his ancestors protected him? But hadn't the ancestors turned their backs on him? Shocked, they agreed to throw his body into the iMbozamo River where it would be eaten by crocodiles. They hurried back to report to Mkabayi, who was equally stunned. Now that Shaka was refusing to go quietly, Mkabayi decided he should be buried with all the decorum befitting a king. The reason Shaka's corpse was untouched is because the large pack of hyenas had descended on his corpse. They dribbled, formed a circle, grunted and dared to come so close. While their demented laughter kept rising, Phampatha valiantly kept them at bay with a long pole. Hyenas were daring when it came to the dead, dying or incapacitated but they were cowardly under any other circumstance. Finally, at dawn, they gave up and scampered to their hideouts, leaving behind their clearly visible paw prints.

The next problem was the digging of a deep grave. Under normal circumstances, the army would dig the grave. Now there were no soldiers in sight because they had all gone to fight a futile war in the north. Mhlangana suggested they throw the body unceremoniously into one of the granary pits but Dingane and Mkabayi refused. Instead, Mkabayi ordered that Shaka be buried in a granary pit with the dignity he deserved. A black bull was then killed by the handful of guards who ventured back in the morning from the wilderness. Shaka's body was wrapped in the bull's hide and monkey creeper cords were used to tie it. Due to rigour mortis, he could not be bound in the usual recumbent posture, so he was buried in the pit, standing.

They also put some of his favourite weapons, food vessels, animal-hide cloaks, feathers, tails and other personal accoutrements next to him. The pit was closed with a stone lid and a heap of stones were raised over the grave and covered with Buffalo thorn bushes. The meat of the slaughtered bull was placed in the adjoining pit before being sealed. This would serve as his dining room in the next world. All other pits were carefully sealed, since the murderers were paranoid. They believed that if they did not seal the pits, Shaka's spirit would escape and seek revenge. More than a century later, in 1944, the British gave away the 60 000 acres of the land where KwaDukuza Palace was situated to a farmer, T Potgieter, for free.

Sadly, the greatest Zulu king was buried by a handful of people, some insignificant. His body servant Jeqe, who was supposed to be buried with him to continue serving him in the next world, was not even present. From Shaka's personal artefacts, Phampatha managed to keep his redwood ceremonial spear and ran about 16 kilometres to alert Ngomane at his Nonoti homestead. She found him seated with one of the king's council members and Shaka's maternal uncle, Nxazonke kaBhebhe Mhlongo who was Nandi's father's younger brother. They were particularly devastated by the tragic news. Sensing that everything was lost, politically at least, they joined the people who were hiding in the iNonoti bush. Phampatha's next stop was Shaka's maternal brother Ngwadi who lived at KwaWambaza homestead near the uMkhumbane River. He lived semi-independently with his own army which Shaka had exempted from the national call-up. Mkabayi and her cowardly nephews decided to neutralise anyone they thought would want to avenge Shaka's death. Phampatha was to be taken alive.

Mbopha anxiously waited for the army to return so that he could be given his half of the empire as promised. But his first assignment was to hunt down and kill Shaka's elderly personal attendants that had witnessed his murder. Ngwadi was to be next because he had killed Sigujana and made it possible for Shaka to be king. Mbopha led the iziNyosi and iziYendane regiments to kill Ngwadi and he knew that he would find Phampatha with him. Phampatha and the young companion given to her by

Ngomane crossed the uThukela River jogging and only stopped to drink a little water from streams. They got lost somewhere in the thick mist on the Melmoth plateau and the youngster returned. Phampatha finally stumbled into Ngwadi's homestead and told him about the catastrophe. Mbopha found them having taken their last stand in the cattle enclosure. Ngwadi managed to kill more than ten of them before he was killed. Still exhausted as she was, Phampatha fought like a tigress no less. When she realised, they were trying not to capture her, she chose to take her own life rather than eventually die at the hands of Shaka's killers. She plunged Shaka's spear into her heart and shouted '*uShaka*'.

Sotobe and his entourage arrived unexpectedly from Cape Town as he was expected many months later. He was enraged and wanted to revenge his friend, but Mkabayi managed to calm him down. On the night of Shaka's murder, the Zulu white subjects were having a party in Farewell's homestead and were admiring the tusks from a hunt earlier in the day. They heard about Shaka's murder from King Mathubane of the Luthuli kingdom and they left Farewell's house and told other whites. They regrouped in a small white settlement called Townsend near Port Natal with some of their Zulu and mixed-race servants. They suspected that Shaka's murderers would also kill them, so most of them - including Isaacs, Cane and Ross who was a member of the iNtontela regiment - sailed to Port Elizabeth immediately. They took some of their servants with them. Only the diehard remained behind such as Fynn, Halstead and Ogle, at least for a while longer.

When Isaacs and his group arrived in Port Elizabeth, their ship was impounded for not having a valid permit. This proved too much for Isaacs who jumped onto the first ship heading to St Helena, vowing never to return to the kingdom ever again. But he could not stay away from the Zulu for long and returned aboard an American ship the *St Michael* in 1829. He took up contract work as the resident shooting instructor for the army in Dingane's palace for which he was paid in tusks. When his contract expired two years later, he left for good and joined the more lucrative slave trade and gun smuggling in Sierra Leone, West Africa. Nathaniel Isaacs, the first Jewish Zulu subject, died a lonely death in Egremont, England, in 1872. Farewell and Cane decided to settle among the Xhosa people but after a year, they realised that their future was among the Zulu. On their way back, they took Dingane's principal aide, Dingane's Lugozolo kaMthiyana Madlanzini, Jantshi, (Nongila's son, the head of Dingane's secret service). They also brought along a few Xhosa servants, a San interpreter Lynx and two fortune seekers William Calamaish Thackwray and

William Walker and they passed through the aMadolo settlement in Mpondoland in September 1829. They later set up camp on the banks of the uMzimvubu River and Farewell decided to pay his respects to the Nqetho, but Cane remained behind.

Nqetho was the marauder-in-chief of the southern lands and killed Farewell and some of his servants in their sleep. Mdlaka received intelligence that his best friend Shaka had been killed after leaving KwaMhlabuyalingana. But he did not share the tragic news not even with the military high command. By the time he arrived at KwaDukuza, his life had changed for the worst. From as far back as the war against Matiwane in 1821 and in all the wars in between, including the recent Soshangane campaign in 1828 he had been commander-in-chief of the army. Not once did he lose a battle but this time, he was returning home with nothing to show for it. The army was only told about Shaka's demise when they reached KwaDukuza. Their anger was tangible, and it was left to Sotobe, forever the diplomat, to calm them down. Mdlaka was uncontrollable and was the only one who spoke his mind without fear in front of the assembly. He said that since someone from the House of Senzangakhona had to be emperor, it had to be Mhlangana and not Dingane, whom he considered a good-for-nothing traitor. He also challenged anyone who disagreed with him to stand up and fight. No one moved. Mkabayi sensed anger and a potential mutiny and she devised a plan to distract them. She whispered something to Ngomane, who then announced that they could perform the *ukusula izembe* ritual immediately and released them. KwaDukuza became a scene of a mass orgy as there were many willing *imidlunkulu* with repressed desires. The orgy continued non-stop for a fortnight and no one dared intervene, lest the passions be directed at those who killed their favourite warrior king.

Mkabayi moved quickly even though it was the mourning period. She rewarded all the military officers who she feared could mobilise the army against her by allowing them to wear *isicoco* and gave them hundreds of cattle. The first casualty was Mdlaka who got a stupendous number of cattle for his distinguished service to the House of Senzangakhona. He lived out the rest of his life in the tranquil foothills of the Drakensberg reminiscing about what life could have been had his friend *iLembe* not been ambushed. Mkabayi ran the kingdom for the third time after the death of her father Jama and nephew Sigujana. She deliberately increased tension between the assassins who now resented each other. They were not even on talking terms anymore but they each silently hoped that Mkabayi would make good on her promise. Dingane was desperate to be his own man but he could not sever his umbilical cord with eMkhosini Valley and meekly went to live at uMbelebele which was the first *ikhanda* built by Shaka, Mkabayi let him stew in fear for almost a month before she summoned him to her private hut at KwaDukuza. She reminded him that he was not going to share the Zulu empire with the untrustworthy commoner Mbopha. In the meantime, Mbopha long suspected that he stood no chance of getting half the empire as promised. But when he was promoted to become the king of aMaNdawe kingdom, south of uMhlathuze River, he accepted it with delight. This was a generous reward for a one-time king's assistant.

Once Mbopha was settled as king of the newly created kingdom, Mkabayi planned his murder. But she decided that whoever would kill Mbopha, had to be killed as well. She decided to check the loyalty of her Chief of Staff, Zidumo, and asked him if he would be willing to kill Mbopha for a promotion. When he agreed, she stopped trusting him because it meant that he would also get her killed for a reward. Even though Mbopha reigned supreme as a king, he was paranoid about his security and was careful about who entered his 'palace'. When Zidumo asked to visit him, Mbopha agreed and found him seated with his favourite wife. But as soon as Zidumo arrived, Mbopha sensed it was his last day on earth. He did not put up a fight, moreover, he now regretted having participated in Shaka's murder. He accepted his fate with dignity and asked to be killed like a soldier, with one stab under the left armpit. Zidumo was killed on the way back to KwaDukuza.

When Mhlangana heard about Mbopha's death, he knew his days were also numbered. Besides, he had heard that Dingane was frequenting Mkabayi's hut, whereas she gave him the cold shoulder whenever he visited her. Mhlangana did not intend to go quietly and increased the number of his followers and prepared to fight. His followers were seen feverishly sharpening their spears. But Mkabayi was too cunning to be outsmarted by newcomers like Mhlangana in the killing game. A few weeks after Mbopha's death, Mkabayi invited Mhlangana to her hut where he found a brooding Dingane already seated. He was informed by Mkabayi's new Chief of Staff, Mkhosana kaZangwana Zungu that the next king would be chosen by ballot. Mhlangana was stunned, sweat started pouring from his lean torso. He began to raise an objection but Mkabayi gave him an icy stare, which rapidly terminated the conversation. Mhlangana left the hut in a daze and started wondering if killing Shaka had been ultimately worth it. Mkabayi's unintended consequence was evolving right in front of her eyes and for a while it seemed like she was not going to be able to contain it. Even before the mandatory year's mourning was over, the empire was divided between Dingane and Mhlangana as they were both being addressed as *Bayethe* by their followers. Mkabayi had to move quickly and she called an *imbizo* at

KwaDukuza. She informed them that the new king was going to be elected through a ballot. No one had ever heard of such before in the whole land of the Nguni but then again, this was vintage Mkabayi. People had to expect the unexpected from her.

On the day of the election, she instructed her nephews to wash in the river without their bodyguards. She said it was because they would be washing with cleansing medicines. Mhlangana again felt outmanoeuvred and baulked at the idea. But his closest allies convinced him that nothing could go wrong because they would be nearby, and he had the numbers on his side. They were guaranteed a certain victory. The nation watched from a distance as the two princes got walked into the river stark naked close to each other near the reeds. After they glared at each other without a word for a while, they washed. Suddenly Mhlangana disappeared under the water and everyone waited for him to emerge but instead they saw bubbles rising. Then an announcement was made that Mhlangana's body had surfaced floating face down among the reeds. Like his name Mhlangana (*little reed*) his life had ended among the reeds.

There were loud remarks of horror and disbelief. Soldiers aligned to Mhlangana faced off with those aligned with Dingane with their spears held in the *mfukulo* position (pointed upward with the blade above the hand and the shaft below it). All that was left was for their commanders to say the word and the slaughter would have begun. Realising that the kingdom was about to disintegrate, Mkabayi used her proven tactic. She jumped in between the enraged soldiers, stretching her hands between them and with her eyes burning like wildfire she sang the national anthem at the top of her voice:

| | |
|---|---|
| *UNdaba, uyinkosi* | *Ndaba is king* |
| *Uyamemeza okaNdaba* | *the son of Ndaba is calling us* |
| *Wasibiza savuma* | *he called us and we agreed* |
| *Uyinkosi yohlanga* | *he is the king of humanity* |
| *Oho, O!* | *Ohho, O!* |
| *Hha, oye!* | *Hha, Oye!* |
| *Jijiji, ajiji!* | *Jijiji, ajiji!* |

It struck a chord and both groups of soldiers slowly joined in and began to do the war dance instead of killing each other. When Mkabayi was satisfied that they had calmed down, she ordered them to stand down. She said they had to do it in memory of *Sigidi* and accept Dingane was now their king. Without missing a heartbeat, the whole army resounded with a thunderous *Bayethe*! So loud were their voices that Shaka surely heard them in heaven. For Mkabayi, it was another mission accomplished with the minimal shedding of Zulu blood. The troops hung around to nurse their wounded pride. They wondered how *Sigidi* could die such a useless death at the hands of cowards who drown their opponents. The rest of the nation was unsure about the future and asked themselves '*ingabe iyozala nkomoni?*' (What does the future hold in store?).

After the near civil war, life was never the same for the grand old lady. Mkabayi suddenly felt extremely tired. Her joints ached and her heart beat as though it was reluctant. Her favourite nephew's palace felt as though it was engulfed by dark and onerous clouds that slithered through its maze. In her mind's eye, she saw all the decisions she had taken ever since she walked through its gates. It felt like a lifetime. Time was moving too slowly she thought. Perhaps if she were to move back up country to KwaNobamba, life would be worth living again. She began to prepare for the long and lonely journey back home. She bid farewell to all the people in the homesteads that reminded her of the times long ago such as the times of her father Jama and younger paternal brother Senzangakhona.

## Emperor King Shaka kaSenzangakhona Laudatory Praises

| | |
|---|---|
| UDlungwana lukaNdaba | the ferocious one of Ndaba |
| UDlungwana loMbelebele | the ferocious one of uMbelebele Division |
| Oludlunge emanxulumeni | that raged in huge homesteads |
| Kwaze kwasa amanxuluma esebikelana | that raged till the next day |
| Ilembe eleqa amanye amalembe ngokukhalipha | the axe that is sharper than other axes |
| UNodumehlezi kaMenzi | Nodumehlezi, son of Menzi |
| Usishaka kashayeki | the unbeaten one |
| Umtaka kaSenzangakhona | the son of Senzangakhona |
| | |
| UShaka ngiyesaba nokuthi nguShaka | Shaka, Im afraid to call him by his name, Shaka |
| UShaka kwakuyinkosi yaseMashobeni | Shaka was the king of eMashobeni valley |
| Uteku lwabafazi bakwaNomgabhi | the joke of the women from Nomgabhi |
| Ababetekula behlezi emlovini | they made fun of him seated by uMlovu River |
| Bethi uShaka akayikubusa | they said Shaka would never rule |
| Bethi kayikubankosi | they said he would never be king |
| Kanti yilapho ezakunethezeka khona | yet he overcame adversity |
| Umlilo wothathe, yebo kaMjokwane | the wild fire, yes son of Mjokwane |
| Oshisa izikhova eziseDlebe | that burns owls at Dlebe hill |
| Kwazwe kwaya kwasha nezaseMabedlana | it even burnt those at Mabedlana hills |
| UNomakhwelo, iNgonyama | the dominant lion |
| UMjokwane kaNdaba | Tall one, the descendant of Ndaba |
| | |
| UVumavumane lukaphephe | Small creature that soars like a flag |
| UDlungwana wavuma na? | Ferocious one, did you agree? |
| Umvumeleni uGodolozi? | Why did you trust Godolozi? |
| Ethi ngowanganeno kwaNandi | thinking that he was on Nandi's side |
| Kanti ukude kwaNtombazi | whereas he was on Ntombazi's side |
| Ilanga eliphandla elinye ngemisebe | the sun that eclipses others with its rays |
| Kaloku liphandle eliseMthandeni | it also blinded the one at eMthandeni Palace |
| Amazwi mabili engiwabongayo | I am grateful for two names only |
| Ngibonga elikaMpandaba nelikaNdunginkomo | I am thankful to Mpandaba and Ndunginkomo |
| Bethi ucu aluhlangani entanyeni | for saying the beads do not fit around the neck |
| Akenibuze kwabase eZinkondeni | please ask the people from eZinkondeni |
| Bathi uHilwayo | they said the underestimated one |
| Bayakumhlaba kwaHlokohloko | would be stabbed at KwaHlokohloko |
| Afa amasi kwafa uqephe | sour milk spilt, the calabash shattered |
| | |
| Inkomo ekhala eMthonjaneni | the bull that bellows at eMthonjaneni |
| Izizwe zonke ziyizwile ukulila | all nations heard it |
| Izwiwe uDunjwa waseluYengweni | it was heard by Dunjwa of oYengweni |
| Yezwiwa uMangcengeza wakwaKhali | it was heard by Mangcengeza son of Khali |
| Yaye yezwiwa ngamantungwana akwaKhumalo | it was also heard by the Khumalo cannibals |
| Umlilo wothathe kaMjokwane | the wild fire, son of Mjokwane |
| Intethe egolwe yizinti zomkhonto kwaMlandela | the locust caught on Mlandela's spear shafts |
| Odabule kuNdima noMgovu | flew between Ndima and Mgovu |
| Ungezwa bethi valela njalo Solunjalose | ignore those who say you should always set traps |
| Abasho kuwe wena kaNdaba | they are not talking to you descendant of Ndaba |

| | |
|---|---|
| *Bashu unyoko uMbulazi* | *they are referring to your mother Mbulazi* |
| *Ovalela ingonyama endlini* | *who trapped a lion in her hut* |
| *Abafazi abenendeni baphuluza* | *pregnant women gave birth prematurely* |
| *Imikhubulo bayishiya isinqindi* | *newly planted crops were abandoned* |
| *Imbewu bayishiya emahlangeni* | *they left seeds among the maize stalks* |
| *Izalukazi zasala semanxiweni* | *old women were left in abandoned huts* |
| *Amaxhegu asala emizileni* | *old men were left by the way side* |
| *Iziqu zemithi zabheka phezulu* | *trees were uprooted* |
| | |
| *Odabule kuBuzane phezulu* | *he crossed at the top of Buzane Mountain* |
| *Wakhethelwa udwendwe lamaza* | *he stumbled upon a long line of deer* |
| *Wadlula kuMcombo zigoduka* | *he passed Mcombo as the cattle went home* |
| *Wabuza izindlela kuDunjwa* | *he asked for directions from Dunjwa* |
| *Kanti ngabe uzibuza kuMbozane* | *when he should have asked Mbozane* |
| *Owandulela ukuya kuNomagaga* | *who ended rushing to Nomagaga* |
| *Lafika iqhude lamvimbela* | *but a rooster blocked his way* |
| *Ilanga eliphume linsizwa* | *the sun that came out without rays* |
| *Lathi liphezulu lansasa* | *but it shone bright at its peak* |
| *Ozulu lizayo khwezani abantwana* | *he was like gathering storm, hide the children* |
| *Abadala bodwa abazozibalekela* | *the adults will flee by themselves* |
| *UDunjwa yedwa limkhandanisile* | *it only destroyed Dunjwa* |
| *Oyewakha amaxhiba oThukela* | *who was building huts near uThukela River* |
| *Lapha kucushwa isilo ngomwowane* | *near the leopard's snare* |
| *Weza noKhungwayo noGobizembe* | *he came with Khungwayo and Gobizembe* |
| *Ohamba ebasa amakloba* | *he who went around stating huge fires* |
| | |
| *Ophehlwe ngeva wanjengomlilo* | *he who was provoked and raged like a fire* |
| *Ondande ngankalo, wabuya ngankalo* | *he who marched slowly on the ridge both ways* |
| *Eya kuBhoyiya kaMdakuda* | *he was going to attack Bhoyiya, Mdakuda's son* |
| *UNdaba ubengababele kuya* | *the son of Ndaba had no intention to attack them* |
| *Wayelanda uMacingwane waseNgonyameni* | *he was after Macingwane at Ngonyama palace* |
| *Ondande ngokhala olude* | *he who trudged slowly on the long ridge* |
| *Wadabula emathanjeni abantabakaTayi* | *he who went across the bones of Tayi's descendants* |
| *Ebebegodola beya kuMacingwane eNgonyameni* | *who froze to death on their way to Macingwane's palace* |
| *Umlunguzi wezingoje* | *the cliff hunter* |
| *Inyathi ehamba isenga amazibuko* | *the buffalo that crosses fords* |
| *Imamba edla umuntu bathi iloyelwe* | *the snake that bites as though its possessed* |
| *Wahlangana nondwendwe lwamankankana* | *he stumbled upon a bunch of hadeda birds* |
| *Mhla eyakudla amaMpondo iziphukuphuku* | *on his way to attack the stupid amaMpondo* |
| *Intaba emahwanqa kaMjokwane* | *Mountain man, with sideburns, son of Mjokwane* |
| *Inkomo yasekhaya kithi KwaBulawayo* | *the KwaBulawayo bull that belongs to us* |
| | |
| *UGasane kade libagasela* | *the attacker that has long been attacking them* |
| *Ligasela uPhungashe wakwaButhelezi* | *he attacked Phungashe of the Buthelezi* |
| *Lwagasela uSondaba eMthandeni ehlezi ebandla* | *he attacked Sondaba in council at eMthandeni* |
| *Lwagasela uMacingwane eNgonyameni* | *he attacked Macingwane at eNgonyameni palace* |
| *Lwagasela uMangcengeza emaMbatheni* | *he attacked Mangcengeza of the Mbatha kingdom* |
| *Lwagasela uDladlama wakwaMajola* | *he attacked Dladlama of the Majola kingdom* |
| *Lwagasela uNqaba kaMbhekane* | *he attacked Nqaba of the Mbhekane kingdom* |

| | |
|---|---|
| Lwagasela uGambushe emaMpondweni | he attacked Gambushe in Mpondoland |
| Lwagasela uFaku emaMpondweni | he attacked Faku in Mpondoland |
| | |
| UDlodlwane luya luhlezi luya ludlondlobele | the young viper that raged with little effort |
| Isidlukula dlwedlwe sibeka isihlangu emadolweni | tough rod that puts its shield across the knees |
| Inyathi ejame ngomkhonto | the buffalo that waited with a spear |
| Phezu koMzimvubu | at uMzimvubu River |
| AmaMpondo ayesaba ukuyiyehlela | the amaMpondo kingdom was too terrified to attack |
| Nani boGambushe, nani boFaku | you too Gambushe's people and Faku's people |
| Ningamhlabi, ukuba nimhlabile | do not stab him because if you do |
| Niyoba kanihlabi yena | you would have not stabbed him |
| Koba senihlabe uPhunga | as you would have stabbed Phunga |
| Nihlabe uMageba | you would have stabbed Mageba |
| Othi esadla ezinye | who while attacking some people |
| Wadla ezinye | he would attack even more |
| Othi esadla ezinye | who while attacking some people |
| Wadla ezinye | he would attack even more |
| Othi esadla ezinye | who while attacking some people |
| Wadla ezinye | he would attack even more |
| Othi esadla ezinye | who while attacking some people |
| Wadla ezinye | he would attack even more |
| Othi esadla ezinye | who while attacking some people |
| Wadla ezinye | he would attack even more |
| Othi esadla ezinye | who while attacking some people |
| Wadla ezinye | he would attack even more |
| Othi esadla ezinye | who while attacking some people |
| Wadla ezinye | he would attack even more |
| Othi esadla ezinye | who while attacking some people |
| Wadla ezinye | he would attack even more |
| Wena weNdlovu | Hail, Elephant |
| Sigidi | Mercury |
| Hlanga lomhlabathi | Reed of the Soil! |
| Ngangezwe lakhe | He who is as big as his nation |
| Bayethe | Hail, Your Majesty |

# 6

# Emperor Dingane kaSenzangakhona

DINGANE HAD TO WAIT out the terror-filled year for the *ihlambo* ceremony before he could be king. When Mkabayi was declared regent at KwaNobamba, it was an unbelievable anti-climax. There was neither a coronation, jubilation nor a ceremony. Dingane kept a low profile at uMbelebele barracks, moreover Mkabayi made him feel inadequate in so many ways. After constructing several palaces such KwaSimanganyawo, he constructed a preposterously huge oval-shaped palace against iSangonyana hill, between the iNzololo and uMkhumbane Rivers a few kilometres from KwaNobamba. He named it uMgungundlovu Palace (*elephant swallower*). The word 'elephant' was a euphemism for 'Shaka' and 'swallower' a euphemism for 'killer'. Which meant he was an 'elephant killer', an impressive oval shaped accolade which resembled two elephant tusks when placed on the ground for his weak self.

It had a diameter of about two kilometres and housed at least 50 000 soldiers, huts were eight deep and from the main entrance he could admire the panoramic eMakhosini Valley. He hosted his last white visitors on the 1$^{st}$ of March 1829 at KwaNobamba. Amongst the guests were Fynn, Dr Alexander Cowie, a British surgeon and Benjamin 'Tiger' Green. They found Dingane and 40 mixed-race Portuguese merchants from Delagoa Bay discussing a bilateral trade agreement with the new Zulu monarch. Hlambamanzi was also present as the senior translator for Dingane. Hlambamanzi now lived in his own homestead eKuweleni on a flat plain between the uMhlathuzana and uMlalazi Rivers at KwaMpofu, Eshowe. Cowie, Green and Hlambamanzi joined the merchants, but when they returned home, Cowie and Green died of fever within five weeks of their arrival in Delagoa Bay.

Dingane was not sure if his subjects were truly loyal to him and embarked on a public relations exercise to endear himself to the people. He went around the empire ordering his subjects to refer to him as the *uMalamulela* (saviour) from Shaka's militaristic lifestyle. He also introduced several sweeping changes, for instance, male regiments were partially demilitarised, regimental courtship was reversed, marriage was no longer a military privilege because anyone could marry whom they liked, when they liked, and he completely demobilised all female regiments. Empire-building wars were abolished along with the death penalty. He proclaimed the law of return for all those who went into exile because of Shaka's wars. Those who had taken to living in dark forests, caves or high up in insurmountable mountain ridges were also promised safe passage back to their ancestral homes. The whole nation welcomed these benevolent acts with great enthusiasm. Dingane became a *Malamulela* indeed. Or was he?

One of the sons of Shaka's archenemy, Prince Somaphunga kaZwide Ndwandwe and his followers were one of the first kingdoms allowed to return to their ancestral land around the Black iMfolozi River and the iNhlungwane Valley near Nongoma. But typical of Dingane, he attacked Somaphunga for no apparent reason at the foot of Hlokohlo Mountain. Dingane's soldiers suffered heavy casualties and retreated. Nqetho was next to take advantage of Dingane's benevolence and made a unilateral declaration of independence from the Zulu empire. He undertook a slow march along the coast to the Qwabe kingdom with his 6000 followers which was on the northern border of the Mthethwa kingdom. Nqetho sent a message to Dingane demanding the return of the wife of his late brother Phakathwayo who was taken away as part of spoils of war by Shaka. Before Nqetho even reached his ancestral lands, the impetuous Dingane changed his mind about the new liberties and refused Nqetho the right to go back home. He claimed that if he allowed Nqetho go back to the land of his ancestors, it would create instability in the empire.

However, he allowed other kingdoms to return to their lands. Nqetho realised it would not be long before Dingane killed him and his followers, so instead of proceeding north, he turned back and fled further south. He crossed the uThukela River and ran along the coast and settled in today's eziMbokodweni (incorrectly spelled 'Mbokotwini') in Magaye's territory. When he had recovered from the long march, Nqetho formed iziNtuthwane and izaNqume regiments and attacked unsuspecting Magaye who had given him refuge. Nqetho kidnapped the women and children and took cattle that technically belonged to Dingane. As per Zulu custom, everything and everyone in the empire belonged to the emperor.

After a few weeks, Dingane's soldiers were seen sharpening their spears near the eziMbokodweni River. It was within a day's walk from Nqetho's camp, close to the uMngeni River in today's New Germany near Durban. Nqetho with his cattle and those belonging to the Cele kingdom, moved deep in the forest and prepared to fight Dingane's regiments. But before the battle, the kind and amiable Magaye was found dead under mysterious circumstances. Everyone suspected Nqetho, who denied having killed him. A few days later, the two armies finally stood toe-to-toe in the *umfukulo* (attack) posture. The command to attack, neither came from Nqetho's nor Dingane's commanders. Perhaps the commands never came because the soldiers were genuinely battle-weary. Nqetho's regiments retreated into the forest, while Dingane's regiments took as many cattle as they could and slowly trudged back like defeated soldiers. Before they parted, they ensured that the gentle Magaye received a dignified burial. Dingane's paranoia on the other hand grew by the day, fuelled by his growing insecurities about perceived threats to his life. He embarked on a killing spree of all the people who were close to Shaka. The secret service investigated Magaye's death and found that he had been at the top of Dingane's hit list. Nqetho was vindicated after all.

This was the beginning of Dingane's dirty tricks of assassinating his opponents by stealth, a foreign and cowardly concept in the psyche of the brave Zulu soldiers. Shaka had taught them the bravery of *ukuqonda umuntu ngqo* (facing the enemy directly). There was great trepidation when the nation heard that Magaye had been murdered in such a cowardly manner. However, Magaye's six sons continued serving in Dingane's army despite what he had done to their father. The entire military high command led by Mdlaka confronted Dingane at uMgungundlovu about Magaye's murder. The lily-livered Dingane denied ordering the assassination and went as far as offering a reward of 100 cattle, a fortune in those days, to anyone who could point out the murderer. Incensed by the reward, Mdlaka publicly called Dingane a liar and blamed him for the assassination. Mdlaka even criticised all his so-called 'radical' actions to make himself the *uMalamulela* of the people. He even threatened to replace him with one of Senzangakhona's weak sons, Mpande. This public humiliation in front of the entire military high command was the last straw for the conceited Dingane. The commander in chief, Mdlaka kaNcindi Mgazini, had joined the Zulu empire as a refugee and promoted to the highest military rank by Shaka because of his exemplary bravery. He was found speared the same way Magaye was killed, and he too died in his sleep.

After feigning sadness at the death of Mdlaka, Dingane announced new appointments. He promoted Ndlela kaSompisi Ntuli, the commander of the iNtontela regiment, to Field Marshal and the commander-in-chief of the army. Ndlela had a meteoric rise in the military because of his exceptional bravery. His family had joined the Zulu fold during Senzangakhona's reign when he was a little boy, when they ran away from being eaten by their cannibal relatives. Nzobo became Ndlela's deputy and Sotobe became the governor of the whole area from the uThukela River to the uMzimvubu River in the south. The cruel and human bile drinking Matiwane and his amaNgwane also returned to the Zulu empire as soon as Dingane allowed it. They were given a large piece of land near uMgungundlovu where Dingane had them closely watched. Matiwane was watched to see if he was still a threat or if he had lost the previous 'fire' that kept him alive. Melancholic, Matiwane often went on long walks with his favourite dog *Bozibozi*, a large brown fox terrier and reminisced about his bloody past with regret. He used to wonder what life could have been had he not fled from Shaka so many years ago. A few months later, Dingane asked Matiwane and all his followers to give him a hand to recover some stolen *inyonikayiphumuli* royal cattle. Matiwane could have been lugubrious but he had not lost his edge and knew something was afoot when he was called to come with all his followers. But this vicious butcher of the weak was done with fighting and tired of life on the run. Given half a chance, Matiwane would have preferred to die watching the sunset, nothing dramatic, just a quiet and uneventful death.

But his ruthlessness towards the innocent had taken its toll on his conscience, he was a truly exhausted and broken man. Before they left, he called his 14-year-old son, Zikhali, aside and solemnly removed one of his *izigxotha* (war medals). He then instructed Zikhali to hide inside one of the huts because he feared he was not going to come back from 'looking' for Dingane's stolen royal cattle. Tearfully, Zikhali obeyed and hid. He later escaped to Swaziland where he married Princess Nomlalazi kaSobhuza I. Matiwane and his followers were told to wait in a cattle enclosure for other regiments to join them. Dingane arrived in the cattle enclosure with his entourage carrying his famous black shield with a single white spot on the left. 'Where are your people?' a perplexed Dingane asked seeing such few people. 'Here they are, this is all that is left of them,' replied a subdued Matiwane. Without warning, Dingane shouted: '*Phezu kwabo*' (jump on top of them), the attack command. The unsuspecting amaNgwane had their necks broken. But before they killed Matiwane, they was first tortured him, his eyes were gouged out and sticks were driven up his nostrils before he was thrown over a cliff near the confluence of the uMkhumbane and iNzololo Rivers. This cliff became known as *iwa likaMatiwane* (Matiwane's Cliff). It was a pitiful end for one of the fearless soldiers and chief strategists of the Nguni people.

Even though he had ruthlessly slaughtered defenceless people, some people believe he could have been a great and resourceful leader had he not been under pressure to survive outside the Zulu empire. Had he led a simple life, he could have established a great kingdom such as those founded by Mzilikazi, Soshangane and Zwangendaba. Dingane's next victim in 1839 was King Mqadi of the Dube kingdom, Shaka's maternal relative. The *amaQadi*, as they were known, were requested to cut *izintungo* (roof frames) for Dingane's huts. Mqadi happily obliged and sent all his soldiers. But Dingane claimed that he had not sent them all and accused him of insubordination. He then ordered all the amaQadi women, children, the sick and the aged to carry *izintungo* to him at uMgungundlovu a considerable distance away.

Some escaped and joined missionaries who had begun to trickle into the empire. As soon as the amaQadi entered the cattle enclosure with the logs, Dingane shouted '*Babambeni*' (seize them) and they were all killed. Dingane tried to trick the Cele people by pretending to care about their welfare. He made the daring 25-year-old Mkhonto Cele the regent because the heir, Crown Prince Magidigidi kaMagaye Cele could only be coconated after the year's mourning. Since the Cele people were specialist boundary log makers, Dingane asked them to erect a boundary around Sotobe's homestead.

They agreed but remained vigilant because they did not want to be taken by surprise like the amaQadi and amaNgwane. They erected the boundary and were not attacked. But after a few days Dingane asked them to join him to kill a lion that had eaten one of his cattle. They obliged. Once they were in that valley, someone shouted, '*Bulalani ibhubesi*' (kill the lion) the attack command. Mkhonto and his regiment were killed but this time Magaye's six sons, who were still serving Dingane at the uMgungundlovu, deserted. They sought refuge among the whites in Port Natal, which was slowly becoming a refuge for all the disgruntled and fearful Zulu.

A year after moving into the uMgungundlovu Palace, Dingane's first white visitors were slave traders from Portugal who were blown off course and shipwrecked at Port Natal in January 1830. Their ship *The African Adventure* left Sofala with 160 African slaves along with the wife of the Portuguese commander in Delagoa Bay and a short comical Chinese deckhand. By the time they ran aground in Port Natal only thirty African slaves were still alive along with the commander's wife and the Chinese man. Dingane was particularly fascinated by the Chinese man and made fun of his floor-length pigtail, which he dragged around the palace floor. When the visitors finally left uMgungundlovu, the Chinese man agreed to remain behind for

Dingane's amusement, and he was often seen pulling at the extra-long ponytail like a leash. The little Chinese man lived in the secluded section at the palace reserved for the mentality ill, dwarfs, orphans, social misfits and the deformed.

The arrival of whites with different agendas peaked for the next five years as they poured into the Zulu empire by land and sea. For instance, three Jewish brothers Joshua, James and Samuel Cawood arrived with their families and African slaves from the Cape. They were pulling six wagons laden with all sorts of merchandise. In April 1830, another group of mercenaries which included Dr Andrew Smith, John Minting, William Parkins, Captain Eddie of the 98th regiment of the British Imperial Army and James Terry, two German brothers, Carl and Frantz Drege, and an Afrikaner, Hermanus Barry, also rolled in. As more whites arrived, the first white Zulu subjects became uncomfortable, especially Fynn. He proposed to Dingane that new families who came to *khonza* in the Zulu Empire be limited to four members only. His reasoning was that the whites would end up outnumbering the Zulu people. Dingane laughed at the idea and sent Ndlela with his deputy Nzobo north with some of the new white Zulu subjects to retrieve the royal cattle stolen by Mzilikazi. They camped around iMpama (*Magaliesberg*) Mountains north-west of the *iGwa* (Vaal) River. But Ndlela's battle plan was surprisingly weak as Mzilikazi escaped unscathed and Ndlela came back with a pitiful number of thin cattle.

Dingane was incensed and like Shaka he ordered the execution of several of his officers for their failed mission. He sent many soldiers to death for very minor offences which led to the desertion of whole regiments. This was a contradiction because he had only recently abolished the death penalty for any crime. Then he went on a killing spree. He went for King Ncaphayi, the king of the amaBhaca kingdom, and Faku and accused them of stealing his cattle. Again, Ndlela let both escape unscathed and returned with even fewer cattle. The whites in Port Natal misunderstood these losses and thought that the Zulu army had lost its invincibility, whereas Ndlela was sabotaging Dingane's delusions. Next was poor Hlambamanzi, whom he suspected of being a double agent because he spoke European languages so well. Dingane ordered Cane to personally kill Hlambamanzi but Cane could not bring himself to do it. Ogle volunteered to do it and in February 1832, after a long bloody gun battle, Jacob *Jacot Hlambamanzi* Msimbithi was gunned down - but only after he had run out of bullets. Cane helped himself to his 80 cattle as payment of killing Hlambamanzi. That was a sad end of someone who had served the Zulu empire so well.

The killings of Magaye and Mdlaka were bad enough, but the killing of Hlambamanzi - a person with such special skills - was the last straw even for Dingane's most fervent supporters. The orgy of senseless killings traumatised everyone and Dingane was publicly condemned. His people stopped calling him *uMalamulela*. Instead, fear gripped the nation and his deranged lust for bloodletting made the military mutinous. It took Ndlela's exceptional skill to maintain order. Dingane's lunacy made Shaka's excesses look harmless. For example, some people were hiding in forests, bushes and caves, while others were streaming south to live in exile under the whites in Port Natal. Sotobe managed to convince Dingane to apologise publicly for his recent wanton killings especially of the military, Magaye, Mdlaka and Hlambamanzi. For some inexplicable reason, Dingane listened and sent royal messengers all over the empire to beg people to either come back from exile or come out of their hiding places. The depopulation was so bad that, for a while, large tracts of land around Port Natal, including KwaNjanduna Palace, a major *ikhanda* on the northern banks of the uMdlothi River were deserted. Dingane gave Sotobe the responsibility of ensuring that all returnees had enough land and cattle to begin a new life.

This is partly why when the first white colonisers came to this part of the Zulu empire, they assumed that it was deserted and declared it *terra nullius*. Some claimed that the local Africans people originated from the Congo Basin and the African Great Lakes region and came down via the Great Rift Valley. They also said local Africans arrived in South Africa at the same time with the colonisers. This distorted view of history used to be taught in South African schools and published in the textbook *History Syllabus for Kaffirs*. The truth is that the prehistoric presence of human beings in South Africa has been proven many times before. For example, the University of Toronto made an announcement in April 2012 that they had uncovered scientific evidence of human occupation at the Wonderwerk Cave in Kuruman, Northern Cape, from a million years ago. The research team reported finding well-preserved ash plant material and burnt bone fragment deposited *in situ* on discrete surfaces and mixed within sediment. Some of their unearthed fragments showed evidence of surface discolouration typical of a controlled burn and not a wildfire or any other natural event. Whereas evidence of human occupation from 100 000 years ago was also scientifically proven at eNgodini (*Border Cave*) near Ngwavuma and an infant's skeleton adorned in shells was discovered in 1942.

The military high command was obliged to react to what was being whispered throughout the valleys and mountain tops. People were saying '*Buzani kuMkabayi*' (let Mkabayi provide a solution), the ultimate custodian of all things sacred in the House of Zulu. By the time the military approached her for a solution, she had heard what people were crying out for. She was aware that Dingane also targeted the *abanumzane* (nobility and aristocrats) with sizeable property; those with many cattle or those with many daughters or wives as well as those who were close to Shaka such as Nxazonke. Dingane had him killed on the same day Phampatha and Ngwadi were murdered. It became clear to Mkabayi that Dingane was perpetuating what he had accused Shaka of doing. She was hard-pressed to remember a single incident where Shaka had shed blood without reason. As far as she was concerned, Shaka's insane acts were justifiable. For instance, the occasions where people felt the killing was unjustifiable when he ordered the killing of *udibi* when they were caught peeping, when he was making love to his women.

Everyone knew that breaking the rule was punishable by death, including the naughty *udibi*. If uFasimba regiment was genuinely mourning the passing of his mother, they should have known better than entertaining erections at the sight of almost naked young women, dancing by raising their shapely legs sky-high in their faces. As Mkabayi sat in her hut, she could visualise Shaka, the beads of sweat on his nose, his love for practical jokes, his offbeat sense of humour and his love for song and dance. Above all, she remembered his love for the Zulu empire, which he put above everything else. Mkabayi sighed loudly, but there was no one to hear her hollow sigh and no mountains to echo her tired yawn. She was in agony, but she knew she needed to act swiftly, even though she had not anticipated doing anything so drastic so soon.

The white Zulu subjects Fynn, Collins and Cane, who had been claiming to be friends of the Zulu people all along, led an attack against Ndlela near Port Natal in June 1833. They waited for him as he returned from fighting Ncaphayi, Faku and other Xhosa kingdoms in the south. Ndlela routed them and only a handful barely escaped with their lives. The ringleaders knew that Dingane would avenge this miscalculated bravado so Collins, Cane, Fynn and the rest of the mercenaries fled south to their friend Faku and arrived in his capital in September 1834. Mkabayi became more vigilant about what was happening around the Zulu empire. She was happy that Ndlela was heeding her advice of bringing back as few cattle as possible and not winning any war except of course, putting the whites in their place. Dingane and Mkabayi also kept track of the large number of whites who were starting to arrive on the southern and northern borders with their wives, children and slaves, as well as large herds of livestock. They poured over the mountains on horses and mobile huts (wagons). What bothered Mkabayi most was that these whites were heavily armed. Those that arrived during Shaka's time were far more obedient and co-operative. For example, they used to *khonza*, they learnt to speak isiZulu, acquired Zulu wives and assimilated. Those who were being spewed from their floating huts (*ships*) or passed from the south going north to trade in Delagoa Bay rarely caused trouble.

The latest influx of whites at the borders appeared arrogant and aggressive. Mkabayi wished there was someone from her past with whom to share her worries, but all her confidantes were dead. Ndlela and the old woman agreed that the only way to curb Dingane's indulgences was to sabotage his egoistic military campaigns and boost the number of Mpande's followers. Ndlela had to continue to retreat from as many battles as possible and encourage the regiments to temporarily defect to Durban. Dingane also became concerned as the number of whites was steadily on the rise and he wondered if they were the *'swallows'* Shaka spoke about when he was dying. Dingane looked around and found that he had no one he could talk to. He merely grunted to himself and continued to grind his short teeth. He even once seriously considered seeking advice from Mkabayi, but his fragile ego would not let him. He still needed to prove to her that he was his own man and Mkabayi made him face his insecurities. For instance, after fleeing from KwaDukuza he had not paid her a courtesy call. He did not even go to gloat about the size of his outrageous palace or how well he thought he was running the empire. Equally Mkabayi had neither visited nor congratulated him.

Afrikaners had a sect called the *Voortrekker* (poineer) whose objective was to colonise the African continent and ambitions to go as far north as Egypt. They called their trip the Great Trek and their first recorded departure from the Cape Colony was in 1834. They left in groups and took their families and the Khoi, Xhosa, Kham, San, Griqua, Goringhaicona, Chainoqua, Goringhaiqua, servants and slaves with them. Their slaves were forced to guide them through the treacherous passes in the great Outeniqua and Drakensberg mountains ranges and where to ford the big rivers such as the *Gariep* (Orange), *uMzimvubu* (Buffalo), *iGwa* (Vaal) and uThukela. They also helped the colonisers avoid malaria-infested areas and cured them of tropical diseases, raging fevers, scorpion bites, snake bite and showed them how to handle prowling lions and raging rhinos through their indigenous knowledge. The group led by Dr Andrew Cowan, Lt Donovan, Rev Anderson and two Kruger brothers ended up settling in Limpopo in an area whose rocks glistened with water. They named the place the *Waterberg* (Water Mountains) and called the local river *'Nyl'* (the Nile) River because they thought that they had finally arrived in Egypt and hoped to stumble upon the awesome pyramids. Piet Uys's group headed to the Zulu empire that had been described as the proverbial Canaan. Uys had heard that the land had abundant rainfall, green rolling valleys, a mild climate and, above all, its indigenous people the Zulu, were admired for their iron-fist discipline.

When Uys arrived in the area around Durban, he could have sworn it was indeed the Promised Land. He rushed to go to *khonza* in uMgungundlovu, but uThukela River was flooded. Uys was struck down by malaria while waiting for the river to subside and they resorted to shouting across the river and requested people to *khonza* for them. But when he recovered, and the river had subsided, instead of going to the capital, Uys went back to the Cape to recruit more Afrikaners to follow him to the Zulu empire, his land of milk and honey. The mercenaries, led by Andries Potgieter, camped south of the Vaal River in October 1836 and were given a baptism of fire by Mzilikazi's commander-in-chief Mkhaliphi Ndiweni. They had several skirmishes and after one of the fights, Mkhaliphi took about forty thousand cattle, around 100 horses and about 60 000 sheep and goats. In this fight, Mkhaliphi was particularly brutal because he even killed all the women and children and spared only two little girls and a boy whom he found hiding in the Liebenberg house and carried them off as a gift to Mzilikazi. The colonisers retaliated in January 1837 and attacked Mzilikazi's palace in Mosega and their last war was fought at Mzilikazi's biggest palace *eGabeni* (Kapain) for over nine days in November 1837.

The next wave of whites who went to *khonza* in uMgungundlovu were different. They called themselves missionaries and preached the *Ten Commandments* based on a book called the Holy Bible. They always emphasised the seventh commandment, 'thou shall not steal' as though the Zulu had problems with theft. But within a few years, they behaved just like the non-missionary colonisers and became as ruthless and appropriated land without compensation. Captain Allen Francis Gardiner arrived in the Zulu empire with his interpreter from the Cape Colony with George Cyrus and a wealthy Polish refugee JF Berken, who was en route to New South Wales in Australia. After sending a message to *khonza*, Gardiner was the first person who tried to make Dingane a Christian. But Dingane sent a clear message to him that he had no interest in his version of an omnipotent, vengeful white God, but was interested in him as a military man. Before meeting the king, he had practised how to be a 'missionary' on both Zulu and non-Zulu residents in Durban without formal training. Dingane wanted him to train the army to use modern weaponry. Dingane was even less inclined to grant him permission to set up mission stations around the kingdom.

Only when Gardiner agreed to conduct training, did Dingane meet with the self-made 'missionary'. He made him tiptoe behind him on his way to eMbelebeleni as he walked with his favourite dog, a black Great Dane *Maklwilana*, which used to belong to Shaka. After listening briefly to what Gardiner had to say, he said that he did not like his God that sends his own 'creation' to eternal hell if they do not convert to Christianity. But he made a concession that the white subjects could practise their religion in Durban and nowhere else in the empire. When Dingane was satisfied that Gardiner was an obedient Zulu subject, he allowed him to preach around the kingdom, but Gardiner chose to be Durban's resident missionary. Gardiner prayed day and night for the Durban lowlives to find Jesus but to find any of the mercenaries, hunters, misfits, thieves, murderers and runaways to be vaguely interested in a loving God, required a miracle. These people had come to Africa looking for elusive riches, power, fame and fortune. Eventually Gardiner managed to persuade a handful to attend his first service, which was held in a tent on the hill overlooking Port Natal. Gardiner named the place *Berea* after reading from the Bible, Acts 2:10-11.

The same tent was also used as the first covered European school in the empire. The first recorded Zulu people to be literate were two girls and four boys. Dingane's aimable overtures to his subjects was not making headway because more and more people continued to escape to Port Natal. The influx made whites jittery and they sent a message to Dingane promising to report all the Zulu who intended to live in Port Natal permanently. Instead of a response, the port was gripped with absolute terror when they heard that Dingane was heading south, in person. They thought he was coming to slaughter them and went as far as sending Gardiner and his servant, Mpondombini, to give Dingane a present.

However, by the time they arrived in uMgungundlovu, Dingane had already left. Dingane was visiting KwaKhangela near Port Natal and whites were the last thing on his mind. A few years later Gardiner finally established a mission near the *ikhanda* of iNtontela called Ogwagwini. But he warned all those he was trying to convert not to use the mission as an 'underground railroad' for those fleeing Dingane's excesses. But Gardiner only made that announcement after he heard that Dingane was screaming blue murder that he had allowed one of Dingane's wives Nona, their children Mamisani, Nombabi, Mphathikazi, the nanny Nongubo and their bodyguard Mbube, who had already escaped from KwaNjanduna Palace to use the mission as their halfway house to Port Natal. When Gardiner found out, he was so petrified of what Dingane would do to him that he personally hunted down the so-called 'Dingane runaways'. He found them living with Nongubo's grandfather Mankanjana and frogmarched them and others to uMgungundlovu but left the children behind. Dingane killed Nona and the runaways immediately and demanded the children back. But one of the whites had already taken them as slaves and refused to hand his 'merchandise' back. The children were finally rescued after a pitched gun battle by a 60-strong force of Zulu men and they grew up under close tutelage of Dingane.

After this dramatic incident, Gardiner claimed that Dingane had made him a 'chief' of all the land between the uThukela and uMzimvubu Rivers from the sea in the east to the Drakensberg in the west. Now that he was a 'chief', he called the first whites-only public meeting in Port Natal but only 17 whites turned up. Without getting permission from Dingane, he allotted them individual plots within the town's boundaries but no Zulu living there was allotted any plot. He fixed the property prices at between six and seven pence a plot for those who could afford it. Those without any money were given the plots for free. Gardiner also proclaimed that only European-style houses and shops were permitted within the town boundaries and anything that resembled a Zulu structure such as round huts would be torn down. The whites were ecstatic to own a piece of land in their own name, something that would have never happened in their countries of birth. On the 23rd of June 1835, Gardiner chaired a meeting in JF Berken's hut attended by about 15 whites, including John Cane; J Collins; Francis; Pickman; Henry Ogle; P Kew; George Cyrus; J Mouney; R Wood; R Carden; R King; J Pierce; EC Toohey and they resolved to rename the settlement. They named it *D'urban*, after the Cape Colony Governor Sir Benjamin D'Urban, a sadist who confiscated the livestock of all the Africans living west of Great Kei River. Unprovoked, he drove them across the river with nothing and many of them died of starvation.

When Gardiner was happy with the progress of the construction of the town, he left for England to recruit more missionaries. His daughter Julia, was the first white child to be buried in Durban on thr 12th May, 1837. During his absence, three American missionaries, Reverends Aldrin Grout, George Champion and Dr Newton Adams, sailed into Durban on the *Dove*. They went to *khonza* and they could establish mission schools such as *uMlazi*, which was established on the 12th of February 1836. Their first pupils were 12 Zulu children and a single white boy, William Wood. Their class was under a tree where they learnt to write the alphabet in the sand. School was too boring for the 14-year-old Wood, so he quit after a few weeks. He went hunting and later lived at uMgungundlovu and participated in shooting lessons with the army. The next American mission was called *KwaNginani* alongside Msunduze River, about 26 kilometres north of uThukela River and about 20 kilometres inland from Mandeni Train Station. Rev Champion preached his first sermon on the 26th of September 1836 to a handful of potential Zulu converts. Reverend Grout and his wife Charlotte established *Groutville* mission near Stanger. They also built a sugar mill called uMvoti (Melville) Sugar Mill. The Grouts joined the first white couple to settle in uMvoti in 1836, Willem Landman and his wife Maria (Piet Retief's daughter).

Four months after Dingane had allowed the Americans to establish mission schools, he mobilised four regiments including the iNdumezulu Rifle Corps, about 30 white Zulu subjects and about forty Durban-based Zulu subjects to attack the Swazis under the command of Ndlela. For a change, the Commander Ndlela did not sabotage the battle, and the Swazi's were thoroughly defeated, and the successful Zulu's came back with numerous cattle. After this battle, Dingane made firearms the only currency for white hunters to buy tusks and other valuable merchandise in the empire. He bought enough ammunition and modern weaponry to establish a fully stocked armoury at the capital. It was run by a San man called Jan Bouwer, the main was shooting instructor as well as responsible for fixing and servicing the arsenal. Gardiner returned with a real English missionary Rev Francis Owen, his wife, Owen's sister and a Welsh maid Jane Williams aboard the *Palmyra*. They established *Hambanathi* mission about 40 kilometres north of the uThongathi River. Rev Owen's first pupils were not only the princes and princesses but Dingane himself, which made him the first literate Zulu monarch. He used to write his own letters to people in Delagoa Bay, Durban and the Cape. But he died not having changed his mind about their God and never converted to Christianity. The borders south of the empire were a hive of colonial resistance by the Xhosa kings, especially King Ndlambe against the British and Afrikaner commandos.

One of the white ring leaders in the forefront of raiding the Xhosa was a colourful Afrikaner character Piet Retief. He is portrayed as a hero with dazzling virtues and a great achiever. Yet, the real Retief was a loud and boisterous man that led an impractical and irresponsible life and dreamt of numerous get-rich-quick schemes. He lived at his parents' home until he was over 30 years old and went on to an unenvious life of failure. He borrowed 30 000 Rixi Dollars (17th Century South African currency) from several people to buy *Kromme Rhee* wine farm but lost his farm due to poor management. Through his excellent powers of persuasion, he borrowed more money in Grahamstown and bought his second wine farm *Elsenburg* which left him bankrupt. He did not give up and bought yet another farm *Waarburg* and again ran it at a loss. His last wine farm *Patryssen Vallei* was repossessed. He decided to reinvent himself and turned his boundless energy and attention to new commercial endeavours. He simultaneously dabbled as an auctioneer, builder, miller, baker and a slave trader. Even then, he ended up poor as ever. His last resort to redemption was to make a name for himself by joining the commandos. Comical as he was, in 1812 he was given the command of 150 men, despite his lack of military training.

While he was on the front, he prayed to survive long enough to execute his next cunning plan. He planned to find an unsuspecting female, preferably a rich one and marry her so that his persistent financial woes would end. A rich widow with nine children, Magdalena Johanna Greyling, fitted the profile. She owned four slaves and a big farm *Mooimeisesfontein* where she reared hundreds of cattle and sheep. Life on the frontier was not meant for a single woman. So, without trying too hard, Retief tried his luck and she agreed to marry him in 1814 and they had six children. By the end of 1821, Retief was a proud owner of almost 40 African slaves but when he encountered financial trouble, as always, he was forced to sell them all to settle his debts.

Twice he sold his strong, well-built African male slave Jeck who came from Mozambique. First to a C Wentzel on the 10th of June 1822 for a 3000 Rixi Dollars debt, then the same slave, a Mrs. Thalman on the 12th of August 1822. This caused serious problems because both parties wanted him badly. Retief's problems worsened in the following two years because he appeared in court 24 times for unpaid debts. He even had to part with his favourite imported English stallion *Tempest* as well as his 25 plots he had accrued around Grahamstown. By 1829 the wife's farm, cattle, sheep and slaves were all gone. Retief tried to stem the loss of his dwindling fortunes by building a Dutch Reformed Church on the farm he was living on. That seemed to work because he was hired by the Stellenbosch Town Council to construct a major road through the town. But he built a road that was riddled with potholes and was washed away during the first rains. He had diverted some of the road construction money into stockpiling grain. He had hoped to benefit from the high prices that would follow, after some engineered crisis but again he failed. He then abandoned Stellenbosch and moved to Grahamstown hoping to pull yet another trick.

Eventually, he led a bunch of Afrikaner dissidents and they wrote an angry article in the local newspaper the *Graham's Town Journal* on the 22nd of January 1837. They called it 'The Emigrants' Manifesto', a vague and abstract article that blamed the English for the lack of justice, liberty, lack of security on the farms, cattle theft and robbery by their Xhosa neighbours. However, their biggest gripe was with the abolishment of slavery. As far as they were concerned, the prospect of life without slaves was too hard to contemplate. When their article did not change anything, the almost 60-year-old Retief found enough energy to run away from his failures and become a coloniser. He dragged his long-suffering wife, some English, German and Afrikaner thrill seekers, their African slaves, mixed-race servants and livestock and slowly trudged north-east. They pulled 1000 wagons into the unknown and prayed for divine intervention the whole way.

They weathered Africa's inhospitable wilderness, harrowing winds, flooded rivers and persistent tropical diseases. They eventually glimpsed the lofty peaks of the Drakensberg (*uKhahlamba*) Mountains after a few months of sheer misery. They prayed, set up camp and admired the breathtaking panorama, their 'Promised Land' and rested. They climbed the majestic mountain range and began their epic descent into the Zulu empire in September 1837. They went through natural mountain passes which they called *Bezuidenhout Pass* and *De Beers Pass*. The sick, old and frail were carried down on stretchers, while the women and children cautiously crawled on all fours unsure what lay beyond each shrub and plant. The men sweated, cursed, pushed and pulled the wagons down the mountain and the short descent lasted the whole week. They established a *laager* (a camp formed with wagons parked in a defensive circle) that they called *Doornkop*. Once they recovered from the arduous journey and descent, they saw no need to ask for permission to occupy the land of the Zulu. After all, they had arrived in their Promised Land.

In the following months, more Afrikaners followed Retief and at times more than a 100 of them poured into the Zulu empire a day. They lived close to one another and they too did not bother to *khonza*. However, they noticed that they were being watched and it spooked them, thinking about the Frontier Wars n and around the land of the Xhosa people. The whites that had arrived before the Voortrekkers pleaded with the newcomers to go to the capital to *khonza* officially, lest they regret it. But the newcomers were arrogant and took weeks to make an appointment, which was noted by Dingane. When they requested an appointment, Dingane kept them waiting for three months and saw them on the 5$^{th}$ of November 1837. Unsure of the reception they could expect at the palace, Retief suggested that 200 of the men should go with him as a show of force. But he was overruled and only six men ended up going with Cane and Halstead interpreted for them. When they arrived at the capital, they found a seething Dingane seated with a terrified-looking Rev Owen, frantically clutching his Bible. Dingane then accused Retief of stealing 300 royal cattle and killing one of the royal shepherds, King Jobe Sithole's grandson. Retief obviously denied it and blamed Queen Manthanisi's son Sekhonyela who was now king of the Batlokwa kingdom (a non-Nguni people). Dingane said that to prove that Retief was innocent, he had to bring in Sekhonyela and the cattle to the capital or face immediate death together with their families. Retief reluctantly agreed. After two days at the capital the mood relaxed, and Retief was informed about the rules and regulations of the empire.

Dingane threw them a lavish party as new subjects and Rev Champion and Rev Owen were also invited. They were entertained with food, song and dance and the mercenaries were happy. So far, the hazardous trip inland had been worth it. The visitors were mesmerised by Dingane's colossal palace as well as its intricate decoration. Retief noted in his diary that: 'It was spherical, 22 foot in diameter, supported in the interior by 22 pillars which were covered in beads and the floor was perfectly smooth and shone like a mirror...' whereas Reverend Owen noted in his diary that: '... the king's hut does great honour to native architecture. It is very spacious, lofty and exquisitely neat, the floor is bright with polished marble, the fireplace tastily devised, and the roof formed of sticks closely compacted together, supported by 20 pillars covered in beads...'

Life among the Zulu people was good for the new subjects. For instance, when Retief turned 67, he threw a lavish party on the 12th of November 1837 and invited Rev Champion, Dr Wilson and Rev Henry Venables, whose mission was along uMbaya River. A few days later, Retief organised a hunting party to find Sekhonyela. They found him after four weeks. He told the unsuspecting Sekhonyela that the visit was to trade in elephant tusks with him. To celebrate the newfound friendship, they drank copious amounts of alcohol and Sekhonyela was tricked into putting his hands into handcuffs. Then Retief took all of Sekhonyela's guns, food, 700 cattle and dragged him to their settlement. The Boers then argued for days about who would hand Sekhonyela, the royal cattle and other loot to Dingane. On the 16th of January 1838, about 200 of them met in Retief's dwelling to make the final decision. The loudmouth and biggest coward in the group, Gert Maritz, said they should not go to Dingane at all. He suggested that they should keep the guns and food as they were not part of the deal but agreed to make Sekhonyela their slave. Initially, no one agreed with him, but they changed their minds after Sekhonyela promised large tracts of land in his kingdom. In the end, about 70 mercenaries including Retief's son, Piet Retief junior, Magdalena's son, Abraham, Barend Liebenburg, Piet Meyer, Jan Robertssen and Hercules Malan as well as their 40 mixed-race servants were brave enough to face Dingane on the 25th of January 1838.

Before they left the camp at dawn, Rev Erasmus Smit led a prayer and benediction in Retief's tent. They sang the 4$^{th}$ and 6$^{th}$ morning psalms at the top of their voices. There was tension as they departed firing shots into the early morning sky. Maritz was so afraid of dying that he did not even attend the prayer meeting. Hence Retief thumped on his tent as he lay curled up in the foetal position and shouted: '*Tot siens, bang broek*' (So long, scaredy pants) and galloped away. They only arrived in uMgungundlovu on a Saturday, the 3$^{rd}$ of February with only 300 cattle and without Sekhonyela. Dingane was incensed when they appeared heavily armed, with few cattle and without Sekhonyela. Dingane pretended to believe them when they said that they did not find Sekhonyela. As usual, there was entertainment and they were encouraged to stay for as long as they wanted. The following day, a Sunday, Retief enjoyed himself so much that in a drunken stupor he started having delusions of grandeur. Oblivious to his fate, he walked about the palace telling everyone that Dingane had given him most of the empire because of the cattle he had recovered. He even waved around a title deed he claimed was signed by Dingane giving him the land between uThukela and uMzimvubu River. These claims made Dingane even angrier because they could not be further from the truth.

On Monday evening, the 5$^{th}$ of February, Retief's men were caught sneaking around on their horses, looking for a way to enter the secluded section of the palace reserved for *imidlunkulu*. The first thing all newcomers to the Zulu empire were warned against, even before being informed about capital offences and the constitution, was never dare go near that part of the palace instead of the warning, they persisted. Halstead pleaded for their lives and claimed that they had gone astray while looking for some of their lost horses – even though it was in the middle of the night. The truth was that they were looking for the ravishing maidens because most of Retief's commandos had come without girlfriends or wives. Despite the profuse apology, it became clear to Halstead that they had crossed the line and their lives were in grave danger. He then suggested that they should leave the following day which they did. Dingane was informed about the attempted intrusion in the early hours of the morning on the 6$^{th}$ of February and he flew into a murderous rage. As far as he was concerned, they had signed their death warrants. Then Ndlela, Nzobo and Sigananda came up with a fail-proof plan to kill them in accordance with Zulu law, as well as to take their much-needed arms.

When Retief's delegation went to bid Dingane farewell in the morning they were requested to attend a farewell function in the main parade ground within the palace. They agreed, and they were also asked to leave their horses, luggage, bags, personal items, saddles and firearms at the entrance of the palace. The festivities began and again, they were hypnotised by the scantily dressed *imidlunkulu* dancing right up to their faces while they were being plied with meat and with even more beer. The uThulwana and iHlaba regiments also sang and danced dressed in their war regalia, commanded by a young Cetshwayo. They sang the following war song:

| | |
|---|---|
| *Yiya, yiya, yiya* | *hey, hey, hey* |
| *Muntu wami KwaZulu* | *my fellow Zulu in the empire* |
| *Babezithela obishini* | *they were responsible for their tragedy* |
| *Muntu wami KwaZulu* | *my fellow Zulu in the empire* |
| *Abafokozana babethi* | *foreigners were convinced that* |
| *Kayikungena eNgome* | *he was not going to go to eNgome forest* |
| *Wangena nawe Nhlanganiso* | *yet you also went in Nhlanganiso* |
| *Wawuphika inkani ukuthi* | *you were so very sure that* |
| *Kuyakushisa eMhlahlandlela* | *Mhlahlandlela Palace would not be burnt* |
| *Awusekho, awusekho* | *it is no more, it is no more* |
| *Heyaye, heyaye muntu wami KwaZulu* | *oh yes, oh yes, my fellow Zulu in the empire* |
| *Wangena, wakhuza* | *you arrived, you gave orders* |
| *Iwawa* | *iwawa!* |
| *Mbo* | *mbo!* |

Retief and his men were to be attacked during the entertainment and the plan was that when the song leader sang *iwawa*, the regiments would respond with a war cry *mbo* and then jump on the lecherous and drunken mercenaries. Indeed, once they sang the attack word, the regiments pounced on them. They were dragged and carried out kicking and screaming to the spot where Matiwane had been killed as no killing was allowed within the confines of the palace. Even though Halstead was petrified, he still could speak isiZulu and as he was being dragged away, he shouted at the top of his voice: *'Lalelani, ngidedeleni bo, ngifuna ukukhuluma nenkosi...'* (Listen, please let me go, I want to speak to the king). But they ignored his pleas and clubbed him to death like the others. The so-called *'bulalani abathakathi'* (kill the wizards) war cry was never uttered. Retief and his 70 white mercenaries; 30 San servants and an unknown number of African slaves were all killed on Matiwane's Cliff. Below is the list of those slain on the day:

'Piet Retief; Abraham Greyling (Magdalena's son); M Oosthuijzen; J Oosthuijzen Mzn; Piet Retief Jnr (Piet's son); D Liebenberg; K Oosthuijzen; K Opperman; D Auckamp; W Basson; C de Beer; J de Beer; M de Beer; S de Beer; B van den Berg; P van den Berg; P van den Berg Jzn; J Beukes Czn; J Botha; C Bothma; C Bothma Lzn; J Brede; B Klopper; L Klopper; F Laubuschagne; H Malan; J van der Merwe; F Pretorius; M Pretorius Mzn; M Pretorius Jnr; J Robberts; G Scheepers; S Scheepers; S Smit; G Visage; J de Wet Jzn; P Meyer; B Liebenberg; P Breed; P Breed Jzn; C

Breijtenbach; L Klaassen; P Cilliers; A van Dijk; M Estherhuijzen; S Estherhuijzen; H Fourie; R Grobbler; J Hattingh; T Holstead; J Hugo Pzn; J Jooste; P Jordaan; A de Klerk; J de Klerk Jzn; J de Klerk; G Klopper; P Klopper; H Labuschagne Sn; B Oosthuizen; J Opperman; J Pretorius; M Pretorius Jzn; I Robberts; P van Schalkwijk; J Scheepers Fzn; M Scheepers Szn; M Taute; S van Vuuren; H de Wet Pzn and C Mare'.

Retief died drunk and left his unfortunate widow Magdalena with nothing. She ended up poverty stricken, selling *koeksusters* (twisted sweet doughnuts) for a living near Potchefstroom. She spent the rest of her days regretting falling for the sweet-talking Retief. Wood witnessed the slaughter because he lived at the palace. He rushed to Rev Owen's house which was nearby and found him reading his Bible. He was totally oblivious to the history taking place around him. The American Missionaries Rev Venables and Rev Brownlee arrived the same day to visit Owen and found him distraught and told them what had happened earlier in the day. When Rev Owen looked through his binoculars and saw the dead whites, he passed out. As he was being resuscitated, a royal messenger arrived to tell them that Dingane said not to worry as their lives were not in danger. But they did not believe him and three days later they all left to live in Durban. Once there they found the missionaries who were based at KwaKhangela had long abandoned their mission because they failed to convince potential Zulu converts about the purpose of a white God.

When Mkabayi heard what had happened at the capital, and for once she was proud of Dingane. What impressed her even more was that Dingane continued to kill more mercenaries and their minions who were too proud to *khonza* as subjects. He wanted to show the rest the mercenaries that he was always to be obeyed and respected in his empire. There was a bloodbath on 17th of February when several white settlements were razed at KwaNobamba, Colenso, Estcourt, along the following rivers, Bushman (*uMtshezi*), Blauwkrantz and Mord. They wiped out the Botha, Roussouw, De Beer, Bezuidenhout and Liebenberg families. They killed at least 41 white men, 56 white women, 200 mixed-race servants and an unknown number of African slaves. They took about 30 000 cattle and an even larger number of other livestock and drove them to Dingane. When the whites in Durban heard about the slaughter, they organised revenge parties. A month later to the day, Cane led a bunch of mercenaries against Ndlela's men calling themselves *The Grand Army of Natal*. It was made up of 15 white mercenaries including Robert Biggar and John Stubbs, 30 mixed-race mercenaries, 400 Durban-based Zulu mercenaries carrying muskets and 1 000 carrying shields and spears.

Cane marched to war in an old straw hat with an ostrich feather. He carried a panther skin-covered elephant gun as well as two battle flags, one flag read *iziNkumbi* and the other read '*For Justice We Fight*'. Cane truly saw himself as half a Zulu 'chief' and half as a member of the European stock. His followers came from all walks of life as well as Zulu refugees. Cane also went with numerous women carrying war rations and cattle for meat like Zulu regiments when they went to war. He marched north and torched many Zulu homesteads where there were only women, the old and infirm as the men were at eThaleni. Cane's biggest carnage was in eLenge where yet more women and children were killed, and their livestock looted. Cane suffered only two casualties, one died from a snake bite and he fatally the other one for stealing. His exploits were greatly celebrated in Durban and when the news reached the Cape, another 14 white families from Stellenbosch packed up and made their way.

To them this was a sign from God that they too, should brave the elements. They took 6000 cattle, 5000 sheep, 70 horses and 21 oxen-drawn wagons with roofs made out of white canvas. They were laden with furniture, farm tools, seeds, food, clothing, medicines, gunpowder and lead for their ammunition. They took their time travelling and occasionally allowing their cattle and sheep to graze beside them. The men rode ahead on horses to find the easiest way and the women and children followed. They read the Bible and sang hymns every morning and evening without fail until they entered the Zulu empire. They also settled without asking for permission. On the 8th of April, Piet Uys and Andries Potgieter led about 350 commandos from Durban and anticipated another easy victory. But they were stunned when they were repulsed by iNjanduna, iMihaye and uThulwana regiments under the command of Mpande, Nongalaza kaNondelumzimba (*Nondela*) Mnyandu and Madlebe kaMgedeza Zungu at the Battle of eThaleni. One of the tactics the regiments used was to pretend to run away. The overconfident mercenaries would then follow in hot pursuit and were ambushed. This is how Piet Uys and his teenage son Dirkie met their bloody end.

An extremely angry Alexander Biggar led a revenge attack six days later and crossed uThukela River on the 14th of April with Robert Russell, Joseph Brown; George Biggar (Alexander Biggar's mixed race son); John Kemble; John Cain; Henry Batt; W Bottomley; Robert Biggar; Richard Lovedale; Robert Joyce; Charles Blanckenberg; J Clark; John Stubbs; Richard Wood; Thomas Calde; William Wood; Richard King; George Duffy; thousands of Durban-based Zulu men; an unknown number of mixed-race and San people. They fought a pitched battle on the banks of uThukela River and the mercenaries were routed and the only survivors were Richard Biggar, (Alexander Biggar's son), Richard Wood (William Wood's father), John Stubbs and Dick King. The triumphant Zulu chased them all the way to Durban. When the whites in Durban heard about the carnage at the Battle of uThukela, they fled from their homes; the majority sought refuge on Captain Rodham's ship the *Comet* anchored at the bay.

Those who managed to board were Rev Owe, his wife and daughter; Dr Towey, his wife and child; Robert Dunn, his wife and children; Mr. Miller and his wife; Mr. Pitman and his wife; Mr. Heyward, his wife and children; Mr. Hull, his wife and children; Mrs. Wood and her son; William Wood; Rev Champion and his wife; Mrs. Rodham; Mr. Biggar Snr; Mrs Adams; Rev Grout; Dr Adams; Charles Adams; Jane Williams; Richard King; Henry Ogle; George Duffy, Jas Brown as well as Capt Allen Gardiner and his wife. The Zulu soldiers under the command of Cetshwayo occupied the empty houses. They helped themselves to the colourful cloth, beads, trinkets, alcohol, weapons and gunpowder. They held celebratory dances every evening for about two weeks within sight of the terrified whites who could clearly see them from the ship. This mental torture was the last straw for Rev Owen. He left for good with his family on the first ship that left the harbour, which was the *Comet* that finally left Durban on the 11th of May. The whites that remained behind, never stopped plotting after the public humiliation. They strongly believed that the Zulu were one of those minor challenges in their quest to colonise the rest of Africa.

The greatest coward, Maritz, had since become the new camp leader in Doornkop after the demise of braver men. He sat in his tent and sent messengers to request reinforcement of ammunition and men from the Cape. But after waiting for five months with nothing or no one coming, he decided to personally go collect it from Durban. But he only managed to obtain ammunition because no one was interested in fighting the Zulu on his behalf. The highly-strung Maritz was struck by fever on his way back and barely made it back alive. He was bedridden for days and finally on the 23rd of September he asked his brother-in-law Rev Smit to administer the last rites. Rev Smit cut an pitiful figure because he was severely crippled and bent over by rheumatism. He had to be carried across the flooded uThukela River in the pouring rain by strong Zulu men, who found that situation very comical. Gert '*Bang Broek*' Maritz was half the man he used to be as he lay dying. He wept like a little girl, agonising about not being able to avenge his friends. His grief-stricken wife, his devastated mother and his miserable four sons and two daughters looked at him without blinking. He was whimpering about his biggest fear that his family had to survive without him in the sea of black faces. Reverend Smit performed the last rites and there was nothing more to say.

*Piet Retief was a colourful character who lived an impractical and irresponsible life full of dreams of get-rich-quick schemes. He was killed with his men after they were caught sneaking into the secluded royal female enclave at Emperor Dingane's palace. (1820 Settlers Museum)*

*Mercenary leader Piet Uys (seated centre) with a group of mercenaries. He was killed at the Battle of eThaleni in 1838 together with his teenage son Dirkie. (SB Bourquin Collection)*

South Africa's first currency. A two rixi-dollar note used in the 18th Century in the British Colonies. (1820 Settler's Museum)

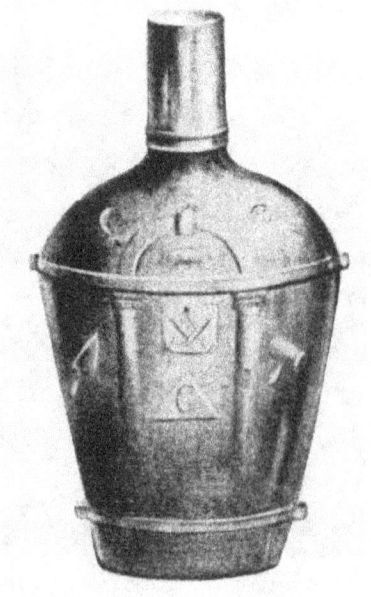

The Freemason flask belonging to Piet Retief which was found with his remains at Matiwane's Cliff. (1820 Settler's Museum)

*The Monument displaying the whites killed by the Zulu at Matiwane's Cliff, near the site of uMgungundlovu palace in uLundi, 2 January 1838. The names of their San servants and African slaves are not listed. (Shalo Mbatha)*

*Piet Retief's grave in Matiwane's Hill. (Shalo Mbatha)*

*Sign posts to Emperor Dingane's palace and to Piet Retief's grave. (Shalo Mbatha)*

**The Afrikaner Vow**

By November 1838, there were enough Afrikaners in Durban who believed they could take on the Zulu army one more time. The new leader Andries Pretoriuslanga was a rabble-rouser rearing to tear into them single-handedly, if possible. He was not prepared to wait for more commandos who had promised to come from the Cape Colony. He decided to charge into battle with a commando of 500 men called the *Wen Kommando*. It included three British mercenaries, Richard Biggar, Robert Joyce and Edward Parker, their wives and children and more than 120 African and mixed-race slaves and servants. They also had about 500 horses, 900 cattle. Their destination was uMgungundlovu and they went past Winterton, Ladysmith and Dundee before crossing the uThukela River at Skietdrift. They camped on the banks of the Washbank (*iTholeni*) River at Danspen.

What happened on the banks of the Washbank River is a matter of historical conjecture. One version is that Andries was suddenly overcome by piousness and assembled his unit into a tent and recited 'a vow'. The second version is that a general meeting was called on the banks of the stream and everyone attended and Sarel Cilliers led a prayer called 'The Vow'. The prayer was meant to bind future Afrikaner descendants to commemorate that day as a religious holiday. And, should they defeat the Zulu, a church was to be built to thank God for his grace, kindness and mercy. The third version is that a meeting took place on the banks of the stream and the 'vow' was taken but the English and their African and mixed-race servants and slaves were excluded. Additionally, Afrikaners who were in the meeting but objected to taking the 'vow' were allowed not to take it. The fourth version is that no meeting ever took place anywhere and no vow was ever made.

However, the 'vow' was honoured three years later when the 'Church of the Vow' was built in Pietermaritzburg in 1841. There is also controversy around the date when it is said to have been made. It is said it was made between the 7$^{th}$, 9$^{th}$, 15$^{th}$ or 16$^{th}$ of December 1838. What is a fact though, is that the 'vow' was never recorded verbatim. What transpired on that stream is based on several incongruous sources. For instance, Andries Pretorius's secretary Jan Bantjies wrote in his diaries that no 'vow' was made but instead, a 'promise' was made to build a house not a church, in case of victory against the Zulu. Whereas Dewald Pretorius, who took part in the battle that ensued, only wrote about what happened on the stream 24 years later. He said a meeting did take place on the banks of the stream and that the 'vow' included the building of churches and schools.

While Andries Pretorius sent an announcement to a newspaper *The Volksraad* in Pietermaritzburg on the 23$^{rd}$ of December 1838 and mentioned the 'vow' in connection with building of a church. But he said nothing about it binding future generations. Pretorius's version of the 'vow' is as follows: '*...we here, have decided among ourselves... to make known the day of our victory... among the whole of our generation and that we want to devote to God, to celebrate with thanksgiving, just as we... promised in public prayer.*' Cilliers wrote about what happened on that day 33 years later. But agreed with Bantjies that a 'promise' was made and not a 'vow'. The promise was to commemorate the day and tell the story to future generations who should remember it for eternity: '*...the day and date, every year as a commemoration and a day of thanksgiving as though a Sabbath... and that we will also tell our children that they should share in it with us, for the remembrance of future generations.*'

Whereas William Louw, the author of Sarel Cilliers' biography in English- reconstructed the 'vow' which had originally appeared in Afrikaans. It was the formidable apartheid intellectual and apologist Gustav Gerdener who ranslated Louw's 'vow' reconstruction back into Afrikaans in 1919. This reconstructed translation is what the Afrikaners adopted as their official 'vow' to this day: 'Here we stand before the Holy God of Heaven and Earth to make a vow to Him that if He will protect us and give our enemy into our hand, we shall keep this day and date every year as a day of thanksgiving like a Sabbath, and that we shall erect a house to His honour wherever it should please Him, and that we also will tell our children that they should share in that with us in memory for future generations. For the honour of His name will be glorified by giving Him the fame and honour for the victory.'

On Saturday, the 15$^{th}$ of December, the iNtibane Mountain (*Vegkop*) shook as 500 mercenaries roared through the *esikhaleni samabhunu* (Boer Pass) and took a defensive position in the valley below. They created a *laager* between the iNcome River and a steep ravine. They formed a shape that resembled the letter *D* with their wagons. They closed the gaps in-between with branches, thorns, hides and everything they could find. The wheels of the wagons were covered with ox hide and lanterns hung on the corners of the wagons while the women, children, servants, slaves and livestock hid inside the *laager*. The flooded river formed the straight line of the *D*-formation and provided a natural line of defence behind the *laager*. The ravine was on the round side of the *D*-formation.

Dingane heard that Pretorius was heading towards the capital. Ndlela on the other hand, decided to go on the offensive and engage the enemy on contact wherever the battle theatre would be. He commanded the elite forces uDlambedlu, uMxhopho, uNokhenke and uMthuyasizwe and was assisted by Nzobo. They found the enemy cowering inside their *laager* and numb with fear as they listened to the blood-curdling Zulu war chants coming from beyond the horizon. The bravado was slowly dissipating as they sat cold and hungry in the pitch-black night and outnumbered in the heart of the Zulu empire. It sounded as though a terrible end was horribly nigh. When the Zulu forces found them, they camped on the hill that is now known as *Intaba kaNdlela* (Ndlela's Mountain). After assessing the enemy's strength and formation, Ndlela was not worried about stealth. He allowed his men to light evening fires where the enemy could see them. They sat around the campfires and they discussed the battle strategy. They teased one another, danced war dances and reminisced about Mgobhozi's crazy war antics and how he used to entertain soldiers before a major battle.

They also sang songs that brought terror to the shaking enemy in the dark. The following day, before dawn on a Sunday morning, on the 16$^{th}$ of December the Zulu army was assembled in its traditional pincer formation. UDlambedlu left horn was commanded by Sikhobobo kaMababakazana Sibiya and deputised by Mpande. At first light they crossed the iNcome River at the *izibuko labafazi* (women's ford) to iNtibane Mountain. Sikhobobo sent a small unit beyond the mountain and found no hidden enemy forces. UNokhenke and uMthuyasizwe were the right horn commanded by Sikhobobo's brother, Henqa. They went to the distant Somgonqo Mountain where they were to intercept any reinforcements of the enemy. The head and chest, uMxhopho, *bahlala phezu kwamahawu* (sat on their shields) which means they waited for the attack command.

When the uDlambedlu found no enemy hiding behind the mountain, they silently surged down the mountain towards the *laager* using the thick morning mist as cover. When Pretorius and his men became aware of the army coming towards them, they shot wildly through the thick mist. But it only slowed down the tumultuous Zulu wave, but it did not stop it. Realising that the mist was not providing adequate cover for his men, Sikhobobo ordered a retreat. It took iron-fist discipline for his excited men to obey his command. But suddenly the Zulu gods were with them because out of nowhere, numerous Basotho mercenaries, wearing their distinct blankets, came rushing to reinforce the heavily outnumbered Pretorius. Sikhobobo could not believe his luck and without waiting for the attack command from Field Marshal Ndlela, he ordered his forces to charge the mounted Basotho unit in hot pursuit. They chased them over the ravine right into the *laager*, shooting and spearing many of them in the back. The mercenaries fired their three canons and

Martin-Henry rifles at everyone advancing towards them. In the melee of the battle, they could not tell the difference between their Basotho allies and the enemy in the heavy mist and gunpowder smoke. However, that did not deter them, they kept on firing and when they ran out of ammunition, hand-to-hand combat ensued. By this time the Afrikaners initial defensive front line was broken and that allowed for the livestock to stampede out of the *laager*. This caused greater mayhem as horses and cattle trampled women and children.

Pretorius was lucky to escape with his life after he was speared in the left hand. He retreated into the *laager* and hid among the screaming women and children. By the time uDlambedlu finally complied with the order to retreat from the carnage at midday, there were some Zulu casualties. For instance, two of Shaka's paternal brothers, the brave Princes Magwaza Nongqobho and Kholekile kaSenzangakhona were not so lucky. Nearly all the Basotho mercenaries were wiped out and even more white mercenaries and their minions were killed. Subsequently, Ndlela lay a siege around the *laager* for a week and hoped that Pretorius would be reinforced. But when he received intelligence about the size of the reinforcement, he left. He ordered uThuyasizwe and uNokhenke to remain behind, split up into smaller units and take cover out of sight. The reinforcements from Pietermaritzburg and Durban rushed over Somgonqo Mountain to bring relief to their brethren. But Henqa's men ambushed them and killed them and took all the supply - food, medicines and above all gunpowder and weapons. When the military command was satisfied that no more reinforcements were forthcoming, they leisurely marched back to the capital. Reinforcements only arrived after the Zulu army had left and they did not pursue them. Instead, they tended to the starving souls, mostly women and children, that had survived inside the *laager*. However, years later, the Afrikaner historians claimed that they were victorious. They claimed that the Zulu army had attacked their *laager* from the river. Hence, they were able to kill them all and the river turned red with their blood. The differing Zulu account of events is hardly mentioned in public discourse.

The controversy about who won this battle is based on the conflicting claims about who was standing where. The Afrikaner historians claim that the straight line of the *laager*'s D-formation was along the ravine. That means Pretorius and his men were facing the river, therefore the Zulu attacked them from the river. Meaning that they swam with one hand, the other hand they held up the big war shield, the spear and a gun and bullets above the water. They also claim that they obliterated at least 20

000 warriors within a few hours causing the river to turn red with their blood, hence they changed the name of the river from iNcome to Blood River. Whereas other historians, including the Zulu, say that Afrikaners were attacked from the ravine and that it is the Afrikaners that were killed in large numbers. The glorious military history of the Zulu army and the illustrious military career of Field Marshal Ndlela does not correlate with the defeat assumption. Furthermore, looking at Ndlela's previous military tactics, it is highly unlikely that he would have exposed his men to direct fire and made them swim with one hand. Supposing Ndlela made his men cannon fodder, he would have been haunted by the question: *'Ngothini kalinda, noNdaba, nabakithi uma ngingabulalisa amabutho eSilo?'* (How will I explain myself to Malandela, Ndaba and my ancestors for causing the death of the emperor's regiments?). It is a question that was instilled in the psyche of all Zulu soldiers as soon as they joined a regiment.

Even though many Afrikaners believed that their ancestors were triumphant, yet when the same Afrikaner ancestors started commemorating the 'victory' only 20 years later and it was commemorated as *Dingane's Day*. The reason why the Afrikaner's 'sacred' day was named after their arch enemy, who was not even at the battle, is a matter of conjecture. The Afrikaners have continued to revere this date. They inaugurated the Voortrekker Monument in Pretoria on the 16th of December 1949. Also, when the Afrikaner political party the Nationalist Party came into power in 1948, it used the 16th of December 1838 to legitimise their alleged uniqueness and historical relationship with God. Then they declared it a public holiday in 1952 and changed it from *Dingane's Day* to *Day of the Covenant* or the *Day of the Vow*.

But for most Africans, especially the Zulu this day was special because as far as they were concerned, the Zulu army proved their military superiority and bravery over the whites. Furthermore, to commemorate the defeat of the Afrikaners by Dingane, South Africa's first revolutionary movement, the African National Congress formed its military wing uMkhonto weSizwe on the 16th of December 1961 and called it *Heroes Day*. After South Africa's first democratic government, it was called *Day of Reconciliation*. This controversial day continues to be celebrated. But it is the perfect example of South Africa's many idiosyncrasies. Afrikaner 'victory' celebrations take place at iNcome on the spot where they believe the battle took place, between the river and the ravine. While the Zulu 'victory' spectacle takes place closer to where the Zulu say the battle took place. These annual celebrations are less than one kilometre apart.

As the Afrikaners licked their wounds in December 1838, the tension between Mpande and Dingane was tangible. Mpande was now being openly lobbied to oust Dingane who was, by now, an outright blood thirsty monster. The grand old schemer, Mkabayi ensured that Dingane was aware that his days were numbered and that haunted him. He accepted that he had also fallen out of favour with the army and was aware that any resistance was futile against Mkabayi. He waited for Ndlela to leave to sort Pretorius and the Afrikaner forces out and since he did not feel safe amongst all those thousands of people, he acted fast. He decided to re-evaluate his life in the damp and dark iNgome forest. His rationale was that he wanted to be where he could easily escape, rather than worry about every footstep approaching his inner royal sanctuary. Hence, he personally supervised the evacuation of about 50 000 people from the capital. He also removed the food supplies, livestock and valuables such as the national treasures *inkatha* (grass coil) and *inhlendla* (the royal harpoon shaped spear) which the Zulu monarch carries to this day.

As they departed, Dingane stood on his favourite spot and took one last sweeping glance at his ostentatious palace and admitted to himself that the size had not achieved its purpose of overshadowing Shaka greatness. He sighed and instructed the army soldiers to torch it. Then he began his long, slow walk into the lower rungs of history with his personal regiment *iziTholatholi* or *iziThoyathoyi*. With a heavy heart, Dingane crossed the uMkhumbane River and climbed the famous iZihlalo mountain in eMahlabathini. He sat down and watched the enormous flames engulf his ego. After reminiscing about his miserable life, littered with more innocent blood than that of the enemy, he crossed the White and Black iMfolozi Rivers. He ended up settling in the area that is part of the Hluhluwe iMfolozi Game Reserve. Here he built a miniature palace and called it *uMgungundlovana* (Little Elephant Swallower) along the iVuna River. When the survivors in the laager heard that Dingane's palace was deserted and on fire, they rushed there hoping to salvage valuables from the fire. They rummaged looking for glass beads, jewellery, tusks, copper, gold and firearms as well as their biggest desire weapons, women and cattle.

Instead they found nothing of value, neither livestock nor women, but mere burnt out trinkets. But they ventured outside the palace and tripped over bones and some skeletons still had their hats or boots on. Their worst nightmare was confirmed by Retief's distinctive flask with the Freemason symbol. That is why there is the belief that that he was a Freemason. They rummage was indeed at Matiwane's Cliff and they buried all their brethren they could find with some dignity and even put a rudimentary cross on their mass grave. They kicked the stones cursed and shot in the air desperately wanting to revenge. But they did not want to risk ending up like their friends and have their bones devoured by wild animals as they grieved. Ndlela was informed by the secret service that some mercenaries were seen around Retief's bones and screaming revenge. Ndlela decided to use their weakness against them. He asked for a volunteer (*idelakufa*) to go on a suicide mission. Astoundingly, nearly the whole army raised their right hand and begged to be chosen. Ndlela was spoilt for choice but decided on a member of the military high command Bhongoza kaMefu Ngcobo. He took him aside, briefed him about the secret mission. After the briefing, Bhongoza openly started reciting Shaka's laudatory praises and the whole army joined him, then they performed *ingomane* and shouted '*Sigidi*'.

As hair-raising and heart-thumping war salutes resounded across the valleys, then Bhongoza broke into a steady jog. They looked at him, as he disappeared into the shimmering horizon without looking back, envious. As the Afrikaners weighed up their revenge options, if at all, the deathly silence was shattered by the sudden appearance of their scouts dragging a 'terrified' Zulu man. They released their pent-up anger on him, thoroughly assaulting him. When they were tired, they wanted to know if he was a member of the military high command. He said he was only a lowly soldier and began to sob. Under normal circumstances, a Zulu man was not allowed to demean himself, especially before a non-Zulu. According to the Zulu adage anyone who is a non-Zulu is a non-human therefore, *isilwane* (animal) - especially whites.

Bhongoza told them that he was running away from Dingane, who had killed his whole family for entertainment, and sought their protection. Instead of showing him any compassion, they accused him of being a spy and hanged him upside down. Before losing consciousness, Bhongoza managed to tell them that he knew where Dingane's prized royal cattle were hidden. They quickly untied him as the prospect of owning royal cattle changed their mood immediately. Then they chained him around the neck and made him run next to the horse, still with his wounds still bleeding. After a few hours walking in the blazing sunlight, Bhongoza showed them the magnificent herd. They stopped dead in their tracks and admired the cattle and for a minute they forgot about Bhongoza. The cattle grazed under the trees at the bottom of the valley. Some drank water from the tiny Ophathe River, unguarded. The whole valley was sheltered in picturesque tranquillity, an idyllic Zulu rural day. Women were leisurely collecting firewood, singing, talking and laughing, while others were drawing water from the stream with their babies on their backs. Under the shade of mimosa trees, herd boys played with mud cow figurines, others were stick fighting and the younger ones were swinging on willow tree branches laughing mirthfully.

The Afrikaners scanned the valley from top to bottom and sensed no danger and thanked their Afrikaner gods. Without wasting any more time, they split into two groups and raced down the valley on either side of the herd, barely containing their excitement. Suddenly, the all too familiar numbing Zulu war chants and hissing shattered the peace. The Afrikaners could not believe their ears. This time, they stared at each other across the trees and hoped to wake up from this terrible nightmare. They squinted through the haze in search of the flayed Bhongoza, but he was nowhere to be seen. It quickly dawned on them that their greed had led them to their demise and the 'aggrieved' Bhongoza was part of an elaborate trap. The army had camouflaged themselves in the long grass with their shields and weapons and at the right moment, charged at the dumbfounded Afrikaners. They were slaughtered and Bhongoza became an instant hero. This incident is the basis of the Zulu idiom, *ukuholela umuntu Ophathe* (to ambush someone).

The Afrikaners had a miserable year. Within 12 weeks they had suffered a huge loss of life, including their women and children. They fought at the Battle of eThaleni, at the Battle of uThukela, and at the Battle of *iNcome* (Blood) River. The slaughter at Ophathe valley on the 27$^{th}$ of December was a late Christmas present for the Zulu army and the last humiliation the Afrikaners suffered in 1838. Dingane amassed more firearms and formed isiThunyisa Rifle regiment, like Shaka's iNdumezulu, deep in the forest. He was fixated on finding a final solution for the Afrikaners and planned grand military campaigns that would have made Shaka envious. Unfortunately, all the plans remained inside his head because no one took him seriously any longer. He would plan a strategy with the military high command, and they would agree with him. But they would do the opposite once they arrived at the battle theatre, just to annoy him.

Even Ndlela was now in the habit of 'losing' wars. The Afrikaners found out that Dingane was increasingly being isolated and they made overtures towards him. They said if he gave them 10 000 royal cattle for the hardship of the wars, they would sign a peace agreement with him and protect him from his own army. To everyone's surprise, Dingane agreed but asked for some time to organise the cattle. Instead, he sent Ndlela and four regiments including John Cane to raid cattle in eSwatini. Ndlela made it clear to Dingane that he did not agree with giving the Afrikaners cattle. But he complied and the battle took place deep in Swazi territory in Mzimpofu near Manzini. After a brief fight, the Swazi capitulated and Ndlela took a few cattle. Dingane was incensed when he saw the lousy number of cattle and seriously interrogated Ndlela's loyalty because the Swazi were not known for their bravery. In fact, as far as Dingane was concerned, fighting the Swazi for cattle was no different than going cattle shopping. But now he had no cattle of value to offer his newfound 'allies' the Afrikaners - which was a problem.

Dingane's decision to retreat to the forest left a leadership vacuum in the Zulu empire. Once again, attention turned to the ageing Mkabayi, who undoubtedly became regent. She viewed the turn of events with great sadness and deeply regretted believing the lily-livered coward and liar called Dingane. He had gone into hiding in broad daylight, which was considered un-Zulu. She secretly agreed with Ndlela and a chosen few that the time had finally come for Mpande to ascend to the throne.

# 7

# Emperor Mpande kaSenzangakhona

MPANDE LIVED AN UNEVENTFUL life for many years at his Emqakavini Palace near eLenge. He later moved to eMangweni Palace near aMatigulu River on the lee side of Ongoye Mountains where he continued his prosaic existence. All he did was gorge himself on food and have many children with his many wives and *imidlunkulu*. He had inherited his mother's black sores that later developed into leprosy. Some of his descendants have the same sores to this day. In his younger days he occasionally went to war and managed to be awarded a few *imiyezane* (war medals) for his surprising bravery. He received a medal for bravery for the Battle of *iNcome* (Blood) River.

Except for living a basic life, Mpande hated his aunt Mkabayi with passion for her role in the killing of Shaka. What bothered him more, was that Mkabayi was never known to have displayed feminine emotions or traits. This made her a freak among her female peers. He also felt that had she married, that experience would have softened her up a bit (*ashukwe isidwaba*) and made her more likeable. In his time, Shaka had a soft spot for the infirm Mpande and they were genuinely fond of each other. Shaka's untimely death left Mpande devastated. Shaka had liked Mpande so much that he gave him many cattle and built him KwaNodwengu Palace near the present-day town of uLundi.

But Shaka didn't stop there, after he impregnated two of his *imidlunkulu* Ngqumbazi kaMbhonde Zungu and Monase kaMtungwa Nxumalo, he passed them on to Mpande as a gift. This is because Shaka doubted whether Mpande's private parts functioned properly because they were ravaged by leprosy. It was customary for wives to be handed over to one of the male relatives if the husband was impotent or died without having children. But since Shaka was king, he could also hand over a lover. This custom is called *ukungena* (inherit the wife of a deceased brother) and the practice was called *ukuvusa umuzi* (to carry on the lineage). This tradition continues today. Mpande also had a protruding bone on one leg. Moreover, he was tormented by being publicly referred to as *umntwana wasemsizini* (conceived under dubious circumstances), which unflatteringly described where he was conceived. Custom dictated that when the king was undergoing pre-first fruits festival sacred rituals, sex was taboo. Hence the hut where the king slept on the night before was guarded by royal women. But in the event that he slept with one of his wives or *umdlunkulu* ordinarily, such a progeny could never rule. Ngqumbazi became the principal wife because she was a princess from the Zungu kingdom and Shaka had sent her family his personal cattle as *ilobolo*. She gave birth to Cetshwayo. But no cows were sent to Monase's family as *ilobolo* and she bore Mbuyazwe. Later Mpande fathered other children with her, Bathonyile and Mantantashiya.

Dingane's absence and antics made Mpande realise that the coveted Zulu throne was within reach. All he needed to do was to out manoeuvre the paranoid Dingane and take care of wily Mkabayi. He was in no mood to let history slip through his fingers too easily. Moreover, he had been around Shaka from early childhood and had learnt one thing – intrigue. He had managed to survive Dingane's deranged purges by pretending to be *isithushana* (mentally slow). By the time soldiers began defecting to him, he was living at KwaGqikazi Palace. This is where he spent many hours plotting his future. He was also trying to understand why Mkabayi pressured him to urgently to form the *uHlomendlini omnyama* and the *uHlomendlini omhlophe* regiments when Dingane was still alive. After forming the regiments, he appointed Nongalaza as the commander of both regiments. Shortly after Mpande had formed the two regiments, Dingane instructed him to send the *uHlomendlini omnyama* to him in the forest as reinforcement as he was going to war against the Afrikaners. Mpande wanted Dingane to lose so he sent him the young and inexperienced *uKhothikhoti* regiment. They were hopelessly lost in the dense forest and returned home.

The regiment's no-show was further proof to Dingane that he no longer had influence over his subjects. But that was not as shattering as the fact that his subjects were now addressing Mpande as *Bayethe*, a title reserved only for a reigning monarch. What incensed Dingane more was that Mkabayi did nothing to stop the unfolding events. Worse still, he was in self-imposed exile and seemingly powerless. Treachery being his best fighting tactic, Dingane sent Mpande a gift of 100 magnificent cattle through two of his trusted royal messengers, Nxangwana kaZivalele kaJama (Zivalele was Senzangakhona's younger brother) and Mathunjana kaSibaca Nkwanyana. It was meant to be a magnanimous gesture to please Mpande. When he received the cattle, he was extremely impressed. He prepared to do exactly what Dingane had hoped he would do, come to the forest and thank him in person. At the time, the relationship between Dingane and his one-time confidant and commander-in-chief Ndlela was at its lowest. Hence when Dingane sent Mpande the royal cattle without consulting him first, Ndlela knew it was trap. The tall, fair-skinned and battle-scarred soldier watched Dingane as he gave the royal messengers the cattle. He stood alone smoking his hemp under an ancient tree while his free hand clutched his *imiyezane* (war medals). As he listened to Dingane speak, Ndlela again visualised the many facets of his life with Shaka - in slow motion. But most of all, he remembered the meticulous detail that Shaka invested in his plans to create and maintain the Zulu empire.

He observed Dingane behave like a snake that he was and concluded that truly, he had to answer to his ancestors about his senseless killing of people, most notably scores of innocent soldiers. Ndlela wondered where the ancient rule of law, that once governed supreme and protected the innocent, had gone. He also asked himself what had happened to justice that was meted out firmly but fairly. He also realised that out of the scores of sons from the House of Senzangakhona, only Mpande and Gqugqu managed to evade Dingane's cruelty and paranoia. The treachery Ndlela was watching was the last straw. The son of Sompisi resolved to act against Dingane's brutality and he knew he could rely on Mkabayi's full support. Ndlela figured that he had fought too many battles, too hard and for too long to let one of the potential rulers of the empire perish without putting up a brave fight. He knew that Dingane's sudden kind gesture was nothing more than a ruse to lure the unsuspecting Mpande to certain death. Then Ndlela called Mathunjana, - his close confidante- aside and asked him to warn Mpande that this was a trap. He also advised Mpande to go and live south of uThukela River, amongst the white Zulu subjects and the Zulu refugees in Durban. While Dingane waited for Mpande to come and thank him in person, he sent two of his loyal war veterans, Nzobo and his personal aide Khambazana to Pietermaritzburg. They were to negotiate a new peace agreement with the Afrikaners in order that Dingane would pay fewer than the 10 000 cattle they had agreed on.

After arriving they were made to negotiate with his nemesis, Andries Pretorius. Instead of conducting a civil discussion with them, he flew into a rage and publicly humiliated them. Even though they were mere messengers, he accused them of dishonesty and greed. Then Pretorius increased the number of cattle they wanted to 40 000. He did not stop there, he court-martialed them for being members of the military high command and held them responsible for the Afrikaner defeat at the Battle of *iNcome* (Blood) River as well as the ambush at Ophathe. Nzobo, who once belonged to Shaka's inner circle, was then killed in the most horrendous manner. They tied his feet together and dragged him behind an ox wagon face down through the streets of Pietermaritzburg until his face was totally scrapped off. Nzobo *Dambuza* kaSobhadli Ntombela, like a true Zulu warrior, never begged for his life nor cried out. Instead as soon as they passed the sentence, he recited Shaka's laudatory praises.

This gratuitous and barbaric death had never been seen before and there was a public outcry by the Zulu as well as some whites. As a result, Khombazana was not tortured but summarily executed in public. The purpose of this primitive act was to instil terror in the hearts of the Zulu who were refusing to comply with white laws. Mkabayi was shattered when she heard how the deputy commander-in-chief of the Zulu army died. Taken aback, she reflected on the highs and lows of her long, eventful life. Alone and overcome by intense grief, she wished she could cry, even if it was a lonely tear. She silently said to herself: *'Kukude emuva', kukude phambili'* (There is no turning back).

Dingane shrugged off the death of the senior member of the military high command as a non-issue. Rumours started surfacing that Dingane was behind their horrific killing because they had been so close to Shaka. Instead of planning a revenge attack, Dingane ordered the savage slaughter of his last two surviving paternal brothers. He had already killed about 20 other sons such as Ngqonjana, Ndunge, Nomkhwayimba and Sondondo. He sent special sadists to disembowel Gqugqu. His mother, his wives and all his children were speared to death. The savage killings shocked everyone especially Dingane's aunt, Mawa, as she was particularly close to Gqugqu. Mawa was a glamorous, amiable old woman who spent hours grooming herself just like her older brother, Senzangakhona. To disguise her advancing state of baldness, she used to wear a handmade wig of wavy, shoulder-length hair. She wove some of her children's hair and braided them into extensions and glued it together with red clay and bits of hard fat from a cow's stomach. She suspected, with reason, that Dingane would also kill her. She then fled south with many of her followers, some royal cattle and livestock. But she was stopped after crossing uMbilo River by Capt Charlton Smith of the British 27th regiment because he suspected it was yet another Zulu invasion of Durban. Mawa then settled right where they were stopped and built KwaHoqo Palace. This is where one of her grandsons Sothondose Nxumalo, joined joined her three years later, when he fled deranged Dingane. This is where the great 1841 drought found her and her followers.

Mpande tried to make himself useful and played God by taking it upon himself to make it rain. He tried everything including using the infamous rain doctor, Mbethe Ngcobo. He managed to 'evoke rain' from a concoction that included a steenbok's stomach pouch. But Mbethe's 'rain' was only a few miserly drops. It seemed Mbethe had made the gods mad because the drought intensified after his hocus-pocus. Shaka must have had a good laugh in his grave because he never trusted any of the so-called 'rainmakers'. This drought is now known as *iqhina likaMbethe* (Mbethe's steenbok). During the drought, many whites moved from the Cape to Durban; the Zulu also migrated south looking for food and joined Mawa. In no time she lived large and reigned supreme once again; she tried cases and held Zulu ceremonies. Her remains are buried in the ruins of KwaHoqo. It was only after Gqugqu's brutal murder that Mpande decided to leave. He left KwaNodwengu in September 1839 with at least 2000 followers and about 70 000 cattle and other livestock.

At that point, he was so obese that he could no longer walk and had to be pulled by Nothekwane kaSilimela, in a specially made bright green carriage. The son of Senzangakhona looked undignified and amusing in that carriage, a sight that would have eternally shamed Shaka. With a heavy heart, Mpande was dragged to the south side of uThukela River. But as soon as they crossed the river, the whites stopped them from reaching Durban because again, they thought it was a Zulu invasion. Mpande was summoned to a meeting with the white mercenaries at eHlawe River and he went with his two advisers, uncles Mkhanyile kaZivalele kaJama (iziMpohlo regiment), Nkunga kaSithayi kaJama (king's council member) and a refugee from Swaziland, Prince Mbilini kaMswazi *(Mbilini waMswati)*. Mbilini, the pretender to throne was born in Hhohho, eSwatini to Nomkhasiso Vilakazi and King Mswati of eSwatini. He was exiled to the Zulu kingdom after he tried to take over the throne.

After surviving a humiliating interrogation by the white mercenaries, Mpande was told to settle on the south bank of uThongathi River. This was about 40 kilometres north of Durban where he built KwaMahambehlala Palace and lived with some of the royal family members such as Langazana. Little did Mpande know that his problems were far from over. The Afrikaners said he needed to prove that indeed he was running away from Dingane. They coerced him to fight with Dingane and promised to support him with white mercenaries, arms and medication that would arrest his leprosy. In return, they wanted land and cattle. The need to become the Zulu emperor was too great for Mpande to resist and he agreed. Mpande's idiotic ambition led to what would plague the Zulu people for generations to come. It was a bitterly sad day for the whole Zulu empire when the two paternal brothers fought at the behest of the white mercenaries. The Zulu called this civil war *ukugqabuka kwegoda* (the breaking of the rope).

Nongalaza, assisted by Jobe and Matuwana, commanded Prince Mpande's 5000 men. They marched along the coast to the battle theatre in Dingane's hideout on the 14th of January 1840. Andries Pretorius had a vendetta against Dingane, but the thought of another fight sent shivers down his spine recalling the blood curdling Zulu war chants. So he chose the longest way possible to the battle theatre, and for his 350 white mercenaries and their 500 Zulu servants it was more of a hunting expedition. Pretorius chose to use the route that made him cross iNcome River where they rested. Ndlela divided Dingane's forces into three groups, the uDlambedlu regiment guarded Dingane, the iziNyosi regiment went to meet the enemy, and the rest of the army that was held in reserve. Ndlela's final instructions to his army before they left was that they should put up a weak resistance and then defect to Mpande.

The two sides finally faced off at Maqongqo Hills three weeks later the 29th of January, and predictably Mpande's forces won. Pretorius and his mercenaries were at least 200 kilometres away during the clash and never saw any action. Instead, they rushed to Dingane's hideout and found him long gone and took about 40 000 cattle. Now they were looking forward to taking land as well. Dingane and his army retreated through iNgwavuma forest, crossed uPhongolo River and hid in Hlathikhulu forest in Swaziland. As they retreated, he led them singing his favourite war song:

| | |
|---|---|
| *Siphakiwe siqonde empini* | we have been mobilised and deployed to go to war |
| *Ngaphesheya kwaleziyantaba* | to go over those mountains |
| *Ngale kwezintaba zentshonalanga* | to go beyond the mountains in the west |
| *Siqonde kwesingaze silithi nhlo* | we are going to places we have never seen before |
| *Sihambela wena Mjunju womhlanga* | we are going on your behalf, sharp reed |
| *Ngonyama! Ndlovu! Mkhululi* | Lion, Elephant, Emancipator |
| *Nkosi yamakhosi* | King of kings |
| *Silo sikaZulu* | Leopard of the Zulu empire |
| *Vezi* | Exposer |

After recovering from the grueling journey, licking his wounds, Dingane analysed Ndlela's battle plan. He realised it was feable and convened a court martial to chair it. He charged Ndlela with treason, found him guilty and sentenced him to die by strangulation with no leave to appeal. Dingane wanted Ndlela to die the most gruesome death possible and hysterically ordered the executioners to strangle him slowly with a leather thong until his windpipe broke. Ndlela stood to attention, poker-faced as Dingane pronounced his sentence. He had started off as a son of a reformed cannibal and ended up being a Field Marshal of the Zulu army that was the strongest military machine in the sub-continent. Ndlela kaSompisi kaGuqa kaMsalela kaNomashingila Ntuli stamped his right foot, after ten silent counts he shouted *Sigidi!* He showed no fear as the executioners nervously tied a knot around his thick neck and slowly pulled on opposite ends of the cord. As though Dingane wanted him to regret having been a great warrior, Ndlela was strangulated with his *imiyezane* on his neck. The military high command did not agree with the way their commander was killed and were horrified when Dingane refused to give him a military burial. He ordered that Ndlela's body be dumped in the forest to be eaten by wild animals. The soldiers, including his confidant and Chief of Staff Hwayihwayi, refused to obey that order. Instead, they gave him a decent burial with some of his personal items. Ndlela's laudatory praises are as follows:

| | |
|---|---|
| Gwabini wemikhonto | bundle of spears |
| ONonjiyela kulala uhlangothi lubomvu | Puzzler who sleeps on the side red side of his body |
| UManxeba angamanxulumana | Scarred one with several wounds |
| Insingizi eNdondakusuka | the hornbill at Ndondakusuka |
| UMagaju njengengwe | Agile one, like a leopard |
| UMahlatshwa ebuhleni njengethole | the Stabbed one in the face like a calf |
| UHlahla vimbela iNtontela | the Branch that protects iNtontela |
| UNdaba zafika nxa | whose story I first heard |
| NgikuDlungwana eMbelebeleni | when I was with Dlungwana at eMbelebeleni |

Dingane did not live long after ordering the killing of Ndlela. After the execution, Dingane built eSankoleni Palace in the ancestral land of the Nyawo people without their permission. They reported them to the Swazi border patrol commanded by Sonyezane Dlamini. Dingane's exaggerated sense of self-importance made him forget that he was a mere refugee in Swaziland and demanded large tracts of land. Shortly after the demand, Sonyezane, Nondawana, Silevana, Sambane and Mdluli Nyawo crept into Dingane's hut and attacked him, but his *iziThoyathoyi* saw them and a fight ensued. As Dingane was running away, he was stabbed with a poisoned spear that went through his thigh and partly disembowelled him as he ran away. He collapsed at the edge of the cattle enclosure and died from the septic wounds a few days later. In the last hours of Dingane's life - as is customary - his *iziThoyathoyi* sat in military order, mute in absolute silence with their shields lying on the ground, indicating that their great living shield was about to expire and lie in the dust. Dingane died thanking his *iziThoyathoyi* and cursing Mpande.

Silevane sold his scalp and his jewellery, that he was known to wear, for a mere 20 cattle. It was gleefully paid out by Andries Pretorius. At the time of his death, Dingane had established about 11 regiments. He lies buried in Lebombo Mountains in Kwaliweni (Gwaliweni) section of the Hlathikhulu forest. It is ironic that the *iziThoyathoyi* buried him next to his greatest nemesis, Ndlela. The only earthly possession that survived Dingane because he never 'officially' had any offspring, is a pentagon chair built out of a solid block of wood. It is displayed at the Voortrekker Museum in Pietermaritzburg.

When Mkabayi heard that her nephews were at war with each other, she became despondent. She feared that these hostilities would mark the end of her lifetime's objective of preserving the Zulu empire. For the first time in her colourful life, Mkabayi wished her father Jama had followed custom and killed her. She regretted that she had ordered Shaka's death based on Dingane's lies. Despite her hardly knowing Mpande very well, she was pessimistic about the House of Senzangakhona. On the other hand, when Queen Langazana kaGubeshe Sibiya heard that Dingane had died, she moved from esiKlebeni Palace where she had been hiding for a while to the *ikhanda* of uNokhenke regiment in eMahlabathini. She resumed her very busy lifestyle and tried cases every day, old as she was. She had led many battles with the iNtontela Special Forces in her younger days, side-by-side with greats like Ndlela.

Langazana was an extremely large and pleasant woman and will be forever associated with a 'mini-war' that broke out between Shaka's *imidlunkulu*. The females of esiKlebeni and KwaDukuza palaces were both under her watch. It so happened that three KwaDukuza girls came across some esiKlebeni girls who were taking beer to Shaka in KwaDukuza. When they saw the quality of the calabash cover of the king's beer, they were not impressed. As far as they were concerned, it was of poor quality and not fit for a king. So, they thoroughly beat them up before allowing them to proceed. It was not over as the esiKlebeni girls planned to revenge. One morning they waited for the soldiers to go to work in the king's fields and some 20 girls took their sticks and knobkerries. They attacked about 40 KwaDukuza girls, three of whom were being princesses. The fight that ensued became a madhouse. The guards and Queen Langazana managed to stop them only for a little while before they started fighting again. They climbed into each other over and over. They hit one another mercilessly while screaming at the top of their voices. Those who dropped their weapons were beaten to the ground, scratched and bitten with tiny mouths. The guards watched, thoroughly entertained by the female fighting tactics. It was the scratching, high kicks and piercing screams that amused them the most. Finally, the esiKlebeni girls fled after 30 minutes.

Langazana later moved to KwaDliwayini Palace near KwaKhangela *ikhanda* during Cetshwayo's reign. She died aged 90 still with a sharp memory during

Dinuzulu's reign. She was the richest and greatest repository of Zulu history of her time. She covered events from before the rise of the Zulu empire to its zenith and near final collapse. Queen Langazana kaGubeshe Sibiya was particularly well versed in all events in Shaka's life and had lived under seven Zulu kings, her father in law Jama, her husband Senzangakhona, Shaka, Dingane, Mpande, Cetshwayo and died during Dinuzulu's reign.

*Prince Mkhungo kaMpande was a member of uMbonambi regiment. He escaped with his sister Princess Bathonyile kaMpande and sought refuge at Ekukhanyeni mission under Bishop Colenso after the civil war between his uncles, Prince Cetshwayo kaShaka and Prince Mbuyazwe kaShaka. (Killie Campbell Africana Library)*

*Ndongeni kaXoki Zulu (Senzangakhona's descendant) was given a farm on the north bank of uMzimkhulu River in 1898 as a reward for guiding Dick King to Mpondoland in 1842. (Killie Campbell Africana Library)*

## Zulu Territory Seized by Afrikaners

After his resounding success at Maqongqo Hills, Mpande was forced to make good on his promise to the Afrikaners even though they had not met their side of the agreement and were nowhere near the battle theatre. Even though it was still the mourning period, the Afrikaners insisted on crowning him as the Zulu monarch. Present were some of the king's council members such as Nkunga, Mkhanyile and Godolozi kaZivalele, Nkabana, Mpaphe, Ambassador Sotobe as well as Mbilini. Mpande allocated land to the white mercenaries somewhere south of uThukela River close to Durban with no clearly demarcated borders. Then they renamed this undefined area the *Republic of Natalia*. They made Pietermaritzburg their capital and called their parliament the *Volksraad*. All the Zulu living south of uThukela River, whether by migration or on ancestral land, found themselves ruled by Afrikaners. Mpande had not discussed this with anyone. Mpande returned to KwaNodwengu in shame and said as far as he understood the agreement, he was merely allowing the Afrikaners jurisdiction to the land not ownership of the land.

Despite having achieved his lifetime dream of becoming the undisputed emperor, he was not at peace. When Mkabayi heard the news of what her nephew did, she nearly died of shock and little did she know worse was yet to come. Even though he had already been crowned, Mpande did not trust Mkabayi who was to remain the regent until the mourning period was over. Guilt made him discuss his fears with Nongalaza, who was now the Prime Minister. He advised him to get rid of Mkabayi as soon as possible. Nongalaza reminded Mpande that the last Zulu king to rule the empire without Mkabayi's influence was her grandfather, Ndaba. Shaka was the only person who had ruled independently from her and for that reason he did not last long. The two were wary of killing her openly because she was, firstly, too valuable to the Zulu empire. Secondly, she was obviously favoured by the ancestors because she was still alive after all the trials and tribulations. Touching her would unleash untold misery and hardship, not only to Mpande personally but to the entire empire. Hence, as soon as Dingane's mourning period was over, Mpande moved swiftly and called a national *imbizo*.

He ensured that everyone was seated before he made a grand appearance. He arrived surrounded by uDloko regiment commanded by King Makhubalo kaNhliziyo kaLukwabithi kaDikane Mbatha and his deputies Mbune kaSomaphunga kaZwide Ndwandwe, Mswazi kaNtokontoko Zulu and Magwala kaMqundane Zulu. Mpande accorded Mkabayi no courtesy or respect accorded to a princess and regent. In fact, he completely ignored her. Instead, he brazenly informed the bewildered *imbizo* that

Mkabayi would be moved from KwaNobamba to the most remote north-eastern border of the empire. Pretending to be kind, he reminded everyone that she was going to live amongst Shaka's favourite people, abaQulusi when in fact, he knew that they could not stand her because she orchestrated Shaka's death. She was going to head a new *ikhanda* eMahlabaneni Palace among the Zwane people in eZungeni Valley. This was west of the Dumbe Mountains near today's Paulpietersburg (*Dumbe*). Mpande glared at her with hostility when he sarcastically said that she was the most qualified commander to be the first line of defence against their enemies, whites, Mzilikazi, Soshangane or anyone else for that matter.

Undeterred by the hostile silence, Mpande continued to announce her new officers that would form her command structure. Her Chief of Staff was Ntanjana kaNdiyane Mbatha. Her senior advisor was Sobhadli Ntombela and her personal bodyguards were Sekethwayo kaNhlaka Mdlalose and Siwangu kaMbikwane Mthethwa. Mkabayi was visibly shocked. She looked at her nephew Mpande as though seeing him for the first time. It had never happened in the Zulu realm that a princess opened a new *ikhanda* (military base). Everyone was stunned, but no one dared say anything. The truth was that the people were still trying to recover from having to pick sides between the sons of Senzangakhona. The result was that Dingane died and was buried in a place they had never seen or heard of before, and Mpande was now standing right in front of them saying things they could not really comprehend. This was undeniably a big calamity and the people remembered that Shaka, with all his faults, would never have let such happen. In addition, Mpande did not even bother to explain why he had unilaterally given mercenaries jurisdiction over part of the empire. Mortified, Mkabayi's will to fight evaporated and for once she chose to say nothing. She braced herself and did what had always taken her out of a tight spot before. She began to hum the national anthem quietly to herself. She suspected that it would be the last time she would hum it in public.

The Zungeni Valley is bleak and harsh. The summers are extremely hot, and the winters are extremely cold. Mkabayi's new *ikhanda* squatted on barren ground. The winds blew relentlessly, raising clouds of dust and often partially obscured the sun. Mkabayi passed her time melancholically and hardly talked to anyone. She recalled the times gone by and many moons ago when Shaka stamped his authority on sub-Saharan Africa with lightning speed and how he was like mercury, unstoppable. She told whoever cared to listen that she often felt as though *uqulusile esidindini somtshiki* (her buttocks were exposed over a mound of grass). She wished for nothing more than to sit in the shade of a mimosa tree in a familiar environment and feel familiar winds blow in her hair and feel familiar warm rain on her ageing skin. Mkabayi missed the breathtaking views and valleys of KwaNobamba, the simmering hazy blue-green mountaintops in the distant horizon. She missed the smell of burning grass crackling in the late summer months and became steadily more miserable.

One day she impulsively confided in Siwangu, whom she had known practically all his life, that she really longed to be in the eMakhosini Valley and wished to see her twin sister Mmama, who was now the commander of Osebeni *ikhanda* and her younger sister Mawa who was commander of iNtontela *ikhanda*. Mkabayi told Siwangu that she felt particularly vulnerable and spoke about her unfulfilled childhood dreams, particularly about having felt obliged to give up her life for the sake of the Zulu nation. What tore at her heart most of all, she confessed, was missing the opportunity of being a wife to the love of her life, *iLala* Prince Lamula kaNgwabini Ngcolosi. But she said that even though she had regrets, she still felt justified for not hesitating to order the killing of anyone who threatened the existence of the Zulu empire. Despite Mpande's treachery, she took comfort in the fact that even though the Afrikaners had declared a *'Republic'* on the land of the Zulu people, they merely had jurisdiction. Moreover, no one could ever own it, instead the emperor was the custodian of the land. He had the authority and responsibility to take care of the land and its people, as well as to distribute jurisdiction of the land to subjects.

Mkabayi also acknowledged her mistakes, Shaka's murder being the most spectacular. For the first time, she openly admitted missing Shaka. She wished to again see his fit and towering figure, holding his long white shield with its single black spot in the centre on his left hand and in his right hand holding his glistening *iklwa*. She could see him in his finest war regalia, the single blue-crane feather, a symbol of royalty, proudly stuck high at the back of his head. She missed his sense of humour, his intricate dance moves and resonating voice when at war or when singing. She would forever see his disarming smile and a glint that always shone in his eyes whenever he was happy. She lamented that her personal sacrifices for the Zulu empire would not be remembered. Instead she would be remembered for being the one who had allowed the death of the greatest African warrior and king and creator of the Zulu empire.

Siwangu stole a glance at her, noticing how the regal princess had aged. Her eyes had lost their sparkle and the famous firm breasts were hanging low, her snow-white teeth were dull, her shapely legs shrunken, as was her long neck. Her once gracefully carried sholders now slouched forward, and she had taken to using a walking stick frequently, complaining about sore knees and a painful back. In a pained voice, she concluded by saying that even though she was not happy at *ebaQulusini* (land of abaQulusi people), she would rather not go back to KwaNobamba. After all, her people had finally managed to get rid of her, something they had not managed to do when she was born. Then she abruptly kept quiet and seemed to peer through the door. Siwangu stepped outside to digest what he had just heard. It did not take him long to decide to share this heart-wrenching monologue with the senior members of *ikhanda*. They realised that Mkabayi's days were numbered and decided to take her back to KwaNobamba and would not seek permission from Mpande. When Sobhadli went into the hut to inform her about their decision, he realised that *selidume ladlula* (it had already thundered). She had passed on.

Princess Mkabayi *ongagugi* kaJama kaNdaba kaMageba kaZulu kaMalandela kaLuzumane had lived a long and remarkable life. From the troubled times when her kingdom was still tiny and insignificant until her death. She was the first female ruler among the Nguni people in Southern Africa. She had led the Zulu nation five times and was the power behind six thrones - she was adviser to her father Jama; she ruled in the place of her younger vain paternal brother Senzangakhona and buried the weak Sigujana. Then she had watched in awe, the spectacular success of Shaka and oversaw the installation of the brutal Dingane. Finally, she had been exiled by the slow and conniving Mpande. She was nearly 100 years old when her tormented spirit left her exhausted body in 1840. Mkabayi has the singular honour to be the only female mentioned among the Zulu kings. Her laudatory praises illuminate her life:

| | |
|---|---|
| *USoqili* | Great manipulator |
| *Iqili lakwaHoshoza* | the manipulator from kwaHoshoza |
| *Elidla umuntu limyenga ngendaba* | the sweet-talking destroyer |
| *Ladla uBhedu ngasezinyangeni* | that destroyed Bhedu by the healers |
| *Ladla uMkhongiyana ngasemaNgadini* | as well as Mkhongiyana by the Ngadini people |
| *Ladla uBheje ngasezanuseni* | and Bheje near the fortune tellers |
| *Ubhoko lukaMenzi* | the trusted walking-stick of Menzi |
| *Olubambe abantu lwabenebela* | that ambushed people and tore them apart |
| *Ngimbone ngoNohela kaMlilo* | I saw it as she destroyed Nohela son of Mlilo |
| *Umlilo ovutha izintaba zonke* | the fire that burnt down all mountains |
| *Inkomo ekhala eSangonyana* | the cow that bellows at iSangonyana hill |
| *Iye yezwiwa nguGwabalanda* | it was heard by Gwabalanda |
| *Ezalwa nguMndaba kwaKhumalo* | born by Mndaba from the Khumalo kingdom |
| *Intombi ethombe yoma umlomo* | the virgin whose private parts dried up |

It was only after the death of Mkabayi that Mpande casually divulged why he felt morally obliged to the white mercenaries. He said they had helped him ascend to the throne and missionaries from Norway had healed his leprosy. With Mkabayi no longer haunting him and being forever grateful for having ascended the throne, Mpande disengaged from the matters of the empire. He also did not sort out the mess he created with his mercenary friends who were demanding more and more land. He even refused to discuss the matter with the king's council. Instead he lived a life of song and dance and had many more children. The whites were quick to notice internal Zulu tensions and rivalries. They did not only encourage them but also started them so long as they could get more land. Hence, they lied, cheated and claimed they 'owned' the land they seized. But this was not new; since Shaka's reign several whites such as Francis Farewell, Henry Fynn, Lt James King and Capt Allen Gardiner had done the same thing. They either forged documents or claimed to have been verbally given some corner of the Zulu empire.

After the establishment of the *Republic of Natalia* Zulu families were evicted from their ancestral land. They were moved to barren and rugged land, swamps or mountain slopes where they and their livestock could not survive. Others were forcibly moved to the place between the uMthamvuna and uMzimvubu Rivers where it was equally bushy, mountainous, strewn with rocks and there was insufficient arable land. Those that resisted were summarily shot in public as a lesson to others. Many poor souls woke up on the morning of the 13th of October 1839 and found that they were homeless, landless and had become squatters in the land of their forefathers. Two days later, Mpande was summoned to the *Volksraad* in Pietermaritzburg and told to come with his heir. Mpande took Cetshwayo, a mere 13-year-old boy, with him. When they arrived, a group of Afrikaners led by Pretorius pounced and held the young innocent boy down. Then they swiftly cut out a piece of his left ear like a cow with a blade. They justified their action by saying that they wanted to ensure everyone knew that he was the crown prince. Cetshwayo returned home bleeding and had to endure the humiliation of being pegged all his life. He never forgave them for the sadistic action. The people were increasingly turning against Mpande and they despised him for allowing whites to run riot in their ancestral lands, south of uThukela River. Moreover, they were slowly encroaching north of uThukela River under the guise of saving Zulu souls from eternal hell by baptising them to Christianity.

As if that was not enough, in May 1842 the British and Afrikaners went to war at the Battle of Congella (*impi yaseKhangela*) over the possession of the Zulu empire. Some Zulu mercenaries took part on either side, while the rest of the Zulu subjects watched in horror as the systematic dispossession of their land began. The British defeated the Afrikaners and the ill-fated *Republic of Natalia* ceased to exist in 1843.

The British then drew boundaries that demarcated the '*Natal Colony*' from uThukela River in the north, the Indian Ocean on the east, down to uMthamvuna River in the south and somewhere along uKhahlamba Mountains in the west. The rest of the Zulu empire territory was referred to as '*Zululand*'. When white people arrived, they found a Zulu governance system that was based on equity and fairness, as well as on the right of association. Hence refuge could be sought anywhere, including where the whites lived in Durban. But for whites to go to war over Zulu-owned land and to claim that they 'owned' the land was preposterous. The fact that no one could 'own' land in the Zulu empire would not change just because the whites said so.

The challenge for the British was that they were so few in number and so they declared the land that they could not occupy, '*Crown Lands*' so that the Zulu could not occupy it. They also devised an ingenious plan to subjugate the now 'landless' Zulu by introducing a slave labour system called *isibhalo*. This was devised as a way for these 'destitute Zulu' to pay government tax. This system forced all Zulu males from the age of 10 to leave their homes and to travel to assembly points within the '*Colony*'. They were used as labour to clear forests to plant sugarcane fields and build railway lines and roads but without pay. By 1902 about 3 500 were working at the Public Works, Railway and Harbour and Military Departments. The British justified these injustices by reminding the men that they had traditionally worked 'without pay' on the Zulu imperial fields. They also passed a law that the Zulu, living south of uThukela River should demand a minimum of 15 cattle as *ilobolo* so that they could own some cattle, to feed their families. Before *isibhalo* was forcefully introduced, the set minimum number of cattle for *ilobolo* was 11 cows and every cow represented something in the life of a female. The British then opened major mission stations and schools in the so-called '*Crown Lands*' such as in Stanger, Driefontein, Pietermaritzburg and Edendale. However, these mission schools could only be attended by the Zulu whose souls had been saved.

The Zulu were increasingly getting angrier and more restless by the day. Mpande was openly despised and Mkabayi was sorely missed. Sensing an insurrection, the British Governor of the Cape Colony and High Commissioner Sir Harry Smith instituted a Land Boundary Commission south of uThukela River in 1846. The sham investigation concluded that all the Zulu living in Natal were 'foreigners'. The rest of the land in the colony was for any white person who wanted it and they could take it for free. The whites were then issued with 'Title Deeds' for the land they occupied. The commission recommended the establishment of pockets of land to be called 'Native Reserves' that would be occupied by the Zulu people and would be governed by a person that would be called an *inkosi* (king). The British would ultimately choose them and their appointees did not necessarily have to be of royal blood. The Zulu governance system was left intact in the so-called 'native reserves'. The *inkosi* could try civil and criminal cases but the reports of these cases had to be presented to white magistrates. When the Zulu also demanded title deeds for their ancestral lands and where they had been dumped, the colonial government refused. Hence, the Zulu viewed the commission as a ploy to legitimise the theft of part of the Zulu empire. Most Zulu people whose land that was seized under the 1839 Republic of Natalia Declaration and the 1843 Colony of Natal Declaration have not been compensated to this day.

Then the British embarked on a two-pronged strategy – to rapidly take more land and to recruit more colonisers who were white to settle in Natal. Moreover, many of them were extremely poor peasants from rural areas in England were forced off the land because of industrialisation. Hence, between 1848 and 1851 about 60 ships left London, Hull, Plymouth, Liverpool and Glasgow. They brought about 5000 colonisers and missionaries. The J.C. Byrne and Company Natal Emigration and Colonisation programme sent about 20 ships from England with an average of 150 colonisers on board. The *Wanderer* left London on the 24$^{th}$ of January 1849 with 15 emigrants and arrived in Durban on the 16$^{th}$ of May. It was followed by the *Washington*, the *Henry Tanner*, the *Dreadnought*, the *Aliwal*, the *King William*, the *Sovereign*, the *Edward*, the *Lady Bruce*, the *Minerva*, the *Henrietta*, the *Sandwich*, the *Globe*, the *British Tar*, the *Emily*, the *Devonian* and the *Bernard*. The *Conquering Hero* left Glasgow with 127 colonisers, the *Ina* had 76 adults and about 40 children and there was one birth on board. The *Unicorn* brought 257 colonisers that included the parents of Col Duncan '*Dune*' McKenzie.

- Prospective emigrants in England were offered passage to Natal and 20 acres of land at unbelievably low rates. The *L*-symbol represented the British pound before the modern pound symbol £. The amounts paid were as follows, *L10* for a steerage passage.

- *L15* was the standard fare. *L19* for an intermediate berth.

- Children under 14 were charged *L5* and entitled to five acres.

- Cabin passengers could travel for *L35*, but they were not entitled to free land.

For the emigrants to take advantage of the land offer, they had to be approved by the British government and be below the age of 45, unless accompanied by an adult offspring. The only acceptable occupations for the emigrants were practical trades such as farming, blacksmith, wheelwright, wagon making, dairymaid, agricultural labourer, shoemaker, and similar jobs. The agreement was that immigrants would disembark in uMzimkhulu River and be taken to Durban by land. They could rename the land they settled on, hence the colonial names such as *New England, Pinetown, Ashburton* and many more. Approximately 189 colonisers arrived in Durban in 1848 from Bremen in Germany.

The first batch of indentured Indian workers disembarked in Durban from the *Truro* on the 17th of November 1860 from Madras. The *Belvedere* docked 10 days later with more Indians from Calcutta. Over 200 000 Indians followed in the next 50 years. Today Durban is the city with the largest settlement of Indians outside India in the world. The Norwegians were recruited in the 1880s by the Natal government. It promised to pay for the transportation costs to the appointed place of settlement and a week's lodging. They were also promised common grazing land of 2000 acres and a 100-acre plot for each family at seven shillings and sixpence per acre payable over ten years. In turn, they had to agree to land near the uMzimkhulu River, not in Durban. They were also to be men of integrity, sober, hardworking, Christian and willing to be of mutual help. So, when 38 Norwegian families arrived in Durban in the 1880s, they were welcomed by missionary Rev Hans Schroeder. He had been living in Durban since 1844, but Mpande had only allowed him to establish missions north of uThukela River in 1851. These were in eMpangeni (1851), Entumeni (1852), eMahlabathini (1860), iMfule (1861), Eshowe (1861) and iNhlazatshe (1861). It took 15 years of trying before Rev Schroeder managed to convert one woman, Mathenjwaze Shange in June 1858, at uMphumulo mission on the south bank of uThukela River, Durban.

*Cartoonist George Cruikshank impression of what would happen to British emigrants who took part in the emigration scheme to the Cape Colony in 1820. (1820 Settlers Museum)*

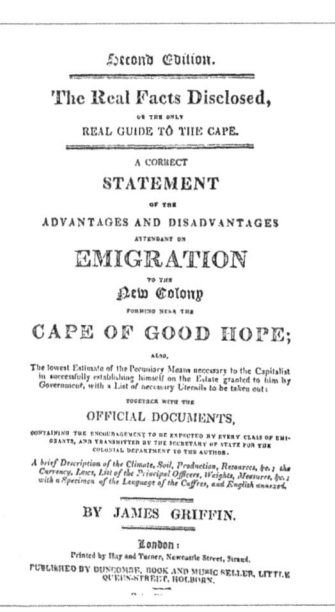

*The Guide to the Cape emigration scheme pamphlet from London to the Cape of Good hope. (1820 Settlers Museum)*

The Afrikaners were aware of Mpande's waning support and Cetshwayo's popularity. So, they encouraged one of Shaka's sons Mbuyazwe to contest the throne and promised to support him. Mbuyazwe was a loud and insecure and boisterous giant. He lived south of the Black iMfolozi River with his supporters *iziGqoza* at his non-descript homestead called Mkweyantaba at Mfaba hills. He is described as looking like 'the palm of the hand' meaning that he was fair. He had Shaka's gait and tuft of hair on the nape of his neck just like Shaka. He was also known as *uMbuyazwe omuhle* as he was extremely handsome, but he had fewer followers than Cetshwayo and was brazen about his leadership ambitions and often seized Cetshwayo's cattle to provoke him. On the other hand, Cetshwayo's temper and strength were clearly inherited from Shaka and he had more followers than Mbuyazwe. He had also commanded several wars with exceptional courage and his bravery during the campaign against King Sekwati of the Bapedi kingdom (a Sotho group) was outstanding. He returned with numerous cattle that could drink extraordinary amounts of water within a short space of time. This feat fascinated the regiments and after it all Cetshwayo's followers called themselves '*uSuthu*'.

Cetshwayo gained even more prestige when he routed the Hlubi kingdom and they ran away and went over the Drakensberg Mountains. When he routed the Swazi as the Commander of the uThulwana regiment along the uPhongolo River by successfully deploying new fighting tactics. He piled wood and old shields in the mouths of caves where Swazis were hiding and set them alight, forcing the Swazi to come out and be killed. This made him a superhero throughout the empire as distinguished himself like his father Shaka and exhibited great qualities of a fine officer. This campaign is legendary in the psyche of the Zulu to this day and referred to as *ukufunda kukaThulwana* (the teaching of the uThulwana regiment) because of the great number of cattle he seized. After such epic victories, the king's council was left with no option but to allow him to build himself a palace, even though he was still unmarried. He built it against the backdrop of Undi mountain range facing aMabedlana Hills, south of uMhlathuze River and called it *Ondini* (uLundi). It was a place of great joy, happiness and serenity. It even had a resident court jester, called Hebe kaJaja Dludla (uThulwana), who followed Cetshwayo everywhere he went. The two became so close that when Cetshwayo finally ascended the throne, the laudatory praise reciter would start acknowledging *Hebe* first. Therefore, when people heard *Hebe* it meant Cetshwayo was nearby. Hence the arrival of the Zulu monarchy has since been preceded by the shouting of *Hebe*.

Cetshwayo had no desire to fight Mbuyazwe who was under his command in Thulwana regiment, despite the repeated provocation. He even asked Mpande to mediate but he ignored him. He invited Cetshwayo and Mbuyazwe to his palace at KwaNodwengu. He then instructed Mbuyazwe and his *iZigqoza* to dance for him. Thereafter, he praised them profusely and gave Cetshwayo a large number of feathers, accessories and skins to dress his *uSuthu*. Mpande then told Cetshwayo that he should teach his followers how to dance like Mbuyazwe's followers. Shaka's son were livid, as one felt insulted that his followers were portrayed as not being able to dance, and the other was jealous of the number of gifts the other had been given. This was not going to end well. When Mbuyazwe realised that war against Cetshwayo was inevitable, he escaped to the fledging economy of Natal and hid in Bishop Colenso's mission in Bishopstowe. But his younger brother Mantatashiya, taunted him and called him a coward, the biggest insult to a Zulu man.

However, Cetshwayo had another problem. Despite being the crown prince, one of Mpande's sons, Mthonga (uMbonambi) was being touted as the next king because his mother, Nomatshali *Msuthukazi* kaSiguyana Bhele was Mpande's favourite wife. Mpande used to affectionately call her *Somapha*. Since he could not risk fighting on two fronts, Cetshwayo sent sent assassins to kill Mthonga. But when they did not find him, they killed his mother Nomatshali and his young son QSompoyiyana, which had not been sanctioned by Cetshwayo. He tried to convey his deepest regret to Mpande, but he did not believe him and held him responsible. Unlike Mbuyazwe who had gone to the British, Mthonga had sought refuge amongst the Afrikaners. Mbuyazwe, in the meantime, was goaded into proving that he was no coward.

He agreed to fight Cetshwayo with the assistance of English mercenaries such as Jack Hill, Joshua Walmsely, Ephraim Rathbone, Joe Pierce, Dick Pierce, Paul du Pre, John *Jantoni* Dunn (not related to Captain Robert Dunn) as well as several Durban-based Zulu mercenaries. The Zulu nation had to witness another civil war (*impi yabantwana*) within a generation but this time between Senzangakhona's grandsons. As far as Mpande was concerned, Shaka's sons were welcome to slaughter each other as his biological son Mthonga was positioned to taking over the throne. The civil war was called the Battle of Ndondakusuka (*impi yabantwana*) and finally took place on a misty and rainy day on the 2$^{nd}$ of December 1856 at Ndondakusuka Hill near iThambo River, a tiny tributary of uThukela River. Cetshwayo did not go to the battle theatre, but instead he knelt on Mbuyazwe's shield which had been stolen from his hut. The Zulu believed that if you knelt on your enemy's shield, victory was certain.

On the day of the battle, Mbuyazwe wearing his war regalia was inspiring his men then forebodingly, the ostrich feather he wore on his head fell to the ground, even though, despite there being no wind. His men regarded this as truly a bad omen. Cetshwayo's men, *uSuthu* looked magnificent as their lithe bodies glistened in the early morning mist, their shields raised high and did *ingomane*. Then they rushed Mbuyazwe's men *iZigqoza* as well as their women and children as they had foolishly brought them to the battle theatre. It was all over at the initial onslaught. Cetshwayo's men killed almost 25 000 people within an hour including at least five of Mpande's sons Shonkweni (uThulwana), Somklwana (uThulwana), Dabulesinye (Udloko), Mantantashiya (uThulwana) and Mdumba (Indlondlo).

Unfortunately, Mbuyazwe's body was never found as some claim that he drowned, others said he died of a broken heart for losing to Cetshwayo. Mpande was inconsolable at the loss of his sons and refused to accept cattle seized from Mbuyazwe's cattle enclosure as a gift from Cetshwayo. Melmoth Osborne who later became the British Resident, was present and was hiding in the bushes and gave a firsthand account of the battle to the colonial government. After the decisive victory, Cetshwayo's men instantly composed a song highlighting the fact that Mbuyazwe had been ill prepared for the battle:

| *Bayaziphangisa, wayeqale bani na* | they are hurrying them away, who had he provoke |
|---|---|
| *O woo hhaye* | well done |
| *Sivimba ngomkhonto eNdondakusuka* | we stopped them with a spear at Ndondakusuka |
| *O woo hhaye* | well done |
| *Sanqoba ngomkhonto e Ndondakusuka* | we conquered with a spear at Ndondakusuka |
| *O woo hhaye* | well done |
| *O woo hhaye* | well done |

As fate would have it, during the battle, a biblical Moses-like story unfolded in the uThukela River. On his last trip, Captain Joshua Walmesly, who was ferrying bullets for Mbuyazwe across the flooded river, heard tiny wails coming from the reeds. When he went to check, he found a naked Zulu toddler in the water desperately clinging on the reeds. Walmesly was unusually moved by the sad sight and picked up the terrified little girl. He wrapped the child in his coat and noticed the two gaping wounds, one on the left arm and the other on the left thigh. He took her home to his wife, Maria and since they did not have any children, they named her *Nomanzi* (Miss Water) and raised her as their own. Nomanzi ended up marrying Walmesly's elderly main servant Sifile and they then moved to Nonoti. Sifile gave the Walmeslys 32 cattle for *ilobolo* as her adoptive parents. However, when the Walmesly couple died, Nomanzi inherited the cattle to the absolute delight of Sifile.

After the battle, the grief-stricken Mpande advised all his wives and children to flee to the whites. Some of his wives, like Queen Nobelungu Mthethwa (who was a princess in the Mthethwa kingdom) and Queen Monase Nxumalo, heeded his advice. But the rest refused to go and live under the whites. Some of the children who fled were Bathonyile and Mkhungo (uMbonambi) who went to Bishop Colenso's eKukhanyeni mission in Pietermaritzburg. Mthonga and Mgidlana (Mbonambi) fled to the Afrikaners in the *KwaYende* (Wakkerstroom) kingdom. Mthonga asked one of his literate followers, Ngema, to apply for a title deed on behalf of the Yende kingdom and it was granted. But the area was erroneously registered as *KwaNgema* instead of *KwaYende* because the Title Deeds Office assumed that the signatory of the request Ngema, was the King of the Yende kingdom. This caused tension in the area and remains unresolved to this day.

When the British government appointed Sir Theophilus Shepstone (*Somtsweu*) Secretary for Native Affairs in 1856, the tension between the Zulu and the colonisers was high. Shepstone was pompous and the epitome of colonial arrogance. He soon became a controversial figure in the history of the Zulu people. He married many Zulu women as well a mixed-race woman called Mitha, a San woman called Christina Brown (he referred to her as Christina with a fat backside) and a Swati Princess called Tifokati kaSobhuza 1. The Swazi princess lived with Shepstone in Durban with a large Swazi royal retinue and they had many children. Shepstone sent two wagons full of gifts and 300 cattle as *ilobolo* to the king in Swaziland. Apart from for looking after his growing family, Shepstone kept an eye on his sickly neighbour Henry Francis *Mbuyazi weTheku* Fynn who finally gave up the ghost in 1861.

When the Zulu Prime Minister, Masiphula kaMamba Mgazini, called a national *imbizo* in December 1857 and declared Cetshwayo the regent, he did not invite Shepstone. Shepstone was furious as he had waited for an invite to KwaNodwengu, (the Zulu capital) for four years. Masiphula did this even though Mpande was very much alive and was still king. This made Shepstone very angry because he was not invited. So, Shepstone decided to go there in 1861 without an invitation or sending a message that he was coming. On arriving at the capital, he ignored all protocol and galloped straight into the king's private quarters followed by his main Zulu servant, Ngoza kaLudaba Majozi. Ngoza was once the personal servant of Mpande's wives, Queen Monase. Shepstone found Mpande morose and detached. He did not even raise his eyes when Shepstone sauntered in. After offering condolences for his dead sons, Shepstone said that he had come to ask for food for Mpande's wives and children who had fled to Natal. Mpande graciously accepted the condolences but referred him to Cetshwayo for any other matter he wanted to discuss. He never uttered a single word after that. At face value, Shepstone's request was fair, but the intention of going to Mpande was to show Cetshwayo that the English still recognised Mpande as the king. Shepstone was forced to eat humble pie and reluctantly went to Cetshwayo. Ngoza, feeling protected by the presence of Shepstone, did the unthinkable. He trespassed into the *imidlunkulu* quarters when Shepstone was talking to Mpande. This would cause Retief and his mercenaries to be killed.

Cetshwayo was informed about the transgression as Shepstone strolled in with Ngoza in tow. They found a fuming Cetshwayo in the company of his council and personal attendants such as Mehlokazulu kaSihayo Ngobese, Nsizwana Xulu and Mnyama Buthelezi's sons, Tshanibezwe and Mbulawa. Even before Cetshwayo found out why Shepstone had come, he asked Ngoza twice why he had gone into the sacred enclosure. On both occasions, Shepstone condescendingly tried to answer on behalf of Ngoza. But Cetshwayo twice ignored him and glowered at Ngoza as he waited for an answer. When he did not answer, Cetshwayo asked Ngoza for the third time and when Shepstone tried to answer again, Cetshwayo exploded: '*Mlungu, kangikhulumi nawe ngikhuluma noNgoza. Ngimfunge uNzibe ekwaSoshangane*,' (white person, I am not talking to you, I am talking to Ngoza. I swear on Nzibe's grave in the kingdom of Soshangane). They begged him to calm down and Shepstone received the message loud and clear and sheepishly apologised. He also added that Ngoza had taken the liberty to greet the *imindlunkulu* because he was once close to them whilst in service to Queen Monase. Then he repeated the request for food. Cetshwayo's initial response was that those starving people in his care were Zulu subjects. Therefore, they should come back home where they would be looked after. But after deliberations with his council, he allowed Shepstone to take Queen Monase's cattle with him.

According to the late Senior Prince Reggie Mandlenkosi kaMagangezintaba kaDinuzulu when Mpande became aware that his days were numbered, he called a few close attendants and said: 'Go to Maphitha kaSojiyisa's homestead and tell him to give you one of his best white bulls. Then take it to the edge of iNgome forest and shout *uwenu uyakubiza uthi woza umphelekezela* (your peer is calling to come and accompany him). A lion will come and attack the bull, but the bull will not run away. That will be your chance to kill the lion. Once you have killed it, wrap my body with its skin before you bury me.' Indeed, they went to the forest with the bull and shouted all night and nothing happened. Finally, in the early hours of the morning, an old lion sauntered out of the forest. They all moved back with their spears ready. The bull did not make a sound or move a muscle. Then the lion attacked it and the men were able to kill the lion.

There were very few tears when Emperor Mpande *Madela Khonzaphi* kaSenzangakhona died in his sleep on the 18$^{th}$ of October 1872 at his palace, KwaNodwengu. He was buried by his personal attendants, Ntinto kaMvubu Xulu, Mvubu kaGwazindlu Xulu, Mundula kaNomansala Ndwandwe, Kwabakithi kaThiwana Sibiya, Mnqumela kaMbangambi, Ntabeni kaNtonongwana and Mpenzeni kaGala kaNodade Biyela (Gala's son who made Shaka call off Ngomane's decrees). Mpande had reigned for 32 long years.

*Ngoza kaLudaba Majozi was Theolophus Shepstone's trusted servant who collaborated with whites against the Zulu people. (Killie Campbell Africana Library)*

*Khula Majozi (sixth from the left) took part in the Poll Tax Uprising in 1906 unlike his grandfather Ngoza Majozi who fought against his own people. (Killie Campbell Africana Library)*

# 8

# Emperor Cetshwayo kaShaka

CETSHWAYO HAD NO CONTACT with the whites until the year-long mourning period was over. But this made the whites uneasy. During that period, the Zulu became aware of the plan to attack them, but the date was unclear. Cetshwayo took these rumours very seriously and clandestinely prepared for war. The Zulu old guard advised Cetshwayo to avoid war at all cost, until the Zulu army was armed with modern weapons too. As the adage goes, 'keep your friends close and your enemies even closer', then the Zulu mind games began. Now that the mourning period was over, the nation was invited to converge at Makheni Palace to inaugurate Cetshwayo.

Prime Minister Masiphula coronated him after his personal doctor Dlephu Ndlovu from Emakhabeleni had perfomed all the necessary rituals. Even the Zulu living under whites in the Natal Colony came because as far as they were concerned, they remained Cetshwayo's subjects. All Zulu regiments came and were commanded by Masiphula, including those based south of uThukela River. They were all awe-inspiring in their military finery. After completion of the official rituals, Cetshwayo was presented to the assembly and like one man, they all rose together, stamped their right foot in unison and roared *Bayethe*!

Cetshwayo and his men went hunting to feed the maltitudes, it was a time of song dance. However, it was the absence of some senior members of the Zulu royal family and aristocracy such as Hhamu kaNzibe kaSenzangakhona (uThulwana), Mnyamana kaNgqengelele Buthelezi, Zibhebhu kaMaphitha and Mavumengwana kaNdlela (uThulwana) at eMakheni that caused some trepidation. Mavumengwana's absence was particularly severe because he had sided with the 'dead' Mbuyazwe. Some of them finally made a sensational entrance followed by hundreds of their followers. Clouds of red dust rose sky-high as they galloped on their decorated horses at full speed, shooting in the air. Everyone cheered and welcomed them. For a while the national strife and tribulations belonged to the past. Even more cattle were slaughtered that evening and they ate, drank and danced better and harder. A turnout of such multitude of people had never been seen in Zulu history. The spectacle gave rise to the Zulu saying that describes an extremely large number of people, *'bangangoZulu eya eMakheni* (they were as many as the Zulu who went to eMakheni).

However, the king's council and military command decided to confuse the enemy and requested Shepstone to crown Cetshwayo. But on both occasions, he did not even bother to respond. He only agreed on the third occasion because the colonial secret service reported that if Shepstone continued ignoring Cetshwayo, the Zulu would form an alliance with the Afrikaners. Cetshwayo's 'white coronation' venue was at uMlambongwenya Palace in KwaHlabisa near Dlinza forest where he was born and where his mother lived. From eMakheni, Dinuzulu was accompanied by thousands of people from all over the empire. Every Zulu wanted to be part of this spectacle, where a Zulu king was going to be 'coroneted' by a non-Zulu. It was a party that no one wanted to miss. They also wanted to show the whites that Cetshwayo had their full support. When he found out about the huge number of people accompanying Cetshwayo, he did not want to be outdone. He begged superiors for a huge imperial contingent to equally impress. But he was only allowed about 100 officers and 300 soldiers carrying an array of weapons including cannons.

They left Durban and used the steep iNsuze Road that ran below the uThukela River and past Eshowe. They crossed over uMlalazi and uMhlathuze Rivers and went up eMthonjaneni Heights. Once they reached a small waterfall in White iMfolozi River where the locals showered, he received instructions not to proceed because Cetshwayo was not done hunting and celebrating at eMakheni. Shepstone felt insulted, but he was forced to follow Cetshwayo's instructions because he was not going to be able to explain the turning back to his superiors. He suffered quietly in the heat and patiently waited not even knowing for how long he would be waiting. Days turned into weeks, and he waited. Sadly, Prime Minister Masiphula also died and the trip was delayed by another four days. Shepstone was not impressed with the delay and it frustrated him greatly, but his ego would not let him beg Cetshwayo to hurry up. The instruction finally came that Cetshwayo was ready for him at uMlambongwenya Palace.

Before marching to uMlambongwenya, Shepstone ordered his soldiers to laod their rifles and revolvers and said: 'Every one of you must be alert at the Coronation.

In the vent that the Zulu attack us, you should die like true Britons, shoulder-to-shoulder'. They finally arrived on the 3rd of September 1873 and found a huge tent that impressed everyone, as they were a novelty those days. Zulu crowds waited with song and dance. Shepstone tried to make a dramatic appearance with an ill-fitting military uniform and tried to look important. He marched into the palace grounds with his soldiers and the Maritzburg Rifles played martial music followed by the Durban Artillery pulling two field guns. The guns were later display outside the Old Fort in Durban.

However, Cetshwayo made a grand entrance with his regiments who stole the show. Even the most hardened cynics got goose bumps at the sight of their colours, feathers, spears, guns and shields. But it was their shining sculptured bodies and toned muscles that were jaw dropping. Shaka's sister Nomcoba made sure she attended the spectacle, despite her old age. After the armies had sized each other up, Cetshwayo and Shepstone sat uncomfortably next to each other outside the tent. They watched the Zulu dance for a while, then Cetshwayo and Shepstone disappeared inside the tent. After a while, Shepstone first stepped out and everyone continued talking as if nothing had happened. When Cetshwayo appeared, the multitudes fell silent. He wore a gold and red gown and delicately balanced a fake golden crown made by the master-tailor of the 75th Regiment. It had ostrich feathers that flouted gravity on the warm spring day. Cetshwayo stood to attention in front of the Zulu dignitaries with a slightly crooked smile. Then Shepstone announced: 'Men of the Zulu nation, I am installing Cetshwayo in your presence. His right ear was cut as the successor to Mpande. Do not ever harm him. Here he is.'

There was a loud '*Bayethe*' from the crowd. Then unexpectedly Shepstone took a piece of paper out of his tight jacket. He said that he was going to announce new laws that would govern the Zulu empire in future. No one protested, not even the Zulu military high command, and everyone seemed amused. The laws were as follows:

- ⊠ No one was to be killed for no reason
- ⊠ The accused reserved the right to bring witnesses and if found guilty, the case would be sent to Cetshwayo
- ⊠ No death penalty could be passed, even if someone was found guilty by the king
- ⊠ Petty crimes such as theft ceased to carry the capital punishment, just a fine.

Then a 17-gun salute followed instead of the 21-gun salute reserved for all royalty. Shepstone's superiors knew nothing about the 'laws' he had announced. The Zulu were not perturbed by the announcement, hence no one interrupted him. Instead Cetshwayo calmly asked Shepstone to demonstrate his 'fire-power' from the two cannons he had brought. Forever vain, Shepstone was flattered. Grinning broadly, he ordered his soldiers to fire one cannon into an empty field. When it was fired, it caused a tremor. Sweat streaming down his red sunburnt face and neck, he asked Cetshwayo to return the favour demonstrate the 'spear power' so to speak.

Cetshwayo conveyed the request to his military high command but Hhamu, Mnyamana (uThulwana regiment) and Mavumengwana refused, whereas Masiphula, Ntshingwayo and Cetshwayo's view carried the day. The iSangqu '*amaTshitshi*', iNgulube, uThulwana '*amaMboza*', iNdlondlo, uDloko, iNtontela, uFasimba, uMxhapho, uDududu, uMbonambi '*iNkonyanebomvu*', uNokhenke '*uZulu ekhenkesile*', uNdluyengwe, uMkhuze, uKhandempevu '*onqandamatshezulu, nyakamumbe bonqaka izinhlavu zabelungu*', uThuyasizwe, iNgobamakhosi, amaPhela, uLandandlovu and uFalaza regiments were first to sing Cetshwayo's favourite war song. They were joined by the female regiments, amaQhwaki, amaDlundlu, amaDuku, iNkelembe, iziNjinga, uGudluthukela, (*uGudludonga*), iSitimane, iNgcugce and iNdlovukayiphendulwa which comprised of the following Princesses, Ndindela, Sigayigayi, Bekiwe and Bathonyile. Whereas Princesses Mbhixabhixa, Mbikose, Nomabhunu, Nokwenda, Sancinza, Bhudu, Ngcobengcobe, Nomanxiwa, Mthabayi, Bathabile, Ziwelile, Nqumile, Popoza, Ntuthwane, Hlayisiye, Vukaphi and Ntonjana belonged to the Mkhandandlovu regiment. The female regiments were draped in their finest war attire and seductively swayed slowly back and forth singing:

| | |
|---|---|
| *Nango-ke okaNdaba* | there he is, the descendant of Ndaba |
| *Nangu ozithulele* | here he is, the quiet one |
| *Ji, akaqali muntu* | Ohh, he never starts arguments with anyone |
| *Uzithulele, akaqali muntu* | he is quiet, and never starts arguments with anyone |
| *OkaNdaba* | the descendant of Ndaba |
| *Izwe lonke, loku ezithulele* | he is the quietest in the whole country |
| *Sidedele siminye abafo* | please give us permission to kill the foreigners |

When they finished singing, the 60 000 soldiers performed *ingomane* and shouted *Sigidi* and the heavens shook. This was the same deafening noise that confused and terrified the Zulus' enemies on the battlefield. Shepstone's unsuspecting horses went berserk, they broke loose and took off in all directions. The mounted officers were thrown to the ground, the rest dropped to the ground taking cover. All this made

Shepstone's soldiers looked weak and unprofessional. His pink nostrils quivered as he too, lost his balance during the pandemonium and fell to the ground. He had to be supported by one of the Zulu soldiers; he was sadly upstaged in the presence of his men. The Zulu crowd enjoyed the spectacle and began to make fun of Shepstone's men and imitated them dive. Masiphula tried to apologise for the embarrassment caused, but Shepstone felt humiliated. Sweating profusely from his back and armpits which left unsightly marks on his military jacket, he ungraciously stormed off in a huff without a proper farewell. He even left behind his gift of cattle. He did, however, ask for them to be delivered to Durban. The truth is that the Zulu had asked Shepstone to conduct the 'coronation' to assess the military might of the British. Shepstone did not realise that the request to show off the 'fire-power' was a ruse to assess the destruction power of the cannons.

One of the tactics Shaka used to ensure men with a strong immune system enjoyed the privilege of fathering healthy offspring was that they marry much younger women. Another reason was younger women would still have enough energy to take care of an ageing husband as the years went by. Marriages were arranged by the state, to ensure that both male and female regiments got married to the appropriate regiment. However, Dingane wanted to destroy every innovation by Shaka and abolished it only to have it reinstated by Mpande. It saved the men the trouble of looking far and wide; they knew where to go and 'fish in a specific pond'. As per the custom, in 1876 Cetshwayo paired off iSangqu (male regiment) with Gudluthukela (*Gudludonga*) (female regiment), uThulwana (male) with iSitimane (female regiment). The 50-year-olds of uDloko and iNdlondlo (male regiments) based at Ezinduneni Mountain where they guarded the spears of deceased kings were paired off with iNgcungce (female regiment) who were only 19 years old. However, when the young women found out that the men they were supposed to marry, they sent the following message to uLundi Palace: '*Tshelani okaNdaba ukuthi ucu kalulingani. Angeke sigane lemidodovu yamakhehla azosishiya khona manje nje, asenze abafelokazi*' (tell Ndaba's descendant that it is impossible to tie a knot with the enthronement beads. We refuse to marry these old men who will soon die and make us widows). This was the greatest scandal to befall the empire ever.

These young women made history for being the first regiment ever to defy a royal decree. This defiance was unprecedented, and the families of the young women pressured them to agree. The majority capitulated, but some ran away and lived among whites in the south, others ran to the Transvaal while others went to live in the caves and forests. Some found refuge at Ekubazeni Palace royal shelter established by Cetshwayo before he became a king it was near Black Imfolozi River. It was a safe place for abused women, runaways and others who were in the process of proving their innocence after being accused of dabbling in witchcraft or some such. Anyone one that needed protection was welcome to live there for as long as they wished. Out of the whole iNgcugce regiment, no more than 10 young women flatly refused to run away or get married. About six or seven were put to death by their male relatives such as their fathers, uncles and brothers who were embarrassed that the young women had the audacity to defy a royal order. They impaled them with spears driven through their anuses (*ukujoja*), a slow painful death. However, when the whites in Durban heard about what had happened, they exaggerated the number and claimed Cetshwayo had ordered the impalement of 10 000 young women. As Cetshwayo was dealing with the insolence of iNgcugce, tensions continued rising between himself, the Afrikaners and the English. Shepstone felt obliged to report the deteriorating relations to Number 10 Downing Street, London.

Already strained relations were aggravated by the chaos in the recently established bankrupt independent state on the north-western borders of the Zulu empire. It was called the *Transvaal Republic* and it was led by a weak Prime Minister Rev Thomas Burgers, whose government was recalcitrant and dysfunctional. When Shepstone realised that no one really had confidence in Burgers, he lied to him and told him that Cetshwayo was about to attack the Transvaal. Then he convinced him that only the English could protect his bankrupt republic. The unsophisticated Burgers believed Shepstone and found it a welcome diversion from the circus he presided over.

The Afrikaners were not only worried about their overheating economy, but they also stopped paying taxes. The infrastructure was in shambles with impassable roads and no water working systems, which compromised sanitary conditions which led to the dilapidating outbreak of enteric fever. They did not hesitate to surrender their republic in April 1877 as a protectorate of the British. They allowed the Union Jack to fly over Pretoria without a single shot being fired. With their fortunes waning and the loss of the Republic of Natalia, the Afrikaners did what they did best, invade land. They then seized large tracts of the land belonging to King Sekwati of the Bapedi kingdom. Many Afrikaner farmers were encouraged to seize the land and were protected by the Afrikaner army. Delegation after delegation of Bapedi told the Afrikaner farmers to evacuate their land, but to no avail. Sekwati had no option but to prepare for war to take his land back. In truth, the Afrikaners could not afford a war. So, they lied and said that they had bought the thousands of hectares of land they occupied from King Mbandzeni from Swaziland for a mere 100 cattle.

After King Sekwati's death, one of his sons Sekhukhune, usurped power and became the king. He developed a friendship with Cetshwayo, and they exchanged gifts that can be found in possession of the Sekhukhune royalty in Limpopo to this day. Sekhukhune waged an armed struggle against the white colonisers and established a military alliance with the Zulu empire called 'The Zulu Pedi Combined Forces' (ZPCF). Zulu military advisers went to advise Sekhukhune and the Bapedi fighters went for military training in the Zulu empire to learn the art of war that gave the and the secret Zulu an edge. The ZPCF fought pitched battles against Afrikaners using some spears but mostly firearms and cannons. The Bapedi had amassed a large arsenal which was payment for working in the diamond mines in Kimberley. The ZPCF's fighting spirit and tactics had a very strong Zulu influences and they inflicted a humiliating defeat on the Afrikaners at Mount Mosega on the 1st of August 1876. The Afrikaners punished Burgers for losing the war to the ZPCF by replacing him in the next general elections with Paul Kruger as president in 1882. When the Afrikaners ran out of steam and ideas to defeat Sekhukhune, they let the British finish what they could not. Hence, The British attacked Sekhukhune four times unsuccessfully.

Then the British enlisted the help of 10 000 Swazi soldiers promising that they could keep the land in the Bapedi kingdom if they won. Sekhukhune was finally subdued on the 28th of November 1879 and managed to escape with some of his people and hid in Mamatatanageng caves, up on Lulu Mountain. But he lost his heir, Crown Prince Moroanoche, and 14 other members of his family. Sekhukhune survived without food and water in a siege that lasted a week. He surrendered and together with his family, they were sent to jail in Pretoria. The British did not keep their promise to the Swazi, instead they made a *detente* with the Afrikaners and carved up Swaziland between themselves. A sickly Sekhukhune was released three years later and killed by his ambitious cousin Mampuru at the Great Palace in Manoge on the 13th of August 1882. However, after Mampuru declared himself the king of the Bapedi, he found himself on the run from the British for killing Sekhukhune. Mampuru tried to take refuge under King Nyabela of the Ndebele kingdom but Nyabela sold him to English and Afrikaner bounty hunters who handed him over to the British authorities. In 1883, over 400 people witnessed the public hanging of a naked Mampuru on the site of today's Museum of Cultural History in Pretoria. But Mampuru refused to go without one final dramatic act. The rope around his neck snapped three times before he was successfully hanged. The majority of the Bapedi who lost their land have not been compensated to this day.

ISandlwana War

In November 1878, a year after the Afrikaners had given up 'their' real estate the Afrikaner Transvaal Republic, a random domestic matter took place in the heart of the Zulu empire. It set off a series of events that changed world history forever. Nandi's relative King Sihayo kaXongo Ngobese of the Qungebe kingdom lived an ordinary life with his many ordinary wives in Babanango. Zulu law dictated that a wife had to ask for permission from her husband before undertaking any adventure, especially something as radical as believing in a white Christian god. For one thing, Sihayo's wives knew that their husband held no brief for the Christian religion. But five of his wives decided to secretly convert to Christianity and knew that whatever Christian rituals, they had signed up for, had to be practised underground.

One lazy afternoon, when Sihayo had gone far away on a royal errand, his Christian wives congregated in a hut and began praying in low tones. But they had forgotten to lock the door. As fate would have it, Sihayo's heir, Mehlokazulu, heard humming like bees coming from the hut. When he went inside the hut, he nearly died of shock from what he saw. He found his father's wives on their knees, bent over with their bottoms up in the air and their eyes shut tight. They were urgently pleading with an unknown *inkosi* to come down to bless and save them. He left unnoticed, but as far as Mehlokazulu was concerned, it was tantamount to adultery. He reported them to his father when he returned and Sihayo was equally enraged. He believed Cetshwayo had been betrayed and it was unmitigated adultery. He couldn't help wondering what magical hold this unknown *inkosi* had on his wives that they were so desperate to be blessed with. After all, he was a wealthy man with many cattle and the Zulu aphrodisiacs enhanced his libido, which could be attested to by the large number of children he had fathered. A brief trial was held, and the wives confessed to having converted to Christianity without the blessing of their joint husband. They were sentenced to death.

Sihayo had heard about this white Christian god whose son was called Jesus and through whom everything was possible. But he personally only knew of *uMvelingqangi* who lived in the sky in a place called *ezulwini* (heaven) whose earthly representative on earth was Cetshwayo who lived at uLundi Palace. Their jurisdiction was unambiguous, so how could his wives want another man to come down and interfere with Cetshwayo's reign on earth. This was nothing short of profanity. The wives managed to escape to Natal across uMzinyathi River which was now under colonial rule. On the 28th of July 1878 Mehlokazulu with his brothers Mkhumbikazulu, Thekwane, Sisiyana and 30 friends as well as some family members went across the river and hunted the women down. They first found one and brought her back to Zulu justice and she was executed by firing squad. Then they went back for the others and found them and on their way home and their sentence was swiftly carried out.

Cetshwayo was not involved or even aware of this domestic affair. Besides, he and the military high command were worried by the large number of Afrikaners who were invading more land, even north of uThukela River now. They had seized land from the confluence of iNcome and uMzinyathi rivers up to uPhongolo River. When Cetshwayo told them to vacate, they claimed to have secretly 'bought' the land from Mpande for a mere 100 cows. Cetshwayo demanded to see proof of the transaction, but there was none. Their relationship dipped to a new low. Once again, pretending to want to find an amicable resolution to the land invasion, the British established a Land Dispute Commission. They tabled a report on the 11th of December 1878 which agreed with Cetshwayo. It found that the land had never been for sale or sold by Mpande to the Afrikaners. But the British pleaded with Cetshwayo to allow the Afrikaners to continue living on that land. Furthermore, they were prepared to *khonza* and become upright Zulu subjects and be ruled by Zulu laws. In any case, the British added, many of the Afrikaners were too old to move. Cetshwayo agreed and the matter seemed amicably resolved - but this was the axiomatic 'calm before the storm'. Forty-two days later, the Zulu dramatically changed the course of world history.

By 1883 the Transvaal Republic had recovered from its early economic woes and the leadership of Paul Kruger had made the Afrikaners considerably more self-confident. Gold had been discovered in the Transvaal and Kruger was in no mood to tolerate more imperial interference. They made it clear to the British that they were not happy with the 1878 Land Dispute Commission's findings. The five-week investigation found that the documents presented by the Afrikaners were fraudulent. For instance, one document alledged a meeting at KwaNondwengu Palace on the 16th March 1861 between Shepstone, Mpande and Cetshwayo took place, whereas Shepstone only got to the palace on the 9th of May; one only had the signature of the Afrikaners who presented it and another had Mpande's alledged signature and witnessed by a whole Afrikaner Commando. They also regretted having surrendered their Republic to British suzerainty and most importantly, they now wanted the British to act instead of protecting them in case the Zulu attacked them first. They even threatened another war against the red coats (British) if they did not change their tune. The British found themselves in an untenable position. They were forced to fight even though they were not yet ready. But on the other hand, they were not concerned because they were the number one undisputed reigning world power as they had never lost a war in any part of the world. But what they did to buy themselves time, is less than honourable.

The British High Commissioner to South Africa and Governor of the Cape Colony, Bartle Frere summarily changed the Land Dispute Commission's findings. He pronounced that the land seized by Afrikaners now belonged to the Natal government, therefore it could do as it pleased with it. At the same time, Shepstone accused Cetshwayo of engineering the killing of Sihayo's five wives. He did not stop there, he said that by merely converting and fleeing across the river it made them 'Natal citizens' who were arrested on 'English soil'. Then he ordered Cetshwayo to hand over Sihayo, his sons Mehlokazulu, Mkhumbikazulu, Thekwane, Sisiyana and the 30 accomplices to stand trial for murder in Natal. He also demanded 500 cattle for Sihayo's actions. Suddenly another matter that had nothing to do with the 'Sihayo Affair' became part of the demands. Shepstone demanded a further 100 cattle because a Zulu border patrol had arrested two whites, for trespassing, David Smith and William Henry Deighton of the Natal Colonial Engineers Department for trespassing on Zulu territory. Again, Cetshwayo knew nothing about it. Previously, some white men had also come to the same border and claimed to have been inspecting a road which had fallen into disuse. The Zulu patrol had warned them to stop creating paths for military wagons through people's homes.

According to a report written by the British First Resident, William Wheelwright who was succeeded by Melmoth Osborn, both Deighton and Smith had ignored the Zulu immigration officers when they tried to communicate with them. He said: 'The fact is that the two white men took no notice of lots of Zulus shouting out from their own (Thukela River) bank. They asked: 'What do you want there? But the whites walked quietly along (the river) as if they had not heard or as if they were deaf, very naturally confirmed the suspicion that they were no good.' Then the Zulu let them enter the low river and only affected an arrest when they were on an island in the middle of the river near Kranskop. Once they had arrested them, they interrogated them as follows:

"What are you doing here?'

"What had the soldiers come to Greytown for?"

"What did the white men want coming down here?"

"They were two others not long ago, then other two few days since and now there is other? You must be coming for some reason?

The Zulu recognised a provocation when they saw it but chose to temporarily lie low because they were not yet ready for war. So Cetshwayo 'agreed' to Shepstone's absurd demands but asked to be given adequate time to organise the cattle. However, Cetshwayo reported the matter to the Natal Governor Sir Henry Bulwer. After investigating, Bulwer ruled that Shepstone should not have implicated Cetshwayo on both accounts. But Bulwer did not cancel the ridiculous cattle fine. While Cetshwayo was busy disputing the allegations, the unstable northern borders were ablaze. Mbilini, his deputy Manyonyoba kaThulasizwe Kubheka, and their followers decided to punish whites for increasingly seizing more land north of uThukela River. They raided German mission stations and Afrikaner farms, killing everyone, including women and children. He also seized thousands of their cattle to his fortresses in eHlobane, eNtombe, KwaThalagu and eMbongeni.

A manhunt for Mbilini and his followers was unleashed but he was always a step ahead. The Afrikaners then reported him to Cetshwayo, but he told them that he did not want any involvement. It is only when Mbilini began killing locals that Cetshwayo took it personally and summoned him to uLundi. But Mbilini begged for the king's indulgence and said that he had no time to go to uLundi as he was busy killing whites and their Zulu collaborators. He also said that his biggest mission in life was to drive the whites out of the empire. The more the white commandos looked for Mbilini, the more he killed whites with horrifying brutality. For some reason best known to them, both Shepstone and Bulwer accused Cetshwayo of harbouring Mbilini simply because they could not find him. Therefore, Shepstone added another 500-cattle fine for Mbilini's actions. For tactical reasons, Cetshwayo agreed and again he asked for more time to organise the cattle. The time he had to comply with the different penalties varied but Cetshwayo successfully negotiated to meet all the demands by the 10th of January 1879. But after agreeing to the time frame, Bulwer suddenly ordered Cetshwayo to a meeting at short notice.

*Mehlokazulu kaSihayo Ngobese (second standing) with his brothers Mkhumbikazulu, Thekwane and Sisiyana and his friends Khambi kaHhamu Zulu and other fighters. Emperor Cetshwayo refused to hand them over to the British to stand trial in the Natal courts over a disagreement about the interpretation of a law. This was one of the major causes of iSandlwana war in 1879 where the British were defeated by the Zulu army. (KwaZulu-Natal Museum Services)*

*Mehlokazulu kaSihayo Ngobese's wives. He was killed during the Poll Tax Uprising 1906 which was the last Zulu conventional war in eMhome Gorge. (Killie Campbell Africana Library)*

# Emperor Cetshwayo kaShaka

*The Zulu Immigration Officers. One such unit arrested two whites, David Smith and William Henry Deighton of the Natal Colonial Engineers Department for trespassing the Zulu empire border in 1879. This was one of the causes of the iSandlwana War. (Killie Campbell Africana Library)*

*Prince Mbilini waMswati I (right) and his deputy Manyonyoba kaThulasizwe Kubheka led abaQulusi regiment that caused a bloodbath at eNtombe River, 1879. Over 80 British soldiers were killed including Captain Moriarity; Surgeon Cobbins; 2 white wagon conductors; 15 African drivers and the rest of the bodies were found littered at the banks of the river. The victorious Zulu also took about 90,000 rounds of ammunition and over 100 kg of gunpowder. (SB Bourquin Collection)*

Looking at the events throughout 1878, it is clear that the British were spoiling for war. Hoisting the Union Jack in Pretoria two years earlier had been easy, so sorting out the Zulu was surely going to require even less effort, or so they thought. Cetshwayo sent a strong delegation of about 50 people, John Dunn and 14 aristocrats led by Vumindaba kaNtethi Biyela (uKhandempevu). They met the British emissaries Shepstone, Fynn, who was now a Magistrate of uMsinga and Forester Walker led by Charles Brownlee on the 11th of December 1878. They sat under a sycamore fig tree now known as the 'The Ultimatum Tree' in Mandeni (*Fort Pearson*) on the south of uThukela River, close to its mouth. Brownlee sat on a chair and looked very asinine insignificant in his colonial uniform. A steady stream of sweat poured out of every pore as he read out the ultimatum signed by Bishop Colenso:

- Surrender of Sihayo' and his three sons for their trial by the Natal courts.
- Payment of a fine of five hundred cattle for the outrages committed by the above and for Cetshwayo's delay in complying with the request of the Natal Government for the surrender of the offenders.
- Payment of a 100 cattle for the offence committed against Messrs. Smith and Deighton.
- Surrender of the Swazi Chief Mbilini and others to be named hereafter, to be tried by the Transvaal courts.
- Observance of the coronation promises.
- That the Zulu army be disbanded, and the men allowed to go home.
- That the Zulu military system should be discontinued and other military regulations adopted, to be decided upon after consultation with the Great Council and British Representatives.
- That every man, when he comes to man's estate, shall be free to marry.
- All missionaries and their converts, who until 1877 lived in Zululand, shall be allowed to return and reoccupy their stations.
- All such missionaries shall be allowed to teach and any Zulu, if he chooses, shall be free to listen to their teaching.
- A British Agent shall be allowed to reside in Zululand, who will see that the above provisions are carried out.
- All disputes in which a missionary or European is concerned, shall be heard by the king in public and in the presence of the British Resident.
- No sentence of expulsion from Zululand shall be carried out until it has been approved by the British Resident.

Alarmed by the British audacity, the Zulu joint committee of the military high command and the king's council held an emergency meeting to consider the ultimatum. All the regiments were called to the capital. The drums of war were loud and clear and the demand to hand over Sihayo was the biggest outrage. The Zulu had never abandoned one of their own before, especially a member of the king's council related to the royal family through Nandi. They debated the ultimatum at length and at the end they voted. Cetshwayo, Zibhebhu, two of Mpande's sons Maduna and Dabulamanzi said they should ignore the ultimatum while another three of Mpande's sons Hhamu, Ziwedu and Sitheku (uThulwana) wanted to submit to the British demands. To break the deadlock, they agreed to solicit the army's opinion, even though they instinctively knew what the army would say. Cetshwayo led regiments stationed around the capital and they marched to KwaLandandlovu Palace the following day. They were joined by all regiments that could arrive within 24 hours. They were dead silent as Cetshwayo explained their predicament. When he finished, the thousands of men assembled jumped to their feet in military precision and performed *ingomane* and shouted '*Sigidi!*'

There was nothing more to say. The die was cast. This unanimous decision to ignore the British reminded Cetshwayo that no Zulu emperor had ever bowed to any ultimatum before. It certainly was not going to happen now, not with the Zulu army in its present mood. Cetshwayo gave his army a long hard look and his chest swelled with pride. He was convinced that the whites were the 'swallows' that Shaka had said would try to destroy the Zulu empire. With a few drops of sweat on his shiny dark forehead, he led the army in singing many times over as though Mkabayi was present:

| | |
|---|---|
| *Uyinkosi yohlanga* | *he is the king of humanity* |
| *Oho, O!* | *Ohho, O!* |
| *Hha, oye!* | *Hha, Oye!* |
| *Jijiji, ajiji!* | *Jijiji, ajiji!* |

After the meeting, Cetshwayo sent the royal war messenger, Bhejane kaNomageja Khoza (iMboza) and his assistant Mnyakanyala nomatsha Xulu, to announce *ukhukhulelangoqo* (national call up) in the entire empire, including in the 'occupied' lands. Bhejane's descendants can be found living in Enseleni near eMpangeni to this day. They are forever proud of their ancestor's role in this war. Firearms and weapons were collected from all households and sent to uLundi. Food was stockpiled in strategic places and some cattle were hidden in forests with no easy access. Female regiments and retired warrior women were mobilised, and they too made their way to the capital. Civilian women reorganised their homes to reflect a kingdom at war. They covered their faces with special herbs, wore their leather skirts inside out, while grass mats, brooms and other household items were kept upright. Livestock, food, valuable items, the weak, the aged and children were moved into caves. Cetshwayo bought more arms; they were serviced and distributed to both male and female regiments. He sent John Dunn, who since the death of Mbuyazwe had become Cetshwayo's new 'best friend'. When Dunn wanted to know the reason for stockpiling arms, Cetshwayo said they were for protection against an Afrikaner invasion. Cetshwayo asked Dunn to write the British a letter assuring them that Sihayo, his sons and everyone involved would be handed over and the fine would be paid.

Cetshwayo also asked that should 30 days pass without some of the ultimatum demands being met, it would be due to flooded rivers, which would prevent the cattle from being timeously assembled. But Bulwer, Frere and Shepstone did not respond to Cetshwayo's 'humble' request. Instead, they accused Cetshwayo of more transgressions such as stockpiling arms, but Dunn defended him. He told them that it was a mere precaution against the recalcitrant Afrikaners. The white men naïvely believed Cetshwayo as they could not bring themselves to imagine that the 'apologetic' and 'passive' Zulu emperor was using the oldest trick in warfare – disinformation. Then the British sent Cetshwayo a stern warning and said he was behaving like a 'spoilt native' for failing to comply with their ultimatum. They also informed him that since they were benevolent, they would grant him an extension only until the 11th of January 1879 and not the 30 days he had requested. But if he did not comply, Frere said a state of war would be deemed to exist between them and the Zulu empire.

Cetshwayo did not meet the deadline because he never intended to do so in the first place. All he wanted the time for, was to buy extra weapons. Moreover, when the British responded to his extension request, the secret service informed him that British forces were en route to uLundi. Even though it was days before the expiry of the ultimatum. Most Afrikaners refused to join the British war, but some did as they had personal scores to settle. Piet Uys wanted to avenge his father Piet and brother Dirkie who were both killed in the Battle of eThaleni. The overconfident and arrogant General Lord Chelmsford, who was Queen Victoria's favourite and a close friend of Frere, was the commander in chief of the British Imperial Forces (BIF). He recruited soldiers from five nations - the British, Indians from India, New Zealanders, Canadians and the Batlokwa, a non-Nguni group. There were also the Zulu who were based in Natal. Chelmsford deployed three columns and two reserve columns. The *Central Column* was commanded by Col Richard Glyn and arrived at Rorke's Drift on the 9th of January and on the day the ultimatum expired on the 11th of January, they crossed Buffalo River. They spent their first night in Zulu territory relaxed, with no Zulu in sight. The following morning, they marched to Sihayo's huge homestead and pounded it to the ground with canons killing several women, children, infirm males and Mkhumbikazulu, who was guarding the homestead. Again, there were no Zulu in sight and the British became more confident. They moved on to King Jobe Sithole's palace that they also razed. They looted over 3000 cattle from both homesteads.

Chelmsford could almost see the glory that would be bestowed upon him for disciplining the warlike Zulu once and for all and without too much effort. Then after a few days of marching, they leisurely camped near uMzanyana River below the insignificant sphinx-like hill called iSandlwana. It was on the 20th of January. This unspectacular hill deep in the heart of the Zulu empire got its name from its house-like shape. The highly mobile *Left Column* was commanded by Col Wood. Whereas Col Durnford (he was present at Cetshwayo's coronation) and Col Rowlands each commanded an additional reserve force. Col Pearson commanded the *Right Column* and crossed the uThukela River on the 22nd of January coming from Eshowe. Pearson received some good news after crossing the river as his men made helio contact with him and informed him that: 'Mrs Pearson is well and delivered a baby daughter'. Had they been Zulu, the baby's name would have been *Nompi* (the one born during the war). The highly mobile *Left Column* was commanded by Col Evelyn Wood. Whereas Col Durnford (he was present at King Cetshwayo's coronation) and Col Hugh Rowlands commanded the additional reserve forces, respectively.

John Dunn (standing left) with local leaders. He fought against the Zulu during the iSandlwana war in 1879; killed 200 Mthethwa family members in cold blood; took their 2500 cattle and also stole their land around Mandeni area. (SB Bourquin Collection)

*The Ultimate Tree along uThukela River near Mandeni. This is where the British gave the Zulu an ultimatum but Emperor Cetshwayo ignored it which was one of the reasons of the iSandlwana war in 1879. (Killie Campbell Africana Library)*

*Nongejeni Zuma was Theophilus Shepstone's servant from his youth until he died in March 1945. His brother Ndabayakhe Zuma was the king of the Zuma people in Nkandla. (Killie Campbell Africana Library)*

The British Imperial Force (BIF) was made up by about 50 000 foot soldiers and cavalry. They were armed with breech-loading rifles, cannons and rocket batteries. They had 1000 ox-drawn wagons carrying loads of five tonnes each. Ironically, most of the British army consisted of Africans called the African Natal Native Contingent (ANNC). Their uniform was a piece of red cloth tied around their foreheads to distinguish them from Cetshwayo's army. However, the Natal non-combatants wore black coats. About 8000 men were from Natal and they made up 16 percent of the BIF. They had been recruited by two brothers Robert and Samuel Samuelson who spoke fluent isiZulu. The King Zikhali kaMatiwane sent 300 men from his amaNgwane kingdom. 200 men answered the call from the Hlubi kingdom; King Homoyi sent 600 men from the Bomvu kingdom; King Macangca sent 100 men from the Mkhabela kingdom; King Nondonise sent 100 men from the Luthuli kingdom; King Sobuza sent 600 men from the junior amaBomvu kingdom and 100 men from the amaMbo kingdom.

King Balungeni sent 200 men from the Mthembu kingdom; King Mzwangedwa sent 100 men from the Cele kingdom; King Somolo sent 100 calvary; King Sikhali supplied 100 men for the 2$^{nd}$ Battalion; King Hlubi's 1$^{st}$ Battalion had 50 men while King Hlubi of the Batlokwa kingdom sent numerous mercenaries. Some of the ANNC members were coerced to fight against Cetshwayo while others gladly sided the whites. Only one in 10 ANNC soldiers in a group was given a gun, even then with only four bullets, the rest were to use their own spears. Some of the Zulu *amakholwa* (Christian converts) mainly from Driefontein, Ladysmith, eNdaleni near Richmond, Rockdale and Edendale, were led by Stephen Mini, Elijah Khambule (*Durnford's interpreter*), Simeon Khambule, Jabez Molefe, Gabangaye kaMatiwane Mchunu and Njengabantu kaSobuza Ngubane (Shaka's one-time *udibi*). The British were so pleased with Njengabantu's dedication that they made him a police sergeant at the Greytown Police Station after the war.

Meanwhile, the Zulu army assembled at uLundi under the very capable commander-in-chief Ntshingwayo (he was Senzangakhona's best friend and was present when he met Nandi for the first time). His deputy was Mavumengwana kaNdlela Ntuli (one of Ndlela's sons). The *izinyanga zempi* (war doctors) performed the mandatory ritual for the war including the killing of a black bull. Next, the regiments moved to eMakhosini Valley where most of the Zulu kings are buried. The members of the military high command recited the Zulu king's laudatory praises at King Senzangakhona's grave. They also informed all other kings buried in the vicinity about the forthcoming war and pleaded for protection to defeat the invaders. They also took an oath that they would die fighting in defence of the empire and would not surrender.

They led about 40 000 soldiers from the following regiments; uMxhapho; uGqikazi; uDududu; uSishizwe, uMzinyathi, uBulawayo; iNdlondlo; uThulwana, iNkwethu, iNdwali, iNsukamngeni, and uNdi formed the forward right horn; uNodwengu (2000) formed the right horn; uNokhenke (2000) and uKhandempevu and part of uMcijo (4000) formed the centre right horn; uDloko and another part of uMcijo formed the left centre; iNdabakawombe; iSanqu; uDukuza; uMthuyasizwe; uMlambongwenya; aMankwenkwe; iNdluyengwe; iziPikili, uBhewula, iShudu, uFasimba; iNgobamakhosi (5000) formed the left horn; uVe and uMbonambi, the sniper regiment (5000) formed the forward left horn; iNdumezulu Rifle regiment and a mounted regiment. They carried one-metre-long guns, long-barrelled guns, double-barrelled guns, 50-centimetre guns used for close-range fighting, long-range guns that used small bullets, cannons, harpoons, spears, shields and an assortment of traditional weapons. The Zulu army looked dazzling as they stood to attention.

Their glistening and sinewy bodies were all shades of yellow, brown and black. Each regiment's distinct colour combinations of feathers, furs, beads and mouth-high shields stood out in the warm summer sun. Their weapon of choice *iklwa* glistened menacingly as were the rest of the weapons. It was truly a breathtaking sight that would have made Shaka proud. Ntshingwayo deployed some of the female regiments, such as uThiyane, amaDlundlu, amaQhwaki and amaDuku, who were trained in the use of modern firearms as the rear guard. Ntshingwayo deployed the regiments in Shaka's pincer formation. The time to defend the honour and dignity of not only the Zulu empire but also Africa's pride had finally come. Before the Zulu army departed from uLundi, they asked their ancestors to plead with the Zulu God to make them victorious. They then sang war songs such as this one composed by Dingane:

| *Woza langa, lashona* | come on out sun, it will set |
| *Lashona* | it will set |
| *Woza langa, lashona* | come on out sun, it will set |
| *Liyawushona kuleziya ntaba* | it will set over those mountains |

The 40 000 men performed *ingomane* and saluted *Sigidi!* The noise vibrated and echoed in the valleys and surely it must have woken up Mgobhozi, Ndlela, Mkabayi and many Zulu braves, long dead and gone. The chest of the main army departed from KwaNodwengu on the 17th of January and covered 80 kilometres in five days. This was a slow march as Cetshwayo had specifically instructed the army not to rush but ensure that they defeated the British. Apparently, it took six months before grass could grow where the regiments marched going to meet the British head on. Chelmsford's army on the other hand could only cover 16 kilometres in 10 days. Once they arrived at the battle theatre, Commander Ntshingwayo recited the laudatory praises of kings Shaka and Senzangakhona and held his shield up and said: '*Nansi intando yakithi*' (this is what we love).

Mehlokazulu kaSihayo (iNgobamakhosi) gave a first-hand account of the battle to Magema kaMagwaza Fuze a literate Zulu who could also speak English recalled: 'The Zulu generals had planned to attack the British on the evening of the 23rd of January as it was going to be a full moon, but the British attacked us a day earlier on the 22nd of January. It was a pitch-dark moonless night and the British came upon us as we lay low inside a maize field and we exchanged gunfire. Their leader Col Dunford retreated and segregated his army. He ordered the mounted ANNC force to attack on the left side and the whites to attack us from the right side. We watched them as they came for us and our commanders ordered us *sihlale phezu kwamahawu* (to sit on our shields). It took iron-fist discipline for us not to rush head on. The day before the clash, the army chest which I was part of, slept on a very rocky place below eNquthu Hill.

We did not see Chelmsford's soldiers, the mounted ANNC, the Batlokwa and white soldiers moving towards our direction, but they did not see us either. Instead, they came across uMcijo near us below Nquthu Hill and they were forced to turn around and fight uMcijo. When the firing started, we rose and advanced towards them shooting. They were shocked to see such a large army and retreated. Mkhosana kaMvundlana kaMenziwa Biyela commanded uKhandempevu and easily sliced through them. Prince Dabulamanzi commanded uVe regiment even though he belonged to Udloko regiment and iNgobamakhosi was led by Sigcwelegwele kaMhlekehle Mngadi and they fought with British forces on a hillock nearby. They would now and then also turn to shoot at us, but we slowly kept on coming. Finally, the British forces disappeared behind a *donga* together with their horses and we occasionally saw their hats when they came up to shoot. We kept on taking cover as we advanced towards them, but we were taking heavy casualties. We ended up retreating to the left, but they did not follow us. The army horns had gone to the hill and we headed to Buffalo River and British forces rushed to protect their base and kept on firing at us.

'We also returned fire and advanced towards them, many died but we kept going forward. When they ran out of ammo for their big guns, they used revolvers and when those ran out, the British forces stood tightly together shoulder-to-shoulder. Then they fought with the bayonets attached to their guns in the hand-to-hand combat. We speared many of them to death and some of us even stripped them and wore their colourful clothes. Whilst on the other side of their camp, some of British forces ran to take cover in their camp. But they were surprised by uKhandempevu and uMbonambi and they all arrived at the camp at the same time. This is where many of them lost their lives and by now the two army horns had enveloped the camp. When they realised that there was nowhere to run, they started firing wildly and ran towards Buffalo River.

'They managed to cut through and run away. We followed them in hot pursuit and we also lost many men, but we managed to slaughter them especially after they ran out of ammunition. The cannons did little damage because we only lost about four men to the cannons in my regiment. We continued fighting ferociously on all fronts, but I must commend one white soldier who fought better than most of them. He stood just below iSandlwana Hill and dispersed rapid fire in all directions. He managed to kill many of us single-handedly. There was even a time when he had all of us lying low and as we planned how to corner him, he was taken out by one of our snipers. By the time I came close to his body, I found that they had already removed his top. Many whites drowned as they tried to cross Buffalo River. This place became known as *eSigubudu* (Ford of Escapees). Out of the hundreds that were fleeing, only about 40 black and white BIF soldiers survived, and they were either on foot or on horses. After defeating them we took two cannons back with us and helped ourselves to some of the items they left behind.

Others got carried away and drank any clear liquid they came across, thinking it was the white man's alcohol but some of it turned out to be paraffin. We buried most of our soldiers in two empty wheat granaries and others were buried in the *dongas* and everywhere we found holes. The BIF soldiers we found lying around as we made our way home. We cut their stomachs open because we believed that if you did not do that, the killer's body would swell up. I also heard that some people cut their heads off. For instance, Magudulwana Mthembu speared two whites and decapitated the third after he was shot in the leg. The headless white fell on top of him and he was pinned down and only freed when we looked for survivors. On the whole the Zulu showed extreme bravery but the British also fought well in a terrain they did not know.'

The death of one of the British Commanders, Col HB Pulleine who was one of the officers decorated with the Victoria Cross yet had performed dismally, was recounted in detail by the Zulu who killed him: 'I approached a lone white tent and saw a white soldier sitting at a table (apparently he was writing a letter to Chelmsford) and he shot me through the neck. I managed to jump and stabbed him dead. Hence I am now called *Maqedindaba* (the finisher of the matter) because my bravery led to the defeat of the British.' Whereas Lieutenant Melville plunged into the 12 metre-wide flooded Buffalo River with his horse in an attempt to save the Queen's colours of the 24th Regiment. He was ejected from his horse and he tried to hang on a jutting rock but the colours slipped from his hand. Lt Coghill had managed to cross the river with his horse in full flight but when he saw that Melville was struggling, he turned back and jumped into the river and saved both the colours and Melville. But the horse was shot dead. They both managed to crawl out of the river exhausted. The Zulu chased them in hot pursuit and killed them in the dense bush. The colours were found further down the river stuck between rocks.

As if to compound the terror unleashed on the BIF by the Zulu, there was a sun eclipse around 2.30pm as the battle was raging. The bloodletting did not stop until the BIF ran away. Some of the white soldiers ca rocks mouflaged their white helmets with tea so as not to stand out. They had stood out from far and became easy prey for snipers. Whereas when Capt Reginald Younghusband realised that he wasn't going to survive together with his 'C' Company, he went around and shook hands of his men, bade them farewell and led them towards the Zulu gunfire. He was shot between the eyes. Despite coming under heavy fire, the Zulu quickly figured that they should lie down after the word 'aim' and leopard crawl forward. This went on until the BIF ran out of ammunition. The rest is history, colourful history. Most of the British officers did not regard the Zulu as a formidable enemy. Even when warned by Col JH Bowker who had seen the Zulu in military action tried to warn them. They had dismissed his concerns and said: 'This little war will be a pleasant military promenade in Zululand'. They sat comfortably in their tents as the war raged. They insisted to be served on fine china, linen table clothes and silverware. They continued drinking wine as the dispatches were coming thick and fast. They toasted to *'our swords'* on Wednesdays and on Saturdays they toasted *'to our sweethearts and wives, may they never meet'*.

The ANNC members, who had been forced to fight, would shoot in the air and once the four bullets were finished, they would drop the gun and run away from the battlefield. Then the whole group ran away with their spears. The battle broke out around 11am and it was all over shortly after the sun eclipse at about 3pm. There was a horrendous number of casualties on both sides. The Zulu suffered many deaths, but the British lost more men. After their victory the Zulu army jogged back to the capital, uLundi. They celebrated for days on end and thanked *uMvelingqangi* and the Zulu ancestors. Many of the old warhorses imitated Mgobhozi and danced his moves when he celebrated victory and others imitated Shaka. Cetshwayo was euphoric because he had humiliated a world power and proved the invincibility of the Zulu army.

The memories of the day Afrikaners held him down and cut out a piece of his ear as though he were an animal, were the last thing on his mind. The joint military high command and king's council were debriefed by each regiment and described how they defeated the enemy. The regiments that were held in reserve felt cheated as they missed out on the action, especially since the whole Zulu army had not fought a decent war, since the death of Ndlela. So uGqikazi, uLundi and uMbonambi regiments commanded by Ndabuko kaMpande, Mankulumana kaSomaphunga Ndwandwe (uMbonambi regiment) and Ntuzwa kaNhlaka Mdlalose (brother to Sekethwayo, Mkabayi's personal bodyguard) sneaked across the Buffalo River at night. They fought with the British the whole night because they wanted to be part of history. In the morning they returned to uLundi singing a song composed specifically for the iSandlwana victory:

| | |
|---|---|
| Siyayivuma inkani | we fear nothing |
| Siyayivuma inkani | we fear nothing |
| Sesabehlula bezile abelungu | we routed the invading whites |
| Imnandi | we are excited by our bravery |
| Siyixoxa enkosini | we are going to inform the king |

The iSandlwana battle produced many extraordinary heroes but some military officers were simply outstanding. Their brilliance under fire and heroic feats will forever be etched in Zulu history. Some of them are Sekethwayo kaNhlaka Mdlalose (Mkabayi's bodyguard), Mhlekehleke Ngema (iNgobamakhosi), Mfusi kaManyala Mdletshe (his descendant is Bonga Mdletshe in KwaHlabisa), Hhemulana kaMbangazeli Sibiya (later commanded KwaNdunu Battle), Mbopha kaWolizibi Hlabisa, Mpandamana kaNdlela Ntuli, Sitshaluza kaMamba Ntshangase was related to Mpande's Prime Minister Masiphula, Mvubu kaNgqengelele Buthelezi, Siganande kaZokufa Shezi (later commanded the poll tax revolt) and many others. The war continued for most of the year throughout the empire.

After the British defeat at iSandlwana, major battles were fought at Rorke's Drift, eGingindlovu, eHlobane. Phalane kaMdinwa Mkhwanazi, Somopho kaSikhala

Mthembu, Mavumengwana kaNdlela Ntuli and Majiya Nzuza fought with distinction at iNyezane, KwaNodwengu and Eshowe. The battle at eKhambula was fought with outstanding bravery by abaQulusi. The defeat of the mighty British reverberated around the world. This made the name of the Zulu people be associated with bravery the world over and Shaka remans a military icon to this day. In the meantime, Mbilini, his brother Thekwane, Manyonyoba and his retinue carried out a private war against the invaders unabated. He caused a bloodbath on either side of eNtombe River on the 12th of March around 3.30pm by killing Captain Moriarity, 61 soldiers, two white wagon conductors and 15 African drivers. His name became synonymous with 'pure evil' among the colonisers. The Battle of eHlobane stands out as having been fought by a large number of female regiments. This is where Thekwane and Mbilini were grievously wounded by Heinrich Filter, a German missionary's son and Field Marshal Wood's interpreter on the 15th of April. Heinrich was later ambushed by Manyonyoba and abaQulusi and was killed him in a horrific way. They were avenging the killing of Mbilini, and they made his mother watch as they tortured him to death. Manyonyoba's greatest personal loss was at the eNtombe Battle where he lost three sons.

*Members of the African Natal Native Contingent were part of the British Imperial Force that fought against the Zulu during the iSandlwana War in 1879. (Killie Campbell Africana Library)*

The Zulu elite Christians in the 19th Century with their handlers. (Seated, left) James Mqwabi, Frank Zulu, Simon Msimang, Walter Msimang. (Middle row left) Stephen Mini, Colonel Wales, Johannes Khumalo, General HP Leader, Timothy Gule John Mthimkhulu, Mathew Msane. (Back, left) John Zuma, Sololmon Xaba, Stephen Xaba, Jabez Molefe, Simeon Khambule, Lazarus Xaba, Micah Kunene, Simon Khumalo, Anea Khumalo. (Killie Campbell Africana Library)

Coloured (mixed-race) soldiers fought on the side of the white colonisers against the Zulu nation during the Poll tax uprising in 1906. (Killie Campbell Africana Library)

Some prominent people who were killed at iSandlwana fighting on the side of the British were Gabangaye kaPhakade Mchunu (grandson of Macingwane) and Captain George Shepstone (Theophilus' son) was killed by Mtweni kaZibana in a hand-to-hand combat. As though that was not enough, the Zulu army put an end to one of the oldest European dynasties. They killed the French Prince Imperial Eugene Louis Napoleon Bonaparte, the only son of Napoleon 111 (Emperor King Napoleon's cousin) and Empress Eugenie. The French were not at war with the Zulu, but the effeminate artist-turned-mercenary wanted to experience active duty with all its brutality. The British government only allowed him to go to Natal on condition that he would not go to the front line. They agreed that he would be based in Pietermaritzburg under the eagle eye of Chelmsford as his aide-de-camp. He then sailed on the *Danube* together with two officer friends from Southampton on the 28$^{th}$ of February 1879 and landed in Cape Town in March.

The doe-eyed 23-year-old prince made time for some real romance in the Cape before he continued with his journey. He fell madly in love with an Afrikaner beauty Sophie Botha, whom he met at the Naval Ball hosted in his honour in Simonstown. The Prince Imperial was so besotted with his *'poppie'* Sophie that he even visited her two days later at her family's farm *Hoogenkraal* under the majestic Outeniqua Mountains. He proposed to her and only had a dressing mirror which he gave her as a gift. However, he urgently sent for the family jewels to be sent from the family's world famous collection including the official French Royal ring. However, during a romantic picnic together with Sophie's two sisters and his two officer friends, tragedy struck as the lovebirds romatically rowed on the Maalgate River. Their canoe capsized and Sophie drowned. Devastated and inconsolable as he was, he did not wait for the funeral and proceeded to Durban. The jewels, sadly, arrived after both the Prince and Sophie had died. The old dressing mirror still hangs in the Supper Room at Hoogekraal farm.

He arrived in Durban on the 31$^{st}$ of March and went to the British Headquarters in Pietermaritzburg to familiarise himself with military life in the time of war. But he became bored from analysing military dispatches and wanted to be the one writing them *in situ*. Chelmsford transferred him to the Royal Engineers where he could see some safe action through reconnaissance missions. He was assigned a French speaker Lt Jahleel Brenton Carey and they went on a few missions and they were never in danger. However, for the trip on the 1$^{st}$ of June he was supposed to be accompanied by Zulu servants, but they 'mistakenly' reported to a wrong tent far away. Obviously, Chelmsford knew that the Prince Imperial was reckless so he ended up being escorted by 12 men; Lt J Carey, Lt W Cochrane, Sgt R Willis, Corp

J Grubb, N Le Tocq, W Abel, G Rogers and about six unnamed Basotho servants. They went deeper than usual, and he took command of the mission stopping a few times because he was dazzled by the breathtaking landscapes of the kingdom. He carefully sketched the panoramic views before continuing.

He was on his grey horse Percy, and he was with his fox terrier *Nero* and the second horse *Fate* when his group galloped up uMhlungwane Hill and descended into a deserted five hut homestead with a cattle enclosure and found warm cinders and a lonely dog. After looking around, they saw nothing threatening and the naïve Prince Imperial was suddenly overcome by desire to drink a cup of coffee in the middle of the African wilderness. After all, it was about 3pm, which was time for high tea in England. He ordered the Basotho servants to rekindle the fire from the thatch, collect water from the nearby iJojosi River and pull the coffee from his bag. They did not post a lookout and some of his men alighted from their horses and relaxed in the middle of a war zone. They drank their coffee, smoked and let their horses graze. Little did they know that a handful of Zulu warriors, Hlabanathunga, Mshingishingi, Khubalo, Langalibalele, Cabanga, Gwebuka and Maganga were observing them.

One of Cetshwayo's bodyguards, Mnukwa Ngodwane, gave a personal account of what transpired to Harriette Colenso: 'We were on a reconnoitre mission on the banks of iJojosi River one late afternoon and suddenly saw a group of whites with a few black mercenaries come towards us. We hid in the tall grass. They stopped not far from us, and some got off their horses including the Prince Imperial. We shot at them whilst four of them were still on their horses but missed and they rode off. The Prince Imperial only managed to place one foot into the stirrup. His horse *Percy* bolted with his gun still on top of it, dragging him on the broken country. He only managed to break loose after about 150 metres. He got up and shot at us with his revolver but also missed. Then we ran towards him. Cabanga was the first person to spear him in the chest followed by Gwebuka and Maganga. We also speared four white soldiers, one of them was called Rogers, and we shot and killed another called Abel in the back and speared to death one of their Basotho servants. I personally took the prince's *inkemba* (sword) which I gave the king, who later handed it over back to the British.'

The soldiers who survived such as Carey were court-martialed and they attested that the Prince Imperial had not been able to remount his horse. In the process the Austerlitz made sword that belonged to Napoleon fell and the horse trampled on his right hand. Then the prince fled on foot and two revolver shots rang out and a spear struck him in the thigh. He pulled it out and used it to block more spears then narrowly missed three close-range bullets. He was stabbed in the left shoulder and as he began to sink, a spear landed in his right eye and brought him down. The Zulu converged on him and the fight was over in less than a minute. The lifeless naked body of the Prince Imperial, with only a bloody locket around his neck was found the following day. He was lying face up with his left arm across his chest, a position of self-defence with 18 spear wounds. His stomach was split open, a Zulu ritual to let the soul escape. His body was embalmed with salt and shipped to England on the *SS Orontes* where he lies buried in the crypt of St Michael's Abbey, London.

The iSandlwana disaster so traumatised the British that Prime Minister Sir Benjamin Disraeli publicly lamented: 'A very remarkable people the Zulus, they defeat our generals, they convert our bishops and they have settled the fate of a great European dynasty'. Disraeli was referring to the Right Reverend Bishop John William Colenso who arrived in Durban in January 1854 as the first Anglican Bishop of Natal. One of his first projects was to convert young boys who were beginning to lose their front teeth (about seven years old) to be converted to Christianity. He requested, through the traditional leadership, that they be brought to his *Ekukhanyeni* (Place of Light) mission. He taught them how to read and write and how to speak English as well as how to use the printing press. Magema Fuze was one of the students and in 1922, when he was in his 80s, he wrote an authoritative book about the history of the Zulu people '*Abantu Abamnyama Lapa Bavela Ngakona* (The Black people and whence they came). Bishop Colenso's isiZulu teacher was William Ngidi and they co-wrote two books. *The isiZulu Grammar* book and *First Steps in Zulu: Being an Elementary Grammar of the Zulu Language*. They also translated the Bible into isiZulu with the help of Ndiyane and Magema. However, Ngidi challenged the 'accuracy' of some sections of the Old Testament such as Noah's ability to capture a pair of every living animal on earth - poisonous snakes, wild Russian bears, male and female mosquitoes, and managed to single-handedly to put them in the ark. Ngidi threatened to stop translating if Bishop Colenso did not come clean about this unbelievable feat. Overwhelmed, the bishop answered in words of a prophet: 'Shall a man speak lies in the name of the Lord?'

But that was the beginning of his problems because his potential converts cross questioned him relentlessly. They asked poignant questions that made him find himself defending every aspect of the Bible. They discussed the Zulu belief system, philosophy and doctrine for hours on end with him. But the final straw was when he couldn't give a satisfactory answer about who Satan's father was. Moreover, this question struck a chord with him personally because he was an admirer of Professor

FD Maurice who had been fired for suggesting that hell did not exist. Bishop Colenso then decided to write a commentary on The Epistle to the Romans and contested many things. He questioned the doctrine of eternal punishment and the Holy Communion being a precondition to salvation. He ended up totally rejecting the early chapters of Genesis as a literal account of creation. Furthermore, the good Bishop could not bring himself to preach that ancestors of newly converted Africans were condemned to eternal damnation because they were not Christians.

He ended up asking whether certain sections of the Bible should be understood as historically inaccurate. He shared his thoughts in a series of Treatises between 1862 and 1879 and published them in his book *The Pentateuch and the Book of Joshua Critically Examined*. It caused a huge scandal in England and he was accused of heresy and was excommunicated from the Anglican Church. But some prominent biblical scholars, such as Abraham Kuenen joined him, and this contributed in the overall development of biblical scholarship. Bishop Colenso was later readmitted to the church, but he made his stand clear on the baptism of polygamists: 'I must confess that I feel very strongly on this point that the usual practice of enforcing the separation of wives from their husbands, upon their conversion to Christianity is quite unwarrantable and opposed to the plain teaching of our Lord. It is putting new wine into old bottles and placing a stumbling-block which He has not set, directly in the way of their receiving the Gospel. Suppose a Kaffir man, advanced in years with three or four wives as is common among them, who have been legally married to him according to the practice of their land (and the Kaffir laws are very strict on this point and Kaffir wives perfectly chaste and virtuous) have lived with him for thirty years or more and served him faithfully and affectionately. What right have we, to require this man to cast off his wives and cause them in the eyes of all their people to commit adultery because he becomes a Christian? What is to become of their children? Who is to have the care of them? And what is the use of our reading to them the Bible stories of Abraham, Israel and David with their many wives?'

*William Ngidi was one of the early Zulus Christians who was converted by Bishop Colenso at Ekukhanyeni Mission, Pietermaritzburg when he was 7 years old. He translated the Bible into isiZulu and also challenged a number of Biblical teachings such as Noah's achievements, the existence of hell, the basis of polygamy as a sin and the Holy Communion as a precondition to salvation*

*Bishop John Sobantu Colenso established Ekukhanyeni Mission in Bishopstowe near Pietermaritzburg but the Zulu challenged him on some of the fundamental Christian views such as the extraordinary feats in the Old Testament, polygamy and the existence of hell. Colenso ended up agreeing with Zulu philosophy and shared his new found thoughts which led to his excommunication from the Anglican Church. He is the Bishop the British Prime Minister Benjamin Disraeli was referring to, when he lamented British defeat by the Zulu army at iSandlwana Battle in 1879: "Who are these Zulus, who are these remarkable people who defeat our Generals, convert our Bishops and on this day have brought the end to a great dynasty?"*

After the humiliation at iSandlwana, the secret service informed Cetshwayo that the British were sending in fresh troops from overseas with even more modern weapons. Hence the Zulu changed tactics and engaged in guerrilla warfare as they were slowly running out of ammunition and it was impossible to quickly buy more. This is the time the British committed unheard-of atrocities among civilians. They tortured and castrated men, raped women, disembowelled small children, broke the legs of cattle they could not loot, torched granaries, homes and plantations. This resulted in the womenfolk not being able to plant which led to the ominous food shortage. The inevitable starvation of his people and the British atrocities weighed heavily on Cetshwayo.

Cetshwayo knew his limitations and in a calculated move he wrote letters to the British through Bishop Colenso and his daughters Harriette (*Dlwedlwe*) and Frances proposing a cessation of hostilities. A humiliated Chelmsford responded by saying that if Cetshwayo wanted peace, everything that had been appropriated from the British. These were 800 Martini- Henrys, 400 000 catridges, an assortment of weapons, horses, artefacts, clothing and cattle. He also demanded that the Zulu army to surrender all their weapons, otherwise there would be no peace. This time Cetshwayo responded through three royal messengers Sithwango, Nkisimane Luhlongwana and Mfunzi Xulu. They were to ask Chelmsford why Cetshwayo should return the arms when his subjects needed them to protect themselves against wanton British atrocities. Furthermore, Cetshwayo reminded Chelmsford that he was the victor and he could not be dictated to by a loser. Chelmsford was so infuriated by being reminded that he was a failure that he arrested them. He accused the royal messengers of espionage and kept them in a secret location around KwaNtunjambili for over six weeks. When Cetshwayo heard nothing from the British and his messengers, he sent a second letter and called for a face-to-face meeting with Chelmsford. He also demanded that Chelmsford should tell 'the snake' Shepstone to be present. This time the letter did not reach Chelmsford because the messengers were nearly arrested like the previous messengers, so they turned back.

Famine had started taking its toll and swallowing his pride, Cetshwayo sent the third letter with 100 cattle and two huge tusks of ivory this time. He also promised to send back two looted cannons within a short space of time. As Cetshwayo had correctly guessed, Chelmsford kept the cattle but returned the ivory tusks and made even bigger demands than before. Chelmsford sent another message demanding that all the thousands of Zulu soldiers based in uLundi are to surrender otherwise, he would continue attacking the Zulu empire. Magema and some messengers were sent to plead for sanity with Chelmsford. They told him that Cetshwayo genuinely wanted peace because his people were staring complete starvation in the face. Moreover, *indlala ibanga ulaka* (hunger makes one unpredictable). But Chelmsford was 'smelling blood' and now demanded to be given the entire royal *inyonikayiphumuli* herd kept at KwaMayizekanye Palace. But the youthful iNgobamakhosi regiment, refused to hand over the cattle. They sent a message that the British would only reach the cattle over their dead bodies. As an act of defiance, they slaughtered many cattle and ate them. They now even refused to surrender the two cannons Cetshwayo had promised to return. The war continued in various parts of the empire and the Zulu fought the whites wherever they met. For instance, one such skirmish at eMthonjaneni Heights next to Dingane's water well was major and lasted for weeks. The British were defeated, and the Zulu helped themselves to the food and weapons they left behind.

After six months of continuous fighting, the Zulu army was war-weary and still undefeated. No army can fight on an empty stomach; the Zulu granaries were empty, and something had to give. Yet the well-supplied imperial forces kept on pouring into the Zulu empire. The Zulu army had nothing to prove anymore as they had annihilated the mighty English army together with their six allied nations in conventional warfare. The Zulu defences were finally breached and the KwaNodwengu Palace was burnt to the ground on the 3$^{rd}$ of July 1879. It was the beginning of the end. The British went on a burning orgy of the palaces in the eMakhosini Valley. They razed uMlambongwenya, KwaMbonambi, eMakheni, KwaMayizekanye and many others as they marched to the capital, uLundi. But by the time they reached uLundi Palace it was virtually deserted because Cetshwayo and the Zulu army were long gone. A small number of soldiers were left behind to strategically buy time for Cetshwayo's escape. After a lousy thirty minutes of resistance, they retreated into the forests. The British claimed to have found the pride and treasure of the nation *inkatha* at uLundi Palace and publicly burnt it on the 4$^{th}$ of July 1879. The palace's diameter was 1000 metres; the cattle enclosure was 40 000 hectares; outside circumference of the cattle enclosure 3 000 metres; between the inner and outer fences close to 1 000 huts were in rows of three, each trio occupying a frontage of 20 metres. Outside the main kraal were two smallers ones, one for milking the royal milking cattle the other to store food.

Nomguqo Paulina Dlamini, who was one of the *umdlunkulu* present at uLundi Palace when Cetshwayo fled, disputed this allegation. She recounted the series of events prior to their departure to Rev Heinrich Filter (whose son was slaughtered by abaQulusi and Manyonyoba). Filter's mission was near Msinga. Dlamini recalled: 'When we heard that the British were at eMthonjaneni Heights on the 2$^{nd}$ of July, preparations were made for the king to flee. We were ordered to collect all the king's personal belongings and national assets such as *inkatha* and *inhlendla*. We were to make sure that they were safely hidden. We lowered them down with an aid of a rope, deep into iNhlansi caves in Hlophenkulu Mountain. We fled from uLundi Palace the following day on the 3rd of July with the king, his family and the royal retinue that included the king's adviser Mkhosana kaZangwana Zungu. We were protected by iNdabakawombe regiment and when we arrived at uMlambongwenya *ikhanda* we heard that the enemy had reached uLundi. We went past KwaMbonambi *ikhanda* by moonlight.

'The king walked whilst others were on horses and he hardly said a word. At daybreak he instructed his bodyguards to take his wives, some of his children, *imidlunkulu* and cattle to Zibhebhu at Bhanganomo for safety. Zibhebhu and the king had been close from the days when they grew up. On that day, we kept on walking without sleep and from that day on, we never slept in any homestead but under the open dark skies. My responsibility was to look after the 11-year-old Crown Prince Dinuzulu. When we reached Ziwedu, who was Cetshwayo's relative, 20 girls were selected (including me) to accompany and look after princesses Simiso, Beyisile, Sililo, Nomdlambi, Sabede, Siyela and many the others. The king ordered us to move only at night. I still remember walking through thorns at night without a footpath to guide us and we could not see where we were going. The most difficult part of our march was when we had to cross the waterless region of oBonjeni. We the Zulu are really a tough people. When we arrived in Bhanganomo we were split up and some of us were taken to eNkalakuthaba homestead. But a little later Ndabuko, the king's relative came and wanted to take the royal herd as well as Dinuzulu and Beyisile (Queen Nompaka's daughter) away. Zibhebhu let the children go but refused to part with the royal herd. This was to be the source of hatred between the uMandlakazi and uSuthu factions for years to come.'

Cetshwayo and his retinue witnessed the burning of the capital from a safe distance and the big clouds of smoke seemed to cover the whole sky. The British looked for king high and low, in caves, forests as well as in people's homes. Many people were tortured to death and their homes torched but they refused to betray their king. At some point the British came across seven girls, a young man and a boy who told them that the king had been caught. Llittle did they know that they were part of the king's entourage and were deliberately misleading them. They finally found him on the 28th of August, just after 16h00 at KwaDwasa, deep inside iNgome forest. When they saw some 20 huts, they knew they had their man. To ensure that Cetshwayo was inside one of the bigger huts, the British asked Martin Oftebro, a missionary's son, to call Cetshwayo. He used Cetshwayo's name given to him by his peers and shouted: '*Magwegwana*'. Cetshwayo recognised Martin's voice as he had known him since he was a little boy. Then he asked him: 'Wasn't your father a friend of mine for a long time for you to do this to me?' Martin did not care as he wanted to go down in history as the one who betrayed Cetshwayo and did not answer. After establishing that he would be surrendering to a Major, Cetshwayo refused to come out. He eventually came out when his people begged him. Moreover, Major Marter was ready to shoot him on the spot. He came out not because of the death threat but because his people said they wanted him to live another day to lead his broken people.

He walked for three days while they rode on horses next to him. They arrived at 10h00 on the 31st of August in uLundi and he was heartbroken when he saw it in cinders with only ten huts still standing, out of the thousands that made up the capital. As he was led to the tent of Sir Garnet Wolseley, who was now the commander of British Imperial Forces in Natal, something extraordinary happened. The defeated BIF army showed due respect to the victorious Zulu king dressed in his military attire. The British formed a 100 metre guard of honour for him to walk through. Major Marter led the procession with a trumpeter, an orderly and a group of officers stood to attention all with drawn swords. They were followed by a company of Dragoon Guards with their accoutrements flashing in the sun and Captains Gibbins and Godsden marched the king. His royal skin hung loosely over his shoulders and his magnificent body flashed through the cloak. He was carrying a long stick on the right hand, looking majestic as more soldiers followed behind. Now, no one saw that coming. What went through his mind when this happened, will forever remain a mystery.

Without any formalities or wasting of time, Wolseley informed Cetshwayo that the Zulu empire had ceased to exist, and the land would be divided among the people who had supported the British invasion. Wolseley's final words to Cetshwayo was that he was no longer an emperor but a prisoner of war and that he would be sent to jail in Cape Town. Then Wolseley got up from his chair came around the desk and ripped off the lion's claw royal necklace from Cetshwayo's neck. Then dismissed him off hand. Cetshwayo did not react because he did not want to give the British an excuse to execute him. Wolseley sent the priceless lion's claw necklace to his wife Louisa in England. He instructed her to remove each claw from the necklace and have it inscribed *Cetshwayo 28 August 1879* and give to their female friends as a gift from wild Africa. Wolseley was an acclaimed sharpshooter who had served in the Crimean War where he had shot unarmed Russians for amusement. He bragged about it in his book *All Sir Garnet* that sent shivers amongst the military elite. He did not stop there and wrote his elderly aunt a letter: 'Man shooting is the finest sport of all, there is a certain amount of infatuation about it and the more you kill the more you wish to kill.'

Prince Ndabuko kaMpande a decorated commander and a member of uThulwana regiment was appointed as the regent after King Cetshwayo's death. Together with Prince Shingana kaMpande and Emperor Dinuzulu, were found guilty of High Treason and exiled to St Helena Island for 12 years, 15 years and 19 years respectively. (Killie Campbell Africana Library)

Emperor Cetshwayo kaShaka defeated the British at the iSandlwana War in 1879. The British forced him to cover his body with a damask tablecloth before he boarded the military ship SS Natal which took him to prison at The Castle in Cape Town. He was later sent to Oude Moulen farm near Stellenbosch. He later went to London where he successfully negotiated his release with Queen Victoria over tea in Osborne House on the Isle of White on 7 August 1882. (Killie Campbell Africana Library)

*Queen Nompaka Sixiphe kaSekethwayo Mdlalose and other queens who accompanied Emperor Cetshwayo to prison at The Castle in Cape Town after defeating the British in iSandlwana War 1879. They were forced to cover themselves with white bed sheets and wear plastic necklaces for the photo shoot. (Killie Campbell Africana Library)*

*Some of the medals created after the iSandlwana War inscribed: 'The Zulu War Medal' (Africana Museum)*

## The Zulu Empire is Divided

After being stripped off his empire, kingship and royal necklace at about 14h00, Cetshwayo, four wives and attendants was transported in a ten mule carriage with grass strewn at the back. But they did not sit on the grass instead they squatted and the men marched next to the carriage for the 140 kilometers to the coast. They went over eMthonjaneni Heights, via KwaMagwaza, past St Paul's church, across uMhlathuze River and through eNkwalini valley and past *esihlahleni samagwala* (coward's tree where cowards ans deserted were killed from Shaka's time). When he arrived at the makeshift Port Durnford dock next to uMlalazi River mouth near today's Richards Bay, he still looked regal. The British soldiers made fun of him and encouraged the resident white women and children to throw stones at him like Jesus on his way to Golgotha. They also threw him a damask tablecloth to cover his big strong body adorned in his military attire. When he refused, they threatened to undress him in public. Only then did he oblige. He was kept waiting for hours before he strode with bold steps that shook the earth under his feet into the military ship *HMS Natal* on the 4th of September. He could go with his principal wife Queen Nompaka *Sixiphe* kaSekethwayo Mdlalose and a few others as well as a small royal retinue.

When the ship pulled away, Cetshwayo went on deck and gazed at the receding coastline of his empire. His heart went out to the crying *imidlunkulu* on the shore and quietly swore to return alive. By the time he arrived in Cape Town, on the 15th of September, he was dressed in a black suit including a black high hat. After being humiliated in a place they had never heard of before somewhere in Africa, 10 Downing Street, London took a decision to destroy the 'savage' Zulu nation entirely so that it would never rise again. So, the capture of Cetshwayo was a big international story and all eyes were on his forthcoming trial. Cetshwayo had been an Emperor for a mere six years. A short but undoubtedly tumultuous reign for the 52-year-old monarch. He had defeated a world power in an astonishing battle and was now their prisoner. Once again, the Zulu nation had no king. But this time, Mkabayi was long dead and gone and the future truly looked bleak. Worst of all, the Crown Prince Dinuzulu was a mere 12-year-old boy. Wolseley had called a national *imbizo* in iMfolozi Valley on the 1st of September 1879 to announce the terms of the peace settlement. Over 200 traditional leaders and their war-weary Zulu soldiers turned up in their thousands. He told them that the Ultimatum demands would now be implemented, which was a shock. But what followed next came as a complete surprise and great consternation. He announced that the Zulu empire had ceased to exist as they knew it and, people who had sided with the British would be rewarded with large tracts of land and title. However, the land in abaQulusi and eMgazini kingdoms north of uPhongolo River would not be affected. He further added that:

- Zululand would be split into 13 kingdoms
- A chief had been appointed for each kingdom
- The chiefs would rule their kingdoms
- Each chief would commence his reign as soon as they had signed or made their mark on the document, they had been given
- Each would adhere to their allocated boundaries
- No one could form an army
- All men could marry when they wished without the need to approach the chief
- All could travel freely in order to find work
- No arms or ammunition were allowed in a kingdom
- No life could be taken without a fair trial. Sentence would be passed by a council of indunas
- Those wanted by British justice had to be handed over
- No British soldiers could be tried by a native court
- No land could be sold
- A British Resident would be appointed who would maintain overall control of the 13 kingdoms
- The succession of chiefs would ultimately be determined by the British Resident

It was bad enough that the British had made all the Zulu living south of uThukela River squatters and beggars. This new affront was unprecedented and one question every Zulu asked was: 'What would Empire King Shaka do?' One thing was certain, the future did not look good as they were now starving since no food had been planted because of the war. Cetshwayo had been put on a ship and was bouncing somewhere on high seas going to a place no Zulu king had ever been before. Wolseley did not explain the criteria of carving out the borders but came up with a new concept for the Zulu. He said that each ruler in the *'new kingdoms'* will be known as *isiphakanyiswa* (elected chief) and their titles would be *inkosi* (the same title of legitimate kings) which would also apply to people who were not Zulu or Africans for that matter. Cetshwayo's fair-weather friend Dunn had defected to his fellow whites during the war and was given the largest '*kingdom*' around Eshowe. Cetshwayo had where he had been living. Wolseley even had the audacity of offering Dunn the opportunity to become the overall '*King of the Zulus*' but he declined.

A non-Zulu mercenary, King Hlubi kaMbunda Molefe of the Batlokwa kingdom. This a non-Nguni group. He got the second largest '*kingdom*' situated north-west of Dunn's 'kingdom' along the Buffalo and iNcome Rivers. King Faku kaZiningo Ntombela a nonentity before the war, fought as a mercenary. Hhamu kaNzibe kaSenzangakhona, who served under Field Marshal Wood at iSandlwana, was given a smaller '*kingdom*' than the non-Zulu in the north-western part of the kingdom. Some of the great fighters that had fought gallantly against the British were also given land, such as Zibhebhu kaMaphitha who saw action at iSandlwana and uLundi. He was given a sparsely populated but mountainous 'kingdom' east of Hhamu's 'kingdom'. King Mlandela kaMbiya of the Mthethwa kingdom was given a 'kingdom' along the coast, north of Dunn's huge 'kingdom'. Other people who were rewarded with land and given the title of '*inkosi*' included crippled Siyunguza *Gawozi* kaSilwane Mpungose, Mfanawendlela kaManzini Zungu, Mgitshwa kaMvundlana Biyela (whose father had fought alongside Mghobhozi), Sekethwayo Mdlalose (Mkabayi's personal aide) Ntshingwayo (the commander-in-chief of iSandlwana war), Mgojana kaSomaphunga Ndwandwe (who was married to Princess Mbixambixa kaMpande) and Somkhele kaMalanda.

The average *inkosi* was paid a monthly salary of £50 while others received a bigger salary depending on their level of collaboration with the British. This caused more problems because it meant that *amakhosi oselwa* (rightful kings) in the new 'kingdoms' were dismissed. The Batlokwa mercenaries, who lived in Ntabazwe, were thanked with huge tracts of land right in the heartland of the Zulu empire at KwaNobamba. They were also given land belonging to King Sihayo Ngobese of the Qungebe kingdom and part of Sekethwayo Mdlalose's land in Nquthu was also thrown in as a bonus. Hence, large numbers of seSotho speakers can still be found in those areas to this day. Wolseley announced that Sir Melmoth Osborn was going to be the British Resident. But did not give him reasons why some of the strongly anti-British Zulu aristocrats were also given '*kingdoms*' and were to be called '*inkosi*'. Unhappy as they were with the turn of events, the Zulu understood that the absence of war did not mean peace. Therefore, they chose not to react to the announcements.

After all, they needed to reorganise their lives under the new dispensation. They desperately needed to find enough food for everyone and strengthen their defences, albeit underground. During the 'peace' that followed the announcements, every *'inkosi'* surprised everyone living in their *'kingdoms'* with draconian laws. People were taxed, payable directly to their *'inkosi'* in the form of cattle. Homes were regularly raided for arms or searched for Cetshwayo's cattle which were stolen when he was sent to exile. Those who resisted were summarily executed and their livestock was looted with impunity. Within months of the establishment of the *'new kingdoms'* the joint committee of the military high command and king's council had no choice but to hold a clandestine meeting. One of their resolutions was that Mnyamana kaNgqengelele Buthelezi was to head the 'Cetshwayo Affair'. Mnyamana then instructed the royal messengers Mgwazeni kaDonda Khumalo, (his father was Shaka's best friend) Mfunzi Xulu and Maduna kaMpande to go to Pietermaritzburg and demand Cetshwayo's charge sheet. The second demand was that the British explain why they did not want the legitimate House of Senzangakhona to rule.

When they arrived in Pietermaritzburg, the British sent them back with the worst British arrogant contempt ever. They were told that only the 'House of Mpande' would be allowed to rule and the 'House of Senzangakhona' would only reign sometime in the future. Even then, it would be in a small and undefined area they called *'uSuthu'* and its *'inkosi'* would have the same status as the newly appointed ones. The Zulu were incensed by the response and sent a senior delegation back to Pietermaritzburg. This time Cetshwayo's relatives Ndabuko, Dabulamanzi and Shingana kaMpande were included. They arrived in Pietermaritzburg on the 24th of March 1880, but they were ignored.

In the meantime, the British people could not believe what had happened in the Zulu empire. They could not imagine being defeated by an indigenous African people. After all, their slogan *'Britannia rules the waves'* was proof that they were an invincible world power. Therefore, the British voters punished Disraeli's Conservative government in the April 1880 elections and voted for the grand old man of the Liberal Party, William Gladstone. Moreover, Disraeli had spent over £5 million of the public purse on a war that ended up badly. British newspapers led with screaming headlines about the demise of Cetshwayo. They whipped up public sentiment about the victorious king being locked up in an old military fort in Cape Town for defending his country from unwarranted aggression. Invariably public opinion swung towards the brave 'kingless' Zulu nation. Bishop Colenso, his daughters and many others, not least Gladstone's Liberal government itself exerted pressure on the Natal colonial government to list Cetshwayo's charge. After all Gladstone's election platform had been: *'What was the crime of the Zulu?'*

Cetshwayo's charges were as follows:

- Amassing arms with the intention of attacking the Transvaal
- Moving troops to the Transvaal border with the intention to undermine British rule in the Transvaal
- Murder of ten thousand iNgcugce virgins for refusing to marry into the iNdlondlo and uDloko regiments in 1876
- General wanton killing of innocent people

However, Cetshwayo's defence was as follows:

- Jantoni, the white chief sold arms to people individually and they paid with cattle. But often Jantoni would take cattle and promise to return with guns and did not. This action caused a great deal of tension.
- Shepstone had put pressure on Cetshwayo to make abaQulusi, *bahlale phezu kwamahawu* (be on high alert) on the Transvaal border in case of an Afrikaner insurrection against the British that would spill into Zululand and Natal.
- Cetshwayo was personally opposed to the killing of the women of iNgcugce regiment but they were killed by their own male relatives. In fact, he had accommodated some of the women at eKubazeni Palace that he had built years before he was king, for the express purpose of providing shelter and protection for women at risk.

Meanwhile, an incident in the Mthethwa kingdom diverted the attention of Melmoth away from the pressing 'Cetshwayo Affair'. Out of the blue, someone calling himself Stimela kaSomveli Mthethwa galloped into oYengweni Palace with many followers. He claimed to have been the direct descendant of King Dingiswayo and had come to take his rightful place on the Mthethwa throne. Mlandela, who was on the Mthethwa throne (Shaka's friend), was now very old and had no desire to fight Stimela. He simply fled to the kingdom of abaQulusi that was still 'independent'. But on his way, his old bones failed to carry him that far, and he died in Dunn's 'kingdom' which he had to cross to reach ebaQulusini. Mlandela's death, under those controversial circumstances, caused a split in the Mthethwa kingdom. Some thought he had run away because Stimela was the rightful heir, while others thought he had gone to *khonza* under Dunn.

The matter was finally taken to Melmoth for resolution. After a brief investigation, he ruled in favour of the old man Mlandela and sent Dunn to remove Stimela. However, Dunn ever the opportunist saw an opportunity to enrich himself and shot Stimela and over 200 of his followers in cold blood. They then looted over 2500 royal Mthethwa cattle. There was outrage among the Mthethwa people, and they wanted justice. But Melmoth did not punish Dunn because he claimed to have acted in self-defence. Yet there were many witnesses who testified to the contrary. Hhamu often killed so many people that it even embarrassed the whites especially in the land of abaQulusi. Melmoth was forced to call an *imbizo* on 31 August 1881 at his Nhlazatshe residence to address the atrocities. The people agreed to attend if there was only one item on the agenda - the appalling treatment of the people by the people Melmoth had given the title '*inkosi*'. The nation was led by the Crown Prince Dinuzulu assisted by Ndabuko, Shingana, Ziwedu, Dabulamanzi, Maduna, Mnyamana and Dikane, who was so old that he had to be on *isikhumba*, a stretcher made from ox-hide. After listening to their singular complaint,

Melmoth had the nerve to stand in front of tens of thousands of the people and not entertain their plight. Instead, he told them, without flinching, that he had decided that Dinuzulu, Ziwedu and Maduna had to go and *khonza* under Dunn and if they agreed, the royal cattle that had been taken by Zibhebhu would be returned in their entirety. Mnyamana tried to protest but Melmoth shouted him down and said that he must not utter a single word because he had refused to be '*inkosi*' or to live under Hhamu. On that very rude note, Melmoth closed the meeting and told everyone to leave. It was as though the crowd had been struck by lightning, the air was thick with pent-up emotions. The Zulu could not imagine their crown prince being a subject of anyone, let alone an untrustworthy white arms-smuggling mercenary. As if to make sense of it all, someone began to sing *ihubo lesizwe* just as Mkabayi used to when she was in a tight spot. They then all slowly dispersed, singing. Clearly, things were not likely to be the same ever again. They went to their respective homes and openly prepared for an insurrection, and also demanded the immediate return of Cetshwayo.

While the British were still planning the destruction of the Zulu people and their kingdom, they had something new to worry about. Afrikaners finally invaded Natal and seized Laing's Nek on the 16th of December 1880. The British put up a fight, but it did not end well for the British and they were defeated at the Battle of Majuba Hill on the 23rd of March 1881. Field Marshal Wood returned to Natal from Britain to negotiate an armistice with the Afrikaners and it was settled on O'Neil's farm at the bottom of Majuba Hill. The Transvaal was consequently restored to self-rule under the British. This is often referred to as the First Anglo-Boer War, even though Africans also fought on either side of the whites. A year later, in April 1882, over 5000 Zulu people marched to Pietermaritzburg and demanded the immediate return of Cetshwayo.

The arrival of Cetshwayo in Cape Town set the town ablaze with excitement. Even though he was wearing western-type clothes for the first time, he looked comfortable and quite stylish. Roads were lined with crowds eager to catch a glimpse of the Zulu hero king, which he found amusing as he was taken to The Castle military fort. He had spectacular view of Cape Town and the Table Mountain from the fort but life was a far cry from what he was used to as a king. For one thing, he was forced to share a two-room tent with four female royal members, his wives and attendants inside the jail premises. He was also under a 24-hour armed guard. He tried to protest as no one could bear arms in the presence of a Zulu king, but they ignored him. Cetshwayo had no contact with the kingdom, which distressed him. But he did not let his captors know how much he was suffering. Despite his personal worries, many high-profile people and celebrities visited him at such Lady Flo Dixie as well as Prince Albert and Prince George (later King George V) of Wales when they were on a world tour. Bishop Colenso and Harriette also came to visit him, and their presence lifted their spirits as they finally heard stories from home after a whole year.

The Colensos were equally pleased to find the king still in good health and fiery as ever, despite his circumstances. Cetshwayo was relieved to hear that female regiments he had trained in the use of guns, amaDlundlu, amaQhwaki and amaDuku, were once again the official home guard because the male regiments were out mobilising the nation for his return. But what broke Cetshwayo's heart was to hear that the British had evicted all his wives from uLundi Palace and told them to find other husbands. They had all refused, choosing instead to go back to their homes. No one was permitted to continue living at the palace including *imihlalandlini* and the palace stood like an empty shell, unattended. But the welfare of his only son Dinuzulu weighed paramount on him. He also inquired after Mthonga if he was still living under the Afrikaners in Wakkerstroom. Cetshwayo continued engaging the British about his return home and tried to strike all sorts of deals. He even offered Dinuzulu to be taken captive in his place as guarantee of his good behaviour. But the Cape Colony's new Governor Robinson would hear none of it.

The continued presence of Cetshwayo in the city centre was causing too much embarrassment for the British. So, he was moved to a farm *Oude Moulen* outside Cape Town but one of his advisers Mkhosana Zungu was sent back to the kingdom. The farm was situated in a small valley surrounded by stark grey rocky hills, a rather depressing and barren sight. It was a far cry from the emerald-green sweeping vistas of the Zulu empire. The environment in Stellenbosch was so harsh that it led one of the king's assistants, Dambuka to commit suicide. Cetshwayo missed the water drawn from his personal bubbling spring in Hlophenkulu Mountain and the feel of the cool waters from Mbilane, his personal bathing river. It was a bitter-sweet surprise when he realised that King Langalibalele of the Hlubi kingdom had been banished in the next farm called *Uitvlugt*. Nothing grew in on this arid farm in summer and in winter it turned into a swamp.

Langalibalele had been arrested by the British together with his son Malambule who had been sentenced to five years. Whereas Langalibalele was found guilty for refusing to register his subjects' firearms which they had bought legally in the diamond mines of Kimberley. His other crime was that he refused to stop his subjects from under-cutting white farmers in the marketplace. He had initially been sentenced to death, but it was commuted to life imprisonment in Robben Island, and later at *Uitvlugt* farm. He was also was lucky to be alive as he had escaped from being eaten by his relatives who were cannibals. They had shaved his head, tied him to a pole and made a fire but he managed break free and swam through a crocodile infested uMzinyathi River which was in flood. Langalibalele was married to Princess Mzamose kaSobhuza, whose younger sister Princess Tifokati was one of Shepstone's black wives. Hunting had always been a Zulu royal sport and Cetshwayo was a crack shot, so was Langalibalele. They often went on long hunting trips and they used these times to plan and to communicate with the Zulu military high command underground. In the meantime, Cetshwayo spent the time at the farm learning how to read and write. He wrote his friend, Lady Dixie and some of the letters ended up in the English press. He also wrote Prime Minister Gladstone's government seeking to secure an audience with Queen Victoria.

Then on the 26$^{th}$ September the Governor Robinson went to the Oude Moulen and told Cetshwayo that the British Government had granted him permission to present his case in person in London the following May. But what's more, he was now a free man and could do as he pleased except return to the Zulu empire. He could keep cattle and hunt small game and was later allowed to go by railway to Cape Town and attend social occasions. He visited the Theatre Royal for the pantomime *The Fair One with the Golden Locks*, attended the sports of the Sutherland and Argyll Highlanders and even had dinner at the house of Mr. and Mrs Arnold. After many excuses and delays, it was a cold wintry day on the 12$^{th}$ of July 1882 when Cetshwayo and his small entourage boarded the *RMS Arab* in Cape Town for London. He had ensured that his two Zulu interpreters, Lazarus Xaba and Hlimbithwa kaXhakaza Mbizankulu came with him. Other dignitaries that accompanied him were his advisers Ngobazana kaVukuza Mpungose, Phosile kaManyosi kaDlekezele Mbatha, Ngcongcwana Zulu and Mkhosana kaZangwana Zungu was brought back. Mkhosana's descendants established big homesteads such as KwaMngani, KwaBambelentulo and eMeveni in different parts of the kingdom. The Natal government sent Cetshwayo white interpreters, Shepstone's son Henrique, Robert Dunn and RCA Samuelson, but Cetshwayo refused to have anything to do with them.

In a twist of fate, as the *RMS Arab* passed through the Bay of Biscay on the coast of Spain, Cetshwayo was told to look through the porthole. He saw the ship the *Lapland* carrying Norwegian colonisers gently sailing past him, heading to where he was not allowed to go, his very own Zulu empire. No one will ever know what crossed his mind as he watched the ship disappear over the southern horizon. The colonisers had left from Aalesund, Norway, in July 1882 on the *Tasso* that dropped them off in England and then they took the *Lapland* which took them to Durban. They arrived in Durban 45 days later. Each coloniser on board was given 2000 Norwegian crowns by their government to support their settlement in the Zulu empire. To qualify, the colonisers needed to have a doctor's certificate of good health and a religious minister's letter of good conduct. Each family was permitted bring two single persons and the ship held 34 families, with a total of about 233 people. They later sailed down to uMzimkhulu River mouth on the 28$^{th}$ of August 1882 to receive the free land they were promised.

They were allotted land through a lottery that distributed 100-acre plots. The names of the heads of the 34 families were: K. Martinsen a merchant; Andersen a bookseller; E. Bjorseth a cabinet-maker; O. P. Valdal a tailor; O. A. Vinjevold a farmer; J. Lillebo a builder; E. Haajem a shipbuilder; Bjorkelund a farmer; N. Gidske a farmer; K. Hageselle a farmer; J. A. Ole a farmer; E. Pahr a teacher; L. Haram a farmer; J. Igesund a farmer; G. A. Kvalsvig a farmer; M. Holte a blacksmith; G. Kjonstad a teacher; J. Kjonstad a farmer; J. Nero a agronomist; Rodseth a goldsmith; C. Lund a landscape gardener; F. Hufft a weaver; J. Pettersen a farmer; P. Trandal a baker; J. Kipperberg a seaman and fisherman; S. Borgesen a bookbinder; R. Brune a boatbuilder; F. Bodtker a carpenter; K. O. Standal a painter; N. Oie a wagon-maker; R. Sandanger a builder; T. Dahle a mechanic and shoemaker, H. Andreasen a farmer and Rev. E. Berg a pastor.

Cetshwayo's ship finally docked at Plymouth on the 5$^{th}$ of August at 05h00. The Calvary Volunteers, created a guard of honour on the dock as he walked to the special train to take him to the centre of London. Hundreds of excited people gathered to see the Zulu king. By the time he disembarked he was dressed in very stylish European clothes, a black suit and the black hat he had worn when he left his kingdom instead of his traditional *isicoco*. They were accommodated at the royal guest house in 18 Melbury Road, Holland Park in London for a month. Today the residence has the English Heritage blue plaque, a commemorative marker affixed to buildings linked to great figures of the past. His meetings with the British government were held in Kensington Palace and many well-wishers camped outside the palace throughout his stay. The meetings had to be interrupted a few times a day so that Cetshwayo could wave from the balcony to a fascinated crowd in the streets below. This public admiration was reinforced by many gifts and large quantities of letters addressed to him that were delivered to Kensington Palace daily. He was admired even by the poorest of the English poor as he received an acrostic from Brighton Warehouse:

C etewayo! Zulu King!

E ngland thee is welcoming

T hy misfortune through sad war

E nglish hearts have watched afar

W hen returned to Afric's shore

A fter thy brief visit

Y oung and old hope thou again

O ver Zululand mays'st reign!

His friend Lady Florence Dixie gave him a strong stunning stallion. The press reported that Cetshwayo exuded statesman like qualities and left all those he interacted with in awe of his 'eloquence' and 'grasp of intellectual discourse', as though they had expected otherwise. The British wanted to impress the Zulu monarch and organised a full itinerary which included amongst other things, a tour of the the London Docks, the Artillery Museum in Woolich and the London Zoo. On his way to visit Lord Granville, they passed the statue of Achilles in Hyde Park, he remarked that it was not too long ago that the British fought like the Zulu, without clothes. He was also invited to visit the Prince and Princes of Wales at Malborough House. They had a great time reminiscing about when they Prince Albert and George were his guests at Oude Moulen. He gave them gifts of well-crafted sticks made from *umsimbithi* wood grown in the Zulu empire and reserved for royalty. In return they gave him a silver headed stick made.

Victoria invited Cetshwayo to Osborne House on the Isle of Wight to tea on the 7$^{th}$ of August 1882. He boarded a train with Lord Kimberley and his entourage and were met by an enormous crowd at Portsmouth Dockyard. They were met by Prince Edward who sailed with them to the island. Throughout their discussions, Queen Victoria addressed or referred to Cetshwayo, as 'Your Majesty King Cetshwayo', not as an ex-king - a far cry from the treatment he was given by the Natal government. Cultural differences came to the fore even before the negotiations could begin. Through his personal Zulu translator Xaba, Cetshwayo asked if he could not negotiate his freedom with the man in her life, as he was aware of her romantic relationship with her man-servant John Brown. After uttering these words, there was dead silence in the room and all the while Cetshwayo kept his eyes glued to the floor. Offended, Victoria glared at Cetshwayo in disbelief and arrogantly told Cetshwayo that she was the 'Queen of Great Britannia' and therefore he had to negotiate with her. The fact that she had no husband she could call her own, was no fault of hers. She also demanded that the king look her straight in the eye as they spoke. But Cetshwayo refused to look at her and warned her of the dire consequences if he did. Victoria insisted, so Cetshwayo raised his eyes slowly and looked directly at her. As soon as their eyes locked, Victoria began to bleed, and the talks were ended abruptly. This bleeding phenomenon happened for a week until, finally, she agreed to talk to him but without them locking eyes.

Negotiations between the monarchs and between Cetshwayo and the Gladstone government were long and hard. But the Zulu delegation never lost their temper and remained focused despite being undermined at times. For instance, they wanted to know why he refused to have John Dunn as his adviser. He responded: 'Who was Dunn? What was Dunn? What could he have been if he had not been saved from being destitute? The English would have never heard of him, it would be to put a spear near to me if I were to keep him close. He stole my property and cattle and made my children starve. I adopted Dunn when he had nothing, he was not sent to me by the government, and he was a nothing. He became somebody under my wing and I allowed him to live as my subject. He pretended to be my friend and lied about me. He lied that my people did not want me to come back. Instead, he took their cattle and land. He punished everyone who wanted me to come back... when I was on the run, I intercepted messages he sent to Zibhebhu asking him to help betray me and in return, he would make it possible for him to become the king of the kingdom. Would you keep a rat in your house that eats your food?

Fortunately, the British public opinion, especially the press, was sympathetic to the Zulu cause. Finally, Gladstone bowed to public pressure and granted Cetshwayo his freedom. But he made him agree to a long list of undertakings. He also admitted to Cetshwayo that their worst nightmare was the existence of the Zulu regiments. They wanted them abolished. Again, Cetshwayo agreed but insisted that the regiments that looked after state fields and royal cattle would not be dismantled. The British grudgingly agreed. The British Defence Ministry was particularly unhappy with Cetshwayo's successful mission in England. Especially that he was going back home a free man and still the emperor of the Zulu people. On his departure, Queen Victoria presented Cetshwayo with a silver cup with three handles (a love cup) inscribed *'Presented to Cetshwayo by Queen Victoria August 14, 1882'*. She also gave him a huge Bible which can still be seen in the uLundi Museum to this day. She also personally gave him a picture of herself and said: 'I respect you as a brave enemy who will, I trust become a firm future friend.'

Cetshwayo left London on the 1st of September 1882 aboard the *Briton* and landed in Simonstown in Cape Town on the 24th of September. But he was made to wait for a whole month in *Oude Moulen* farm before being allowed to go home. The British tried to keep Cetshwayo's homecoming date a top secret, but the secret service found out. Word spread like wild fire that *okaNdaba* (Ndaba's descendant) was coming home, a free man but with limited powers. Thousands upon thousands of people gathered at Port Durnford where he was expected to arrive. Hence the settlement grew to become eSikhaleni (previously called *eSikhawini*). The multitudes waited patiently for days on end happy, singing and dancing. But the British continued feeling threatened by Cetshwayo's growing popularity. They tried to disperse the crowds, but they refused to move. Angry and helpless, and probably afraid, Shepstone personally threatened to shoot into the crowd if they did not go away. Only then did the people retreat to the nearby oNgoye Mountains. When Cetshwayo finally docked in the blistering heat on the 10th of January 1883, there was hardly anyone to welcome him.

Instead, a devious looking and now visibly aged Shepstone stood in the sun, half the man he used to be since his son George had been killed by Mtweni kaZibana at iSandlwana. He offered Cetshwayo to ride in a cart to uLundi Palace but Cetshwayo refused and chose to walk on solid ground, as he needed to connect with the land of his forefathers. He secretly sent word to his people that they should assemble at Dingane's water spring at eMthonjaneni Heights. By the time he arrived there a week later he found thousands of people waiting for him. During the day they celebrated but under the cover of darkness Cetshwayo and the joint committee of the military high command and king's council strategised the way forward. Despite tight British army security around Cetshwayo, he managed to sneak to the eMakhosini Valley. He performed the royal rituals and thanked his ancestors for protecting him, and announced that he was back. He was obviously upset when he found out that large tracts of land north of uThukela River were now to be governed directly by the Natal government, something they did not raise with him in London.

Those areas were now the 'Zulu Native Reserve' (*iLizevu*) whose boundary was uMhlathuze River near Eshowe and this *iLizevu* included land given to Dunn, Hlubi and Zibhebhu. All Cetshwayo was left with was a thin strip of land between uMhlathuze, uPhongolo and Black iMfolozi Rivers. But what angered him the most was Dunn's sudden rise over the Zulu people, something he had objected to when Prime Minister William Gladstone's government had requested him to make Dunn his adviser. He described in detail his first encounter with Dunn when he came to *khonza* under him. Cetshwayo remembered what Dunn was when he had first arrived in the Zulu empire. He was nothing more than a hungry vagrant beggar. Out of *ubuntu* ethos, he had given Dunn dignity by allowing him to marry two of his cousins, Princess Sigodi kaMpande and Princess Sobejile kaMpande whose mother was Princess Malanda kaVelani of the Mkhwanazi kingdom. Dunn also married many ordinary Zulu women and his principal wife was a mixed-race woman who was a Christian, Catherine Fihlaswe *Gadeni* Pierce.

Cetshwayo was restored to the throne 10 days after his arrival by the same now shrunken Shepstone, on the 29$^{th}$ of January 1883. Cetshwayo tried to bring life back to normal and started by hurriedly rebuilding the capital on the old grounds and called it *uNdi olumahlikihlikana* (the rugged uLundi mountains). The joint committee called a meeting of utmost importance with Shepstone and demanded answers about Cetshwayo's future. They wanted to know what was to happen now that he had limited powers, no cattle, with most of his subjects now living in '*new kingdoms*' under cruel '*chiefs*' and hardly any land. A very uncomfortable Shepstone sat under an umbrella with sweat pouring down his prune-like red neck but he put up a brave face. As he was beginning to talk and defend the indefensible, '*inkosi*' Zibhebhu, who was now estranged from Cetshwayo, galloped in.

He deliberately disrupted the tense meeting and with content totally ignored Cetshwayo, his one-time confidant. He only spoke to the shivering Shepstone, and without dismounting galloped off again covering everyone with dust. Shortly thereafter '*inkosi*' Mfanawendlela was equally theatrical, providing a welcome distraction for Shepstone, who could not defend the colonial government's actions. After not getting adequate answers from Shepstone, the joint committee resolved to revenge all the injustices suffered by the people at the hands of the '*new chiefs*' as well as for the torching of their capital, uLundi.

Cetshwayo then began the hard task of rebuilding what was left of his empire. All those who had fought against the British at iSandlwana and had been appointed as '*chiefs*', disbanded and took their marching orders once more from Cetshwayo only. Three months after Cetshwayo's enthronement, as promised, Ndabuko led the Zulu army against Zibhebhu and uMandlakazi regiment on the 30th of March 1883 at the Battle of uMsebe. The battle theatre was at Ndinhlane in the valley between Ngxongwana and Hlophekhulu Hills. The army poured into the valley at lightning speed and a ferocious fight ensued near the river. Thousands of bodies of uMandlakazi regiment were left lying along the riverbank, a truly grotesque sight especially after they lay half-eaten by crocodiles. Zibhebhu barely escaped but his five brothers were killed and uMandlakazi regiment was thoroughly routed. However, Cetshwayo lost a great a crack sniper, Mayibane Xulu.

The old warhorse Zibhebhu was not done yet. He led his uHlabisa regiment and some British and Afrikaner mercenaries and attacked the uLundi Palace on 21st July 1883. They ambushed a joint committee meeting which included many senior members of Zulu royal family, aristocrats, the king's council and military high command. No one ever imagined a blood bath within the confines of a palace, moreover at the capital. This was a sacrilege as blood was not allowed to be spilled within palace grounds, something Zibhebhu knew but did anyway. Many custodians of Zulu heritage, culture and history were killed in one swoop inside the grounds of the palace.

Five of Mpande's wives were killed as well as one of Cetshwayo's sons Prince Nyoniyentaba, whose mother okaMajiya was severly wounded but managed to escape. Other heroes and prominent people who were also killed defending Cetshwayo were Godide, (Ndlela's son) who was the commander of KwaBulawayo regiment; Dikane Mbatha (a great orator and Shaka's adviser); Zibhebhu's paternal brother Hayiyana kaMaphitha who was on Cetshwayo's side; Ntshingwayo kaMahole Khoza (commander-in-chief at iSandlwana); Sekethwayo kaNhlaka Mdlalose (Mkabayi's last personal aide). Cetshwayo tried to organise resistance but it was too little, too late. He barely escaped with his life and again he witnessed the burning of his recently rebuilt capital. Once again, Cetshwayo was on the run. This time he crossed uMhlathuze River together with a few soldiers and tried to hide in nearby bushes but Zibhebhu's uHlabisa regiment caught up with them. Sikhuni kaNkovu Nxumalo, a renowned sniper from Msebe, threw a spear that stabbed Cetshwayo in the thigh. But as soon as Sikhuni realised that he had stabbed the king, he apologised profusely and tied the king's wound and let him escape with his bodyguards.

Zibhebhu almost managed to complete what the whites could not, and the House of Senzangakhona went into turmoil. Once again, the king's whereabouts became anyone's guess. But word finally got out that Cetshwayo was alive and had recovered from his stab wound and was in the Nkandla forest. Sigananda provided refuge to Cetshwayo at his eNhlweni homestead on the edge of the Nkandla forest. When Zokufa (Sigananda's father) heard Cetshwayo was in the forest, he led the iNkominophondo regiment on a search-and-rescue mission. They found that Sigananda had moved him to Dlaba's fort with his wives and they were taken to Manziphambana fort that belonged to Zokufa's father, even deeper in the forest. It was comfortable and big enough to accommodate the king's retinue and soldiers. Cetshwayo was with his principal wife Queen Nompaka who had been everywhere with him, in the iNgome forest, in Cape Town, in *Oude Moulen* farm and now the Nkandla forest. Melmoth sent many messengers to beg Cetshwayo to come out of the forest and move into a special government house in Eshowe. He even promised that he would live in royal splendour but Cetshwayo was not interested.

Cetshwayo was aware that Melmoth was two-faced because he was busy encouraging non-royals to take over the throne by any means necessary. Some of the pretenders encircling the Zulu throne were Hhamu, Zibhebhu and Mfanawendlela. What's more, Melmoth had not only armed Zibhebhu to attack the capital, but he had personally recruited at least four white mercenaries to go with uMandlakazi regiment. These mercenaries were to report directly to him afterwards about the outcome of the attack and whether Zibhebhu was really against Cetshwayo. After the uLundi bloodbath, Melmoth seriously considered installing the young boy, Dinuzulu as the king even though Cetshwayo was still alive. This was to confuse matters and create tension between father and son. When he received no support to install Dinuzulu, Melmoth threatened to send the army to eject Cetshwayo from the forest. This was a thinly veiled threat to have him killed in the process. Cetshwayo only agreed to come out on condition that Melmoth agreed to let him live at KwaGqikazi near aMatigulu River in Eshowe.

Melmoth refused, so Cetshwayo ended up running what was left of his empire from an old friend Khekhe's homestead in Eshowe, called KwaJazi. Relations between Melmoth and Cetshwayo were cordial and business like and they often held meetings because Zulu philosophy believes in constant engagement. After one such meeting, Melmoth asked Cetshwayo to stay for lunch. During the meal Cetshwayo suddenly passed out but recovered later. After that incident, his health was never the same. He deteriorated rapidly, forever complaining about stomach trouble. The day Cetshwayo died, he called the king's council Shingana (Udloko), Ndabuko (Mbonambi), Dabulamanzi, Ziwedu, Mnyamana and Mankulumana to his side and confirmed Dinuzulu as his heir. Sinking fast, the king asked his heartbroken young son to come closer to him. With tears streaming down his pale face, Dinuzulu haltingly approached his dying father.

Cetshwayo made him promise to revenge against Zibhebhu and to the last drop of his royal blood. Cetshwayo also promised Dinuzulu to assist him defeat Zibhebhu, from beyond the grave. Dinuzulu merely nodded vigorously as his voice would not escape through his trembling lips. An official statement in Natal was made that Cetshwayo had died 'due to fatty degenation of the heart' whereas the prestigious publication the *British Medical Journal* supported the theory that Cetshwayo had no heart disease. On the 8th of February 1884, Cetshwayo *uJinindi omnyama, uMagwegwana* kaShaka kaSenzangakhona died in Khekhe's homestead in Eshowe. His body was placed in a sitting as per the Zulu custom and wrapped in a black ox hide and bile from a goat was put on his hair because he was the king. Cetshwayo died without knowing that one of his wives, Queen Zihlazile *okaQethuka* Magwaza had given birth to a son, Prince Nkongolozana, who was known as Manzolwandle. The king's council then appointed Ndabuko kaMpande as regent.

The issue of the burial of the king became contentious and no matter hard the royal family pleaded, Melmoth refused to allow Cetshwayo to be buried at the royal burial grounds in eMakhosini Valley. A month went by and Melmoth remained adamant that the king be buried at Eshowe. On the 8th of April, Cetshwayo's grief-stricken widows such as Nompaka, Nomvimbi and others rushed to Melmoth's house to revenge and demand that he buried at eMakhosini Valley. When Melmoth saw the murderous women coming for him, the pride of everything British in Africa, fled from the unarmed African women on a horse. It was a spectacle to behold as the angry women ransacked and pulled Melmoth's house apart piece by piece, including the roof with their bare hands and screaming at the top of their voices. This stance worked as a few hours later, Melmoth granted the permission to bury their husband. It had taken a few furious women to solve a problem that had been dragging on for weeks. The royal family together with a man called Hambangana who was an *ikholwa* placed his body, still in the seated position, inside a coffin and began the arduous task of taking the king's remains to eMakhosini. But there was a strong British patrol along the road they had to use which was likely to delay them. So, they used the long way and approached eMakhosini through the Nkandla forest. Unfortunately, the wagon fell apart in the broken forest terrain. He ended up being buried on 23rd April deep in Bophe Ridge in the Nkandla forest by Luhungu Shezi. He was interred with some of his personal belongings near iNkunzana River in the Shezi kingdom. Luhungu's descendants still take care of the grave to this day.

*Prince Imperial Eugene Louis Napoleon Bonaparte was the only son of Empress Eugenie and Napoleon III (King Napoleon's cousin). He joined the war even though the French were not at war with the Zulu. Prime Minister Disraeli was referring to the French monarchy when he lamented: 'Who are these Zulus, who are these remarkable people who defeat our Generals, convert our Bishops and on this day, have brought the end to a great dynasty?' (Killie Campbell Africana Library)*

*A white settler washes on a stream as his young Indian servant looks on holding a water bucket. (Killie Campbell Africana Library)*

# 9

# Emperor Dinuzulu kaCetshwayo

As CETSHWAYO TOOK A nap one lazy afternoon in 1868 he dreamt his ancestors telling him that three of his wives were pregnant with boys. Then they told him to make the son who was going to be borne by a fair skinned short beauty, Nomvimbi *Somakhoyisa* kaMsweli Mzimela the heir and call him Dinuzulu (*Zulu wrath*) because the ancestors were upset about the last two civil wars. Nomvimbi *okaMsweli* lived at KwaGqikazi under the watchful eye of Mbixambixa kaMpande who was the guardian of the national treasure *inkatha*. The other two wives *okaMadwala* lived at eziHlendleni Palace and *okaMagoda* lived at KwaNobamba. Indeed, they all gave birth to boys the same week as Cetshwayo's ancestors had predicted. But *okaMadwala* and *okaMagoda's* sons died when they were both two months old.

To ensure that no harm befell Dinuzulu, the royal family assigned six male bodyguards Nobiyana kaMholo Mzimela, Ntwayibana kaKhwani, Mpatsha kaMadwala, Lwezi Ntombela, Sitambi kaMasiphula kaNtshangase and the old war hero Sikhobobo. Dinuzulu was pampered and loved by all. His father called him *Mamonga woSuthu* or *uMahelana asoNdini olubomvana*. He grew up to be a tall, handsome and fair-skinned young man with striking big eyes that smouldered when angry. He was soft-spoken with a ready smile and his ears were decorated with long earrings. He adorned his great body with his trademark three-metre long *umyezane* war medals made from willow tree bark. He became a skilled fighter and a military strategist, like his grandfather Shaka. This is the same *umyezane* war medal that the founder of the Boy Scout Movement Lord Robert Baden-Powell replicated when he created the Boy Scouts' Wood Badge.

When Dinuzulu was 5 years old he witnessed his father's coronation, he was also present when the uThulwana and iNgobamakhosi regiments viciously tore into each other. He also watched in awe as this father's army defeat the British empire at iSandlwana. By the time Dinuzulu was 11 years old he had already been on the run from his father's enemies, lived like a fugitive in the forest and twice witnessed the torching of his home, uLundi Palace. Hence, he grew up under no illusion about the sad state of Zulu affairs when he ascended the throne. Luckily for him, his mother *okaMsweli* was an accomplished woman. She built the eNyokeni Palace in the highlands of KwaNongoma and her legacy lives through the annual world-famous virgins only annual ceremony in September called *umkhosi womhlanga* (reed dance) and is attended by over 50 000 Zulu girls. She was a warrior in her own right and had been a commander in several battles. For instance, she fought with exceptional bravery at the Ndondakusuka Battle on the side of Cetshwayo where her father Msweli Mzimela was killed by Mbuyazwe's forces. The young women from Msweli's homestead were moved to various palaces as *umdlunkulu* so did she, and who caught the king's eye. She had a profound influence over Dinuzulu and the following laudatory praises highlight her battle readiness as the baby had to suckle on its knees as in case she had to jump into action:

| | |
|---|---|
| Ithole lakokaMsweli | the calf of the daughter of Msweli |
| Elanyisa liguqile | that suckled on its knees |

Dinuzulu grew up in a different environment and circumstances from all previous Zulu kings and emperors. He grew up in proximity and contact with whites, especially the Afrikaners who were Zulu subjects. He grew up playing childhood games with them along riverbanks and in the open fields when they each herded their father's cattle. Consequently, Dinuzulu did not think twice about trusting them. He thought their loyalty to him as the future Zulu monarch would surpass their eternal greed for land and livestock. He was forever preoccupied with the promise he made to his dying father and he also wanted to show the British that even though the Zulu empire had been emasculated, the Zulu defiant spirit did not die with his father, Cetshwayo. He did not want to wait until he was king to take revenge, and when an opportunity presented itself, he organised a reprisal attack against Zibhebhu. He rallied his father's regiments and recruited Afrikaner mercenaries including his childhood friend, Louis Botha (later to become the first Prime Minister of the Union of South Africa).

They had both grown up on the farms of *eMsinga* (Greytown) and like many Afrikaner children who grew up raised by Zulu servants, Louis spoke impeccable isiZulu. Louis was six years older than Dinuzulu and referred to himself as Dinuzulu's 'older brother'. He helped to recruit more white mercenaries because Zibhebhu's forces were better armed than Dinuzulu's forces. Louis organised Lucas Meyer (*Lukhazi*), Jacobus van Staden, Swart Dirk Uys, Paul Bester who commanded 800 Afrikaners, while Adolph Schiel commanded Germans from the Luneburg (*Msinga*) area. Meyer and van Staden went as far as piling stones together, put a stick with a hat on top and swore their allegiance to Dinuzulu, then formed a mercenary regiment called *Dinuzulu's Volunteers*. The Afrikaners only supported Dinuzulu because of their pathological hatred of the British, while the British supported Zibhebhu for the same reason and both had an insatiable greed for cattle and land. The agreement with Dinuzulu was that he would pay the Afrikaner and German mercenaries with cattle. They said that as much as they trusted him, they needed surety that he would return their cattle after the battle. So, they demanded his coronation before the war, so that no other person could claim to be king after the victory.

Dinuzulu and what was left of the Zulu military high command were initially opposed to the idea, but uSuthu needed any help they could secure and ultimately the regent Ndabuko after much soul searching agreed. That is why on the 20th of May 1884 the king's council enthroned Dinuzulu as the Emperor of the Zulu Empire within the confines of uLundi Palace. At noon the following day, Dinuzulu and his entourage arrived at a laager called *Zaalf* in iNyathi Hill near eHlobane and he was led to an upturned liquor box which served as a throne. Then one of the mercenaries, Andreas Laas poured a few drops of castor oil on Dinuzulu's hair and declared him 'the king' as the Afrikaner blue and white flag flattered above. When Dinuzulu asked what the meaning of the flag was, the Afrikaners told him that it was their lucky charm. Only 10 000 Zulu subjects that bothered to show up for the farce and there were about 350 Afrikaners in 70 tents. Dinuzulu was merely 15 years old.

The battle was fought on a wintry morning on the 5th of June 1884 but uncharacteristically wet. It was regarded as a good omen for the Zulu army because they believed that any activity that was accompanied by rain was a blessing from the ancestors. Dinuzulu led his army to the battle theatre on his black horse followed immediately by the war veterans and the high command including Sikhobobo, Mswazi, Mbenge and Hhemulana. They commanded the Buthelezi, Mgazi, Ntombela and Mdlalose regiments as well as the remnants of the awesome abaQulusi regiment. They swept past iVuna River expeditiously like lightning, singing a song Dinuzulu had composed specifically for this battle: '*Wayihlaba wema nayo*'.

They went to Bhanganomo and razed Zibhebhu's huge Ncasengisekhona homestead to the ground and killed everyone and everything that did not manage to run or hide. They also destroyed all Zibhebhu's homesteads in their path. After the attack it became clear that the so-called Afrikaner and German assistance was more a show of strength than active combat. They deliberately followed Dinuzulu's army from a safe distance behind. The battle theatre was in the valley surrounded by uBombo Mountain range, uMkhuze River, eTshaneni and Gasa Mountain.

King Soshangane had named the mountain after one of his ancestors Gasa kaManukuza. His descendants still bury their dead chiefs from Mozambique, as they regard it as sacred. The battle uncovered a new breed of great fighters last seen in the days of Shaka such as Mgilija. One of Zibhebhu's battle plans was that they would start by stabbing Dinuzulu's horses. They arrived at the battle theatre singing:

| | |
|---|---|
| *Awakhonkothe* | *let them bark* |
| *Singamanketshane* | *we are the wild dogs* |
| *Ayakhonkotha* | *they are barking* |
| *Ngqu ngqu ngqu ngqu* | *ngqu ngqu ngqu ngqu* |
| *Imbaxalazela* | *they are dragging themselves* |
| *Uxamu ulele emzileni* | *there is a giant crocodile on the path* |
| *Zasezikhala izilwane zansondo* | *the wretched animals howled* |
| *Seziphikelele kuzo iziGqoza zathi* | *rushing towards iziGqoza saying* |
| *Washesha Washesha Washesha* | *Hurry Hurry Hurry* |

Once at the valley, Zibhebhu's men went silent and set huge tracts of grass on fire. It created a huge smokescreen that concealed their real numbers and movement. Dinuzulu and his men stood still and looked for the uMandlakazi regiment through the dense smoke without success. For a long time, nothing could be seen or heard except for the bursting inferno. Then a shot rang out from Zibhebhu's forces and Mgilija raced down the mountain, through eTshaneni pass and charged towards the enemy as though he was possessed and slaughtered many of them. The skirmish continued for about an hour and Zibhebhu's men went down shouting '*Washesha*'.

Zibhebhu lost over 10 brothers in the Tshaneni Battle, but he survived because he was seen watching the fight from high up in the safety of a ridge. Standing next to him were two of his white mercenaries John Eckersley and Henry Grosvenor Darke. He fled to a newly formed native reserve (*iLizevu*) in uMhlathuze Valley where he lived in shame. In any case, he had no home to go to as all his homesteads were in cinders. After the battle, Zibhebhu instructed the traitor who had given their position away to hack off one of his legs with a blunt axe. Dinuzulu led his triumphant army on a long slow victory march back to KwaNongoma and collected around 60 000 cattle from Zibhebhu's homesteads and returned them to their rightful owners. He also rewarded his forces with a fair share of the loot, including the pusillanimous Afrikaners and Germans who shot at the enemy from a safe distance. Dinuzulu's laudatory praises highlight the revenge attack:

*Indaba engiyizwe ngisemncane*      *I heard the story when I was still young*
*Ngaze ngakhula ngayibona ngamehlo*      *I saw it with my own eyes when I grew up*
*Ukuba izimpondo zimila enjeni*      *that horns grow on a dog*
*Engabe enkomeni zesabani*      *I wonder what they fear growing on a cow*

Despite the success of destroying Zibhebhu's force, Dinuzulu was unhappy that Zibhebhu was still alive even though he was living like a pauper under the British. As the years went by, Dinuzulu was to suffer the humiliation of a disintegrating empire on his watch. But he was powerless to change the course of history. His woes began when his mercenary regiment *Dinuzulu's Volunteers* claimed that he had not only promised them cattle but that he had promised them land to create 240 farms of 1 000 morgen (250ha) each and 560 farms of 2 000 morgens (500ha) each as well. Then Meyer followed up the claim with a Proclamation which said: 'Lines and beacons will be fixed after the ground had been inspected' which is proof that they had no idea where the land was situated which they were supposedly promised.

Before long the number of mercenaries spiked to over 1 000 and lots were drawn and they began to occupy any land they fancied from uMkhuze River in the north, down to St Lucia Bay on the border of the uMhlathuze Valley. Dinuzulu denied promising them anything more than cattle, but they insisted on the land and he was helpless. He could not stop them from forcibly moving his subjects to caves, barren, mosquito-infested marshlands or to stagnant pools and anastomosing streams. They also helped themselves to land belonging to the abaQulusi kingdom, after the Swati government said they were witnesses when Dinuzulu made that promise. The Swatis lied because the Afrikaners had promised them some land if they lied on their behalf, but the Afrikaners reneged.

Once again, the Colenso family wrote letters and sent petitions to England and Pietermaritzburg trying to stop the Afrikaners from stealing more land. They even took the matter to court in Pietermaritzburg. But these efforts were wasted because Dinuzulu only managed to salvage a small piece of land between White iMfolozi, eBabanango, eMthonjaneni and eSihlungu valleys. He was only successful because he said he couldn't have promised them land that held many Zulu ancestral graves belonging to Kings Malandela, Phunga, Mageba, Ndaba, Jama, Senzangakhona, Queen Mother Mthaniya (Shaka's grandmother), Princess Nomcoba (Shaka's sister) and many other members of the Zulu royal family. Nothing could deter the Afrikaners as they went on to declare an independent state in that area.

They called it the *Vryheid Republic* (Freedom Republic) on the 5th of August 1884. Its capital was Vryheid which boasted only one long street. Lucas Meyer was its first and only president. When Dinuzulu refused to yield on more land, the Afrikaners prepared to attack him. As though that was not enough, on the 5th April 1885 a suave German calling himself Amil Nagel, appeared from nowhere and asked for an audience with Dinuzulu. After listening to him, Dinuzulu was reminded of many other land concessions that were purported to have been signed by his grandfather Shaka who was illiterate. He produced a document with signatures he claimed belonged to Dinuzulu, Anderbeko (*Ndabuko*) and Astungam (*Shingana*) dated the 1st June 1885. He said he was representing the German Land Colonisation Company of Berlin and had come to buy the whole Zulu empire for a mere £2 500. He also said that payment would be affected 25 times a year at instalments of £100 or the equivalent in weapons. In return the Germans would:

- Allow the Zulu to continue living on the land for free
- The land invaded by the 100 Afrikaners now belongs to the Germans
- The rules and regulations of the Zulu kingdom will be passed in Berlin
- Every nationality living in the Zulu kingdom would be under the German government
- Dinuzulu would remain king but Berlin reserved the right to install all future heirs
- The Hermansburg mission stations had to be given 6 000 acres each
- In the event of war, the Zulu had to support the Germans
- The Zulu nation were now be ruled by the German Imperial government

Dinuzulu weighed his options and realised he needed extra help to contain the Afrikaners. So, with a heavy heart, he approached his archenemy, the British and asked for assistance. Remembering what his father Cetshwayo had done to them, the British turned on him. They said they were going to punish him for seeking help from the Afrikaners for the eTshaneni war without their permission. Then they quickly moved and seized all what was left of the Zulu empire in 1887, including the one-horse town of the Vryheid Republic. Later, through fomented crises and Machiavellian tactics of fragmentation, the British government convinced its electorate in England that although Zulu power had finally been crushed, it had been necessary to annex their territory. This was to ensure that even the rural Zulu knew exactly, who was now in charge. There was no opposition from the British electorate when the Union Jack flew in remote St Lucia Bay.

The proud Zulu people had finally been colonised. After this momentous and devastating declaration, an uneasy peace prevailed and Dinuzulu did the best he could despite the mammoth setbacks. He lived a perpetual nightmare that the very little land that was left, had been snatched from right under his nose. He could not bear to think about all the wars of resistance that had been fought by Zulu kings to preserve the empire. He felt responsible that the demise of his people had happened on his watch, it had slipped right through his inexperienced fingers. To find some measure of relief from his anguish, he took to drinking white people's alcohol.

The British further divided what was left of the Zulu empire into six magisterial districts Eshowe, Nkandla, eMthonjaneni, Nquthu, KwaNdwandwe and Lower iMfolozi. They also stripped Dinuzulu as the Sovereign of the whole Zulu empire and reduced him to a mere 'Paramount Chief of uSuthu'. There were no clear boundaries to his land, but it covered some parts of KwaNongoma. This was yet another blow, but the Zulu did not give up hope and Dinuzulu relied on the indomitable Zulu spirit to soldier on. Despite the terms that secured his father's freedom of never forming regiments ever again, Dinuzulu defiantly formed the following regiments uCijimpi, uFanozulu, uMagazini, iNdaba kandondondo, uNtabengenaliba, uPhefeni and uVukayibambe (Prince Maphumuzana became a member of this regiment). After living under the British protection in the *iLizevu* of iNyoni in uMhlathuze Valley, Zibhebhu was either a hopeless optimist or a downright fool. He insisted on going back to his home at Bhanganomo because he said that he did not enjoy living as a homeless wanderer.

When Dinuzulu found out about his request, he tried to stop him, but the British allowed him to return. True to his character, Zibhebhu went on a killing spree in Bhanganomo and he killed everyone he suspected was against him. He even turned on his one-time ally, '*inkosi*' Mfanawendlela. Zibhebhu was truly bloodthirsty and hunted for easy prey. He attacked Cetshwayo's longest serving adviser Msushwana Mdletshe (iMboza) and killed him in broad daylight. He then jumped over his corpse twice in full view of everyone, a Zulu sacrilege. This was too much even for the British and to try calm things down and put to bed the enormities, they held a sham trial. As expected, he was found not guilty. This was the last straw for the many people living around Zibhebhu's KwaMandlakazi homestead. They moved en masse to live under Dinuzulu near his palace.

People from all over the empire pleaded with Dinuzulu to act against the barbaric excesses of the '*chiefs*' especially Zibhebhu. Dinuzulu sent a deputation to the British urging them to stop Zibhebhu's atrocities, but they did nothing. He realised that talking was not yielding any results and decided to go directly to the people and hear for himself. Saddled high on his favourite black stallion, Dinuzulu looked imposing as he crisscrossed the Black iMfolozi Valley. He wore a black hat and a long black cape that covered the horse as well. Again, he led his army singing a song he had composed especially for this mission *'Sangena koBhevula'*. Closest on either side of him were his armed bodyguards who rode in strict military formation. On the right-hand side rode 20 soldiers from the aMagangana regiment dressed in all black and on his left rode 20 soldiers from the aMahuzu regiment dressed in khaki gear from head to toe. Immediately behind them, abaQulusi followed in a rhythmic jog behind the horses. They kept this formation as they went all over collecting evidence against Zibhebhu. They told stories of absolute savagery they had suffered. As a true descendant of Shaka and despite his limited resources, Dinuzulu declared war against Zibhebhu again.

At dawn on the 21$^{st}$ of June 1888, he went into the dense KwaCeza forest and the now 18-year-old monarch again led from the front. Dinuzulu's forces were better armed this time but were heavily outnumbered, so he was still not guaranteed success. Moreover, he was not going to receive assistance from neither the British nor the Afrikaners this time. When they reached a strategic point at the top of Ceza Mountain, Dinuzulu looked at his enthusiastic army and admitted to himself that the campaign's success was up to the benevolence of his ancestors now. So far, they had been more than kind to him, but this time the stakes were too high. He therefore was left with no option but to try out something new, the white God. In full view of his fired-up and raring-to-go army, he suddenly swung off his horse. His black cape followed him and floated in the air as he dropped down on one knee. In military precision his 20 000 men simultaneously joined him. They all fell silent, closed their eyes in unison, and waited for Mbulawa Paul Mthimkhulu, the army chaplain and doctor to open the Bible. Without looking up - as though in a trance - he slowly read from Deuteronomy 30:1-20.

History was made that morning because it was the first time that a Zulu king had prayed to a Christian god. His grandfather Shaka and his father Cetshwayo, knew about the white contradictory God who sent his own children to eternal damnation, but was also merciful at times. Dinuzulu was converted on the spot, making him the first Zulu king to become a Christian. Young as he was, Dinuzulu was a brilliant tactician and a military strategist of note. For instance, he sent a group of nimble youngsters to cut some trees and created his ultimate secret weapon, called *amathandalaza*. This was a tree trunk that was sharpened on each end and positioned in such a way that when struck by a bullet, it would boomerang towards the direction of the bullet. The tree trunks became, in fact, an *ersatz* army by themselves. Then he deployed the older regiments up the mountain and sent the young and fleet-footed iMbokodo *'ebomvu kaMagayisa'* and uFalaza *'thatha kuyehlela'* regiments below, deep into the forest and they hid near the Black iMfolozi River. This time an even bigger British contingent accompanied Zibhebhu's 15 regiments such as iNyoni emhlophe, iKuvukeni and Bhanganomo regiments. However, they failed to negotiate the dense treacherous terrain, so they resorted to firing wildly into the trees, hoping to hit the Zulu army.

As Dinuzulu had anticipated, some of the bullets struck *amathandalaza* tree trunks. Thus Dinuzulu's *'ghost army'* struck terror into Zibhebhu's men. They could not believe their eyes, trees or logs behaving like human beings and coming alive when struck by a bullet. They panicked and shot grossly off-target, fearing every tree or log would come alive. The 'invisible' Zulu army only appeared when Zibhebhu and his British mercenaries ran out of ammo and a blood bath ensued. The British, who were spoiling for a fight, began shelling Dinuzulu's men heavily. Then Dinuzulu sent word to them that he was not fighting the British but was in hot pursuit of Zibhebhu's forces, then the British reluctantly stopped. Dinuzulu managed to push Zibhebhu's powerful forces back, well beyond eNkonjeni's British military base camp some 60 kilometres away. Zibhebhu's men scattered and some took cover at the camp. Some of them had run as far as KwaNdunu Mountain and beyond Black iMfolozi River to hide. But Dinuzulu led uFalaza, iNgobamakhosi, uPhefeni and uFanozulu regiments and they shadowed them through Zibhebhu's territory where they camped in Sisusweni's homestead overnight. Then they first marched past the KwaZiphethe Palace near KwaNongoma Court and headed to KwaNdunu Mountain.

At daybreak on the 23rd of June 1888, Dinuzulu fired the first shot at Mancwangeni's homestead in Ndabayakhe the one that killed Sigwabugwabu, Zibhebhu's close ally. The final showdown took place at just before 6am when they approached each other in silence. Their spears were held in the attack position. Zibhebhu's men had tied red ribbons around their foreheads and necks which fluttered in the morning breeze. Dinuzulu's forces had tied white cow tails on their elbows and necks. When the two armies were about 350 metres apart Zibhebhu's men shouted *'Washesha'* and charged, simultaneously Dinuzulu's men shouted *'uSuthu'* and also charged. They clashed and the white cow tails of Dinuzulu's men flapped wildly as they savagely tore into the enemy. After a prolonged vicious fighting, Zibhebhu's forces were finally routed and never to rise again. Zibhebhu escaped by playing dead underneath his regiments' corpses. He only emerged when he was certain that Dinuzulu's forces had retreated into the caves in Ceza Mountain to camp.

A prominent victim of the KwaNdunu Battle was one of Shepstone's *'inkosi'* Mgojana Ndwandwe, who was married to Dinuzulu's great-aunt (on his father's side) Mbixambixa. Her husband was an interesting character; first he had agreed to become an *'inkosi'* when Cetshwayo was in prison. But he gave it up when Cetshwayo returned and aligned himself with him. He was present when Zibhebhu attacked uLundi and he escaped with Cetshwayo and witnessed him getting stabbed in the thigh. But after Cetshwayo had fled, he went back to the palace and watched it being burnt down by Zibhebhu where he switched his allegiance again back to Zibhebhu. He then abandoned Mbixambixa and found new wives at KwaMandlakazi, Zibhebhu's homestead. Mbixambixa was so embarrassed when she found out that she too abandoned their marital home and returned to her people at KwaGqikazi Palace. She was very close to Dinuzulu because she was present at his birth. When Dinuzulu left for the battle, she made him promise to personally kill Mgojana wherever he found him. But when Dinuzulu caught Mgojana, he could not bring himself to kill him because he had grown up around him. Instead, he shot him in the thigh and ordered Shumiselani Mabanga to finish him off. Sadly, Mgojana's son was also killed when he tried to save his father. Dinuzulu regretted both their deaths because of their close relationship.

Dinuzulu's battle plan and execution was so perfect that he did not lose a single man in KwaCeza and KwaNdunu. He attributed the resounding success of both battles to the Christian God as per his Zulu ancestors. After winning these battles, Dinuzulu's supporters as well as his prestige grew in leaps and bounds. He could not thank the white God enough. For the first time in his short life, Dinuzulu felt reassured and happy, and for once enjoyed being young. The Zulu based in Natal lived a terrible life under the whites and Indians. But young people were the most exploited because as soon as they were old enough to work, they were destined to work in white and Indian households. Others were made to work in the mines, sugar plantations, railway lines or any place that required hard labour from sunrise until sunset and at night during full moon. Moving north and joining people who still lived a traditional life was attractive, so thousands of young Zulu men joined him daily, even though he was a king he was in their age group.

The youth in the Zulu hinterland spent a lot of time outdoors herding cattle, swimming in the rapids and raging rivers, diving in dangerous waterfalls, climbing mountains, wrestling crocodiles and taking part in stick-fighting competitions. They hunted for their dinner, joined Dinuzulu's 'banned' regiments and roamed free in the countryside in groups on horseback. They also traded and bartered in rifles with other regiments or with Portuguese merchants from Mozambique or with Afrikaner or British mercenaries. They were also willing to fight in a war when the need arose.

They hunted wild animals for sport in dangerous forests or trapped small animals just for the fun of it. Their most exciting pastime though remained to *ukuqomisa* (charming girls) at water-wells or rivers to their heart's desire.

They also hung around at the edges of forests to find the girls who were collecting firewood. They did everything to impress them with the hope of getting lucky. The regular *ijadu* (matchmaking festivals) were the highlight. Every self-respecting young person could unashamedly show off their dancing and singing talents. Life was good under the teenage monarch who was considered a modern-day *Robbin Hood, Zorro, Iron Man* and a *Samurai* all in one. The British were infuriated as they had not expected Zibhebhu to lose. So, they needed something to curtail Dinuzulu's popularity. Then they started rumours throughout the kingdom that Dinuzulu was wanted by the British because of unspecified, yet extremely serious 'charges'.

All the while, the young warrior king was innocently roaming the Zulu countryside like any teenager would. He was blissfully unaware of the bounty on his royal head. What worried everyone was not only that the British could easily kill Dinuzulu which would come as no surprise but what was worse than him dying, was that he had no offspring. This was a major crisis as far as they were concerned. But as soon as Dinuzulu heard that the British were looking for him, he returned home and strategised the next move with the king's council. One thing was for sure, the British wanted to destroy the Zulu monarchy more than anything.

Therefore, they needed to create a crisis to justify their dubious intentions. Aware of the fact that it was much against everyone's advice, Dinuzulu decided that he was going to confront the British about his impending arrest in person. After a little persuasion from his principal adviser Mankulumana, he agreed to spend at least a week with his favourite girl, in seclusion. This 'exercise' was an attempt to produce an heir, in case the British killed him in Pietermaritzburg. The debonair young monarch had several girls to choose from and Mahayihayi kaMahu kaSojiyisa thought she would be the one because their families had been so close. But Dinuzulu had his own favourite, Princess Mahambogwini kaHlokolo Ndwandwe. Her father had fought with distinction at iSandlwana and died defending KwaNodwengu Palace.

The British had cut off his head after the war and took it to London where it was displayed. Even though Hlokolo's lineage on both sides of his family was 'pure' Zulu, he looked Caucasian. He was totally devoid of melanin, he had a sharp nose, blond hair and a blond beard. Perhaps Hlokolo was an albino or a genuine anomaly. His head has never been returned to his family or to the Zulu monarch to this day. The nation held its collective breath when they heard the news about a desperate attempt to produce an offspring within the next nine months or so. They were hoping against hope that firstly, Mahambogwini was fertile enough to fall pregnant within a week and secondly, that she should produce a boy child. She proved her fertility in nine months alright, but unfortunately for the nation, she gave birth to a little girl. She was named Phikisinkosi *Phikisile* which means 'disagreed with the king'. Her middle name was Harriette, (after Bishop Colenso's daughter who loved Zulu people with all her heart). Princess Phikisile later married the intellectual giant Dr Pixley ka iSaka Seme, the co-founder of the ANC in 1912. They had four sons and a daughter.

Dinuzulu chose to go to the British in Pietermaritzburg rather than Eshowe where Zulu affairs were handled. The royal entourage consisted of Mankulumana, Mgwaqo and about 10 people including advisers, chefs, council members, hairdressers, dressers, baggage carriers. They travelled by train and stayed at St Albans College. But before Dinuzulu reported to the British, he spent a few days sightseeing with Harriette and they even visited the Pietermaritzburg museum. People lined up the streets to catch a glance at him and saluted him and gave him gifts. But it was too much for some whites to see these two together in an open carriage driving through sleepy Pietermaritzburg, being drawn by four donkeys and escorted by 12 bodyguards on horseback. Furthermore, the British were taken by surprise when Dinuzulu turned up in their capital without fear and they therefore refused to attend to him. They sent him back to the Native Affairs department in Eshowe on the 21$^{st}$ of November 1888.

The truth, however, is that the British sent him back because they were still trying to think what they could charge him with. He was sent back to Eshowe under the guard of three Natal police officers who put him on a train called *dabulukusa* (cut through the night till dawn). They were forced off the train at uMdlothi in the north just outside Durban just for the fun of it. Dinuzulu was then handed over to the Zululand police in the middle of uThukela River which served as a border. They then had to walk the rest of the 140 kilometres to Eshowe. It was only in the dying days of 1888 that Dinuzulu was charged with a list of offences. Suddenly his uncles were also charged with the same charges, and so were some members of the military high command and the king's council. The charges were:

- High Treason
- Public Violence
- Seeking help from the Afrikaners without British permission
- The murder of Zibhebhu's people
- The murder of Tonge, a white man who was killed by Mphikwa a resident of Zululand who claimed to have been carrying out Dinuzulu's instructions

Once charges were laid, Dinuzulu again chose to go to Pietermaritzburg to turn himself in. This time he was accompanied by several Zulu dignitaries and aristocrats as well as one faithful white subject, Jim Henderson. He waited for the police together with Harriette and Agnes Colenso at eKukhanyeni mission. He was arraigned at 15h00 on the 10<sup>th</sup> of December by Col MacKenzie and he allowed Mankulumana, Mgwaqo and Ncaphayi to be present during the proceedings that lasted a mere 40 minutes. He was incarcerated in a cell in Pietermaritzburg prison for few weeks. Later he was moved to a prison at Eshowe and dumped in a tiny cell, measuring four by three metres. The inmates did not like the idea that their king was degraded in this way, so they vacated the nearby cells to make more room for him. When Magema heard that king had been arrested, he gave up his job in Pietermaritzburg and went to Eshowe. He then started his own printing press business so that he could be close to the king. Dinuzulu used his time wisely as Magema taught him how to read and write as well as the English language.

He pleaded not guilty to all charges and refused to let any of his advisers to be his witnesses, in case they incriminated themselves. But the British managed to collect evidence against his followers such as Mthatheni, Ndabayakhe (Bhambatha's son), Somkhele (King Mlandela Mthethwa's father), Lugoloza, Masekwana, Dlemdlemu as well as Dinuzulu's brother-in-law Nsukuzonke kaHlokolo Ndwandwe. During Dinuzulu's trial, two overzealous Afrikaners, Paul van der Berg and Wilhelm Joubert, made a citizen's arrest and abducted Dinuzulu's relatives, Dabulamanzi the crack sniper and his son Mzingeli in Vryheid. They were kept under arrest in a jail even though there were no charges against them. But later Dabulamanzi was charged with being a member of the abaQulusi regiment, for violence, for attacking Afrikaner homesteads and for cattle rustling. However, they were sprung from jail they ran to an area under British rule. Instead of protecting them, the British handed them back to the Afrikaners in Vryheid. In the process, Paul gunned down Dabulamanzi at point blank range in front of Mzingeli in the streets of Vryheid on the 22<sup>nd</sup> of September 1886. The first bullet went through his left hip and the second bullet went through his right elbow and left wrist. Paul also shot at Mzingeli twice but missed. This cold-blooded murder caused outrage throughout the kingdom. It was a bitter reminder that they had become powerless at the hands of whites. That was the sad end of the exceptional sniper Dabulamanzi.

Dinuzulu was found guilty of High Treason on the 15<sup>th</sup> of January 1889 and sentenced to 10 years imprisonment. His two uncles Prince Shingana and Prince Ndabuko were also found guilty and sentenced to 12 and 15 years respectively. The three of them were to serve their sentences in exile, on St Helena Island, a small windswept island in the middle of the Atlantic Ocean. Dinuzulu argued for days with his captors about the size and final composition of his St Helena entourage. After reaching an agreement, he was taken to Durban under heavy police and army guard. He boarded the *SS Anglian* with only two of his wives, Queen Silomo *okaNtuzwa* Mdlalose and Queen Zihlazile *okaQethuka* Magwaza. Some of the people who travelled with him were Mbulawa Paul Mthimkhulu, personal attendants Mubi (*Bubi*) Mthuli kaNondenisa and Nyosana kaMadwala and his brother Mkholokotho Mthembu, Mbhodiya an old midwife as well as a hairdresser. His uncles Ndabuko and Shingana were accompanied by one wife each. Xamandolo Zungu one of Ndabuko's assistants and some white government interpreters, including a non-Zulu African interpreter Anthony Daniels from the south coast. But Dinuzulu refused to use him. The passage to St Helena was uneventful except for the mortal fear of drowning. Like his father, the 20-year-old monarch was also confident that he would return to his people alive.

St Helena Island has a fascinating history and was both a penal colony and a refuelling point during the slave trade. The residents call themselves '*Saints*' and the island's slogan is: '*St Helena has only one entrance and no exit*'. They docked in St Helena harbour at 11h00 on the 25th February 1890 but were only allowed to disembark the following day. Several residences were considered for them such as Primrose Lodge, High Knoll and Rosemary Hall. Governor Sir Reginald Laurence Antrobus welcomed them with great respect and they were taken to Rosemary Hall, a grand whitewashed old colonial home on the north side of the island which was found to be the most suitable. It was accommodation fit for royalty with breathtaking sea views, large grounds with stables, 518 metres above sea level and was about 6km from the capital Jamestown. It was also far from the prying eyes of the public. A few days later, as they were adjusting to life in the middle of the sea, a few days later they heard some voices outside their door weakly chanting: '*Bayethe, wena weNdlovu*'. Stunned, everyone looked at one another and wondered if more of the king's subjects had been brought without the king's knowledge. But instead, they saw three black men on their knees at the gate bowing respectfully. They were let inside, and they humbly told Dinuzulu their sad tale of how they ended up on the island. They had been kidnapped from a river in Congo when they were little boys playing along a river. They were grabbed by white men who put them aboard a steam ship. The three men were now called Cummings, George and Williams.

There was also a Zulu man who had also been stolen from the Zulu empire called Mbilimbili. He could recall some of the Zulu children's nursey tales such as '*Chakijana, Bogcololo*' as well as the name of their king, Nqaba kaMbekwane Khumalo. This made Dinuzulu wonder how many more of his subjects had been stolen and sold to slavery and where on earth they had ended up. He made a silent prayer for all of them and asked the Zulu ancestors to take care of them. The men became regular visitors at Rosemary Hall. The story of these unfortunate men confirmed what was regarded as Zulu folklore that *isiququmadevu* (a steam ship) would scour beaches and riverbanks looking for children to be sold as slaves overseas. Dinuzulu was also introduced to the men's daughters, Ms Martha Williams, Ms Cummings as well as to Ms Cressy and her sister at a state banquet held in his honour. They were all with sun-kissed cinnamon skins.

The weather on the island was far from being idyllic as it was often cold and extremely windy. When the blistery winter set in, they all suffered from bronchial diseases. The king's physician Mbulawa ordered medicines from home, but they did not help. They were then moved to a smaller place called Maldivia House, in a valley where there were no vistas. When they protested about the cramped conditions Antrobus refused to move them. After a while, with the money sent to him by his subjects, Dinuzulu built himself a house in Francis Plain where he could entertain his visitors in private. There was tension when some of the Queens became pregnant. According to custom they had to live in seclusion and only their mothers could attend to them. But the British refused to build them their own house or allow them to go back home. The British were in fact punishing Dinuzulu for being able to 'impregnate' some of the 'men', who had permission to visit him.

However, the truth was that the so called 'men' were in fact some of his wives who managed to fool the officials and received permission to go to the island under the pretense of taking the king his special herbs, food and other Zulu specialties. Cultural clashes left both parties bemused, and it would have been awfully funny if it wasn't so serious. Shingana was severely ill and urine tests were necessary, but he refused to either give urine samples or have a catheter inserted into his manhood. With all the dignity a Zulu royal could muster, he told the white doctors that his two small children, Prince Bhunya and Princess Nozinhlanzi, who were born on the island, would suffer life-threatening illnesses if he subjected himself to what they wanted.

Being stuck on a tiny island did not seem to make Dinuzulu lose his panache. Frances Colenso once described Dinuzulu's swagger as 'someone who trod the earth as though he owned it'. He was very much part of the society of Jamestown and continued to be a fashionista supreme. The Governor tried to make life for the young king and his people as comfortable as possible even though the colonial government would overrule recommendations, he made that favoured these Zulu captives. He threw lavish dinner parties in Dinuzulu's honour and invited him to cricket matches. In return, Dinuzulu hosted high-society balls for St Helena's glitterati where he was the centre of attention, especially admired by the ladies. The economy of the tiny island grew quite substantially during the 'Zulu era'.

This is because the king and his retinue were awash with money donated from the kingdom and except for the few outdoor activities, there wasn't much to do except shop. Dinuzulu wrote letters to his mother and read a lot. In doing so, he became well-versed in international affairs gleaned from the local newspaper and available books. For instance, he once took part in the island games and helped defeat the navy team in a tug-of-war contest. He was so benevolent that he donated a one pound, which was a fortune those days to a local poor white man. Dinuzulu took to sleeping on a bed instead of on *icansi* (a grass mat), he also ate with a fork and knife and drank from glasses. He spent hours riding all over the island as he was an accomplished horseman. Since he always loved music and had composed many songs, it was only a matter of time before he became an accomplished pianist and after lessons by Ms Birchill, he played drums like a professional. He even joined the church choir at St James Anglican Cathedral, which is the oldest Anglican Church south of the equator. He had intimate relations with several local women. But it was his relationship with Dona Magellan, a wealthy Portuguese high-society widow that kept tongues wagging on the island. He fathered at least 10 offspring and Zulu royal descendants can still be found on St Helena to this day. Some of the children he fathered with '*Saints*' that passed away were four-month-old Princess Nomfino who died on the 8th of May 1891 and three-year-old Princess Mohlozana who died on the 17th of March 1894. They were buried in the white section of the St James Cathedral while Africans and slaves were buried as paupers and dumped into holes without any dignity in threes around the island.

Queen Zihlazile gave birth to Dinuzulu's first son Nyawana David followed by Bhekelendoda Samuel and a daughter Mphaphu (*Mphashana*) Victoria. Queen *okaNtuzwa* Silomo's children who lived, were Prince Maphumuzana Nkayishana Solomon (*iSolinomona*) and Prince Mshiyeni Arthur Edward who made a dramatic entry into the world on the eve of their departure back home. She also had Princess Magogo Sibilile Mantithi Constance Ngangezinye in Eshowe. The children grew up close to whites and became immersed in the western way of life. They were taught English by a distinguished '*Saint*' educator, Rev E.A. Barraclough. But Dinuzulu also imported two distinguished isiZulu language teachers and interpreters, Magema

Fuze and Bubi Mdluli. They not only taught the children isiZulu but also exposed them to deep Zulu culture. This ensured that they did not lose touch with the glorious Zulu history. Magema described the island as a place where unlike in the old country, thunderstorms, snakes, scorpions, leopards and lions were unknown. Other members of the Zulu entourage also had busy social lives. For instance, Mbulawa married a '*Saint*', Caroline Brown. They had an extravagant wedding that included being driven around in seven carriages drawn by several magnificent horses. Ndabuko's male aide Xamandolo, married Alice Ann Williams and Anthony married Ellen Ann August.

Harriette Colenso was finally allowed to visit Dinuzulu in St Helena in November 1897. She gave him a detailed report about what was going back home. She told him that Queen Mother okaMsweli his mother, had been appointed regent and governed the empire exceptionally well and that Mnyamana kaNgqengelele Buthelezi who headed the 'Cetshwayo Affair' had passed on. But the miserable and lonely death of the Zulu arch enemy Theophilus Shepstone in Pietermaritzburg in June 1893 made them both think about karma. She also told him about her personal loss, the passing of her mother Sarah on Christmas Day of 1893. She described Egyptian biblical-like plagues that befell the kingdom, the 1895 locusts invasion, a dilapidating drought and to top it all, the rinderpest of 1896-7 that swept across Southern Africa and wiped out about 97 percent of the cattle owned by the Zulu. She shared some details about the Bathlaping Revolt also known as *Ntwa ya bana ba Mokgothu or the Langeberg Uprising*.

The British had shot all the Bathlaping cattle claiming that their cattle were contaminated, whereas the cattle that were shot were grazing at the same place with the healthy British cattle. When Bathlaping resisted, they were evicted from their land and sent to Western Cape wine farms as slave labour. Then the British took their land around Phokwane, which lies north-west of the Zulu empire, and dished it out for free to whites. Dinuzulu was particularly interested in what was happening to Bathlaping because they were his subjects. His grandfather Shaka, had conquered them and they became a Zulu protectorate. Hence some Zulu regiments were garrisoned there as an outpost. For unknown reasons, King Dinuzulu and Shingana and Ndabuko ended up serving only seven of the 10-year sentence. The steamship, *SS Umbilo* piloted by Captain Cox picked them all up on Christmas Eve in 1897.

There were hundreds of *Saints* well-wishers at the harbour. Dinuzulu's entourage consisted of his two Zulu queens, two female intimate companions who were *Saints* and Harriette; eight royal children; one Zulu interpreter; two female attendants, and an old nurse. Shingana and his wife Nozinyoni and their two sons and a daughter who were born on the island; Ndabuko and his wife Nozingwe; Xamandolo kaMagidigidi Timothy Zungu and his *Saint* wife Alice Ann and their child; Mbulawa and his *Saint* wife Caroline and their child. Mkolokotho; Mhofana; Myosama; Mbhodiya; Nsuluko Radasi; Magema Fuze who now walked with a limp after a fall at night; Madden and others. Their luggage weighed about 40 tonnes and included 10 dogs, six donkeys, a parrot, rabbits, fowl pens, a canary, a monkey, a piano, a harmonium and other things.

When they arrived at the Durban harbour on a Friday morning in January 1898. they were met by only a few people, because Dinuzulu's arrival had been kept secret. They travelled by train to oThongathi and then embarked wagons that took four days to reach the uThukela River which was less than 100 kilometres away. It was a hazardous journey as it was raining and the wagons either became stuck or broke in the mud. The last of the donkeys from St Helena died on this part of the trip. They were welcomed by a fierce storm in Eshowe and were forced to set up camp under tents for a few days. Then the news of their arrival quickly spread, and everyone was ecstatic to have their king back from exile. The Prime Minister Mankulumana brought the king up to speed about the affairs of the kingdom during his eight-year incarceration. The highlight was that his favourite wife Mahambogwini, had matured and had been assisting his mother, okaMsweli to carry out royal duties.

When rumours emerged that Dinuzulu was going to be released early, okaMsweli sprang into action and formed two regiments which were to be his bodyguards, uDakwakusutha (aka *uDakwa*) and iNgubokakhundlase; Felaphakathi at eKubazeni palace without permission from the British. To everyone's fury, the British had several nasty surprises waiting for Dinuzulu when he arrived. They informed him that he had been demoted to a mere '*inkosi*' and that he had been restricted to an even smaller area within the area of 'uSuthu', still to be demarcated. Furthermore, they made contributing to the royal household illegal. Instead of this traditional way of sustaining the Zulu royalty, the British would give Dinuzulu a measly stipend of £500 per month. This paltry amount was supposed to take care of the king's advisers, *imimhlalandlini*, *izinduna*, regiments, the military command, the king's council, helpers, *udibi*, the king's personal attendants, palaces, *amakhanda*, the large extended royal family and the nation's widows and orphans that depended on the king for their survival.

*Emperor Dinizulu's entourage on the porch of Maldivia House during his imprisonment in St Helena Island, 1897. (Seated left) Prince Ndabuko kaMpande, Dr Delby, Mbhodiya (wet nurse) Nyosana kaMadwala (personal attendant), Harriette Colenso, Mubi (Bubi) Mthuli kaNondenisa, Paul Mbulawa Mthimkhulu (the Royal doctor and army chaplain), Prince Shingana kaMpande and his son Prince Bhula, Emperor Dinuzulu. (In no particular order) Princess Victoria, Anthony Daniels (translator), Nosingwe, Princess Nozinhlanzi, Nozinyoni, Prince Maphumuzana Nkayishana Solomon, Queen Silomo kaNtuzwa Mdlalose, Queen Zihlazile okaQethuka Magwaza, two local Saints. (Killie Campbell Africana Library)*

*Emperor Dinuzulu kaCetshwayo's signature. He learnt how to read and write during his incarceration in Pietermaritsburg prison under the tutelage of Magema Fuze who also taught him English (Killie Campbell Africana Library)*

*Emperor King Dinuzulu kaCetshwayo with his military medals. This picture was taken in 1883. (Killie Campbell Africana Library)*

The same amount of money was also supposed to pay for all the food during national ceremonies and rituals, as well as for the whole nation during times of drought. This was an attempt to remove the dignity of the Zulu empire. But the British were not done yet. They ordered him to stop living in a traditional Zulu *iqhugwane* (round grass hut) but live in a four-corner European-style grand estate in Eshowe. He also had to report to the police both in Eshowe and Pietermaritzburg on a regular basis. Dinuzulu initially obeyed the orders but after six weeks, he left for Nongoma. He then began to visit his subjects throughout the empire and ignored the British demarcation of where they said he had jurisdiction as the king of the Zulu nation. Then he did what looked ordinary and harmless on the surface - he extended his mother's eNyokeni Palace and built himself eMahhashini Palace on the highlands.

This is where he used to keep his horses in the summer months. Discussions between the Zulu of every rank dealt with one topic only, the return of the land to the Zulu and by any means necessary. Moreover, his subjects still recognised him as their king, from as far south as uMkhomazi area up to iNgwavuma area on the northern border. Young men started trickling into eMahhashini and as in the days of old, began to till the royal farms and tended the royal cattle. Whilst at eMahhashini Palace, they would sing, dance, learnt how to do *ingomane*, practiced Shaka's pincer (*izimpondo*) war formation (*head, chest, shoulder and horns*) and disguised it as elaborately choreographed dances. 'The dancers' were separated into age groups and Dinuzulu gave each group a name. The British became nervous about this activity at eMahhashini palace because they could recognise Zulu regiments, however well-disguised. But he reassured them that the young men meant no harm, that they were no standing army but were merely 'dance troupe' regiments.

The British half-believed him, besides, they were more worried about a conflict looming with the Afrikaners than they were about the 'demoralised' Zulu nation. Once again, the Zulu were using the age-old tactic of deception. No self-respecting Zulu king would choose to be without an army, never mind what the British said. Tension between the British and the Afrikaners grew steadily and reached fever pitch. War seemed inevitable between the two white colonising groups.

The British Under-Secretary of Native Affairs Robert Samuelson was uncomfortable with the thought of '*trained entertainment regiments*' who were within a striking distance of Natal. He then wrote a letter to Dinuzulu on the 10th of September 1899 and asked him to plead with his subjects and especially the traditional leaders not to side with the Afrikaners. Dinuzulu was amused by this request and never bothered to respond. Neighbouring countries were also apprehensive about the war, but the Swati nation had even a bigger dilemma. They had to be prepared to give an appropriate answer in case they were requested to assist either group, as their kingdom was now a Transvaal Republic protectorate. The untimely death of their young King Bhunu (*Ngwane V*), two months after the war broke out made matters worse. His mother Queen Labotsibeni (*Gwamile*) became regent for 22 years and her temper was legendary. The Swazi even believed that drought was caused by her, because even the rain was afraid of her rage. When the country's longest river iMbabane turned red, they believed that it was because she had dipped her big toe in it. The truth is that the red colour of the river came from seepage of iron ore from beneath the river bed. Labotsibeni managed Swaziland affairs à la Mkabayi and participated in politics in the Transvaal, beyond her borders.

Tension between the British and the Afrikaners grew steadily and reached fever pitch. War seemed inevitable between the two white colonising groups. By now, the British had carved out two colonies the Cape Colony and Natal for themselves while the Afrikaners had established the Transvaal and the Orange Free State as two independent Boer republics. The Afrikaners, however, found time in 1899 to pass a law in their republics that prohibited Africans from walking on sidewalks (pavements) in towns. This absurdity must have provided comic relief in the highly charged situation. The war between the Afrikaners and the British finally broke out on the 11$^{th}$ of October 1899. Even though the war was regarded as a 'white man's war', it ended up including Africans which is why it is now known as the South African War. But many mercenaries from all over the world also took sides. The British were joined by mercenaries from Canada, Australia and New Zealand. The Afrikaners were supported by the French, German, Italian, Dutch, Russian, Scandinavian Corp and Americans of the Irish Brigade. The Afrikaners besieged the diamond town of Kimberley (*Siege of Kimberley*) in October 1899. When the British tried to go in and relieve the town in a battle they wish to forget, they were defeated by a highly competent General De La Rey at the Battle of Magersfontein. It was fought on the border of the Cape Colony and the Orange Free State Republic on the 11$^{th}$ of December 1899. The Afrikaners even destroyed the bridge over Orange River in Hopetown to stop the British contingent from crossing it to reach Kimberley. For Afrikaners, it was a war of survival against the hated British as well as against the sea of hostile Africans. For the British it was a war to establish their supremacy in southern Africa.

When the war broke out, thousands of able-bodied men - especially the abaQulusi regiment who were dispossed of their land because of the *New Republic* - went to eMahhashini Palace to defend their king. It was also a tactic to avoid being forced to fight on either white side. How things had changed, the British found themselves despairingly assistance from Dinuzulu. His conditions to help them were obvious. They then quietly reinstated him as Emperor of the whole Zulu empire and that was the end of the 'Paramount Chief' title. The British initially drafted the Zulu as non-combatants such Sukabekhuluma *Chakijana Sigilamkhuba* kaGezindaka Sithole (generally called *Chakijana*) who was the grandson of King Jobe Sithole and Dinuzulu's personal aide as scouts, wagon drivers and dispatchers. But before long, they issued Dinuzulu with about 3000 weapons. Then they asked him to form a regiment he called iNkomendala Rifle regiment of about 6000 men who would use modern weaponry.

Lord Kitchener was now commander of the British forces in South Africa after serving in the Sudan. Queen Victoria's favourite grandson, a Sandhurst Military Academy graduate, Prince Christian *Christie* Victor of Schleswig-Holstein served under Kitchner and took part in the attempt to relieve the Siege of Ladysmith. But instead of dying under fire something he would have preferred, Christian died miserably felled by typhoid after a bout of malaria. He died at the uThukela front on the 23rd of October 1900 and was buried in a Pretoria cemetery. He is the only member of the British royal family whose remains are still on South African soil. Kitchener carried out his notorious 'scorched earth' policy and destroyed farms, houses and crops and he initially sent Afrikaner prisoners of war to concentration camps. But later sent Afrikaner women and children as well as African men who had fought along the Afrikaners. Thousands died of starvation and disease.

However, African women braved death and smuggled in food and medicines into the concentration camps, particularly to Afrikaner women, as they understood the pain of watching your children starve to death. Sometimes the African children under the age of 10 years old were used as they could easily go through the fences around the camps. Kitchner began shipping prisoners of war to St Helena Island. The *SS Milwaukee* military ship piloted by Captain Webster, escorted by the *HMS Niobe* departed on the 10th of April 1900. Aboard were 21 officers and 514 soldiers, amongst them was Col Schiel and Gen Piet Cronje with his wife Hester and their African servants. Cronje lived in a big residence *Kent Cottage* and the rest lived in the harshest part of the island, Deadwood Plain and Broadbottom Plain. General Ben Viljoen arrived on the 25th of February 1902 aboard the *Britannic* and by then there were about 6000 prisoners of war. They ended up being enterprising and even started a newspaper called *Kamp Kruimels*.

Afrikaner commandos resorted to guerrilla and terror tactics because they were slowly losing the war. The Zulu fought back and one of the highlights of these skirmishes took place at Dleke Mountain on the 27th April 1901. Even though Dinuzulu was present, the commander of the regiments was Mankulumana and routed the Afrikaners who fled and left behind their ammunition and thousands of livestock and horses behind. In retaliation of their loss, the Afrikaners went on a destruction trail in Zulu homesteads around eNquthu, eNkandla, eMthonjaneni, eMahlabathini, Vryheid, oBonjeni, eNgwavuma, eMahloni, KwaMthashana (*Holkrantz*), eMakhwabi and eNtabamhlophe areas. When the Afrikaners were seen coming, everyone had to hide in the caves and forests.

But one day, a veteran of iSandlwana and eHlobane, the elderly Mlazana kaManzini Zungu (iNgobamakhosi) who lived at KwaMthashana, refused to run and hide at the KwaMatshekazi caves. His frail body was riddled with scars and splinters

*Lord Kitchener sent Afrikaner prisoners of war to St Helena Island during the South African War. The first ship SS Milwaukee piloted by Captain Webster and escorted by the HMS Niobe departed on 10 April 1900. Some of the prisoners were 12 year-old Gert Janse van Vuuren and his 80-year-old grandfather Douw Gerbrandt Steyn from a farm in Potchefstroom, Transvaal. They both returned alive to South Africa. (Killie Campbell Africana Library)*

he had sustained during the ferocious eHlobane Battle which had left him blind. Leaning on his stick for support, he defiantly waited for the wild alcohol-fuelled Afrikaners to arrive. As expected, they grabbed him and dragged him around his homestead, tortured him, and then gouged his eyes out. They cut his head off and tore his body into pieces, skewered parts of his body and pinned them on poles at the cattle enclosure for all to see. They threw parts of his body into grain stores and other pieces were thrown into the iNgulana River which was for drinking water. After seeing these heinous acts from afar, both his family and neighbours knew it was time for revenge. They then secretly amassed weapons as they did in preparation for the iSandlwana war. Afrikaners on the other hand mistook the 'non-retaliation' by the fierce abaQulusi around Vryheid and Ntabamhlophe as a sign of cowardice.

At midnight on the 1$^{st}$ of May, Afrikaners poured into the area of abaQulusi and once again razed unguarded homesteads, burnt or confiscated Zulu grain and drove the cattle to their stronghold at KwaMthashana. But this time they kidnapped women and children as sex slaves and took them to Vryheid. When they passed the Nquthu Police Station, the Afrikaners found 50 Zulu men in custody and kidnapped them at gunpoint. But when abaQulusi saw their half-naked women and children arriving in Vryheid, they took strategic positions around where they were kept captive. As if that was not enough, almost a week later a particularly cruel Afrikaner commando Jan Potgieter, sent the commander of abaQulusi Sikhobobo (uDlambedlu regiment) an insulting message. He called a public gathering and had the message read out for all to hear it. He said that Sikhobobo and his abaQulusi were no better than fowl lice. He also dared him to come to their laager in Holkrantz to collect his cattle and women before they were 'all consumed'.

The Zulu forces did not waste time. Sikhobobo was deputised by Mehlokazulu, Sidunge and Sikhokonke. Together they led abaQulusi regiment and attacked the Afrikaners the same night on the 6$^{th}$ of May. By sunrise the bloodbath left at least 56 dead and 48 wounded Afrikaners, and a few abaQulusi soldiers were also killed. Sikhobobo kidnapped three Afrikaners and recovered about 4000 cattle and livestock and freed their kidnapped women and children. This battle is known as the *Holkrantz Massacre* because of the number of Afrikaners killed by the Zulu in one night. The victorious abaQulusi celebrated all the way to eMahhashini Palace where they briefed Dinuzulu about their resounding success. They sang a song they composed after the victory:

| | |
|---|---|
| *Nanti izwi, nanti igama* | *here is a voice, here is a name* |
| *AbaQulusi* | *of the abaQulusi people* |
| *Zinsizwa nithini na* | *brothers in arms, what are you saying?* |
| *Kumnyama ehlathini* | *the forest is dark* |
| *Sengathi angakaphinde* | *if only he could do it again* |
| *OkaNdaba ayihlomise* | *if only Ndaba's descendant can start another war* |
| *Yithi abashokobezi bempi* | *it is us, the guerrilla fighters* |
| *Sangena ngomnyama* | *we arrived at night* |
| *Ngomnyama kwaMthashana* | *we arrived at night in kwaMthashana* |
| *Ziphi? Naziya* | *where are they? There they are* |
| *Uyamqala okaNdaba* | *you are picking a fight with Ndaba's descendant* |
| *Sizwa bethi laduma* | *we heard them say it thundered* |
| *Laduma, lagoqana* | *that it thundered and became cloudy* |

After a series of losses against the British, the very brilliant Afrikaner General Jan Smuts was mandated to start the terms of his people's surrender with Lord Kitchener. This culminated in the meeting of six Afrikaner leaders, Schalk Burger, General Louis Botha, Koos de la Rey, M.T. Steyn, General Christiaan de Wet and General J.B. Hertzog, who met at the Klerksdorp train station. After much bargaining, the Afrikaners signed the Vereeniging Peace Treaty on the 31$^{st}$ of May 1902. That was the bitter end of Afrikaner independence, but they could keep their republics under British sovereignty. A year later, in 1903 the British rewarded Dinuzulu with a mere 250 cattle for his war effort. But they demanded their 3000 weapons back. But it goes without saying that Dinuzulu was reluctant to surrender all the firearms. He returned them in drips and drabs, a tactic that would work in his favour three years later. Nevertheless, the Zulu spirit of resistance was once again gaining momentum.

# Emperor Dinuzulu kaCetshwayo

*(Left) Khubela Qwabe, member of uKhandempevu regiment. It was commanded by Mkhosana kaMvundlana Zungu. (Right) Mthimuni Mandlanzini member of uVe regiment. It was commanded by Sigcwelegwele kaMhlekehle Mngadi (Killie Campbell Africana Library)*

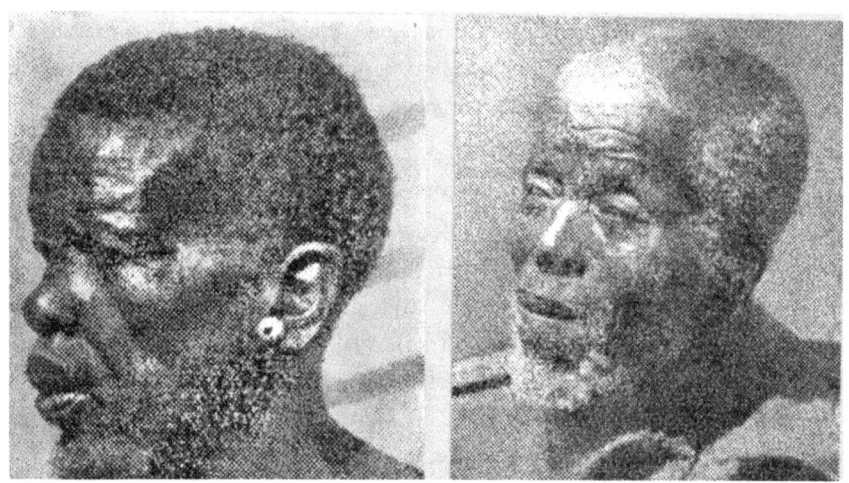

*(Left) Mbongozo Mbonambi member of the uMbonambi regiment commanded by b Prince Ndabuko kaMpande. (Right) Inkosi Zumeka of uMxhapho regiment (Killie Campbell Africana Library)*

# 10

# The Poll Tax Revolt

THE POLL TAX revolt was brought about by several interconnected events that compounded the increasingly unbearable life of the Zulu. First, the 1896-7 drought, locusts, rinderpest and East Coast fever had put pressure on the economy of Natal, wiping out 97 per cent of Zulu cattle. Secondly, doing census was alien to the Zulu psyche, so when the British made it mandatory in 1904 the Zulu thought it was another form of control and further dispossession. They then refused to co-operate. Then followed a severe hailstorm that destroyed all crops and washed away many farms. But it was the violent tornado on the 31st of May 1905 that was the last straw for Sir George Sutton's colonial government of Natal.

This ushered in a new Prime Minister Charles Smythe who obviously urgently needed funds to repair the economy. What better way of raising revenue than by the introduction of new tax laws. He therefore imposed poll tax of £1 (R2) per head. This was the third taxation imposed on Zulu men because they were already being taxed for each hut and dog they owned. An instruction was issued to magistrates on the 22nd of November to assemble all traditional leaders and *'chiefs'* in one place to explain the reasons behind the new poll tax law. The date of collection was to start on the 20th of January 1906, but the Zulu were given up to the 31st of May before action would be taken against them for non-compliance. But for the Zulu this tax was tantamount to paying a fine for being alive, so it was labelled *khandampondo* (a pound for the head).

Many traditional leaders and ordinary people clandestinely went to the eMahhashini palace to tell Dinuzulu after the due date that they would not be paying. But they found that he had paid three days in advance, on the 17th of January. He had even paid for all the males living or working in his palaces. This, however, was another diversionary tactic because he privately encouraged those he could trust not to pay. At the same time, underground mobilisation of the regiments was in full swing and it became apparent that war was going to erupt over this sensitive matter. Zulu leadership reverted to one of Shaka's old military tactics of identifying the 'enemy' through a code.

When two strangers met, one would ask: '*Uthelaphi?*' (Where do you pay tax?). If the response would specify the place where they paid their tax. But the ones who would respond by saying: '*Insumansumane, imali yamakhanda*' (It is a pipe dream, the money for the head), would continue further together. Some 'chiefs' reported those who refused to pay to the British. Whereas both the traditional leaders and 'chiefs' who failed to collect the tax from their subjects were deemed to be rebels by the colonial government. That is why some traditional leaders only collected a portion, others asked to be given more time to collect it and others simply did not bother to collect it totally. Three days before the due date, an overzealous farmer Henry Smith from Camperdown coerced his Zulu farm labourers to pay.

They became very upset with him and planned to resolve their problem permanently. On the same day they waited for him to watch the African sun gently setting between the hills in the distant horizon as he sat on his veranda sipping brandy. Then they stabbed him with a garden fork, and he died a gruesome death. Similar incidents of white farmers forcing their workers to pay before the due date were reported to Dinuzulu from all corners of the empire as well as from Natal. For instance, on the 29th of January farm owners forced their workers to pay at Butler's Store in eNsuze. Other workers were forced to pay the following day at Gaillard's Store near uMvoti. When Magistrate TR Bennet was collecting tax in Henley on the 7th of February, *inkosi* Mveli who was on the side of the British warned him about the presence of 27 spear-wielding men in the vicinity singing against the payment of *imali yamakhanda* (the money for the head/poll tax). The following day, the police found the men in Richmond at Henry Hosking's *Trewirgie* farm and arrested them.

People quickly gathered and demanded their release. But by the end of the day, two more people were arrested and one of their leaders Mjongo kaMphumo was shot and killed by the police. The crowd retaliated by killing two policemen Sidney Hunt and George Armstrong. The incident brought about martial law two days later. A notoriously cruel Col McKenzie arrived with 1000 soldiers to raid Zulu homesteads, find the instigators and destroy crops around Richmond. A day after his arrival, 12 more people were arrested and tried by a court martial and sentenced to death within a week. But before they were shot, they were made to dig their own graves. They did so without trepidation and fear. Mqokwana kaMncindo Ngcobo, Makhanda kaMncindo

## The Poll Tax Revolt

Ngcobo, Nsiba kaMncindo Ngcobo, Thawini kaMpongongwana Dlamini, Dambuza kaMpongongwana Dlamini, Mpukunyane kaSibhamu Ndlovu, Msongelwa kaMachi Dlamini, Mambuka kaMadutshana Bhengu, Mantayi kaMjongo Bhengu, Mjaja kaMatubane Ngcobo, Mbathi kaMazwi Bhengu and Bunjana kaMjongo Bhengu marched with vigour and stood in front of their graves and they recited Shaka's laudatory praises with pride as they were being shot.

This caused an upheaval in the Natal colonial government resulting in Prime Minister C J Smythe and his entire cabinet to briefly resign while the British government tried to halt the killings but to no avail. Winston Churchill who was as a member of the British parliament also condemned the killing and called the Natal government 'the hooligan of the British Empire'. After the murder of the 'Richmond 12', the Zulu from all over the empire and Natal started assembling in Nkandla forest and *bahlala phezu kwamahawu* (became combat ready). The commander was now the aged Sigananda (Shaka's *udibi*) and his deputies were Mehlokazulu, Shayinja, Mangathi (Ndlela's grandson) and Dinuzulu's personal aide Chakijana.

'The Richmond 12' recited King Shaka's laudatory praises as they were led to their death and forced to dig their own graves. They were killed by a firing squad for refusing to pay poll tax in 1906. Mqokwana kaMncindo Ngcobo, Makhanda kaMncindo Ngcobo, Nsiba kaMncindo Ngcobo, Thawini kaMpongongwana Dlamini, Dambuza kaMpongongwana Dlamini, Mpukunyane kaSibhamu Ndlovu, Msongelwa kaMachi Dlamini, Mambuka kaMadutshana Bhengu, Mantayi kaMjongo Bhengu, Mjaja kaMatubane Ngcobo, Mbathi kaMazwi Bhengu and Bunjana kaMjongo Bhengu. (A Verbeek)

# The Poll Tax Revolt

Col Duncan 'Dune' McKenzie was notoriously cruel and sadistic towards the Zulu during the poll tax uprising 1906. (Natal Mercury)

Lt-Colonel George Leuchars led a militia force to Gobizembe Ntuli's homestead, took his 1200 cattle as well as 3500 sheep and goats. Then he shelled it for 20 minutes without prior warning. In addition to this personal punishment, the Ntuli kingdom was divided into three parts. Natal Mercury)

King Dinuzulu's defence witnesses during his Treason Trial in Greytown, 1908. (KwaZulu Natal Archives)

# The Poll Tax Revolt

On the anniversary of iSandlwana on the 22<sup>nd</sup> of January, the Magistrate of KwaMaphumulo, Ernst Dunn was threatened by hundreds of people led by Sambela Ntuli when he arrived to collect the new tax from Allen's Store. They chanted and performed war dances around him and refused to pay *imali yamakhanda*. But he was saved by King Gobizembe kaMkhonto of the Ntuli kingdom. The two Ntuli brothers ruled over 1652 huts with a firm but kind hand and tensions around their KwaMaphumulo were particularly high because people had been forced to live on barren land with little water. By the 22<sup>nd</sup> of February, the government had collected a paltry £1100 since inception in January.

Then in March, Lt-Col George Leuchars sent an ultimatum to Gobizembe to hand over the 300 men who had danced so threateningly around the magistrate within six days. This was an impossible request, but Gobizembe was able to hand over about 20 men only. The following day, without warning, Lt-Col Leuchars surrounded Gobizembe's homestead and shelled it for 20 minutes. Lt-Col Leuchars took his land and fined him 1200 cattle plus 3500 sheep and goats. In addition to this personal punishment, the Ntuli kingdom was fragmented into three parts and handed over to Sibindi Ngubane. He was permitted to create a new 'Ngubane kingdom' which never existed before for his collaboration with the British. More kingdoms were added to his kingdom over the years. Col McKenzie went to Mthwalume to hunt for people refusing to pay the tax. He had a show down with Charlie Fynn (Henry Fynn's son) who was leading the anti-poll tax campaign and fined him and his followers 1500 cattle.

King Bhambatha kaMancinza of the Zondi kingdom who is associated with this war grew up in eMsinga and was a very controversial character. His mother was the daughter of Phakade Macingwane (Macingwanes' son) and he ascended to the throne in 1890 at the age of 25 years old when his father died. He regularly appeared before Magistrate J Cross in Greytown for various transgressions. For instance, jealousy made him try to have the iSandlwana Service Award of his uncle Magwababa cancelled but failed. In the following five years he was involved in seven criminal cases, 37 civil cases for debt and misconduct and all judgements were against him. He was once fined 20 or three months imprisonment. He was also implicated in two cattle-rustling cases which led to his suspension as a king for four months. He was also accused of starting a boundary dispute with his neighbours, the amaBomvu near Kranskop that lasted for years with periodic loss of life.

The Zondi kingdom was expected to pay the poll tax on the 22<sup>nd</sup> of February but they did not. Instead on the 3<sup>rd</sup> of April, Nhlonhlo led the Zondi forces to the centre of Greytown with Bhambatha at the rear. But when the whites heard that Bhambatha was going to attack them, there was pandemonium. They barricaded themselves in Marshall's Hotel overnight and sent their servants into the hills and forests. The Zondi men marched through town armed and each one of them was wearing *ibheshu* (traditional male leather apron). This was a clear act of defiance because Zulu men were not allowed to enter any town in the Natal Colony without wearing trousers. They went to Magistrate Cross and told him that he would receive the poll tax over their dead bodies. In retaliation for this open defiance, Magistrate Cross deposed Bhambatha as the king of the Zondi kingdom and ordered him to report in person to Pietermaritzburg. In retaliation, Bhambatha ambushed Col Mansel's police who were escorting white women and children from Keats Drift to Greytown. Four policemen, A Aston, J Greenwood, E Brown and J Harrison, were killed while Brown was dragged into the bushes and his lifeless body was later found mutilated. That was the last straw for Lt-Col Leuchars. He led a force to Bhambatha's eMkhontweni homestead and fired heavy artillery but Bhambatha managed to escape. The bounty reward for his capture was set at £500 dead or alive. Together with his two attendants, Mgoma and Nkantolo, his children Nonkobose, Ndabayakhe, Kholekile and his favourite wife Siyekiwe Zuma who was pregnant to Dinuzulu for protection. They were accompanied by Jolwane who knew the way through the forest as they walked by night and they rested at Gezindaka Sithole's homestead.

One of Gezindaka's sons, Chakijana had been visiting home as he as working in Johannesburg and had stepped out to visit his favourite girl. When he returned, he found the visitors and his father asked him to accompany them to Dlebe and he left them at Nsukuzonke's homestead, which was not far from uSuthu palace. The men arrived at eMahhashini Palace seven days later and the women and children staggered in two days later after them. After a few weeks Bhambatha decided to go back, leaving his family behind. Dinuzulu did not trust Bhambatha's sudden decision of going back home and instructed Chakijana to go back with him but keep an eye on him. On his return, Bhambatha found that he had been deposed in favour of his brother Funizwe and Magwababa had been made a chief. Driven more by revenge than a sense of justice for all, Bhambatha joined the fighters gathered in Nkandla forest and dreamt of a triumphant return to the Zondi throne.

On the 3rd of May, the Native Commissioner of eMahlabathini Magistrate Stainbank spent the day forcibly collecting tax and around 20h00 he was killed at his camp on the south bank of White iMfolozi River as he spoke on the phone with his boss in Nkandla. Chakijana was accused of the murder but he denied it and even after a massive manhunt, the culprit was never found. However, according to

# The Poll Tax Revolt

the Zulu eyewitnesses, Stainbank was shot by a white man who lived near White iMfolozi River and had a history of stealing cattle belonging to the Zulu as well as illegally grazing his cattle on the land reserved for Zulu cattle. After repeated warnings, Stainbank found him guilty and fined him a hefty fine. This made him very angry and he was sworn to revenge on the magistrate for 'fining him for stealing cattle belonging to a bloody Kaffir'. Out of the blue, six year later, Matayana was held responsible for the death of Stainbank. However, it turns out that he had taken the law into his own hands and killed Gence, who was caught sleeping with one of Dinuzulu's wives. Killing without a fair trial, was anathema according the Zulu law, hence he was made to pay by being made a scapegoat.

After the murder of Stainbank, the British declared martial law because the war was more ferocious than they had anticipated. The British killed innocent people under the pretext of looking for the anti-poll tax ring leaders. They also asked for help from England and more arms were shipped and from the Transvaal, the gold barons sent down 500 volunteers at their own expense. The anti-poll tax battle theatre was Nkandla forest and the story of this war cannot be told without mentioning the heroic feats of its 100-year-old commander Sigananda. During the reign of Dingane, when he began killing people for no apparent reason, Sigananda was one of the people who escaped into exile south of uThukela River. He lived in the Zondi kingdom under Bhambatha's father Mancinza (a policeman at the magistrate's office in Greytown) for about 15 years. During the Ndondakusuka war, he fought on Cetshwayo's side. Hence when Cetshwayo became king, he recalled Sigananda north of the uThukela River. He made him the king of the fiercely independent Ncube kingdom in 1870.

For the battle, the old pincer formation was used and Sigananda led the attack on the colonial forces on the 2$^{nd}$ of May 1906 at the eMhome (*Mome*) Gorge. There were about 2500 colonial forces reinforced by about 400 Zululand Native Police (*Nongqayi*) who were made to wear red and white armbands to distinguish them from Zulu forces. Njengabantu kaSobuza Ngubane fought on the side of the whites, even though he had been Shaka's *udibi*. Sigananda's army had 1200 men and they also used the weapons Dinuzulu did not return to the British after the South African War. The battle was fought savagely face-to-face, the conventional way, with both British and Zulu snipers hard at work. Sigananda's army used an assortment of modern weaponry, guns, cannons, spears as well as innovative projectiles such as iron pot legs for their *uqhwasha* (home-made gun). Bhambatha was deployed as part of *isifuba* (chest) section, but he fought for a short time and slipped away and hid in the rear with women and children. But the women saw him being beaten him up and called him a coward, the worst insult amongst the Zulu. He got away and escaped to Macala Mountain on his horse and hid in a cave. But after a few days Sigananda sent Mehlokazulu and Chakijana to convince him to come and fight.

Moreover, the colonial troops had burnt Cetshwayo's grave on the 17th of May. Bhambatha told them that he was afraid to go back with them because he suspected that he would be shot for desertion. After they promised him that he would be spared, he came out and half-heartedly fought in the Msukane Gap Battle at the confluence of the iMhome and iNkunzane Rivers. This is where Chakijana was shot in the leg and taken to iNhlazatshe Mountain caves as his wound was life threatening. Around midnight an unsuspecting Norwegian missionary Rev Otto Aadnesgaard was kidnapped from his eMahlabathini mission, blindfolded and taken to the cave to treat Chakijana. Sigananda and his army retreated to Bophe (*Bhobe*) Ridge above Mhome waterfall, not too far from Cetshwayo's grave. But they suffered heavy casualties and scattered. Some hid in crevices and caves but continued fighting, others engaged in guerrilla warfare, and the rest retreated to the eMahhashini Palace. After almost 20 days of heavy fighting, Sigananda sent his son Ndabaningi to Col McKenzie at the military post in Mhome Valley to end hostilities. He also offered to 'surrender' and Col McKenzie agreed and gave him until 11am on the 20th of May. But Sigananda did not turn up. Instead Ndabaningi arrived at the British camp in the evening and claimed that he could not find his father. Col McKenzie believed him and extended the deadline for another two days.

On the day Sigananda was supposed to surrender Col McKenzie received another message from the old man asking to be allowed to surrender between Gcongco and Denga Ridges which were the closest military posts to him. He claimed to be 'too old' to negotiate the treacherous valleys to reach Mhome Valley. Again, McKenzie believed him said he should report at 11am two days later. Many colonial forces as well as about 14 horses died trying to ascend the steep cliff of the Gcongco and Denga Ridges. The truth is that Sigananda had duped McKenzie by tempting him to use the risky shortcut that would cause heavy fatalities. When the British finally arrived, it was 5pm due to the treacherous terrain. They found no one and when they returned without the 'old fox', McKenzie was livid. He ordered his soldiers to arrest any Zulu they suspected to be a leader of the uprising.

Rumours surfaced that Bhambatha was 'hiding' in eNsingabantu forest in eQhudeni Mountains. Without proper intelligence, the colonial forces marched through treacherous terrain at night hoping to catch him. They had planned to arrive at eNsingabantu at by 4am but the mist slowed them down and they only arrived

# The Poll Tax Revolt

at 7am. To their fury, there was no Bhambatha. Frustrated, cold, wet and hungry, McKenzie's men ordered their return to Nkandla immediately. The poor troops had walked about 100 kilometres in two days and had nothing to show for it. This was due to disinformation to the enemy by the Zulu military command; Bhambatha was never there in the first place. The frantic search for Sigananda did not stop, and the colonial army managed to find his son Mandisindaba. He was together with the extended Shezi family and they surrounded his homestead and prepared to pound it with heavy artillery, only then did they surrender. Troops were dispatched to eMvalasango forest where they suspected Sigananda and the Zulu military high command had taken cover. McKenzie received intelligence that Mehlokazulu was leading around 200 men to the confluence of iMhome and iNsuze Rivers. He then sent the following letter to Colonel W Barker of the Transvaal Mounted Rifles:

> 'Zululand Field Force,
> Camp, Nomanci [sic] Ridge,
> 9th June 1906
> From O.C. Troops to Col Barker

On receipt of this dispatch, you will please move AT ONCE with all available men (leaving sufficient for the defence of your camp) to the mouth of the Mome Valley. I have information that an impi is coming from eQhudeni to enter the Mome Valley between this and tomorrow morning. Please try to waylay this impi and prevent them from entering the Mome and at daylight block the mouth of the Mome at once. It is anticipated that they will not enter the Mome till daylight. I have reliable information as to almost the exact spot Sigananda is in and I am moving down to surround him. He is supposed to be just below the Mome stronghold, a little lower down than where we burnt his cattle enclosure. I will cut off this position at daylight and drive down towards you, so please do all you can to prevent his escape, and co-operate with me generally. At daylight, please send the Zululand Police and Native levies up to Sigananda's cattle enclosure, which you burnt the day we attacked the stronghold, where they will join my forces. You must take your gun and Maxims in case you meet the impi, which is reported to be of strength. Look out for my signals.
ADDRESSED: COLONEL BARKER,
CETSHWAYO'S GRAVE
Very urgent
Sent 10.30 p.m'

Guerrilla war raged all over the forest and major battles were fought in eThathe Gorge, Gun Hill, Stronghold, eManzimpambana. The last stand was at eMhome Gorge on the 10$^{th}$ of June. This is where several veterans of the military high command were killed such as Mtheli, Nondubela, Mavukuthu, Lubuhlungu, two African Christian pastors, Moses and Mbulawa Paul Mthimkhulu (Dinuzulu's pastor). Mehlokazulu kaSihayo Ngobese also finally met his fate and he died wearing a new attire, riding trousers, a shirt, socks and an overcoat. A wild banana tree marks his final resting place. Some people believed that Bhambatha was also killed in this battle while others believed that he deserted again. Other reports claimed that Bhambatha was shot in the head by *Nongqayi*. To ascertain his death, Sergeant Calverley was sent to Mhome Gorge to obtain proof of Bhambatha's death. He found a body in the bush near Mhome River partly decomposed and decided that it was Bhambatha, but people who knew him disputed it. Calverley decapitated the body and took the head to McKenzie where it was kept in brine. It is said that the head was returned to the forest on the 3rd of June and buried with 'its body' on the right bank of Mhome River. The edition of *Nongqayi* magazine of the September 1925 displayed a photograph of a skull mounted on a shield claiming that it belonged to Bhambatha. Whatever the truth is, the decapitation of the 'unlucky' Zulu man led to an uproar both locally and internationally. The end of Bhambatha remains shrouded in controversy to this day.

All wars are fought on behalf the reigning Emperor hence no war or battle is named after an individual. Instead, they are named after the places they were fought. Therefore, the appropriate name would be eMhome Battle. It was the British that made his name rise to heights equal to powerful kings in the Zulu historiography. It further boggles the mind, how someone who performed so poorly in a war so significant in Zulu history could end up having his name attached to one of the major wars of resistance. History cannot overlook Bhambatha's shady character, dishonesty, theft, unsound disposition and motive for participating in the war. Furthermore, his vanishing from the final battle scene, the absence of confirmation of his death, the lack of positive identification of his severed head and the fact that his wife Siyekiwe, refused to mourn him because she believed he was still alive, are hallmarks of a violent opportunistic life. In the evening of the 13th of June, Sigananda simply walked to the military post in the forest and surrendered.

It was Sergeant Calverley who was sent to pick him up and he threw the ancient man into an old rickety cart and pulled it to Nomangci military camp at the outskirts of the forest. When Sigananda was transferred to Nkandla prison on the 16th of June and court-martialed five days later. He was found guilty and sentenced to death, he showed no emotion when the sentence was passed. When they asked him how he had managed to elude capture for so long he merely said: 'I never had occasion to move very far. When your big guns shelled in one direction, I got behind a rock in the opposite direction. On the day that you burnt my eNhlweni umuzi (homestead), your troops passed quite close by but did not see me.' Sadly, the 100-year-old died alone in a dark and damp cell awaiting execution at midnight of the 22nd of June 1906.

This Zulu hero had known Shaka personally and taken part in all the wars of resistance against colonisation. He was thrown into a hole in the most undignified manner and buried like a pauper because his remains were still the property of the colonial government.

*Greytown Town Hall, 1906. (J Powell)*

*The eMhome Gorge battle theatre where the Zulu fought their last conventional war during the Poll Tax Uprising 1906. (Killie Campbell Africana Library)*

*Thrings Post Store in KwaMaphumulo where Gobizembe Ntuli, Meseni Qwabe and Ndlovu kaThimuni Zulu (Dinuzulu's relative) killed Sangried, a Norwegian shop owner as well as a soldier during the Poll Tax Uprising 1906. (Killie Campbell Africana Library)*

*Gobizembe Ntuli, Meseni kaMusi Qwabe and Ndlovu kaThimuni under arrest for killing Sangried, a Norwegian shop owner as well as a soldier during the Poll Tax Uprising 1906. (The Mercury)*

## The Poll Tax Revolt

Tilongo kaNgunezi, Meseni kaMusi Qwabe and Ndlovu kaThimuni arrive in St Helena Island in 1907 to serve their sentences with hard labour, together with another 22 prisoners for being part of the leadership of the Poll Tax uprising in 1906. (The Mosquito)

Mahatma Gandhi whose rank was Sergeant-Major, led the Indian militia against the Zulu during th Poll tax uprising 1906. (Standing top row from the left) Coopoonsamy, Kunji, Ajodhasing, Moothoosamy, Appalsamy, Sheik Dada Mia, Kistama, Mahommed Essop. (Middle row from the left) Jamula Din, Barbu Hari (Corporal), UM Shelat (Sergeant), MK Gandhi (Sergeant-Major), HJ Joshi (Sergeant), SR Medh (Sergeant), Khan Mahomed, (Seated front row) Sheik Madar, Mahomed, Bomaya, Poon Narekan. (Indian Opinion)

# The Poll Tax Revolt

*The 100-year-old Sigananda kaNcube Shezi in the dock during his Treason Trial for leading the Poll Tax uprising in Nkandla 1906. (Killie Campbell Africana Library)*

*Sigananda kaZokufa kaNcube Shezi (seated) was eventually captured by the British forces in eMhome Gorge for being the commander of the Poll Tax Revolt in 1906. The 100-year-old was sentenced to death by firing squad but died during the night before he could be shot (Killie Campbell Africana Library)*

# The Poll Tax Revolt

*Sukabekhuluma Chakijana Sigilamkhuba kaGezidaka Sithole was the first to stand trial on 3 November 1908 in Greytown Town Hall which had been fitted out for the mass Poll Tax Uprising trial. He was found guilty of high treason and sentenced to seven years hard labour. (Killie Campbell Africana Library)*

*Mangathi kaGodide Ndlela kaSompisi was one of the deputies of Sigananda kaNcube Shezi during the Poll Tax uprising in 1906. (Killie Campbell Africana Library)*

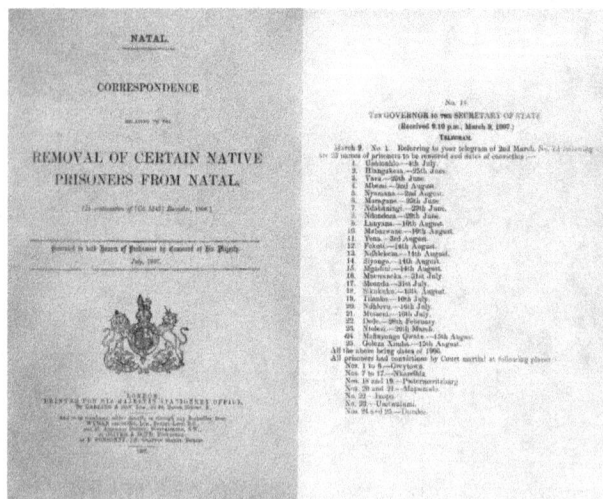

*The Telegram that was sent to London by the Natal authorities informing them about the men who were found guilty for taking part in the Poll Tax uprising in 1906. (The Mercury)*

## The Poll Tax Revolt

*Mankulumana kaSomaphunga Ndwandwe of the uMbonambi regiment (centre) had been recently released from Newcastle jail in 1910 together with his commanders. They had been arrested together with Emperor Dinuzulu for their involvement in the 1906 Poll Tax revolt. (Killie Campbell Africana Library)*

*The 25 men found guilty for taking part in the Poll Tax Uprising marching through the streets of Durban on their way to serve their sentences in St Helen Island. Mqondi and Thobazi were sentenced to 10 years; Ntelezi, Mhlekazi and Lunyana were sentenced to 15 years; Fokothi and Magcwaneka were sentenced to life terms but they died on the island and their remains are still in St Helena. Those who were lucky to make it back but barely alive were Nhlonhlo and Mbazwana were sentenced to 20 years; Ngadini and Siyonga were sentenced to 15 years; Sikhukhukhu, Mahangana, Fava, Goloza, Dede, Nyamana, Ndondoza, Mamfinyongo and Tilongo kaNgunezi were sentenced to 10 years and Mbeni was sentenced to 6 years. (The Mercury)*

# The Poll Tax Revolt

As eMhome Gorge was on fire, more uprisings were taking place throughout the Zulu empire and the Natal Colony against the poll tax. Colonial forces continued to be brutal to those who refused to pay. They murdered King Mashwili kaMngoye Mthethwa (Dingiswayo's grandson), his advisers, his firstborn son and 547 followers in one clean sweep. Mashwili lived at the old Mthethwa palace, oYengweni, and ruled over 188 huts in Lower Thukela area and 38 huts in parts of KwaMaphumulo area. After killing Mashwili, the Mthethwa kingdom was handed over to the newly constituted 'Ngubane chiefdom' under Sibindi who was also ruling the Ntuli kingdom. These provocative decisions can be attributed to some of the problems that continue to haunt the present traditional leadership landscape to this day. The Mchunu kingdom under Macingwane regarded the Zulu royal house as their natural enemies because they had been trying to destroy each other from the time of Senzangakhona.

So, when *impi yamakhanda* erupted, King Silwane kaGabangaye of the Mchunu kingdom sided with the colonial forces. However, siding with the whites did not protect Silwane from being deposed when he was no longer useful to them. He was exiled to the Bhaca people in the south under the care of the Mavundla kingdom where he died a pauper in March 1912. In KwaMaphumulo, a Norwegian shopkeeper Sangreid and a soldier were killed, but a guest W.C. Robbins was severely wounded at Thrings Post store by Gobizembe Ntuli and Ndlovu kaThimuni Zulu. The next ambush on the colonisers took place at Otimati River. Ndlovu's followers attacked 60 members of the Natal Mounted Rifles who were escorting wagons across the river. Ndlovu together with 25 leaders were finally arrested in July 1906. Likewise, Ndlovu's kingdom was also given to Sibindi Ngubane. This was one of the last major skirmishes in the *impi yamakhanda* war.

This was the last conventional warfare between the Zulu and the British and they fought it out in the dark forest of Nkandla. Out of the blue and without Dinuzulu's knowledge, the colonial government installed Manzolwandle kaCetshwayo (Dinuzulu's younger paternal brother) as a '*chief*' of three districts near Nquthu on the 23rd January 1907. This was to weaken Dinuzulu's authority over his loyal subjects. The ceremony was attended by other '*chiefs*' who had been appointed by the colonial government such as Gadaleni, Makhafula, Matshana kaMondise, Mayime, Mjantshi, Mpiyakhe, Nongamulana, Sishisili and others. Demoralised as the Zulu were, life went on as usual at eMahhashini as Dinuzulu was still regarded as *iSilo samabandla onke*. His secret service also provided regular reports about the '*new chiefs*'. The colonial government tried to link Dinuzulu with the poll tax war for many months but found no tangible evidence.

About 4 700 prisoners stood trial many got six months to two years with floggings. But the military high command whose ages ranged from about 20 to 70 years old, and others were found guilty of murder, attempted murder and various charges. They were handed down long sentences and sent to St Helena in June 1907 aboard the steamship *Inyati*. Initially, they were to serve their sentences in Mauritius, but they ended up not going because there was an outbreak of beriberi disease on the island. When they arrived in St Helena, they were given khaki jackets, which were embossed with either 'L' for life sentence or with the number of years to be served at the back. They were housed in Ladder Hill Barracks and did hard labour, constructing roads or working in the local quarries. The prisoner's food rations were hardly enough to keep body and soul together:

- 12 ounces of mealie meal for breakfast
- 12 ounces of mealie meal for lunch
- 18 ounces of mealie meal for dinner with salt
- Some vegetables during the week
- 11 pounds of fresh beef per man per week
- 1 blanket to sleep on
- No tea, coffee, milk or tobacco

On a lighter note, when Dinuzulu left the island years earlier, he was not aware that one of his '*Saint*' women, Emma Henry, was pregnant. When she heard that 'the Zulu' were on their way, she thought that they were coming to take her child to the Zulu empire. She hid him until she was certain that they had not come back for her son, Prince George Edward kaDinuzulu. The prince was affectionately called 'chief' around the island. Nevertheless, Dinuzulu was finally arrested by a large contingent of police and soldiers in the evening of the 7th of December 1907. They arrested him in front of his family at eMahhashini Palace and hid him in an ambulance they had come with, because they feared that Dinuzulu's subjects would stop them. He was taken to KwaNongoma Court and then transferred to Pietermaritzburg prison.

Two days later, he was moved to Greytown together with a number of those who fought against the poll tax such as Mankulumana and Mgwaqo who were both convicted of high treason on three accounts and sentenced to nine and 15 months accordingly. In passing sentence, it was considered that they had already spent 15 months in prison. Chakijana was the first one to stand trial on the 3rd November 1908 in Greytown Town Hall which had been fitted out for the occasion. He was found guilty of high treason and sentenced to seven years hard labour. A young man who bore long dreadlocks Jombolwana kaHloma, was sentenced to death and executed in December for killing Sitshitshil, a British collaborator. He was so hated that Nomapekepekana who wa also anti poll tax, composed a song about him *'umdumo wezimpukane yongena egolo lesiphakanyiswa uSitshitshili* (swarms of flies will enter the vagina of chief Sitshitshili). He substituted the word anus and used the name of the female private part in order to insult him.

The trial of Dinuzulu brought the sleepy little town into the limelight with international headlines. The Natal government cancelled Dinuzulu's salary without authorisation from London when they arrested him. The Colenso family brought this to the attention of the House of Commons and Winston Churchill chaired the discussion about the matter. The debate was heated, and Lord Crewe read out a letter that condemned the Breach of Contract because it was one of the conditions of Dinuzulu's release from St Helena Island. As Dinuzulu sat in his cell and awaited his fate for the 23 charges he was facing, he was comforted by the fact that he had clandestinely commanded the war against the colonial forces to the bitter end. He could not join the war openly because Natal government spies were watching his every move. His people were also proud of his achievements at such a young age and under extremely trying circumstances. The Zulu nation began collecting money for their Emperor's defence. Embarrassed, the Imperial government in London offered to pay Dinuzulu's salary to his family. But the now seriously embarrassed Natal government relented and, also offered to pay for Dinuzulu's defence.

Obviously, the Zulu gods were with them because they received good news from London. One of the top English legal eagles Advocate EG Jellicoe KC, had decided to defend the young Zulu king *pro bono*. Advocate Jellicoe had been following events in Natal with great sympathy for the Zulu royal family and arrived in Natal on Sunday the 19th of January 1908. He quickly got to work and sought an audience with his high-profile client. But the prison officials refused him access to Dinuzulu, even with strong support from the Colensos, he tried all avenues to meet Dinuzulu but failed. A few weeks later Advocate Jellicoe was left with no option but to return home. He called his experience a 'judicial outrage' committed by the Natal government. He said that:

- Dinuzulu was deprived of any opportunity of obtaining evidence in his favour
- Evidence in Dinuzulu's favour was suppressed
- Witnesses in Dinuzulu's favour were imprisoned
- The witnesses signed statement supposedly made by them began with the words 'its tue, according to the authorities…'

After Jellicoe's departure, another high-profile advocate offered his services to defend Dinuzulu, also pro bono. Advocate William Philip Schreiner QC had been the eighth Prime Minister of the Cape Colony. But he had quit politics after serious disagreement with the British over the South African War (Anglo-Boer War). He now threw his considerable talents into defending Dinuzulu. He was assisted by W Campbell, F Dumat and R Samuelson and of course the indomitable Harriette Colenso.

Once the case was underway, to the shock and surprise of many, Bhambatha's wife Siyekiwe turned chief state witness against her one-time benefactor. When she heard that many people had died in eMhome Gorge, she ran away from Dinuzulu's protection at eMahhashini. She had been living there with her family for 18 months. She went to a colonial garrison at Shonengashoni in KwaNongoma. She claimed that she had overheard her husband Bhambatha plan the war with Sichotho (King Jama's great-great-grandson), Ngqengqengqe, Mgwaqo, Nkantolo, Chakijana, Mangathi and Dinuzulu. She also claimed that the old man Mankulumana gave her husband a handgun and Mauser bullets, covered in a white cloth. This shocked the whole kingdom. Such treachery. Many people were also arrested on suspicion of supporting Dinuzulu. This included some members of the military command. However, this time Dinuzulu was allowed witnesses to testify on his behalf.

Hundreds volunteered and travelled from all over the kingdom, including from Natal. But the oldest chief witness was an elderly man, Ngobazana who had accompanied Cetshwayo to England. He was so old that he was unable to walk and was carried on *isikhumba* (a stretcher made from ox-hide) and was permitted sit in a chair during his testimony in court. He made it clear that he personally did not want to pay poll tax and neither did any self-respecting Zulu. But he said they only paid because they were instructed to do so by Dinuzulu. He also defended the right of ordinary people as well as the so called 'rebels' to settle near their monarch in times of war, famine and any other catastrophe as this was a part of Zulu tradition. Another interesting witness was an Afrikaner, Fredrick Meyer from Paulpietersburg (Dumbe) who had grown up with Dinuzulu and testified strongly in favour of the king's good character. The case lasted for 60 days and Dinuzulu was under cross-examination for 11 days. There were 48 Zulu and 47 European witnesses for the Crown and 52 witnesses for the defence, four Europeans and 48 were Zulu. The Zulu Crown witnesses requested to turn their backs on Dinuzulu because they were ashamed to testify against their king. The eloquent defence by Schreiner exposed the moral bankruptcy of the questionable methods used by the prosecution in its desire to secure a conviction on the serious charges. The Crown was so desperate that at some point the Attorney General Thomas Carter screamed at one of the Zulu witnesses, screamed: 'What! Would you dare to contradict a white man?' The result of this protracted affair was not surprising, as Schreiner destroyed all their evidence. He also argued that had Dinuzulu thrown his full weight behind the uprising, the war would have been far more extensive.

Schreiner's closing argument was phenomenal in his brilliant career as an advocate. When judgement was handed down, he was gratified that he had crushed white supremacy. One of the heated exchanges between the Carter and Dinuzulu was when he asked him if he was a Christian or not. Dinuzulu retorted by saying: '*Kangizile lapha ukuba ngizokhuluma lezo zenkolo. Amukho nokunguyena engimaziyo oyikholwa nongekholwa kulelizwe, engimazi ukuthi uyikholwa uKhristu kuphela.*' (I did not come here to talk about religion. There is no one that I know who a true believer is, or non-believer on this earth, the only one that I know of is Christ). The Colenso family, especially Harriette tried to secure Dinuzulu's release by other means. They wrote petitions both to the Natal government and British government in London but to no avail. As though the case was not dramatic enough, suddenly the Carter turned to Harriette. He charged her on two accounts of treason. But he was unsuccessful in convicting her for the allegation that she had taught the Zulu people the British national anthem *God Save the* Queen but had substituted the British queen's name with Dinuzulu's name. The other charge was that she taught them the following song:

| *Kukhona ijele elikhulu kude le* | there was a big prison far away |
| *Ngaphandle kogange lomuzi* | outside the perimeter of this house |
| *Lapho inkosi yethu iboshwe khona* | where our king is held prisoner |
| *Eyayilungele ukusifela sonke* | he was prepared to die for us all |

On the 3$^{rd}$ of March Dinuzulu's highly anticipated verdict greatly embarrassed the Natal government as of the 23 original charges, two were withdrawn and acquitted of eighteen. But he was found guilty of high treason in that:

- He had harboured and concealed Bhambatha's wife and children for fifteen months
- He had harboured & assisted Bhambatha & Mangathi during the actual progress of the rebellion
- He had harboured numerous rebels at various times between May 1906 and the date of his arrest

Dinuzulu and Mankulumana were sent to a prison in Newcastle in the north of Natal. They arrived at the town's railway station on a wintry morning in April 1910. Dinuzulu disembarked from the train decked in convict garb and a cap. But he had artistically thrown across his shoulders a large dark blanket which entirely enveloped his big body. He was still a dandy to the core. Winter was early in Newcastle that year. Everything was frozen and sometimes there was no running water, but Dinuzulu endured with dignity. Seven fellow prisoners volunteered to vacate their cells to provide more space for Dinuzulu and his royal retinue. The first prime minister of the Union of South Africa was General Louis Botha (Dinuzulu's subject and friend). As far as General Louis Botha was concerned Dinuzulu did not receive a fair trial and granted him and Mankulumana a full pardon. The condition of the pardon was that Dinuzulu would never be allowed to live in the empire until death. Mankulumana was released first on the 20th of May and Dinuzulu was released on the day the Union was formed, the 31st of May 1910. The rest of the Zulu imprisoned at St Helena were pardoned on the 23rd of December. Unfortunately, not all of them made it back alive. Those who died on the island were Mqondi and Thobazi (10 years); Ntelezi, Mhlekazi and Lunyana (15 years); Fokothi and Magcwaneka (life). Their remains are still in St Helena to this day.

Those who made it back, but barely alive were Meseni Qwabe, Ndlovu kaThimuni Zulu and Ndabaningi Shezi (life with hard labour); Nhlonhlo and Mbazwana (20 years); Ngadini and Siyonga (15 years); Sikhukhukhu, Mahangana, Fava, Goloza, Dede, Nyamana, Ndondoza, Mamfinyongo and Tilongo kaNgunezi (10 years) and Mbeni (6 years). When they arrived in Durban, two of the 18 were carried on stretchers because they were too ill to walk. They all looked wasted and had aged dramatically, even though they had served only three years. In total, about 4500 prisoners were freed throughout South Africa through a general amnesty. General Botha bought Dinuzulu a farm called *Uitkyk* which was about 400x23 hectares in Middelburg. But Dinuzulu renamed it KwaThengisangaye (*KwaThengisa*) Palace (a place where one was betrayed). He was joined by his seven wives and 37 children, including the Crown Prince Maphumuzana, David, Mankulumana, attendants and two white nurses. Being in exile a few hours away from Zululand was better than being on a remote island in the middle of the ocean or being locked up in a tiny prison cell in nearby Newcastle.

Dinuzulu tried to live a normal life out on the farm. His subjects could consult him about Zulu state affairs at any time and they could stay as long as they wished. His subjects came regularly and often brought him presents and money. He ended up living a very busy life and the number of *imihlalandlini* (palace dwellers) increased.

## The Poll Tax Revolt

He farmed, hunted and of course continued acquiring more wives and ended up with about 40 in total, like his great great-grandfather Senzangakhona). The number of his children also grew, and he had to build them a school on the farm. The graves of some of his children Muyiyane, Nonkantolo, Lawrence and some of his wives including Miriam Mbatha from eMalahleni are still visible at the corner of the ruins of the farm. Just as he did on St Helena, Dinuzulu entertained his family, friends, guests and dignitaries. He demonstrated his polished piano and drumming skills. Dinuzulu had been plagued by debilitating Bright's disease which started in St Helena due to the cold climate. He often went to a specialist in Kroonstad. But his health progressively worsened and the treatment did not work. Towards the end of his short life, he refused treatment and only wanted to be prayed for. Like his father, Dinuzulu told his advisers and senior members of the royal family who the heir was to be. He spent hours reminiscing about his short, troubled life. He listened to his favourite songs he had composed such as '*Wayihlaba wema nayo, Sangena ngobhevula*' and his favourite hymn *Masibonge uJesu ngoba wasifela*.

The Zulu nation contributed money to send the 42-year-old monarch for specialist care in Germany, but the money arrived too late. On the other hand, secret plans were advanced between Harriette Colenso and Gen Botha that Dinuzulu be allowed to return to the empire. Emperor Dinuzulu *uMamonga woSuthu* kaCetshwayo died peacefully on the 18$^{th}$ of October 1913 at KwaThengisangaye Palace in Middelburg. He was surrounded by his family and adviser Mankulumana was with him to the end. Ndabankulu kaLukhwazi Ntombela was sent to inform the rest of the royal family in eMakhosini Valley about Dinuzulu's death. Dinuzulu's body was embalmed by two whites from the government. He was escorted to his final resting place by his wives okaNtuzwa, okaHlokolo, okaHlobane the royal family, his some of Cetshwayo's wives, his son-in-law and legal adviser Pixley ka Isaka Seme, Mankulumana, Harriette Colenso, Magistrate Colenbrander, Falezwe kaShingana, Zenzo, Mpikanina, Mkebeni, Mdumela kaDabulamanzi, Dokotela kaMgidlana Mbuzini, Ndabankulu, Zidunge kaNtshingwayo Khoza (his father was a commander at iSandlwana), Masimba KaNokhokhela Buthelezi, and others.

There were about 3000 people who bid him farewell when he left KwaThengisa. He was put on a train to eMakhosini Valley and there were hundreds of people at all the stopovers. By the time the body arrived at KwaNobamba there were thousands more, including some of his children such as Magangezintaba, Mdlenevu, Mpembeni, Nswabo, Mgungunyane, Magogo and many more. But there was one notable absence - Manzolwandle did not come to the funeral. At the gravesite, some people wanted the coffin opened so that his subjects could look at their king for the last time. But the request was turned down because his body had badly decomposed. This is the source of the rumour that it was not Dinuzulu's body inside the coffin. By 1966 his widow, okaHlabane was still taking care of his grave.

However, the late Senior Prince Reggie kaMagangezintaba kaDinuzulu did not share this view. A cool gentle breeze connected us with history as we sat under the ancient trees at his KwaQambushilo homestead at KwaNongoma. The sprightly, tall, regal and handsome octogenarian showed very little emotion until we discussed his grandfather's burial. In a calm steady voice, he said, 'It took a long time to travel from Middelburg to eMakhosini in those days because of poor roads. My grandfather's coffin was first put on a train that ended up in Vryheid. Then it had to be transferred to an ox wagon that carried it all the way to KwaNobamba. The trip lasted over a week and it was summer, so it made sense to put him in a sealed metal coffin. We should be concentrating on fixing what is broken in our empire rather than worrying about mere speculation. Reviving the Zulu nation to its former glory should be a priority. My grandfather's last rites were done by Rev Reuben Thwala of the Pretoria Wesleyan Church because that is what my grandfather wanted, and the family had to comply with his last earthly wish. Sadly, one of wives Silomo who had been through thick and thick with him, died shortly after him'.

Today only the foundation of the palace and school remain while the ruins of the once large stone cattle enclosure remain. Fresh winds blow quietly through the open spaces. It is as though no mirthful laughter of Zulu princes and princesses ever brought joy nor there was ever an echo of homesick sighs from the elderly members of the royal family. The farm has a different name now and the prized cattle of the current Afrikaner owner graze its pastures. Luckily, the current Afrikaner owners of the farm revere what was once the center of the Zulu people's universe. They are always ready to recount its history to anyone who cares to listen.

*The ruins of the front entrance of King Dinuzulu's kwaThengisangaye Palace in Middleburg, Mpumalanga where he died. South Africa's first Prime Minister General Louis Botha bought the farm for him when he was released from Newcastle prison and was not allowed to live in the Zulu kingdom ever again. The school where the royal children attended still stands in the background. (Shalo Mbatha)*

*The ruins of what was once King Dinuzulu's cattle enclosure in kwaThengisangaye Palace in Middleburg, Mpumalanga. (Shalo Mbatha)*

*Queen Miriam Zulu was 75 years old when she died at KwaThengisangaye Palace in Middleburg, Mpumalanga (Shalo Mbatha)*

*Princess Muyiyane kaDinuzulu was only 6 months old when he was buried at kwaThengisangaye Palace in Middleburg, Mpumalanga (Shalo Mbatha)*

Princess Nonkantolo kaDinuzulu headstone at KwaThengisangaye Palace in Middleburg, Mpumalanga (Shalo Mbatha)

Prince Lawrence kaDinuzulu headstone at KwaThengisangaye Palace in Middleburg, Mpumalanga (Shalo Mbatha)

# 11

# The African Insurrection

AFRICANS FROM DIFFERENT ETHNIC groups and from all walks of life followed Dinuzulu's tribulations with apprehension. They had started organising themselves from the 1900s as they realised that they needed to act collectively if they were to survive the colonial onslaught. A sense of an insurrection was evident in the Afrikaner republics and British colonies. This is because Africans were aware that the whites were planning to dissolve their republics and colonies and form a unitary state that excludes Africans from political decision making. This led the prominent Zulu intellectual Dr Pixley ka Isaka Seme, who was studying at Columbia University, in the America publish an article *The Regeneration of Africa* in 1906. He states that: '...the African already recognises his anomalous position and desires a change. The brighter day is rising upon Africa. Already I seem to see her chains dissolved, her desert plains red with harvest, her Abyssinia and her Zululand, the seats of science and of religion, reflecting the glory of the rising sun from the spires of their churches and universities. Her Congo and her Gambia whitened with commerce, her crowded cities sending forth the hum of business, and all her sons employed in advancing the victories of peace greater and more abiding than the spoils of war.'

Meetings between African people were held around the country, culminating in the holding of a South African Native Convention in Bloemfontein in 1909. This meeting was driven by African intellectuals and traditional leaders and they passed wide-ranging resolutions. One resolution was that the Imperial government in London was bound by both fundamental and specific obligations to ensure that Africans were given equitable justice as was extended to whites. They also not only supported Dinuzulu's actions, but also demanded a national Constitution that gave Africans equal rights that guaranteed freedom for the incarcerated Zulu Emperor.

South Africa's mixed-race people and Indians were later included in the discussions around universal human rights and justice for everyone. Mixed race people were also feeling the heat of discrimination and they formed their first political party in 1902 called the African Political Organisation (*APO*). Its purpose was to represent the interests of the elite coloureds only and it had nothing to do with black Africans. Their leader Dr Abdullah Abdurrahman was a charismatic grandson of Malay slaves. He was educated as a medical doctor in Scotland and established the first Coloured Teachers' League of South Africa (*TLSA*) that still exists today. Indeed, as the Africans suspected, the Afrikaner and British united and formed the Union of South Africa in 1910. It was based on the Transvaal Republic's principle of no equality in church or state. But the Union's main agenda was land ownership, and not much else.

After the establishment of the Union of South Africa in 1910, the young black intelligentsia such as lawyers, journalists, teachers, pastors, social workers, nurses and intellectuals like the Zulu philosopher Dr Pixley ka Isaka Seme had regular meetings. The agenda was a singular urgent item, the course of action about what had befallen the indigenous owners of the land, the Africans. Seme and another Zulu visionary Alfred Mangena set up the first African law practice in South Africa. It was called *Seme and Mangena Attorneys* at the corner of Diagonal and Kerk Streets in Johannesburg. Some of their prominent clients were the Swati royal family. During the 1906 poll tax revolt, Mangena was reading law in London. He made a name for himself by petitioning the British government twice on behalf of those who were facing court martial in Natal. He also initiated a political court case in London against the Governor of Natal for having proclaimed martial law and the representative of the Natal government ridiculed him publicly in London. But Mangena enjoyed a good fight and managed to vindicate himself by suing the representative for libel. Seme and Mangena were staunch Zulu traditionalists and like many from Shaka's time, they believed that the salvation of the African people lay in coming together. This dream had not gone up in flames when the British burnt down uLundi Palace in 1879. The visions of freedom and independence from colonial clutches, especially attaining their ancestral lands, remain in the hearts of many young Zulu to this day.

One of the first laws the new Pretoria government under General Louis Botha formulated was the 1911 Draft Natives Land Act. It proposed to dispossess all Africans 87 percent of their best land in South Africa. All black people throughout the Union knew that if the Act was promulgated, it would be the beginning of the end of life as they knew it. This threat compelled Seme to take the lead in resisting it. He wrote yet another ground-breaking article in October 1911 called *Native Union* pleading with Africans to unite. The article was published in several African owned publications such as in Sol Plaatjie's newspaper *Tsala ea Batho*, in Mark Radebe's *Ipepa loHlango* and in John Dube's *iLanga lase Natal* newspapers. Seme also issued *inhlabamkhosi ka-1912* (Clarion Call of 1912) and begged Africans to unite under the slogan - '*MZulu, MXhosa, MSuthu Hlanganani*' (Zulu person, Xhosa person, Mosotho person come together) based on a song composed by Reuben Caluza.

In the same year, fellow African intellectuals tasked renowned author Sol Plaatjie with the arduous responsibility. He was to organise Africans throughout the country as well as in the rest of the African continent. They were to come together and discuss the threat posed by the unity of colonisers who excluded them. Delegates from different societal formations were invited to go to a meeting in an insignificant Wesleyan Church in Bloemfontein (*Mangaung*) on the 8th of January 1912. Over 100 fired-up delegates arrived. They arrived by car, horseback, foot, wagons, bicycles and on trains. It included traditional leaders such as the Zulu Crown Prince Maphumuzana Solomon kaDinuzulu, the Queen Regent Labotsibeni from Swaziland, King Montsioa of the Barolong kingdom, King Lewanika of the Lozi kingdom in Zambia, King Letsie II of Lesotho, King Dalindyebo of the abaThembu kingdom, King Sekhukhune II of the Bapedi kingdom and King Seretse Khama I from Botswana. Other delegates came from Southern Rhodesia (*Zimbabwe*), Tanganyika (*Tanzania*), Nyasaland (*Malawi*) and the Congo (*DRC*). Other people that came were nationalists, Marxists, Africanists, urban dwellers, rural dwellers, the rich and the poor. In a moment of unparalleled greatness, Africans took one of the most epoch-making decisions ever taken on the African continent. They all went down on their knees in the tiny church.

They prayed in unison for divine intervention. When they were satisfied that God had heard their prayers, they got up and elected the first office-bearers. They called the new organisation the South African Native National Congress (SANNC). Rev John Langalibalele Dube, a Zulu *ikholwa* (Christian convert) was elected the first president in absentia. Seme became the treasurer general, Richard Msimang and George Montsio were elected to the executive. The delegates respected traditional authority and made it a right for traditional leadership, queens and kings to be automatic Honorary office-bearers within the SANNC. Hence, Dinuzulu was elected its first Honorary President in absentia, because he was languishing in exile at KwaThengisa. The name SANNC was changed to the African National Congress (*ANC*) in 1923 and this organisation is still in existence to this day more than 100 years later. The first ANC President Rev Dube was born in an American mission called iNanda. His grandfather Mqadi had been killed when Dingane massacred the amaQadi kingdom in 1839. Luckily his grandmother Mayembe managed to escape with his father Khakhonina and found refuge in Lindley's American mission. Mayembe became the first Zulu female convert in 1849 and was given the Christian name *Delilah*. She was told that the white God would not recognise her if she continued using her Zulu name.

But the Zulu tongue could not contort, and they ended up calling her *Dalitha* or *Dalida*. She often gets confused with Dalida Seme (Pixley's older sister) who worked as a missionary in Inhambane, Mozambique. Similarly, Khakhonina ended up being called *James* and was the mission's first African pastor. Dube's first wife Nokuthela Mdima, a dark-skinned beauty, was also a Christian and she published *A Zulu Song Book* in 1911. After their marriage broke down in Durban, she went to live in the *Driefontein* farm that belonged to the South African Native Farmers Association. She died on the farm on the 26th of January 1917 and lies buried in grave number CK 9763 in the Brixton Cemetery, Johannesburg. CK stands for *'Christian Kaffir'*.

The 1912 mammoth achievement of establishing the ANC gave many sectors of the African society confidence to come into their own. For instance, many Christian converts such as Isaiah Mudliwamafa kaMayisela Shembe broke away from white Christian churches. He established the *iBandla lamaNazaretha* (Nazareth Baptist Church) so that they could worship God in line with Zulu tradition. They played drums, walked barefoot, burnt *impepho* (sage) and married many wives. Shembe also preferred Sabbath observance to the worship on Sunday because he was reacting against what whites preferred. Moreover, the Dutch Reformed Church, which was established by Afrikaners in the 1800s, prohibited Africans and whites from worshipping the same God under one roof. But what perplexed the Zulu most of all was the fact that they, as a people that took their God very seriously were to treat the white man's holy book, the Bible with *izikhali zamantungwa* (deep veneration).

The Zulu Christian converts were a rare breed in the empire those days. However, whites especially the missionaries needed to be able to identify them from a distance in the sea of Zulu non-believers. Therefore, Christian converts were forced to wear uniforms to church so that they could stand out in public. It is still only Africans who continue to wear uniforms, when the white Christians still do not wear them. Furthermore, Christian converts were also forced to stop living in round huts and had to build rectangular houses as proof that they had truly converted. They were also forbidden from having *umsamo* (ancestors' sacred space) where the Zulu communicate with their departed inside a hut. This Zulu worship was equated with devil worship. To ensure that the revolutionary impetus did not dissipate, the Swati Queen Regent Labotsibeni provided all the capital needed to start a pro-ANC national newspaper called *Abantu-Batho*. It was published in Sesotho, isiXhosa, isiZulu and English. The Swazi royal family continued to support the newspaper for the following 20 years, to ensure that Swazi interests within the ANC remained protected.

The success of the ANC's newspaper encouraged Mangena and the fiery orator Sefako Mapogo Makgatho to publish a newspaper called *African Native Advocate*. It was edited by Tiyo Soga, the son of the extraordinary Xhosa intellectual Allan Kirkland Soga. Since Seme had formed an association for African farmers in 1913, it then bought several farms such as *Daggakraal*, *Vlakplaas* and *Driefontein* where Nokuthela Dube in Wakkerstroom in today's Mpumalanga Province. But the brutal Natives Land Act was passed on the 20th of June 1913 stopped the further buying of farms. This meant that Africans were given a mere 13 per cent of the land, which was barren. All arable land was now in 'white' areas. As if that was not enough, Botha and his Minister of Native Affairs, J.B. Hertzog went to all corners of the country and encouraged white farmers to expel Africans from their farms and replace them with poor whites. But they dared not go to the Zulu empire.

The SANNC decided to appeal directly to London and to European governments about all the laws that were planned to degrade Africans further. During yet another protest trip to London in 1914, Plaatjie spent the long lonely nights in the belly of the ship *Kenilworth Castle* writing a book. He described the horrendous effects of the Natives Land Act and dedicated it to Harriette *Dlwedle* Colenso. The delegation was met with enthusiasm by ordinary English people, but the British establishment had no time for them. Plaatjie continued to write many articles in local newspapers especially in the London Times. When Plaatjie finally went back home, he published his seminal book *Native Life in South Africa* in 1916. The book described the consequences of the Natives Land Act in horrifying detail. He pointed out that from the Friday morning of the 20th of June 1913 even criminals who were hanged had the right to a proper grave, but under the Act, little children, whose only crime is that God did not make them white, sometimes had no right to be buried in the country of their ancestors. He wrote that:

'…Kgobadi had also been forced off the land by the Land Act. The '*Baas*' said that Kgobadi, his wife and his oxen had to work for R36 a year. Before the Land Act, Kgobadi had been making R200 a year selling crops. He told the '*Baas*' he did not want to work for such low wages. The '*Baas*' told Kgobadi to go. So together with his father-in-law, they had nowhere to go. They were wandering around on the roads in the cold winter with everything they owned. Kgobadi's goats gave birth. One by one, they died in the cold and were left by the roadside for the jackals and vultures to eat. Mrs Kgobadi's child was sick. She had to put her child in the ox-wagon, which bumped along the road. Two days later, the child died. Where could they bury the child? They had no rights to bury it on any land. Late that night, the poor young mother and father had to dig a grave when no one could see them. They had to bury their child in a stolen grave.'

On another trip, Plaatjie led John Dube, Josiah Gumede, Selope Thema, Henry Ngcayiya and Levi Mvabaza to the Versailles Peace Conference of January 1919. They were hoping for some recognition for being loyal to the British during the First World War, but they were completely ignored. The Archbishop of Canterbury, Randall Davidson, only agreed to meet them after eight months on the 25th of August 1919 in Lambeth Palace. Plaatjie begged, inter alia, for the granting of the Zulu claim on land based on the Royal Proclamation and Zululand Land Annexation Act of 1897. This Act allowed the annexation of all the land belonging to the Zulu people and beyond the uThukela River without any consultation or reparations. Davidson refused to get involved. Plaatjie did not give up when the rest of the delegation returned back home. He proceeded to America and Canada where he met giants such as Marcus Garvey, WEB Du Bois and many other African American intellectuals who supported him.

# The African Insurrection

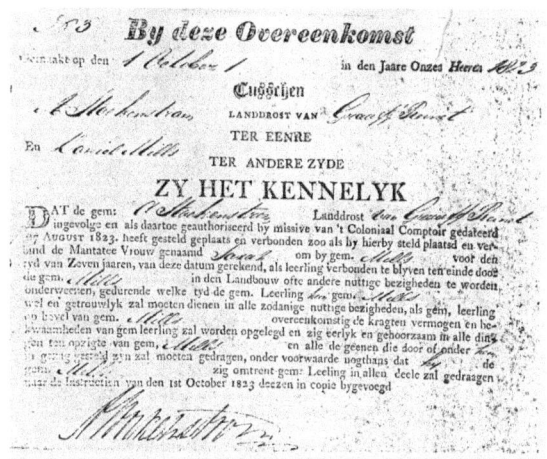

*An Agreement to certify that Sara who belonged to Mantantise's group was bound to a white man, Daniel Mills for seven years. (Cape Archives)*

*A picture of a happy mixed race slave after he got his freedom through the General Order when slavery ceased in Cape Colony. (Killie Campbell Africana Museum)*

# 12

# Emperor Maphumuzana kaDinuzulu

IT IS CUSTOMARY THAT the heir is announced before the burial of the king so that he turns the first sod with a spear on his father's grave. However, King's Dinuzulu's heir had not been officially announced, which held up the burial for two days while the matter was being resolved. This also put pressure for the matter to be quickly resolved because the government was threatening to install a royal pretender to the throne, Khambi kaHhamu kaNzibe kaSenzangakhona. On the day of the funeral, some members of the royal family and Dinuzulu's confidantes such as Lokothwayo kaZembe Mngadini, Mvingana kaNompande Mzimela, Kobiyana kaMholo Mzimela and Nobiyana (he was one of Dinuzulu's bodyguards from birth) said Nyawana was the heir because he was the first son. Hence the veteran Mankulumana announced that Nyawana was the new Emperor.

There were icy stares, others saluted him with Bayethe while others protested. During the heated argument the cortege left for the gravesite. There was more drama at the gravesite as to who was to turn the first sod. The senior royal members authorised Mphaphu to turn the first sod, then the burial took place according to Zulu custom. The following day, thousands more arrived even from the Natal Colony. The royal family and advisers, led by Mankulumana, met behind closed doors to try and understand what had happened the previous day. After a lengthy discussion, the pretender to the throne was duly relieved of his 24-hour reign and he agreed to step down without protest. Then the urbane and sophisticated 20-year-old Prince Maphumuzana Nkayishana Solomon was proclaimed the Emperor of the Zulu by Mankulumana. There was a thundering sound when the people shouted *Bayethe*. Celebrations lasted for a week and the Zulu based in Natal also turned up in their thousands. This was Mankulumana's last coronation.

Maphumuzana was only five years old when he arrived in the empire but spoke perfect isiZulu through the tutelage of isiZulu teachers, Magema and Bubi. He made history by being the first Zulu Emperor to be born in St Helena on the 2$^{nd}$ of January 1893. He experienced a plethora of problems during his reign because the world of the Zulu people and the rest of Africans South Africa had changed forever. The Zulu on either side of the uThukela River were desperately expecting the young monarch to save them from the dreadful 1913 law. As he was still figuring out the best solution with the king's council, a whites-only electorate voted General Jan Smuts into power as prime minister in 1919.

Smuts was a member of the secret Afrikaner organisation called the *Broederbond* and he was not only a larger-than-life character in South Africa, but on the world stage as well. For instance, he was the only person in the world to have signed two world peace treaties that ended the First and Second World Wars. He also drafted the League of Nations Charter and the United Nations Preamble and assisted in establishing the British Commonwealth. He was so influential that when the German East African colonies Tanganyika, Burundi and Rwanda were divided into mandated territories, there were plans to rename Tanganyika (*Tanzania*) Smutsland. He was so close to the first President of Israel, Chiam Weizmann that when asked to write his epitaph, he described Weizmann as the greatest Jew after Moses. Smuts was regarded as such an intellectual giant that his *alma mater* Cambridge University rated him in the same league as the distinguished economist John Milton and philosopher Charles Darwin.

However, his most incredible achievement was to be invited to become a member Churchill's War Cabinet even though he was not a British citizen. He was also appointed as the Prime Minister of the United Kingdom, if Churchill died or otherwise became incapacitated during the war. But Churchill lived for another 25 years and the contingency was never put into effect. Despite his near genius, the person his friends called *Slim Jan* (smart Jan) only came second after another brilliant Afrikaner Jan Hofmeyer. A young distinguished child protégée, an exceptional scholar and outstanding politician. He had the intellectual ability of often holding six to seven ministerial portfolios simultaneously and managing them remarkably well. But his finest hour was when he was Minister of Finance and had to present the national Budget. He did it in the most melodramatic way possible. He used to mesmerise Parliament with his complete mastery of facts and rattle off large amounts of complicated data and figures from memory, without reading. So, he was called *Slimmer Jannie* (cleverer little Jan*)*. Despite all his brilliance, Smuts was a product of his time and environment, even though he should have known better. He strongly believed in racial separation that he articulated in his book *The Theory of Holism*. He linked his views with his political and military activities and belief in white supremacy. Acclaimed author Julian Tudor Hart described Smuts' holism as: '...a soapy term which evades necessary conflict which fitted with his belief in excluding the African majority from democracy'. But Smuts was not alone in these racist views.

Another public figure, the famous proponent of passive resistance from India, Mohandas Mahatma Gandhi shared similar sentiments. These two admired each other so much that before Gandhi went to India in 1914, he presented Smuts with a pair of sandals he especially made by hand for him. Then when Gandhi turned 70, Smuts returned the sandals with a note full of fond walking memories. For example, Gandhi's announcements during the poll tax revolt, expressed his unambiguous feelings very clearly, '...I bore no grudge against the Zulus, they had harmed no Indian. I had doubts about the 'rebellion' itself. But I then believed that the British Empire existed for the welfare of the world. A genuine sense of loyalty prevented me from even wishing ill to the Empire.' He did not stop there, he also published an article in the Indian Opinion newspaper: '...Kaffirs are as a rule uncivilized, the convicts even more so. They are troublesome, very dirty and live almost like animals.' Gandhi further protested about the social classification of Africans with Indians in South Africa and described Indians as '...undoubtedly infinitely superior to the Kaffirs...' *Gandhi whose rank was Sergeant-Major, later led a militia of Indians against the Zulu during the 1906 Poll Tax uprising. He led - Coopoonsamy, Kunji, Ajodhasing, Moothoosamy, Appalsamy, Sheik Dada Mia, Kistama, Mahommed Essop, Jamula Din, Barbu Hari (Corporal), UM Shelat (Sergeant), MK Gandhi (Sergeant-Major), HJ Joshi (Sergeant), SR Medh (Sergeant), Khan Mahomed, Sheik Madar, Mahomed, Bomaya, Poon Narekan.*

Smuts demonstrated his hatred of blacks in 1920 when he passed the Native Affairs Act of 1920. It paved the way for the government-appointed District Councils in the Zulu empire. In the same year, a number of poor working-class whites, Africans, Indians and Chinese from Vrededorp in Johannesburg were killed by the police. Instead of coming to their rescue, Smuts evicted the survivors from Vrededorp. He even offered the Indians a state-funded emigration scheme to return to India. In 1923, he ordered the massacre of 190 Africans in Bulhoek near Queenstown when they refused to be forcibly moved to another location. The Bulhoek leader Enoch Mgijima survived the massacre and was imprisoned for six years with hard labour. In response to this outrage, Maphumuzana formed a political party in 1923 called *iNkatha yakwaZulu*. It was named after the traditional Zulu sacred coil, a symbol of unity and strength.

Even though Maphumuzana had been crowned, he had neither a proper country nor an income. Needless to say, the Zulu were insecure about the future and survival of their nation once again. Under the circumstances, Maphumuzana resorted to only what the Zulu knew best; he prepared for war. Even though it was prohibited and difficult, he formed *uNqabakucetshwenwangabezizwe* (refuses to allow foreign interference) regiment. He also moved to the eZibindini Palace at eMakhosini Valley near White iMfolozi River where his mother lived. Thereafter he built his own palace near KwaDlamahlahla, a western-style house in KwaNongoma. The Zulu royal household had been slowly impoverished by the long litany of wars and shrinking land mass. What had made things worse was that he received no stipend from the British even though they had made it illegal for the Zulu royal family to be supported by their subjects. So, he associated with lawyers, teachers, pastors, trade unionists and journalists and they talked about the ways and means they could regain their dignity. He always reminded them that he was ready for action as his regiments were combat-ready. These meetings made the Smuts government nervous and interpreted them as a move to reassert the Zulu authority. Therefore, institutions that would westernise Zulu youth were established, and the Anglican Church quickly built the Zulu Native Training Institution (*ZNTI*) in KwaNongoma. Their main target was the sons of Zulu traditional leadership and royal family members. The thinking of both the church and the Smuts government was that if the aspirations of the Zulu mission-educated professionals could not be suppressed, they might as well be channelled into the administration of the Zulu Reserves.

Moreover, their conquering methodology throughout Africa was to employ the three Cs - *commerce* (to loot both human and natural resources under the guise of trade), *Christianity* (to justify their cruelty and malicious intentions under the guise of it being God's will) and *civilisation* (to destroy their self-worth and culture under the guise of education and development). However, the Africans recognised that these *Cs* culminated in the last *C,* conquest. In time, Maphumuzana expressed his disconcerting views publicly even about the role of the British in his shrunken empire. To punish him for his anti-British views, he was coerced to attend a public ceremony in Eshowe in June 1925 in honour of the British Crown, Prince Edward VIII. Maphumuzana was told to invite his people and about 60 000 men turned up. He met his men near uMlalazi River where they camped overnight. They slept under the skies in their respective regiments even though they were officially banned. It was the first time that all the regiments came together in almost 50 years, since 1879 at iSandlwana. They wore their full 'war regalia' and there were thousands of onlookers, people who came to witness the spectacle.

Maphumuzana upstaged Prince Edward by arriving in a convoy of four enormous blue open coupés with leopard skin seats, driven by white chauffeurs wearing white gloves. He sat majestically in one of them. He slowly alighted from the car and the Zulu crowds went berserk as the *inyosi* belted out his laudatory praises. Once seated, he spoke loudly to his entourage and ignored the proceedings. When his turn came to speak, he said that it was not right that General Botha had informed him that he did not recognise him as anything under the sun, not as a chief or *inkosi* whatsoever. Maphumuzana demanded respect from powers that be as a king of the powerful Zulu nation. He deliberately flicked his royal whisk directly at Edward's face, taunting him. After his speech, Prince Edward presented nine chiefs with silver plated sticks and gave Maphumuzana a gold-studded cane. In return King Maphumuzana gave Prince Edward a pair of magnificent elephant tusks, mounted on a hardwood base with a gold shield engraved '*To HRH the Prince of Wales on behalf of the Zulu Nation*'.

Thereafter, the regiments surged back and forth singing and looking awesome in their headdresses, shields, sticks, spears, skins and finery. Mankulumana was wearing his *ibheshu* and a leopard claws necklace, in contrast John Dube was wearing a suit as many of the African petty bourgeoisie. Visitors from around the world were in awe and watched excitedly. This included numerous clergy from different dominations such as the Latter-Day Saints missionaries, Leon Stinger Saunders and Kenneth Claude Woodruff from Salt Lake City, Utah in America. Once they returned home, they recounted the colourful event of the day to American audiences with much enthusiasm.

After the ceremony Maphumuzana and Edward held a private meeting at the train station. One of the outcomes of that meeting was that the House of Windsor recognised him and the Zulu empire. General Botha's government said and did nothing about the turn of events. The meeting obviously made Maphumuzana bold in his demands. First, he formed a new regiment named after the gift he gave Edward *uPhondolwendlovu*. Then in October 1925, he held a meeting with traditional leadership at eMahhashini Palace and announced that whites had to leave the Zulu empire forthwith. As Edward left for Pietermaritzburg, a near disaster took place and the Zulu would have been truly blamed. Edward and his entourage boarded his chartered train for Durban. But a few kilometres into the journey, the train lost control in the meandering Zulu landscape. The second last coach derailed and hung at a precariously dangerous angle that could have killed him if it had tilted over. Edward was unhurt, and he was more amused than bothered and assisted in the rescue effort. This is the same Edward that later became King Edward VIII of

England. He gave up the throne to marry the American divorcee Wallis Simpson, which left the English people aghast.

King Maphumuzana's lifestyle was mainly western and the Zulu nation watched with interest as his first wife was a Christian from iNhlazatshe. Queen Christina Ntombembi (*Khelethina*) okaMathathela Sibiya was a 15-year-old dark beauty who was a teacher in a missionary school. Maphumuzana courted her for a long time and used to send her many gifts such as a comb, a silk scarf and brooches. He was under the impression that she was an unsophisticated country girl and wanted to impress her and took her shopping at Denny Dalton's store in Babanango. He was surprised to find that she was quite smart and knew exactly what she wanted. She bought a coat with a matching hat plus some dress fabric. Their wedding was a mixture of both the Zulu custom and Christianity. For instance, they held hands during a Zulu wedding ceremony when they were not supposed to touch, under the Zulu custom. They partied late into the night at the eZibindini Palace and he gave her a cow as a wedding present. However, *okaMathathela* was under the impression that she would be the only wife because Maphumuzana was a Christian. They had four children such as Bhekuzulu Nyangayezizwe Cyprian, Princess Greta and others. But he had other ideas as he married between 30 and 70 other wives who were non-Christian (*amabhinca*) such as Queen Sokwenza kaMbulawa kaMnyamana Buthelezi, Malele kaSintwangu Cele and many others.

However, they all shared two traits - they were either from Zulu nobility or from families of great fighters that defended the empire with their lives. For instance, Malele's brother, Matshana Cele killed Magistrate TR Bennett during the 1906 poll tax revolt. Sokwenza's grandfather was King Cetshwayo's adviser. This came as a shock to *okaMathathela* and *okaMbulawa* did not make things easy for her. She felt that okaMathathela was below her rank therefore her son Prince Thandayiphi Absalom had a shot at the throne, even though he was not the firstborn son. Poor okaMathathela tried the life of being *esithenjini* (in a polygamous marriage) but she wanted a different life for herself and created a right royal scandal. She unceremoniously walked away from KwaDlamahlahla Palace and left her young children behind and went to live by herself in Durban. Then there were rumours that she had taken up paid employment as a domestic worker.

This was inconceivable of in the history of the Zulu empire, hence a royal search party made up of strong men went to look for her all over Durban. She was finally found on her knees scrubbing the floor of a poor white woman. When the search party recovered from the shock, they forced her to return to KwaDlamahlahla Palace with them. She realised that resistance was futile and went back with them. But after enduring a few months of scorn and ridicule at the palace, she ran away again. The king sued her for desertion in the white man's court, which ruled in his favour. She was then ordered to return to her husband. She reluctantly returned but absconded again but this time she made sure that she left for good. Despite the number of challenges, Maphumuzana remained a popular king fondly called *uMqwalajuba*. He encouraged his subjects to pursue education as a new weapon of resistance. He also preferred peaceful resolutions to disputes especially in succession battles. These were caused by the many 'chiefs' installed by the whites to cause anarchy. Maphumuzana managed to maintain fragile peace with Hhamu who had not given up on his ambition to sit on the Zulu throne. But when he realised that the royal family did not trust him because he fought on the side of the whites during iSandlwana, he created a personal fiefdom called *Ngenetsheni* named after his homestead. Many people were not happy with him as he forced his authority on people that had nothing to do with him. So, on the 4$^{th}$ of March 1933 Maphumuzana was invited to solve yet another Ngenetsheni problem at Khambi's homestead. But Emperor Maphumuzana Solomon Nkayishana kaDinuzulu collapsed during the discussions and never recovered. The cause of his death remains mysterious to this day. After the one-year mourning period, all his many wives with male children claimed that their son, was the heir. As the scramble for the throne was resolved, one of the king's brothers Mshiyeni (also born on St Helena Island) was made regent. As fate could have it, the temporary power went to his head.

He woke up one morning and single-handedly made elaborate plans to crown one of his nephews Prince Victor Phikokwaziyo Zulu at his Sokesimbone homestead. When everyone laughed at his audacity, he hunted for the next royal victim. His eyes fell on Thandayiphi David and together with his mother Queen okaMbulawa, made it clear to everyone that he was the chosen one. Moreover, okaMbulawa was born from a better pedigree than the Christian peasant whose family had no glorious military history. But Queen okaMathathela would have none of it. Since she no longer lived at the palace, she sent word to the royal family that her late husband had chosen Bhekuzulu as the heir. Obviously, no one believed her as she was regarded a renegade and years went by and there seemed to be no resolution in sight.

It was sheer drama on the 23$^{rd}$ of September 1944 when Prince Bhekuzulu led about 100 supporters to Native Commissioner's office, the Zulu referred to it as *KwaNdabazabantu* in KwaNongoma. He demanded to be enthroned but the white man refused. Then Bhekuzulu produced a school history book '*Izikhali Zanamuhla*' written by the respected Zulu historian, RRR Dhlomo which confirmed that he was the heir. Prince Mshiyeni was so desperate to continue with the enthronement of Prince Thandayiphi, that he issued an order withdrawing the book from circulation throughout the empire, including in schools. Equally desperate for justice, okaMathathela took the matter to the white's man court. This brazen act did not only capture the attention of the Zulu nation or South Africans but of the whole world. She produced a letter and claimed that it had been written by King Maphumuzana in 1933 when Prince Bhekuzulu was only nine years old. It read: *'I give this letter to you to be cared for and kept in your custody so that if I die before putting my house in order, you can reveal it so that everyone would know that my successor is Cyprian Bhekuzulu.' Signed by Maphumuzana.*

The court decided to engage handwriting experts to verify the handwriting and the letter was taken to Pretoria. On the day of the verdict, thousands of people as well as regiments turned up in court wearing their traditional gear. Defiant as ever, Queen okaMathathela strutted in late with an aura of invincibility. She sat on her own and nodded towards her son who was surrounded by his supporters across the aisle. People stared at her in disbelief and wondered where she found her strength from to challenge a huge institution like the Zulu royal family. The results confirmed that indeed, the handwriting belonged to Maphumuzana. Without going out of the court or waiting for the official announcement by the regent, the regiments inside the court turned towards Crown Prince Bhekuzulu and saluted *Bayethe*!

The official laudatory praise reciter recited King Shaka's laudatory praises. They left the court and it was a matter of time before the proper enthronement took place. Frustrated by the outcome of the court, Mshiyeni resigned with immediate effect leaving a leadership vacuum again in the empire again. Princess Mkabayi was long dead and gone and she was sorely missed for her age-old wisdom. The royal family then made Sifile Sibiya, a son to one of the Zulu princesses to be regent. It had taken five years to resolve the succession battle.

*Prince Mshiyeni kaDinuzulu made a dramatic entry into the world in St Helena Island on the eve of their departure to Zululand where his father Emperor Dinuzulu was incacerated. Mshiyeni became the regent and unsuccessfully tried to install his favourite Prince Victor Phikokwaziyo as the monarch at his Sokesimbone homestead instead of the Crown Prince Bhekuzulu kaMaphumuzana. (Killie Campbell Africana Library)*

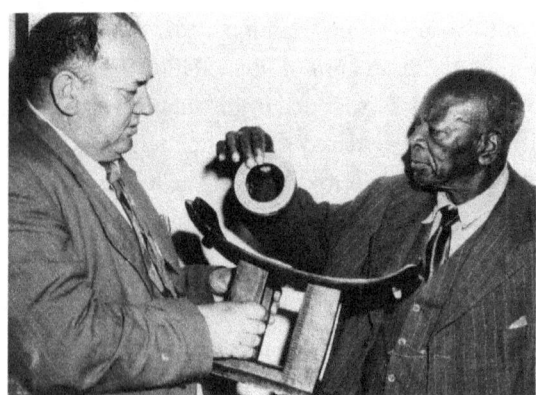

*Prince Victor Phikokwaziyo Zulu holding Emperor Shaka's ivory bracelet and shown Emperor Dinuzulu's headrest by a Natal government official. (Killie Campbell Africana Library)*

*Sifile Sibiya (centre) was made the regent after the death of Emperor Maphumuzana kaDinuzulu as there was a royal succession dispute. He is with his uncle Mpengula kaMaphumuzana (right) and an assistant (Killie Campbell Africana Library)*

# 13

# Emperor Bhekuzulu kaMaphumuzana

THERE WAS MUCH JOY at eNsindeni Palace in eNkonjeni the day Queen okaMathathela gave birth to Bhekuzulu on the 14$^{th}$ of August 1924. Zulu subjects rejoiced because the future monarch was once again born on Zulu soil, unlike his father King Maphumuzana who had been born in exile on St Helena Island. Crown Prince Bhekuzulu grew up in an environment where Western education and industrialisation were the order of the day. Access to their ancestral lands was already unknown to tens of thousands of the Zulu born outside the Zulu empire. Those still living in the kingdom, they were also mere one form or the other 'tenants'. By the time he ascended the throne in 1948, the Nationalist Party (NP) had been voted into power by a white only electorate which ushered in the Apartheid regime. The first Prime Minister under Apartheid regime was Rev DF Malan a racist demagogue who on any good day would whip up Afrikaner emotions with rhetoric.

For instance, he managed to snatch a seat General Smuts had held for 24 years in Standerton by the following theatrics. Whilst canvassing, Malan jumped on top of a table and asked the crowd three times: '*Op wat staan ek?*' (What am I standing on?). Three times they replied: '*Predikant staan op die tafel*' (The Preacher is standing on top of a table). He then said: '*Nee man sien julle nie, op wat staan ek? Lieve vader, van genade*' (No man, can't you see where I am standing? Dear Father of grace). Then he vigorously shook his head angrily and said: '*Ek staan op die kafirs se kop*' (I am standing on the head of a Kaffir – a derogatory term for an African). The frenzied crowd screamed: *Hoor! Hoor!* (Hear!Hear!) This was the beginning of trouble for the 24-year-old monarch as the NP government announced that it recognised him only as a '*Chief of uSuthu*' in undefined boundaries around KwaNongoma. The British had pulled a similar stunt on his grandfather King Dinuzulu but later when they needed his support, they rescinded it. His father Maphumuzana was at one point, not recognised as anything, neither a *chief* nor *inkosi* but that changed after the English royal visit. But this time, attempts to destroy, undermine or dilute the Zulu empire since the arrival of whites in the 1820s were finally looking like a real possibility. This announcement meant that only the Zulu living within the 'undefined' borders of a small area called *oSuthu* had a king - excluding millions of others. The shrunken size of the Zulu empire was one thing, but the young Crown Prince Bhekuzulu had to deal with something more vicious that had all the hallmarks of lasting forever – a social engineering system called Apartheid. This system was also negatively impacting on all Africans this time. However, times were changing in the empire as the Zulu were more vocal and demanded justice.

Deputations went to Pretoria on several occasions until the Pretoria government capitulated. A right royal affair was staged and thousands upon thousands of people attended the coronation ceremony of Crown Prince Bhekuzulu at eVuma Farm in Eshowe on the 12<sup>th</sup> of December 1951. The Pretoria government and all colonial powers henceforth recognised him as King of the Zulu nation, which extended beyond the geographical area of *oSuthu*. However, the government told him that he was not allowed to form the white man's worst nightmare, Zulu regiments. Like his forebears, King Bhekuzulu ignored their paranoia and within a year he formed uMkhuphulangwenya, uNqabakucasha and uKhiphinkunzi regiments. He also managed to finish what his father had started to build, King Shaka's somewhat diminutive monument in Stanger. The unfolding events in the Zulu empire did not go unnoticed in Pretoria, the capital of the Union of South Africa. So, after seven years of watching every move in the empire, the apartheid government engaged the Zulu empire.

The Minister of Native Affairs, Dr Hendrik Verwoerd, summoned Zulu leadership to a meeting in KwaNongoma. He had gone there to convince them to accept apartheid policies. This was because some laws such as the Bantu Authority Act of 1951 that governed Africans in the rest of South Africa, did not apply within the confines of what was left of the Zulu empire. In the blistering heat on the 6<sup>th</sup> of October 1955, a fuming Bhekuzulu sat with his equally enraged 300 traditional leaders. They passively listened to Verwoerd as he sugar-coated the idea of apartheid while subtly threatening them. He portrayed a rosy-coloured picture that it would allow the Zulu to run their own affairs, independent of Pretoria. The meeting was very tense, and negotiations swayed back and forth, as the Zulu are master negotiators. But it became clear that no progress was being made and they reached an impasse.

Then King Bhekuzulu used an old Zulu tactic to buy time and demanded more time to consider the 'glorious' apartheid plans. But Verwoerd refused and said that it was in fact, *fait accompli* and to conclude the matter he said without flinching: 'Do not throw honey at honey birds'. It was now obvious that Zulu reputation was no longer enough to terrorise anyone into submission. They were now negotiating from a position of weakness. Bhekuzulu had no regular income and his subjects were impoverished. He consulted with his subjects over a few months and most of them clearly refused to capitulate. However, after much serious soul-searching and pragmatism - he gave in. So, the abhorred *Tribal Authorities* were instituted in the rural parts of the kingdom. All 'surviving' ancestral lands were declared 'white areas or white farms'. Which meant that no Zulu or Africans for that matter could ever become a citizen of what they deemed to be 'a white area or a white farm'.

This was the precursor of the formation of the so-called *Bantustans* or *Homelands*. These were arid areas where Africans were forcefully moved to, once they became unemployed or became old. For example, a Kunene family had bought a very large farm *Boschhoek* near Glencoe from whites in 1870. But when the government discovered precious minerals in that area in 1968, it threw out its 5000 dwellers without compensation. Most of the people were appalled that the king had 'yielded' which made them 'foreigners' in the land of their forefathers. They strongly considered taking up arms against the Pretoria government and the king had no problem with that. Moreover, what was left of their empire had been fragmented into 250 portions spread over 29 separate pieces of land and not sharing borders. This is what made up the 'Kwa-Zulu Bantustan' and was ruled by commoners and people known as 'chiefs' appointed by the whites.

These 'chiefs' were imposed mainly on communities that were radically against the Tribal Authorities. Whereas the *amakhosi oselwa* (rightful kings) who refused to collaborate with the new system, were simply killed, deposed or exiled. The missionaries compounded matters and made their Christian converts elect their own 'chiefs' every five years on what they deemed to be 'missionary land'. One such prominent 'chief' was Albert Luthuli, Africa's first Nobel Peace Prize Laureate. He was born in Solusi Mission near Bulawayo, Zimbabwe, where his father was a missionary for the Seventh Day Adventist church. The African peasantry was at the coal face of apartheid oppression and they began an insurrection in 1957. The ANC and smaller black political parties were in the forefront of fighting the unjust laws. Some of the hotspots were in Thokazi, KwaNongoma; Ingquza, Mpondoland; Sekhukhune, Limpopo and Zeerust in the North West Province. These pockets of armed resistance were brutally suppressed by the government with a large loss of African life and many people were tortured, given long prison sentences or hanged. Some parts of the urban areas also went up in flames such as in the middle-class township of Dube, Soweto, where over 50 people were killed.

The atrocities against Africans made David Pratt, a white man, attempt to kill Verwoerd, who was the Prime Minister in 1960. He shot him twice with a 0.22 automatic pistol in the face at the Rand Easter Show, but Verwoerd miraculously survived. After his arrest, Pratt killed himself by tying two bed sheets to his bedposts and calmly inserted his head in between the sheets and became an instant gymnast. He miraculously somersaulted repeatedly until he succeeded in strangling himself to death. Dimitri Tsafendas finally succeeded in stabbing Verwoerd to death in Parliament in 1966. Dimitri was of mixed-race descent; his father Michaelis was Greek and his mother Emelia Williams was his 17-year-old domestic worker from eSwatini when she gave birth to him in 1918.

King Bhekuzulu succeeded in juggling his people's traditional needs with evolving modern politics. He managed to have a normal life and was the first Zulu king to be married in a Christian church. He married Queen Joyce Thoko Jali; Queen uMaZungu (*uMaGwabini*), they had three sons; Queen uMaNdebele, they had a son; Queen Priscilla Masuku, they had two daughters, the late Princess Royal Nonhlanhla, and Princess Thembi. The current monarch His Majesty King Zwelithini was born to the late fair-skinned Queen Thomozile Jezangani kaThayisa Ndwandwe. Princess Thembi said her father loved nothing more than to hear his children sing. She recalled the singing sessions as we sat in her house in Newcastle with fond memories: 'We used to look forward to our father's visits at KwaKhethomthandayo Palace where we lived because as a king, our father lived in a number of palaces. Whenever we heard his car pull up, we would rush to him and stand in line ready to sing for him. Even when we were at boarding school, we made sure that we learnt new songs so that we could impress him when we got home. He even made us sing solo which was really good fun. But when it came to singing solo, as far as we were concerned, the king was a disaster. He only wanted to sing the hymn *Silent Night*.

But in all fairness, he sang it extremely well, but we wanted him to sing other songs as well. He would merely laugh at our frustration and continue to sing his 'song' with his eyes closed *Silent Night, Holy Night...* What we could not reconcile though, was his image as a tough crown prince and his singing of *Silent Night* with so much gusto.' Emperor Bhekuzulu Cyprian *Bhusha kanayifi* Nyangayezizwe kaMaphumuzana finally succumbed to diabetes at Benedictine Hospital, KwaNongoma, on the 17th of September 1968. He was only 44 years old. His paternal brother Prince Mcwayizeni Israel kaMaphumuzana was appointed regent at his Nxangiphilile homestead, because the Crown Prince Zwelithini was too young to rule.

## Emperor Bhekuzulu kaMaphumuzana

*Emperor Bhekuzulu Nyangayezizwe kaMaphumzana kaDinuzulu with his favourite horse. He was crowned on 12 December 1951 after his mother, Queen Christina okaMathathela Sibiya proved in court that he was the rightful heir.*

# 14

# Emperor King Zwelithini kaBhekuzulu

HIS MAJESTY KING ZWELITHINI was born three months after apartheid came into in force. Therefore, his whole life experience was shaped by living both as a black man and as a Zulu monarch in a racist environment. The king's birth was prophesied by a stranger from Johannesburg, long before Queen Mother *okaThayisa* was pregnant. The stranger told the royal family that if they wanted the king to live for a long time, he had to be delivered into a white calico fabric and not breast fed by his biological mother. The stranger also said that he had to be raised by his grandfather's wife Queen uMaMtshali. All these instructions were followed and to date, he has been the longest serving monarch in Zulu history.

He grew up in a modernised world but his was an ordinary Zulu rural life. He herded livestock in the adulating fields, rode horses, swam in fast-flowing rivers, dived into deep waterfalls, trapped small animals and took part in *ijadu* (matchmaking festivals). Even though he was particularly good at stick fighting, his number one love was soccer. He was a talented striker who bedazzled with his fancy footwork. Whenever he touched the ball, his fans, especially the girls, would go berserk. They would scream: '*One, One*' which was the number emblazoned on his soccer jersey. Girls could not help being enamoured with him, because he was a very handsome young man. His closest relatives call him *Mbongi*, a name given to him by his late paternal sister Princess Nonhlanhla. This was keeping to the natural order of things as all other kings had *amagama obunsizwa* (a name given by one's peers).

King Senzangakhona was called *uQegwa*, Emperor King Shaka was *iLembe* or *uNodumehlezi*, Emperor King Emperor King Dingane was *uNjunju*, Emperor King Mpande was *uKhonzaphi*, Cetshwayo was *uJinindi omnyama* or *Magwegwana*, Emperor King Dinuzulu was *uMamonga*, Emperor King Maphumuzana was *uMqwalajuba* and Emperor King Bhekuzulu was *uBusha*. King Zwelithini king grew up in a large royal family which consisted of paternal and maternal brothers, sisters, aunts, uncles, cousins and grandparents. There were also *umhlalandlini, imidlunkulu, udibi*, queens, queen mothers, advisers, aides, king's representatives, helpers, healers, midwives, regiments, *izinyosi*, the king's council, military advisers, attendants, widows and orphans. All these people make up the occupants of a single palace and strict protocol for everyone living or working at the palaces is observed. For instance, all members of the royal family except for the king are addressed as *Mageba, Sithuli sikaNdaba* or *Ndabezitha* as a sign of reverence. The king is addressed in numerous ways only applicable to him such as *iSilo, iMbube, uBayethe, iNgonyama, uHlanga lomhlabathi, uNgangezwe lakhe, uNgasitha* and many more. The females in the royal realm also use the *hlonipha* genre to emphasise their feminity. Non-royals residing or working in the palaces are addressed in their appropriate totems. For instance, as my family name is Mbatha, I am referred to as *uMaShandu, uMthiya, uManyosi, uSontshikazi* and off course *Ndabezitha* as well.

History always has a way of repeating itself. Like some of his forefathers, the king's life has been infused with intrigue, treachery and a whiff of scandal. Even though there was no confusion about him being the heir, life still dealt him a lousy card. For him to successfully ascend the throne, he had to stay one step ahead of his royal detractors. This was despite the vicious, dark apartheid cloud that was continuously hovering above every black person's psyche. Tragedy struck, early when the king lost both his mother Queen *okaThayisa* and his other mother Queen *okaMasuku*, whom he was very close to, within a short space of time. He therefore lived an emotionally lonely childhood. But his life began to unfold when he was at KwaBhekuzulu College. This is where his late paternal sister Princess Nonhlanhla, helped him take his future into his young royal hands. She managed to spring him from the college after she uncovered a plot to kill him during a 'hunting' trip.

She took him to her house in the Mpumalanga Province and he lived with her family because she was married to Simon Sikhosana, the first Chief Minister of KwaNdebele Bantustan. But when the news broke that Nonhlanhla had taken the heir to exile, a furore bordering on a revolt erupted within the royal circles. The Zulu nation was confused about the royal shenanigans that they were not privy to. Once again, the royal family was split into two - some did not support Nonhlanhla's actions while others commended her. As arguments were raging, life seemed to be passing by at a rapid rate for the serene heir, as he laboured under an assumed name in some KwaNdebele rural store. He called himself Percival Dlamini from Swaziland; he even tried to speak Siswati. But as time wore on, the nation became impatient with the absence of the crown prince. Moreover, they had not been given an official explanation. Even worse, he had no offspring. Against the backdrop of the Zulu intrigue and conspiracy theories, Africans were in a state of low intensity insurrection against apartheid all over South Africa. This made it imperative for Crown Prince Zwelithini to ascend the throne as a matter of urgency. The Zulu nation needed assurance that when apartheid was overcome, they would still be a nation. It also became clear that the crown prince needed to find a wife and fast.

Indeed a few weeks later, Nonhlanhla and Sikhosana picked up Crown Prince Zwelithini from where he was hiding and working, and they left for the kingdom in the middle of the night. Their first stop was his girlfriend Buhle Mathe's boarding school in Amanzimtoti. They had an urgent request in mind, but she could not oblige because she was in the middle of writing exams. But perhaps, there is some wisdom in having more than one girlfriend at a time. They then sped off to Ivungu High School, KwaCeza, where another girlfriend Sibongile Dlamini was also writing exams. But after being disappointed the first time, the three conspirators had to change tact. They decided that Sibongile would be 'convinced' to marry Zwelithini through guerrilla tactics. Once Sibongile was lured into the car, she was made to sit between Princess Nonhlanhla and Sikhosana, with the crown prince driving despite not having a driver's licence. Sikhosana was comfortably snoring in the back seat because of what he had imbibed along the way to calm his nerves. They sped away from the school with an unsuspecting Sibongile in the middle of the night. By the time it dawned on her that she was eloping, she cried bitterly. She begged them to let her finish her schooling first.

But the Crown Prince gently explained to her in his ever-calm voice that while she was making a valid request it was a selfish one. He explained to her that the survival of the House of Senzangakhona rested on her shoulders. Moreover, her cooperation would be highly appreciated by the whole queenless Zulu nation. Poor Sibongile found herself in a similar predicament like Mthaniya and Mahambogwini in the past. As the crown prince was convincing her to co-operate on an offer no girl would easily pass, they were looking for a place where they could buy her cosmetics and some personal stuff. She had left school with nothing. Princess Sibongile realised that resistance was futile. Moreover, all things considered, an opportunity to marry a future king and be the first queen usually comes once in a girl's lifetime, if at all. She was not going to let this one pass by, and stopped crying. The royal siblings exchanged glances and thanked their ancestors. Despite several royal hurdles and sabotage by the internal palace politics, Sibongile's *ilobolo* and wedding were fast-tracked.

In record time lucky Sibongile and Crown Prince Zwelithini were married. Once those ceremonies were out of the way, preparations for the coronation began in earnest. More tension ensued in the palace corridors as some royal family members felt that the Prince regent Mcwayizeni was doing a great job. He also thought so and saw reason to step down. He therefore resisted holding any formal discussion about his stepping down, whereas others were even suggesting that a commoner should be made king. The debate raged on even in the newspapers. After many false starts, a royal family meeting was eventually convened.

The crown prince had to face off with Prince Mcwayizeni and demand what was rightfully his, tense as it was. He summoned all the courage his youth could muster, knowing that his greatest supporter, Princess Nonhlanhla, was in his corner. When the meeting started, the crown prince politely asked to speak first. He turned to Mcwayizeni and respectfully asked for the keys of KwaKhetha, the car and his father's overcoat and permission to be allowed to access the cattle enclosure. Dead silence followed. His request was a polite Zulu way of wanting to ascend the throne. Prince Mcwayizeni and his supporters were stunned by such audacity. They were under the impression that the meeting was to discuss general royal issues. But when they realised that the crown prince wasn't bluffing, the regent capitulated in shock. The crown prince had to move fast because he heard that Prince Mcwayizeni had identified an 18-month-old prince as the new 'rightful' heir.

Preparations reached fever pitch and the Zulu nation was looking forward to the coronation. But the actual date of the enthronement became a moving target because of royal squabbling and sabotage. Other pretenders to the throne used politics to frustrate the young crown prince and started a Coronation Trust Fund in August 1971. The nation was asked to donate money for the ceremony. The fund was riddled with so many problems that in the end it could not be used, but the Zulu nation never stopped donating money and patiently waited for the coronation date. On the other hand, the white government was in a conundrum because the apartheid system did not have a plan to deal with a 'new Zulu Emperor'. They did not have a ready response should Zwelithini want to renegotiate all his father's agreements with them.

The big day finally came on an uncharacteristically cold, wet and misty day on the 3rd of December 1971. Thousands of happy people dressed in their colourful traditional attire as well as well-wishers poured in from all over the country and from many parts of the world. The venue was the newly-built KwaKhetha amphitheatre. The thrilled crowds arrived on foot, carts, trucks, donkeys, horses, motorbikes, cars, buses, trains, private aeroplanes and helicopters. Zulu virgins pranced about bare-breasted and the regiments looked splendid in their military uniforms. Crown Prince Zwelithini, was a mere 23-year-old as he stood to attention in a black suit with a leopard sash in front of his people. The awkward Minister of Bantu Administration and Development MC (*indlovu elinebatha*) Botha, presented Zwelithini with a 'Letter of Appointment'. Hundreds of regiments performed *ingomane* and shouted *Sigidi*. Then the assembled Zulu nation got to their feet and in unison saluted *Bayethe!* The ancient mountains and valleys of KwaNongoma came alive.

Emperor King Zwelithini kaBhekuzulu was the seventh to be crowned after King Shaka created the Zulu empire. Over 1500 cattle, 6000 goats, thousands of chickens and 50 impala were slaughtered. There were rivers of traditional beer, mountains of *ujeqe* (Zulu corn bread) and hillocks of vegetables. It was indeed a right royal joyous affair. The king received many gifts from his subjects, South Africans and from all over the world. But the gift that stole the show was a snow-white stallion. The rationale behind Emperor King Zwelithini's 'Letter of Appointment' was only known by the white government. It is laughable that at some point they had even organised a fake golden *isicoco* that was to be placed on the king as his crown. Zulu coronations had surely come a long way as King Shaka had been enthroned by Ngomane; King Dingane was enthroned by Mkabayi; King Mpande was enthroned by the joint king's council and military high command; Theophilus Shepstone enthroned Cetshwayo with a fake golden crown; General Botha had enthroned Dinuzulu with a few drops of castor oil on the head; King Maphumuzana was crowned by Mankulumana Ndwandwe; King Bhekuzulu was crowned by the royal family and now King Zwelithini was enthroned with a 'Letter of Appointment' by the Apartheid government. Perhaps, it was sending a clear message to the king that he could be 'fired' or 'retrenched' from his reign at any time, if he defied Apartheid laws. It was obviously wishful thinking because Emperor King Zwelithini outlasted the Apartheid regime as he is still on the throne. The 'Letter of Appointment' should be kept as the last vicissitude of white oppression on the Zulu nation.

After the coronation, the politics of the day throughout South Africa concentrated on getting the universal franchise. This was the panacea for all political woes. The question on every Zulu's mind was whether the young monarch would prevail. The pressure on traditional leadership and affairs did not only come from the apartheid government but also from the large population of powerful and influential urbanised Africans. These were the over five million Zulu living in Diaspora, outside the borders of the Zulu empire but within South Africa. This started when Zulu men were forced to go and work in the gold mines in Gauteng, mainly leaving their families behind.

They then over time created new families that had no affinity with Zulu rural life. To make life bearable in the depressing, degrading, debasing and inhumane hostels in Gauteng, the Zulu developed a new music and dance genre called *isicathamiya* and *umngxobanyawo*. This very popular style of music could be associated with acappela music with the soft tapping of the floor. The famous Ladysmith Black Mambazo exposed it to the rest of the world.

King Zwelithini became part the revolution because his subjects were being maimed and killed every day. He became closely associated with the formation of a now defunct political party called *Inala Party*. However, his active involvement in politics was banned by the KwaZulu Bantustan government. This was an outrage because the Zulu monarchy had always been active in modern party politics. For instance, King Dinuzulu was the first Honorary President of the ANC in 1912. His son King Maphumuzana formed the *iNkatha yakwaZulu Political Party* in 1923. Yet, Zwelithini was expected to be a passive constitutional monarch. The KwaZulu Legislature tried to convince him that being a constitutional monarch would maintain the royal mystique, but Zwelithini had a differing opinion. He continued speaking out against injustices from Pretoria and their collaborators. The Legislature was so enraged by his forthrightness that they forced him to take the following oath: 'I, Zwelithini Goodwill kaBhekuzulu presently iNgonyama of the Zulu, pledge to the KwaZulu Legislature Assembly here present and to the Zulu nation my solemn word that I withhold myself from any participation in any form of politics and from any actions or words which may possibly be interpreted as participation in politics. I pledge further that I will honour in thought, word or deed the letter and spirit of the Constitution of the KwaZulu Government.'

After the king was forced to take the oath, he practically stayed away from the Legislature. But he continued making public political statements denouncing apartheid. There was even a rumour that he had requested the Mozambican liberation movement (FREELIMO) to assist all Africans. This rumour was the last straw for the uLundi politicians as they then banned the king from leaving KwaNongoma area without the approval of the KwaZulu government. This was catastrophic because never in the history of the Zulu had subjects restricted their king from going where he pleased. As if that was not bad enough, he was further forbidden to give media interviews without the approval and presence of the KwaZulu Minister of Justice. Furthermore, a Judicial Commission of Inquiry was set up not only to consider the king's alleged utterances but also to investigate his refusal to attend the very Assembly that he was supposed to head. He was summoned to the Commission to defend himself. However, instead of answering the questions they put to him, he calmly reminded them about the pledge they forced him to sign was to 'not to participate or comment on political matters'. He then refused to answer any further questions, as they were indeed political in nature. There was uproar in the Legislature and members were so angry with him that they swiftly recommended that his already paltry salary be reduced to R100 per month.

Soon thereafter, the king stood up, jumped over the benches and went into the men's bathroom. From there he climbed through the window and escaped to KwaKhangela leaving everyone at the Legislature dumbstruck. The commission was aborted, and both his dignity and his previous salary were restored. It was a painful experience for the king to have to answer to his subjects outside the long tried and tested traditional systems. This scandal that made all the Zulu that were self-respecting hang their heads in shame. Under normal circumstances, these tactics were a specialty of colonisers. For a while, it looked like the king was going to be left alone and allowed to salvage what was left of the ego of the Zulu nation. As white oppression mounted against the resisting Africans, the United Nations declared Apartheid a crime against humanity in 1973. The international boycott of South African products and general sanctions were beginning to negatively impact the economy in a big way. Therefore, the apartheid regime needed all the allies possible, as international pressure was mounting and fast becoming unbearable.

Without any warning, in 1977 the Prime Minister BJ Vorster reminded the Swazi government that the British still owed them land for the 10 000 soldiers they provided for the war against King Sekhukhune of the Bapedi nation. Then Vorster offered them the land along the northern border in iNgwavuma. The Swazi government welcomed the unexpected good fortune. But both Vorster and the Swazi government were shocked by the reaction of the Swazi and the Zulu who lived in iNgwavuma. All right-thinking South Africans also weighed in on the matter and it created another unwelcome uproar internationally. The Vorster administration had obviously misread public opinion and hoped to gain new friends especially the British government by their 'magnanimous gesture'. They misinterpreted what was happening to King Zwelithini in uLundi. They had thought that they could get away with giving away Zulu territory without any resistance from the Zulu nation.

Vorster was shocked when the, apparently, 'disbanded' Zulu regiments were mobilised in the kingdom as well as in hostels in today's Gauteng. The regiments made speeches and said they were prepared to die defending every centimetre of what was left of their Zulu empire. Many people moved north towards the Swazi border and lived in the forests and caves and discussed the war strategy. They also sang war songs, danced war dances and drank *intelezi* (war medicine). The women also went into a war footing and moved large amounts of food, livestock and valuables into caves of uBombo Mountains, just like it was done during King Shaka's empire building wars. They covered their faces with special herbs, wore their leather skirts inside out, while grass mats and brooms and other household items were kept upright. The regiments were ready to take the Swazi head on. After all, they had last fought a good war in the heart of the Nkandla forest during the poll tax revolt in 1906. To cover up the public relations disaster, Vorster's government began a smear campaign against the king. They claimed that it was his idea to cede the land. They claimed that he had been 'overwhelmed' by the love of Queen Mantfombi kaSobhuza II (she is a princess from eSwatini) and wanted to give that land to his in-laws. In disbelief, the king called an urgent *imbizo* in KwaNongoma to defend himself against the monstrous allegations.

After listening to his side of the story, no one objected. They told him that they believed him and confirmed their full allegiance to him. They agreed that what was left of the Zulu empire was to be safeguarded by any means necessary and they all roared *Bayethe!* The matter was put to rest and celebrations began with song and dance. Regiments were instructed to stand down, the women folk came out of the caves and forests. The Zulu nation exhaled, so did the rest of South Africa. The king had survived yet another day with his dignity intact. However, before he knew it, he had to fight for his survival against the backdrop of apartheid's *Third Force* instigated civil war in the empire. The two biggest political parties the ANC and the Zulu based Inkatha Freedom Party (*IFP*) which had been formed in 1975, were slaughtering each other for political supremacy. This savagery also took place in the Zulu empire as well as in Gauteng, where even non-Zulus died.

Emperor King Zwelithini kaBhekuzulu

*Emperor Zwelithini kaBhekuzulu on his coronation day at KwaKhethomthandayo Palace holding a 'Letter of Appointment' given to him by the Apartheid government. (Killie Campbell Africana Library)*

**The Soweto Student Uprising in 1976**

The residential area called Soweto was established in 1944 as an African dormitory for the City of Johannesburg where Africans were not allowed to live as per the laws of apartheid. This came about because poor whites pressured the Johannesburg Municipality to remove Africans from suburbs close to the city centre. The Africans lived in areas such as Sophiatown, Martindale, Newclare and Alexandra Township but many of these areas were declared white only areas and were subject to forced removals. But the Africans fought the forced removals. Zulu activists such as James Sofasonke, born near Durban, were in the forefront of resistance. It is estimated that between 1960 and 1980 over 5 million Africans were moved from one part of the country to another against their will. This was to create room for white people to live wherever they pleased.

Revolutionaries all over South Africa, especially in Gauteng, never stopped plotting the overthrow of apartheid albeit working underground. Hence when Voster's government passed a law that made Afrikaans the compulsory language of instruction for all subjects for African students, it was the beginning of the end of apartheid domination in South Africa. Students from Soweto revolted, and it culminated in a protest march on the 16$^{th}$ of June 1976. The government responded by firing at least 16 000 rounds of ammunition at the students on that day alone. Hundreds of students were killed and thousands more were injured in the months that followed. The events of the day were captured by iconic picture of the lifeless body of Hector Pieterson. He was carried by Mbuyisa Makhubu, who currently lives in Toronto, Canada. The picture was flashed across the world and the whole country became ungovernable.

Again, the urbanised Zulu were in the forefront of the Soweto Uprising. For example, Paul Langa from the Zulu royal family was the commander of the *Suicide Squad* of the Soweto Students Representative Council. After heroic acts of sabotage, he was caught and sentenced to death but after the intervention of the international community, his sentence was commuted to life and he served it in Robben Island prison. He served his sentence with three of the country's former presidents - Nelson Mandela, Kgalema Montlante and Jacob Zuma.

Another young Zulu fighter who made international headlines was Andrew Sibusiso Zondo from KwaMashu, Durban. He was a member of uMkhonto weSizwe and the ANC instructed him to bomb Amanzimtoti Shopping Centre, south of

Durban. He managed to kill numerous whites and the 18-year-old was caught. After a brief trial, he was sentenced to death in 1985 by the notorious hanging judge, Justice Ramon Leon (the father of Ambassador Tony Leon, former leader of the Democratic Alliance Party, Democratic Alliance). However, the resistance movement was also joined by liberal Indians, mixed-race descendants and a few whites. The fearlessness of the Zulu can also be seen through Robert *Pepe* McBride, a Zulu of mixed-race descent, who joined the *uMkhonto weSizwe* and carried out spectacular guerrilla missions around the country. He managed to kill the highest number of the white police in high command and some civilians in Durban. However, his greatest act of bravery, last seen in the days of King Shaka, was the springing of one of his comrades Gordon Webster under heavy fire from Edendale Hospital, Pietermaritzburg, in broad daylight.

Apartheid finally tethered towards its demise in 1990 and all political parties were unbanned, and some political prisoners were freed. Then a national conference *Constitutional Issues in a New South Africa* was organised in October 1990. All races were invited and one of the burning questions was the future of traditional leadership. By then, King Zwelithini had lived an unenviable life as a monarch under siege while his subjects living under traditional leadership expected miracles from him. The Zulu empire played a critical role the following year when over 92 organisations formed the *Patriotic Front* in Durban. This was the precursor to the Convention for a Democratic South Africa (*CODESA*). On the other hand, some supporters of the then ruling National Party were suspicious of CODESA and as a result a white only referendum was held about it. Remarkably, the results endorsed the participation of whites in CODESA. Similarly, many Zulu people living under traditional leadership in the empire were suspicious of the ANC because of its stance on traditional leadership. The ANC's stance was that institutions of 'hereditary rulers' and 'chiefs' shall be transformed to conform to democratic principles embodied in the Constitution. It was only after the formation of the Congress of Traditional Leaders in South Africa (*CONTRALESA*), that there was some level of détente between the two.

As the discussions were raging, the IFP withdrew in protest of the exclusion of the representatives of the Zulu royal family and the KwaZulu Bantustan. The king demanded a special status because the Zulu had defeated the British, a world power at iSandlwana. As well as the fact that the Zulu had fought the last conventional war against oppression in Nkandla in the 1906 Poll Tax Revolt. But his demands were dismissed with contempt. Once again, the Zulu empire's future was at stake, but this time Princess Mkabayi was a distant memory and it was critical that the king seized the moment. After careful consideration, he woke up one morning and put on his military attire. He walked slowly into the KwaZulu Legislature with his regiments in tow. The assembly watched in awe as he only wore the military gear at special occasions. Without mincing his words, he declared that the Zulu empire would seek to secede from the Republic of South Africa and revert to King Shaka's borders, by any means necessary. That announcement made international headlines and the Zulu recieved attention they wanted at CODESA. Negotiations on the future status of the Zulu monarchy were reopened and then the Zulu perspective was considered on all matters from then on.

The king's threat was so real that even President FW de Klerk asked to meet with him. The king turned up with over 50 000 chanting Zulu men and women dressed in traditional gear in Durban. The next meeting was held in Pretoria and both cities came to a standstill when the 'belligerent' Zulu marched through the city centers. The Pretoria meeting took place at the Union Buildings and for a day its magnificent gardens belonged to thousands of Zulu regiments. But even after that show of force, it became obvious that the pendulum of history had permanently swung the other way. It was clear that getting the land back through *impi ebomvu* was not going to happen, at least at that time. But they were comforted by the fact that the Zulu *inkani* (will power) had prevailed. However, the king managed to convince the ANC to promote the dignity of the position of the Zulu king and of the Zulu royal household in the new South Africa. The ANC also further promised to recognise the Zulu Emperor as a king with Constitutional powers, prerogatives, rights and obligations. The Zulu Emperor shall be enthroned in such a manner as may be agreeable with him, which may include a coronation by the Chief Justice of the country.

The king's popularity soared to even greater heights among his subjects because he had proven the Zulu *inkani* was still potent. It also meant that when it came to the art of negotiation, the Zulu were better than the rest. No other king in South Africa was afforded the special privileges such as the Zulu monarch enjoyed. The trials and tribulations as well as the constant humiliation the king endured under the KwaZulu Legislature were now a faraway nightmare. Emperor King Zwelithini will go down in history as having safeguarded the land of his forefathers in the new dispensation.

Despite the success of the exclusive recognition, the thorny issue of land ownership was still not resolved. Again, the king went to the KwaZulu Legislature and raised the land ownership matter. Then a miracle happened a mere two days before the first democratic elections. The KwaZulu Legislature passed the incredible Ingonyama Trust Land Act of 1994, which granted the Zulu king 90 per cent of the KwaZulu-Natal province for his subjects, into perpetuity. Without spilling a single drop of Zulu blood, the king achieved constitutional guaranteed land ownership.

The first democratic elections were finally held on the 27$^{th}$ of April 1994 and the ANC won by a landslide. Nelson Mandela became the first African president of the Republic of South Africa. It was a fitting honour for the first commander-in-chief of MK whose purpose was formed to kill and maim whites for apartheid atrocities in 1960. From 1994 onwards, the Zulu monarchy asserted its presence in the new South African political landscape. Today, the king is the custodian of Zulu traditions and customs and has revived ancient customs that defined the Zulu nation from pre-Shakan times. The most recent was the reintroduction of *ukusoka* (male circumcision) done in hygienic settings (hospitals and clinics). Another custom he revived was the annual colourful virgins only *umkhosi womhlanga* (reed dance) held over two days in September which according to the Provincial Department of Arts and Culture has become the main tourist attraction in the province. The annual *umkhosi wokweshwama* (first fruit ceremony) held in December includes the killing of a black bull by young men with their bare hands.

The process starts early in the morning before sunrise when the cattle are released from the cattle closure. Then the bull gets isolated and the bravest young man wrestles it to the ground, whilst the rest pummel it with their bare fists until it dies. After killing it, the young men are formed into a regiment. This death-defying act caused a big controversy and was subject to a lawsuit in November 2009. Opponents alleged that the method of killing the animal was cruel and barbaric. But the case was thrown out of court by Judge Nic van der Reyden who said that to tell the Zulu people not to slaughter a bull at the first fruits festival, would be tantamount to telling Catholics not to take communion. To date the king has formed the following regiments, uDakwayikusutha, uCijimpi, uKhandempevu, iNala, iziNyosi, iZichwe, iziNyosi and uThulilwezichwe just to name a few.

The king is passionate about the welfare of his subjects and often travels abroad to garner support for his charities such as the *Bayethe Foundation*. He also takes care of the indigent living in South Africa or Zulu descendants abroad or those living in the Diaspora. Several universities have conferred Honorary Doctorates on him, both locally and abroad for his leadership and charity work. The king is the only Zulu monarch to rule for more than four decades and has outlived all his predecessors. Today, the king lives in KwaNongoma with Queen Sibongile Dlamini at KwaKhetha Palace; Princess Queen Mantfombi Dlamini at KwaKhangelamankengane Palace; Queen Buhle Mathe at KwaDlamahlahla Place; Queen Thandekile Ndlovu at KwaLinduzulu Palace; Queen Nompumelelo Mchiza at eNyokeni Palace and Queen Zola Mafu at uLundi Palace. His extended family as well as his children and grandchildren also live at the various palaces.

On the 7$^{th}$ of June 2016, the king made a far-reaching announcement that he was going to grant title deeds to people currently occupying land owned by Ingonyama Trust. He said that since the Trust had been established to administer the land traditionally owned by the king for the benefit, material welfare and social well-being of the Zulu nation, it therefore, made sense to embark on that process that would empower the residents and guarantee economic development for rural areas. King Zwelithin's fiercest face-off with the democratic government came when there were mooted moves to repeal the Ingonyama Trust Act, which had made him the custodian of the land on behalf of his subjects. The king deemed this attempt to be at the same gigantic proportion as the provocation that led to the thorough defeat and humiliation of the British by the Zulu army in 1879 at the iSandlwana Battle. Hence the monarch called the Zulu nation to uLundi on the 4$^{th}$ of July 2018 under the banner of *Imbizo kaZulu* (the clarion call of the Zulu nation) - the strongest show of force in recent times.

The imbizo coincided with the anniversary of the uLundi Palace being razed to the ground by the British – a war crime. King Zwelithini kaBhekuzulu, the only Zulu monarch who has never sent *amabutho* (regiments) to battle, reminded his detractors amongst other things that, *ngiphuma emasendeni ensizwa eyaba isiqhwaga, ngoba yashaya isiqhwaga sombuso wamaNgisi*, (I am a descendant of a fierce Zulu warrior who stood up to the British empire). The tens of thousands that descended in uLundi including Zulu regiments in full war regalia, women also in war regalia, members of uMkhonto weSizwe in uniform, the youth, *izinduna* (king's representatives) from migrant labour hostels across South Africa, well-wishers as well as representatives of kingdoms from around the African continent all eagerly awaited the king to give *umhlahlandlela* (the way forward). The huge crowd hung on to every word of as he lamented that this was one of the many attempts to dispossess the Zulu of their land. Moreover, it was only about a third in size of what the Zulu Empire was originally.

He however, called for peace and further engagement. When the people were given an opportunity to speak, regiments, like in the days of old, announced that they were ready to lay down their lives in defence of the little land they had left. One of the women took to the podium and let it be known that the women *bazoqhubeka ukuvikela umhlaba nangamasikela imbala* (were forever prepared to protect the land with everything at their disposal, including using sickles). After the show of force which was on a weekday, the national government made an about-turn on the move. South African President Cyril Ramaphosa had to go to the land of the Zulu nation and meet the king in a small seaside town of Richards Bay and make amends in person to allay the king's fears.

## Emperor Zwelithini kaBhekuzulu Laudatory Praises

| | |
|---|---|
| *Indlondlo enophaphe ekhanda kaMenzi* | Viper with a feather on the head, son of Menzi |
| *Ndaba kawulalele lomuntu omemezayo* | Ndaba, listen to the person who is screaming |
| *Umemeza ngathi uyakhala, ukhala isililo* | it is as though that person is crying, wailing |
| *Uthi igula likaJama lichithekile* | saying contents in Jama's gourd are exposed |
| *Lichithwa yingqwele endala* | they were exposed by the expert stick fighter |
| *Ngeyakithi kwaMalandela* | who is one of us, in the land of Malandela |
| *Ubesibindi Buthelezi* | you were brave Buthelezi |
| *Ngokukhuthazela umtakaNdaba* | to have supported the descendant of Ndaba |
| *Bemthuka bemcokofula* | when they insulted and humiliated him |
| *Bethi uZwelithini kayikubusa* | and they said Zwelithini will never rule |
| *Bethi kakubayinkosi* | they said he will never be king |
| *Kanti bamgcoba ngamafutha emphepho* | whereas they anointed him with royal oil |
| *Yakithi kwaMalandela* | he is one of us, in the land of Malandela |
| *USodidase* | Great Confuser |
| *Inkonyane encane kaNdaba edida imibala* | Ndaba's small camouflaged calf |
| *Umphikeleli wensizwa* | the pursuer of young men |
| *Ngoba ephikelela amadoda akwaZulu* | because they were from KwaZulu |
| *Esephelelwe ngamandla* | and they had run out of steam |
| *UMaphokophela longayi, insizwa eyisinikinikana* | Determined one, with many difficulties |
| *Ogijime ngandlelande, ngalo uvivi* | who ran a long distance at dawn |
| *Eyakwadadewabo uNonhlanhla* | and went to his sister Nonhlanhla |
| *Owayegane emaNdebeleni* | who was married to the Ndebele nation |
| *Nani maNdebele seniyoguga nidelile* | you, the Ndebele nation, will get old happy |
| *Enike nabona izinyane* | that you saw the cub that belongs |
| *NgeleSilo likaNdaba* | to His Majesty King Ndaba |
| *Ohlamba izandla ngamakhanda amadoda* | who wiped his hands on men's heads |
| *Wathi yiwona ayomhlabanela* | and said that they will fight for him |
| *Shintsha, washintsha ibhulakifesi* | change your ways, you changed breakfast |
| *Walenza idina* | and made it your dinner |
| *Kuye kwagcwala izifunda zemifula* | there were floods in valleys and rivers |
| *Esinye ngesoMkhuze esinye ngesoThukela* | they flooded uMkhuze and uThukela valleys |
| *Gijimani ngezindlela zonkana* | run and inform everyone you meet |
| *Niyobikela abangakezwa* | and tell those who haven't yet heard |
| *Nithi lukhulu luyeza luyanyelela* | tell them that something big is slowly coming |
| *Silufanisa neNdlovu emnyama yasoNdini* | it looks like the great elephant from uLundi |
| *Izoshisa izikhotha ngezakwaNongoma* | it is going to burn the KwaNongoma valleys |
| *INkonyane encane kaNdaba* | Ndaba's small calf |
| *Ekhwele phezu kwendlu Emgazini* | that ascended to the roof of eMgazini Palace |
| *Bathi oyise noyisemkhulu* | his male relatives remarked and said: |
| *Hhawu!!* | Oh no! |
| *Ngasitha, Ndaba* | Your Royal Highness, descendant of Ndaba |
| *Usuyahlola* | you will cause bad luck |
| *Kanti yibona abahlolayo* | whereas it was them who will cause bad luck |
| *INtulu ebande ngodonga kwaBhekuzulu* | Lizard on the wall of Bhekuzulu college |
| *IMvukuzane kaNdaba evukuza ebusuku* | Ndaba's mole, that burrows at night only |

| | |
|---|---|
| Iye yabonwa ngumame ngowaseMaNdebeleni | it was noticed by a woman from the Ndebele nation |
| UBhejane odla abakayise | Rhinoceros that attacks its own family |
| Phuma esiqiwini mtakaNdaba | Ndaba's son, get out of the Game Reserve |
| Kade bekuvalele | they have imprisoned you there for too long |
| Zajabha izihlwele uhalahala bemloyisa | many were disappointed when you triumphed |
| Bethi ngeke igide kwaKhetha | they said you will not be coronated at KwaKheth |
| Yagcagca kithi oNdini olumahlikihlikana | yet you did at oNdini olumahlikihlikana |
| Ngonyaka nonyaka usuhlasele ngothando | you invade with love year after year |
| Phesheya koMzimvubu | across uMzimbuvu River |
| Sibone ngoThabo Mbeki benoJacob Zuma | we saw Thabo Mbeki and Jacob Zuma |
| Ukuthi bazobhula amazolo | ensuring that your problems are solved |
| Wena weNdlovu | Hail, Elephant |
| Hlanga lomhlabathi | Reed of the Soil! |
| Bayethe! | Hail, Your Majesty! |

# The Royal Zulu Lineage

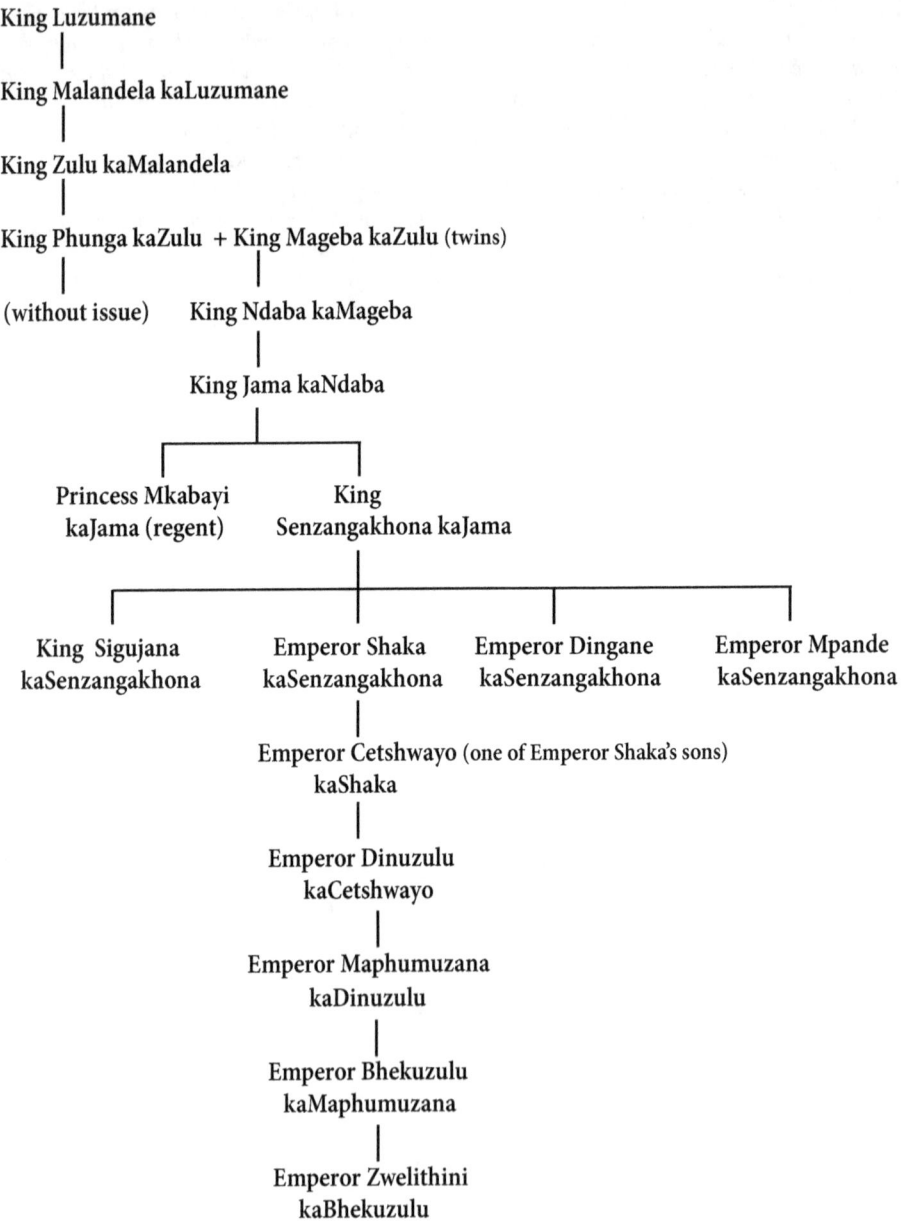

*His Majesty King Zwelithini kaBhekuzulu (right) perusing my first book, uZulu umlando nobuqhawe bukaZulu. Dr BV Mthethwa (centre) is reciting the king's laudatory praises. Shalo Mbatha (author) and her dad, Alex Mbatha look on. (Lolo Mbatha)*

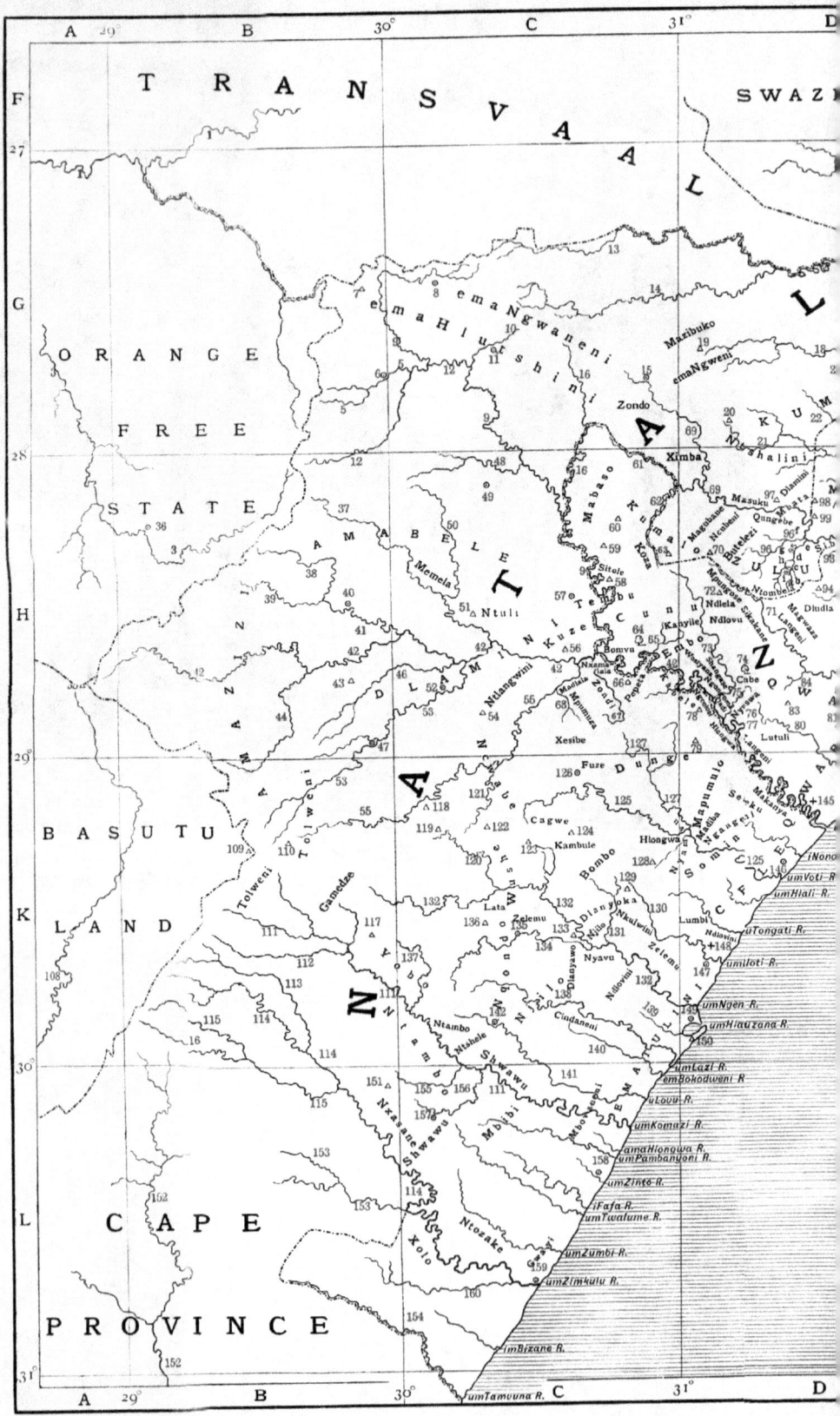

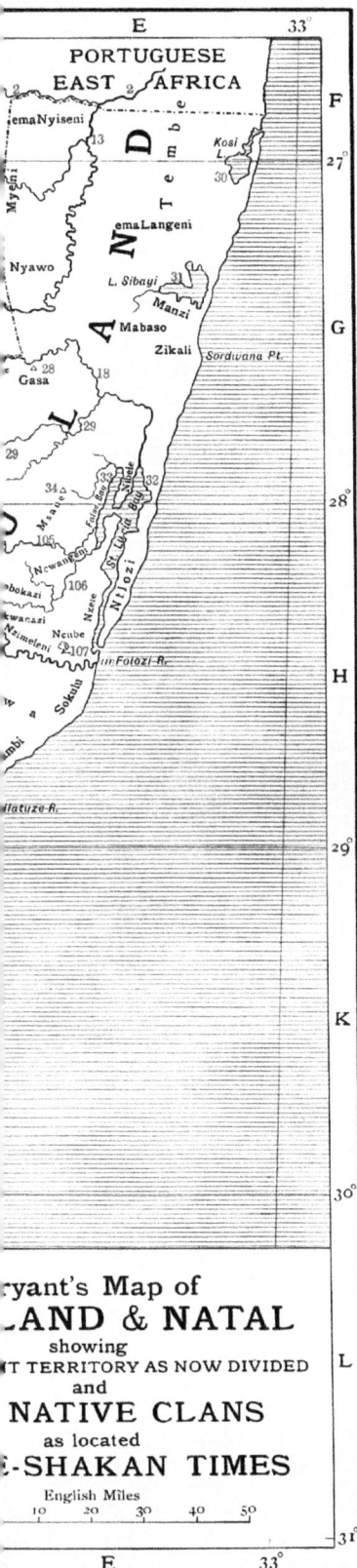

## RIVERS, MOUNTAINS AND TOWNS

K = Kraal.  M = Mountain.  R = River.  T = Town.

| Map Sect. | No. | | | Map Sect. | No. | |
|---|---|---|---|---|---|---|
| BF | 1 | iGwá (Vaal) R. | | — | 88 | umHlatuzana R. |
| EF | 2 | ūSutú R. | | — | 89 | eNkwenkwe Hill. |
| AG | 3 | iNyamakazi (Wilge) R. | | — | 90 | iMfule R. |
| BG | 4 | Klip R. | | — | 91 | eNtseleni R. |
| — | 5 | iNcandu R. | | — | 92 | eNtsangoyana M. |
| — | 6 | Newcastle Town. | | — | 93 | ūPàtè R. |
| — | 7 | emaJuba M. | | — | 94 | emTónjaneni Heights. |
| CG | 8 | Wakkerstroom T. | | — | 95 | umKúmbáne R. |
| — | 9 | umZinyati (Buffalo) R. | | — | (a) | emGúngundlovu Kraal (Zulu's Grave). |
| — | 10 | iNcuba R. | | — | (b) | Retief's Grave (kwaMatiwane). |
| — | 11 | Utrecht T. | | | | |
| — | 12 | iNgágáne R. | | | | |
| — | 13 | ūPòngolo R. | | — | (c) | kwaBulawayo K. |
| — | 14 | ūBivane R. | | — | (d) | esiKlebèni K. |
| — | 15 | Vryheid T. | | — | (e) | emBelebeleni K. |
| — | 16 | iNcome (Blood) R. | | — | (f) | eNtuzuma Hill. |
| DG | 17 | iNgwávuma R. | | — | (g) | kwaNobambá (present) K. |
| — | 18 | umKúze R. | | — | (h) | kwaNobambá (old) (Senzangakóna's Grave). |
| — | 19 | eHlobane M. | | | | |
| — | 20 | kwaNtabankulu M. | | — | (i) | iNzololo R. |
| — | 21 | Black Mfolozi R. | | — | 96 | emPembèni R. |
| — | 22 | isiKwébezi R. | | — | 97 | iNtlazatshe M. |
| — | 23 | iNgòme M. | | — | 98 | isiHlalo M. |
| — | 24 | tBululwane R. | | — | 99 | amaBedlane Hills. |
| — | 25 | tVuna R. | | — | 100 | kwaHlopèkulu H. |
| — | 26 | umMona R. | | — | 101 | óNdini K. |
| — | 27 | iNkunzane R. | | — | 102 | kwaNtabankúlu H. |
| EG | 28 | eTshaneni M. | | — | 103 | emaYiwane Neck. |
| — | 29 | umSunduze R. | | — | 104 | imBekamuzi. |
| — | 30 | Kosi Bay. | | EH | 105 | tHluhluwe R. |
| — | 31 | Lake Sibáyi. | | — | 106 | iNyalazi R. |
| — | 32 | S. Lucia Bay. | | — | 107 | iDukuduku Forest. |
| — | 33 | False Bay. | | AK | 108 | isaNgqu (Orange) R. |
| — | 34 | emTékwini M. | | BK | 109 | Giant's Castle M. |
| AH | 35 | Mont-aux-Sources. | | — | 110 | Mt. Erskine. |
| BH | 36 | Harrismith T. | | — | 111 | umKómazi R. |
| — | 37 | iNdaka (Sundays) R. | | — | 112 | umKómazana R. |
| — | 38 | iNgúla (Klip) R. | | — | 113 | iPòlela R. |
| — | 39 | iNgwányane (Sand) R. | | — | 114 | umZimkúlu R. |
| — | 40 | Ladysmith T. | | — | 115 | iNgwángwáne R. |
| — | 41 | umNambiti (Klip) R. | | — | 116 | iNdawane R. |
| — | 42 | ūTukela R. | | — | 117 | iMpendle Hills. |
| — | 43 | Doorn Kop M. | | CK | 118 | kwaNtoningi (Mt. Arrochar). |
| — | 44 | iNjisuti (Little Tukela). | | | | |
| — | 45 | Champagne Castle. | | — | 119 | emHólweni (Mt. West). |
| — | 46 | umSuluzi (Blauwkrantz) R. | | — | 120 | umLambòngwènya (Karkloof) R. |
| — | 47 | Estcourt T. | | | | |
| CH | 48 | Sand R. | | — | 121 | iNyamvubu R. |
| — | 49 | Dundee T. | | — | 122 | Karkloof Hills. |
| — | 50 | tBusi (Waschbank). | | — | 123 | imPumulonja (Mt. Gilboa). |
| — | 51 | eLenge (Job's Kop). | | — | 124 | kwaNtabakayikònjwa (Blinkwater). |
| — | 52 | Weenen T. | | | | |
| — | 53 | umTshezi (Bushmans) R. | | — | 125 | umVoti R. |
| — | 54 | umHlumbá M. | | — | 126 | Greytown T. |
| — | 55 | iMpofána (Mooi) R. | | — | 127 | iHlimbitwá R. |
| — | 56 | umSinga M. | | — | 128 | óZwatini (Great Noodsberg) Hill. |
| — | 57 | Pomeroy T. | | | | |
| — | 58 | kwaHlazakazi M. | | — | 129 | iNtlangakazi (Mt. Sargeaunt). |
| — | 59 | eSandlwana. | | | | |
| — | 60 | eNqutú Hills. | | — | 130 | umDloti R. |
| — | 61 | iMvunyana R. | | — | 131 | umQeku R. |
| — | 62 | eNondweni R. | | — | 132 | umNgèni R. |
| — | 63 | isiPèzi M. | | — | 133 | emKámbátini (Table Mt.) |
| — | 64 | eQúdeni M. | | — | 134 | umSunduze R. |
| — | 65 | iMfongosi R. | | — | 135 | Maritzburg T. |
| — | 66 | óPisweni M. | | — | 136 | iMbúbu (Zwartkop) M. |
| — | 67 | eNadi R. | | — | 137 | iNcwadi R. |
| — | 68 | iMpanza R. | | — | 138 | umLazi R. |
| DH | 69 | White Mfolozi R. | | — | 139 | umHlatázana R. |
| — | 70 | tBabanango M. | | — | 140 | emBókodweni R. |
| — | 71 | umHlatúze R. | | — | 141 | uLovu R. |
| — | 72 | eTáleni Hill. | | — | 142 | Richmond T. |
| — | 73 | iNtsuze R. | | DK | 143 | kwaGingindlovu K. |
| — | 74 | iNkandla Forest. | | — | 144 | iNyezane R. |
| — | 75 | iMambá R. | | — | 145 | eNdondakusuka. |
| — | 76 | iMpapála Flat. | | — | 146 | kwaDukuzaKraal (Stanger T.). |
| — | 77 | isiWa samaNqe. | | | | |
| — | 78 | kwaNtunjambili (Krantzkop). | | — | 147 | Verulam T. |
| | | | | — | 148 | kwaNjanduna K. |
| — | 79 | isiNyambóti (Elaid's Kop). | | — | 149 | Durban T. (Port Natal). |
| — | 80 | amaTigúlu R. | | — | 150 | Bluff Range and Bush. |
| — | 81 | eShowe T. | | BL | 151 | amaBedlane Hills. |
| — | 82 | umLalazi R. | | — | 152 | umZimvubu (St. John's) R. |
| — | 83 | eNtumeni Hill. | | — | 153 | iBisi R. |
| — | 84 | iMvuzane R. | | CL | 154 | umTámvuna R. |
| — | 85 | emaNdawe Hill. | | — | 155 | ūFáfá (Lufafa) R. |
| — | 86 | uMpehlela Hill | | — | 156 | iXobó R. |
| — | 87 | emaTèku R. | | — | 157 | Ixopo T. |
| (a) | | emTándeni Kraa | | — | 158 | umZinto T. |
| (b) | | Nandi's Kraal. | | — | 159 | Port Shepstone T. |
| (c) | | Bulawayo Kraal. | | — | 160 | umZimkúlwana R. |

## Epilogue

LOOKING BACK, MY LIFE has seen many coincidences. I could have never guessed that a random act of being born into my family and surviving exile would make me a convert of the *Bicycle Philosophy* - never stop pedalling otherwise life will throw you to the ground. The first coincidence was to attend school in eMzimpofu, Manzini in Swaziland. This was the battle theatre between the Swati army and the Zulu army under Field Marshal Ndlela kaSompisi Ntuli.

When I returned from exile, I bought my first house on Toby Street, Westdene in Johannesburg. Little did I know that I was staring at history as Dr AB Xuma's *Empilweni* house was across the street. Dr Xuma was an outstanding gynaecologist and obstetrician and one of the brightest presidents the ANC ever had. It is now the *Sophiatown Museum*. I was offered a job at Robben Island where I walked where historical giants had served time such as King Shaka's interpreter Jacob *Hlambamanzi* Msimbithi; King Langalibalele kaBhungane of the Hlubi kingdom; Dimitri Tsafendas who killed the architect of apartheid, Hendrik Verwoerd and the founding member of the Pan African Congress (PAC) Robert Sobukwe whose internment created legal history in 1977 because his imprisonment was renewed annually and generally known as '*The Sobukwe Clause*' as well as Nelson Mandela who became South Africa's first African president.

My ancestors answered my prayers and I worked at the University of Zululand deep in the rural areas of the empire. I lived KwaDlangezwa near the *ikhanda* of the Special Forces uDlangezwa regiment under the Ongoye Mountains. I drew my water from uMhlathuze River whose mouth was at Dunford Harbour in eSikhaleni (*eSikhawini*) where King Cetshwayo was put on a ship and sent to Cape Town as a political prisoner.

**Selected Bibliography**

Afrika, L. (1989). *African Holistic Health*. USA. Adesegun, Johnson and Koram.
Alberts, P. (1983). *The Borders of Apartheid: The Chronicle of Alienation in South Africa with a Portfolio of Photographs on Bophuthatswana Today*. Cape Town. The Gallery Press.
Barthorp, M. (1991). *The Anglo-Boer Wars: The British and the Afrikaners 1815-1902*. London. Blandford Press.
Becker, P. (1974). *Tribe to Township*. Great Britain. Granada Publishing Limited.
Beinart, W. (1982). *The Political Economy of Pondoland 1860-1930*. Cambridge. Cambridge University Press.
Bekker, S. (Ed). (1992). *Capturing the Event. Conflict Trends in the Natal Region 1986-1992*. The University of Natal. Center for Social and Development Studies.
Bell, T. & Ntsebeza, D. B. (2001). *Unfinished Business. South Africa Apartheid & The Truth*. South Africa. Redworks.
Bennet, N.R. (1971). *Mirambo of Tanzania*. New York. Oxford University Press.
Biko, S. (2004). *I Write What I Like*. Johannesburg. Picador Africa.
Binns, C. T. (1963). *The Last Zulu King: The Life and Death of Cetshwayo*. The University of Michigan. Longmans.
Binns, C. T. (1968). *Dinuzulu: The Death of the House of Shaka*. London, Longmans.
Bird, J. (1888). *The Annals of Natal 1495-1845*. Pietermaritzburg. General Books.
Bosman, W. (1907). *The Natal Rebellion of 1906*. London. Longmans.
Bond, J. (1971). *They Were South Africans*. London. Oxford University Press.
Bourquin, S. & Filter, H. (1986). Paulina Dlamini: Servant of Two Kings. Killie Campbell Africana Library.
Bourquin, S. & Johnston, T.M. (Eds). (1971). *The Zulu War of 1879* as reported in *The Illustrated London News*. Durban. Cyclostyle.
Brookes, E. H. (1924). *The History of Native Policy in South Africa*. Cape Town. Lovedale.
Brookes, E. H. et al. (1965). *A History of Natal*. Pietermaritzburg. P. Davis.
Bryant, A. T. (1905). *Zulu – English Dictionary*. Mariannhill. Pinetown. T. Nelson.
Bryant, A. T. (1909). *Our Country: An Elementary History of Natal*. London. Struik.
Bryant, A. T. (1919). *The Origin of the Zulu*. Native Teachers' Journal. Vol 1, No 1. London. Struik.
Bryant, A.T. (1929). *Olden Times in Zululand and Natal*. Pietermaritzburg. Shuter & Shooter.
Bryant, A. T. (1949). *The Zulu People as they were before the White Man came*. Pietermaritzburg. Shuter & Shooter.
Bryant, A.T. (1964). *A History of the Zulu and Neighbouring Tribes*. Cape Town. Struik.
Bulpin, T.V. (1986). *Natal and the Zulu Country*. Cape Town. Treasury of Travel.
Bundy, C. (1979). *The Rise and Fall of the South African Peasantry*. Berkeley. University of California Press.
Butler, G. (Ed). (1974). *The 1820 Settlers. An Illustrated Commentary*. Human & Rousseau. Cape Town.
Clingman, S. (1998). *Bram Fischer: Afrikaner Revolutionary*. Claremont. David Philip Publishers.

## Selected Bibliography

Cohen, D. (2004). *People who have Stolen From Me*. Johannesburg. Picador Africa.
Colenso, F. E. (1884). *The Ruin of Zululand: An Account of British Doings in Zululand since the Invasion of 1879*. London. W. Ridgway.
Colenso, F. E. & Durnford, E. C. L. (1880). *History of the Zulu War and its Origin*. London. Crystal Palace Press.
Colenso, J.W. (1855). *Ten Weeks in Natal: A Journal of a First Tour of Visitation*. Cambridge. Macmillan.
Coetzer, O. (1996). *The Anglo-Boer War: The Road to Infamy, 1899-1900*. London. Arms & Armour Press.
Cope, T. (Ed). (1968). *Izibongo: Zulu Praise Poems*. London. Oxford University Press.
Corder, H. L. (1946). *The Truth & Nothing But*. London. The Rustica Press.
Cope, N. (1993). *To Bind the Nation: Solomon ka Dinuzulu and Zulu Nationalism 1913-1933*. Pietermaritzburg. University of KwaZulu-Natal Press.
Crwys-Williams, J. (2004). *In the Words of Nelson Mandela*. South Africa. Penguin Books.
Danes, R. (1901). *Story of the Boer War. 1899-1901*. London. Cassell & Co.
Dallek, R. (2003). *John F. Kennedy: An Unfinished Life*. Great Britain. Penguin Books.
Davidson, B. (1969). *The African Genius*. Toronto. Little Brown & Company.
Delius, P. (1983). *The Land Belongs to us: The Pedi Polity, the Boers and the British in the Nineteenth Century Transvaal*. Johannesburg, Ravan Press.
De Villiers, F. (Ed). (1983). *Bridge or Barricade? The Constitution. A First Appraisal*. Johannesburg. Jonathan Ball.
Dhlomo, R. R. R. (1947). *UNomalanga kaNdengezi*. Pietermaritzburg. Shuter & Shooter.
Dhlomo, R. R. R. (1956). *UCetshwayo*. Pietermaritzburg. Shuter & Shooter.
Dhlomo, R. R. R. (1956). *UDingane kaSenzangakhona*. Pietermaritzburg. Shuter & Shooter.
Dhlomo, R. R. R. (1968). *UDinuzulu kaCetshwayo*. Pietermaritzburg. Shuter & Shooter.
Doke, C.M. & Vilakazi, B.W. (1948). *Zulu – English Dictionary*. Johannesburg. Witwatersrand University Press.
Dube, J. (1909). *The Zulus Appeal for Light and England's Duty*. London. Evans Bros.
Dubow, S. (2000). *The African National Congress*. Johannesburg. Jonathan Ball.
Duff, A. (1998). *Both Sides of the Moon*. New Zealand. Vintage.
Du Plessis, E. J. (1973). *Suid-Afrikaanse Berg en Riviername*. Cape Town. Tafelberg Uitgewers.
Du Preez, M. (2003). *Pale Native: Memories of a Renegade Reporter*. South Africa. Zebra Press.
Du Toit, B. (1978). *Ukubamba Amadolo. Worker's Struggle in the South African Textile Industry*. London. Onyx Press.
Dyantyi, M. (2002). *The Runner*. Johannesburg. Wits Writing Centre.
Etherington, N. A. (1978). *Preachers, Peasants and Politics in South East Africa, 1835-1880: African Christian Communities in Natal, Pondoland and Zululand*. London. Royal Historical Society.
Evans, M. S. (1906). *The Native Problem in Natal*. Durban. P. Davis & Sons.
Everett, P. L. (1990). *Zulus*. New York. Permanent Press.
Farwell, B. (1976). *The Great Boer War*. London. Allen Lane.

Faye, C. (1923). *Zulu References for Interpreters and Students.* Pietermaritzburg. City Printing Works.
Fuze. M. (1922). *Abantu Abamnyama Lapa Bavela Ngakona.* Pietermaritzburg. University of Natal Press.
Fynn, H.F. (Stuart, J. & Malcolm, D.) (Eds). (1950). *The Diary of Henry Francis Fynn.* Pietermaritzburg. Shuter & Shooter.
Fynney, F.B. (1878). *The Zulu Army.* Pietermaritzburg. Shuter & Shooter.
Gardiner, A. (1836). *Narrative of a journey to the Zoolu country in South Africa. Undertaken in 1835.* London. Bradbury & Ethan Printers.
Gibson, J.Y. (1911). *The Story of the Zulus.* London. Longmans.
*Geloftedag: Christusfees of Baalfees?* (Afrikaans: Day of the Vow: Christian Festival or Festival of Baal) ProVeritate, Vol 10. No 8.
Gillings, K.G. (1989). *The Bambata Rebellion of 1906: Nkandla Operations and the Battle of Mome Gorge, 10 June 1906.* Military History Journal. Vol 8. No 1.
Greaves, A. (1997). *A Brief Study of the Origins of the Zulu Nation and its Development until War in 1879.* Journal of the Anglo Zulu War. Historical Society 1.
Greaves, A. (2001). *Isandlwana. Cassell's Fields of Battle.* London. Cassell & Co.
Greaves, A. (2005). *Crossing the Buffalo. The Zulu War 1879.* London. Weidenfeld & Nicolson.
Greene, R. (2000). *The 48 Laws of Power.* London. Profile Books Ltd.
Gregersen, J. (1997). *Isandlwana. The Book of Contemporary Quotes.* Johannesburg. Ravan Press.
Grout, L. (1893). *The IsiZulu:* A Revised Edition of a *Grammar of the Zulu Language.* Boston. The Library, 1894 *Social History of Colonial Natal.* Pietermaritzburg. University of KwaZulu-Natal Press.
Guy, J. (1979). *The Destruction of the Zulu Kingdom: The Civil War in Zululand 1879-1884.* London. Longmans.
Harries, C.L. (1929). *The Laws and Customs of the Bapedi and Cognate Tribes of the Transvaal.* Johannesburg. Hortors Ltd.
Hartley, A. (2003). *The Zanzibar Chest. A Memoir of Love and War.* London. Harper Collins.
Hattersley, A. F. (1940). *Portrait of a Colony: The Story of Natal.* Cambridge. Cambridge University Press.
Herbert, E. (1990). *The Second Anglo-Boer War. War Gaming in History.* Hertfordshire. Argus Books.
Heydenrych, L. (Guest, B. & Sellers, J.) (Eds). (1985). *Enterprise and Exploitation in a Victorian Colony.* Pietermaritzburg. University of Natal Press.
Hodge, N. (1984). *To Kill a Man's Pride.* Johannesburg. Ravan Press.
Holden, W.C. (1913). *History of the Colony of Natal.* London. Kessinger Publishing.
Hughes, H. (2011). *First President: A Life of John L. Dube, Founding President of the ANC.* Johannesburg. Jacana Media.
Jackson, E. L. (1903). *Saint Helena: The Historic Island from its Discovery to the Present date.* London. Ward, Lock & Co.

## Selected Bibliography

Jenkin, T. (2003). *Inside Out: Escape from Prison.* Johannesburg. Jacana Media.
Jenkinson, T. B. (1882). *Amazulu — The Zulu: Their Past History, Manners, Customs and Language.* London. M. W. Allen.
John, K. (1939). *The Prince Imperial.* The University of Wisconsin-Madison. Putnam.
Joyce, P. (1999). *A Concise Dictionary of South African Biography.* Cape Town. Francolin Publishers.
Junod, H.A. (1912). *The Life of a South African Tribe.* London. David Nutt.
Keegan, T. (1988). *Facing the Storm: Portraits of Black Lives in Rural South Africa.* Claremont. David Philip Publishers.
Keet, B.B, (1956). *Whither, South Africa?* Stellenbosch. University Publishers and Booksellers.
Kenney, R.U. (1976). *Piet Retief. The Dubious Hero.* South Africa. Human & Rousseau.
Khumalo. R. S. (2004). *UPhoko Volume 1. The History of Surnames and Names.* Pietermaritzburg. Reach Out Publishers.
Khumalo-Seegelken, B. (2000). *'Uyadela wen' usulapho'. AbaQulusi in and around the Anglo Boer War 1899-1902.* National Conference on the Role of Blacks in the Anglo-Boer South African War 1899-1902. Durban.
Khuzwayo, E. (2004). *Call Me Woman.* Johannesburg. Picador Africa.
Kirby, P. (1934). *The Musical Instruments of the Native Races of South Africa.* London. Oxford University Press.
Kirby, P. (Ed). *(1955). Andrew Smith and Natal.* Cape Town. A. A. Balkema.
Knight. I. (1996). *Go to your God like a Soldier: The British Soldier Fighting for Empire, 1837-1902.* London. Greenhill Books.
Knight, I. (2002). *Isandlwana 1879: The Great Zulu Victory.* Oxford. Osprey Publishing.
Kochanski, H. (2001). *Sir Garnet Wolseley: Victorian Hero.* London. Continuum.
Kotzé, D. J. (1950). *Letters of the American Missionaries 1835–1838.* Stellenbosch. Pro Ecclesia-Drukkery.
Krieg, E. (1974). *The Social System of the Zulu.* Pietermaritzburg. Shuter & Shooter.
Kruger, R. (1959). *Goodbye Dolly Gray: The Story of the Boer War.* London. Cassell & Company.
Kunene, M. (1979). *Emperor Shaka the Great.* London. Heinemann.
Laband, J. (1992). *Kingdom in Crisis: The Zulu Response to the British Invasion of 1879.* Manchester. Manchester University Press.
Laband. J. (2001). *The Atlas of the Later Zulu Wars 1883–1888.* Pietermaritzburg. University of Natal Press.
Lambert, J. (1995). *Betrayed Trust: Africans and the State in Colonial Natal.* Durban. University of Natal Press.
Langa, J. (1982). *Shaka.* Salisbury. Longman.
Lee, R. B. (1979). *The !Kung San: Men, Women and Work in a Foraging Society.* United States of America. Cambridge University Press.
Liebenberg, B.J. (1975). *Opstelle oor die Suid-Afrikaanse historiografie.* Pretoria. Lloyd's Greater Britain Publishing Company.

## Selected Bibliography

Liesegang, G.J. (1974). *A survey of the 19th century stockades of southern Mozambique: the Khokholwene of the Manjacaze area*. Lisboa. Instituto de Alta Cultura.
Lock, R. & Quantrill, P. (2005). *Zulu Vanquished: The Destruction of the Zulu Kingdom*. London. Greenhill Books.
Locke, A. (2004). *New Negro, Harlem Renaissance*. Philadephia. Chelsea Publishing.
Lucas, T. J. (1879). *The Zulu and the British Frontiers*. London. The Library.
Ludlow, W. R. (1882). *Zululand and Cetewayo*. London. Oxford University Press.
Lugg, H. C. (1949). *Historical Natal and Zululand*. Pietermaritzburg. Shuter & Shooter.
Lugg, H. C. (1975). *Life under a Zulu Shield*. Pietermaritzburg. Shuter & Shooter.
Luthuli, A. (1978). *Let My People Go*. Britain. Collins.
MacKeurtan, G. (1948). *The Cradle Days of Natal (1497-1845)*. Pietermaritzburg. Shuter & Shooter.
Marks, S. (1986). *The Ambiguities of Dependence in South Africa*. Johannesburg. Ravan Press.
Marks, S. (1970). *Reluctant Rebellion: The 1906-08 Disturbances in Natal*. Oxford Claredon Press.
Marquard, L. (1969). *The Peoples & Policies of South Africa*. London. Oxford University Press.
Mason, D. (2003). *A Traveller's History of South Africa*. Phoenix. Windrush Press.
Mbatha, S. B. L. (1997). *Nawe Mbopha kaSithayi!* Pietermaritzburg. Shuter & Shooter.
McBride, A. (1976). *The Zulu War*. London. Osprey Publishing.
McLynn, F. (1992). *Hearts of Darkness: The European Exploration of Africa*. New York. Carroll & Graf Publishers.
Meer, F. (1987). *The Trial of Andrew Zondo: A Sociological Insight*. South Africa. Skotaville Publishers.
Meintjies, J. (1974). *President Paul Kruger*. South Africa. Purnell Book Services Ltd.
Meli, F. (1989). *A History of the ANC: South Africa Belongs to Us*. Britain. James Curry.
Mendes, P. R. (2003). *Bay of Tigers*. Johannesburg. Jonathan Ball Publishers.
Mgxashe, M. (2006). *Are You With Us? The Story of a PAC Activist*. South Africa. Mafube Tafelberg.
Miller, A. (1954). *Mamisa iqhawe leSwazi*. Pietermaritzburg. Shuter & Shooter.
Miller, W. T. (1957). *A History of Rhodesia*. London. Longmans.
Mitchison, N. (1970). *The Africans from the earliest times to the present*. London. Granada Publishing Limited.
Mitford, B. (1883). *Through the Zulu Country*. London. Kegan Paul, Trench & Co.
Mngadi, J. M. (1979). *Imiyalezo*. Pietermaritzburg. KwaZulu Booksellers.
Mofolo, T. (1981). *Chaka. African Writers Series 229*. London. Heinemann.
Mokae, G. (2004). *Robert McBride – A Coloured Life*. South Africa. South African History Online. Vista University.
Molefe, L. (2003). *Ngiwafunge AmaBomvu*. Pietermaritzburg. Travis Publishing.
Moodie, D.C. F. (1888). *The History of the Battles and Adventures of the British, the Boers, and the Zulus: In Southern Africa from the time of Pharaoh Necho to 1880 with copious chronology*. London. Cass.

## Selected Bibliography

Morris, D. R. (1972). *The Washing of the Spears: A History of the Rise of the Zulu Nation.* London. Jonathan Cape.
Mostert, N. (1992). *Frontiers.* London. Pimlico.
Msimang, C. T. (1991). *Inkosi yinkosi ngabantu.* South Africa. Kagiso Education.
Msimang, C. T. (1991). *Iziziba zoThukela.* South Africa. Via Afrika Limited.
Muila, I. M. (2004). *Gova.* South Africa. Botsotso Publishing.
Mulemfo, M. M. (2005). *Thabo Mbeki: An African Renaissance Voice.* South Africa. Durrant & Viljoen.
Nasson, B. (1999). *Uyadela wen'osulapho: Black Participation in the Anglo-Boer War.* Johannesburg. Ravan Press.
Nathan, A. J. (1999). *Boer Prisoners of War on the Island of St Helena.* October Military History Journal, Vol 11. No 3/4.
Ndelu, B. B. (1962). *Mageba Lazihlonza.* Pietermaritzburg. Shuter & Shooter.
Ntuli, D. B. Z. (1992). *Woza Nendlebe.* Pietermaritzburg. Shuter & Shooter.
Nxumalo, O. E. H. M. (2003). *King of Goodwill: The Authorised Biography of King Goodwill Zwelithini kaBhekuzulu.* Cape Town. Nasou Via Afrika.
Odendaal, A. (1984). *Black Protest Politics in South Africa to 1912.* Totowa, N J. Barnes & Noble Books.
Omer-Cooper, J.D. (1966). *The Zulu Aftermath.* London. Longmans.
Orwell, G. (1965). *Nineteen Eighty-Four.* London. Heinemann Educational Books.
Packenham, T. (1979). *The Boer War.* London. Weidenfeld & Nicolson.
Parr, H. H. (1880). *A Sketch of the Kaffir and Zulu Wars.* London. C. Kegan Paul and Co.
Paton, A. (1961). *South Africa and Her People.* London. Butterworth Press.
Phillips, W.P. (1998). *The Death of the Prince Imperial in Zululand 1879.* Hampshire. Hampshire County Council Museums Service.
Plaatjie, S. (1914). *Native Life in South Africa.* Johannesburg. Picador Africa.
Rasmussen R.K. (1978). *Migrant Kingdom: Mzilikazi's Ndebele in South Africa.* Cape Town. Longman.
Rhoodie, E. (1989). *PW Botha: The Last Betrayal.* Melville. SA Politics.
Rive, R. & Couzens, T. (1991). *Seme: The Founder of the ANC.* Johannesburg. Skotaville Publishers.
Ritter, E.A. (1957). *Shaka Zulu: The Rise of the Zulu Empire.* London. Granada Publishing.
Roberts, A. & Thloloe, J. (2004). *Soweto Inside Out. Stories about Africa's famous township.* Johannesburg. Penguin Books.
Russell, R. (1901). *Natal: The Land and its Story.* Pietermaritzburg. P. Davis & Sons.
Ryan, C. (1990). *Beyers Naudé: Pilgrimage of Faith.* Claremont. David Philip Publishers.
Rycroft, D. K. & Ngcobo, A. B. (Eds). (1988). *The Praises of Dingana. Izibongo zikaDingana.* Durban. Killie Campbell Africana Library.
Shabangu, S. S. (1979). *Bamngcwaba ephila.* Pietermaritzburg. Shuter & Shooter.
Samuelson, R. C. A. (1929). *Long, Long, Ago.* Durban. Mariannhill Press.
Samuelson, L. H. (1929). *Zululand: Its Traditions, Legends, Customs and Folklore.* Durban. Mariannhill Press.
Shain, M. & Mendelsohn, R. (2000). *Memories, Realities and Dreams: Aspects of the*

*South African Jewish Experience*. Johannesburg. Jonathan Ball Publishers.
Sisulu, E. (2003). *Walter and Albertina Sisulu: In our Lifetime*. Claremont. David Philip Publishers.
Sithole, J. & Carton, B. & Laband, J. (Eds). (2008). *Zulu Identities: Being Zulu, Past and Present*. Pietermaritzburg. University of KwaZulu-Natal Press.
Smith, E.W. (1952). *The Life and Times of Daniel Lindley (1801-80): Missionary to the Zulus, Pastor of the Voortrekkers, Ubebe Omhlope*. New York. Library Publishers.
Smuts, J. C. (1926). *Holism and Evolution*. London. Macmillan.
Snook, M. (2005). How Can Man Die Better: *The Secrets of iSandlwana Revealed*. London. Greenhill Books.
Soga, J. H. (1931). *The Ama-Xhosa: Life and Customs*. Lovedale. Lovedale Press.
Steinberg, J. (2002). *Midlands*. Johannesburg. Jonathan Ball Publishers.
Stuart, J. (1913). *A History of the Zulu Rebellion 1906*. Pietermaritzburg. University of KwaZulu-Natal Press.
Stuart, J. (1924). *uBaxoxele*. Pitermaritzburg. University of KwaZulu-Natal Press.
Stuart, J. (1925). *uKulumetule*. Pitermaritzburg. University of KwaZulu-Natal Press.
Stuart, J. (1929). *uTulasizwe*. Pitermaritzburg. University of KwaZulu-Natal Press.
Stuart, J. & Webb, C. & Wright, J.B. (Eds). (2001). *The James Stuart Archives* Vol 1 – 5. Durban. University of KwaZulu-Natal Press.
Tracey, H. (1948). *Zulu Paradox*. African Music Society Journal. Johannesburg. Silver Leaf Books.
Van Diemel, R. (2001). *In search of Freedom, Fair play & Justice. Josiah Tshangana Gumede: 1867 - 1947*. Cape Town. Belhar.
Van, Warmelo. (1935). *A PreliminarySurvey of the Bantu Tribes of South Africa*. Pretoria. The Government Printer.
Verbeek, A. (1982). *Victorian and Edwardian Natal*. Pietermaritzburg. Shuter & Shooter.
Verwey, E. J. (Ed). (1995). *New Dictionary of South African Biography*. Pretoria. HSRC Publishers.
Vilakazi, A. (1962). *Zulu Transformations: A Study of the Dynamics of Social Change*. Durban. University of KwaZulu-Natal Press.
Vilakazi, B.W. (1939). *UDingiswayo kaJobe*. London. Sheldon Press.
Voigt, J. C. (1899). *Fifty Years of the History of the Republic in South Africa* (1795-1845). London. Negro Universities Press.
Walker, E. (1937). *W. P. Schreiner: A South African*. London. Oxford University Press.
Walshe, P. (1970). *The Rise of African Nationalism in South Africa: The African National Congress 1912-1952*. Berkeley and Los Angeles. University of California Press.
Walt, v.d., J. (2007). (3rd Ed). *Zululand True Stories 1780- 1978*. Richards Bay. Richards Bay Printers.
Welsh, D. (1971). *The Roots of Segregation: Native Policy in Colonial Natal 1845-1910*. Cape Town. Oxford University Press.
Wheeler, D. L. (1968). *Ngungunyane the Negotiator: A Study in African Diplomacy*. The Journal of African History. Vol 9. No 4. Cambridge. Cambridge University Press.

Wilkinson-Latham, C. (1978). *Uniforms and Weapons of the Zulu War*. New York. Hippocrene Books.
Williams, B. (1946). *Botha, Smuts and South Africa*. London. Hodder & Stoughton Limited.
Williams, C. (1987). *The Destruction of Black Civilization*. Chicago. Third World Press.
Willoughby, W. C. (1900). *Native Life on the Transvaal Border*. London. Simpkin, Marshall, Hamilton, Kent & Co.
Zulu, Z. (2005). *Umongo kaZulu: The Marrow of the Zulu Nation*. Cape Town. Lotsha Publications.
Zungu, A. Z. (1933). *Usukabekhuluma*. Pietermaritzburg. Shuter and Shooter.

**Unpublished Secondary Sources**
Burrows, R. (1966). *Dinuzulu and the Natal Government, 1907-1909*. B. A. (Hon) Thesis. University of KwaZulu-Natal University.
Carton, B. (1906). *Blood from your Sons: African Generational Conflict in Natal and Zululand, South Africa 1880 – 1910*. Unpublished PhD Thesis. Yale University.
Etherington, N. A. (1971). *The Rise of the Kholwa in Southeast Africa: African Christian Communities in Natal, Pondoland and Zululand, 1835-1880*. Unpublished PhD Thesis. Yale University.
Gasa, E.D. (1999). *John L. Dube, his Ilanga Lase Natali and the Natal African Administration, 1903-1910*. Unpublished PhD Thesis. University of Zululand.
Genge, M. (1999). *Power and Gender in Southern African History: Power Relations in the Era of Queen Labotsibeni Gwamile Mdluli of Swaziland, ca. 1875-1921*. PhD Thesis. Michigan State University.
Hadebe, Z. P. (2002). *Ucwaningo olunzulu ngokuqanjwa kwabalingiswa nezindawo kanye nemithelela yakho emibhalweni yesiZulu*. Ukufeza izidingo zeziquzu zobudokotela benzululwazi eNyuvesi yakwaZulu.
Hadebe, M. M. (2003). *A contextualization and examination of the impi yamakhanda (1906 Uprising)*. Unpublished MA Thesis. University of KwaZulu-Natal.
Hughes, H. (1995). *Politics and Society in Inanda, Natal: The Qadi under Chief Mqhawe, 1840-1910*. Unpublished PhD Thesis. University of London.
Khathi, T. M. (2002). *Ikhono likahagolwana Jiyane ekusebenziseni izithombe izifengqo nesakhiwo ezibongweni zeNkosi uDingane*. Ukufeza izidingo zeziqu zobubudokotela benzululwazi eNyuvesi yakwaZulu.
Khumalo, V. (2004). *EkuKhanyeni Letter-Writers: Notes towards a Social History of Letter Writing in KwaZulu Natal – South Africa, 1890-1900*. Unpublished PhD Thesis. University of Michigan.
Khuzwayo, A. S. (2007). *Ukuvezwa komlando ezibongweni zamakhosi amabili akwazulu uDingane noMpande*. Ukufeza izidingo zeziqu zeMasters eNyuvesi yakwaZulu-Natal.
Mabuza, M. E. (2008). *Ukucwaninga amandla encazelo yegama nemiphumela empilweni yabantu abakhuluma isiZulu nabanye abakhuluma ezinye izilimi zesintu e-Afrika*. Izidingo zeziqu zobudokotela enzululwazini eNyuvesi yaseNingimuzi.
Madlala, T. N. (1985). *The role of Prince Thimuni kaMudu kaJama in Zulu History*

*with Special Reference to the activities of his sons Ndlovu and Chakijana and their descendants.1842-1980*. MA Thesis. University of Zululand.
Malibe, M. J, (2009). *Ubunkondlo obutholakala ezithakazelweni zesiZulu*. Ukufeza izidingo zeziqu zeMasters eNyuvesi yakwaZulu.
Masina, E. M. (2006). *Zulu perceptions and reactions to the British occupation of land in Natal Colony and Zululand, 1850-1887: A recapitulation based on surviving oral and written sources*. Unpublished PhD Thesis. University of Zululand.
Mersham, G. (1987). *Political Discourse and Historical Television Drama: A Case Study of Shaka Zulu*. PhD Thesis. University of South Africa.
Msibi, I. S. M. (2002). *Ucwaningo ngongobumqoka nokubaluleka kwezilwane esizweni samaZulu*. Ukufeza izidingo zeziqu zeMasters eNyuvesi yakwaZulu.
Mzimela, M. B. (2006). *Ucwaningo olunzulu ngeqhaza elibanjwe ukulwa nezimpi ekukhulisweni kolwimi lwesiZulu*. Ukufeza izidingo zeziqu zeMasters eNyuvesi yakwaZulu.
Ndhlovu, B. C. (2000). *The Natal Government's Policy towards amakhosi in the former Kingdom of KwaZulu, 1846-1910*. MA Thesis. University of Zululand.
Sabela, R. T. (1989). *KwaZulu Legislative Assembly*. Unpublished MA Dissertation. University of Zululand.
Smith, K. I. (2005). The Commandants: The Leadership of the Natal Native Contingent in the Anglo-Zulu War. MA Thesis. University of Western Australia.
Ximba, E. Z. (2009). Cultural and heritage tourism development and promotion in the Ndwedwe municipal area: Perceived Policy and Practice. MA Thesis. University of Zululand.
Zulu, B. (2002). From the Lüneburger Heide to Northern Zululand: A History of the Encounter between the Settlers, the Hermannsburg Missionaries, the Amakhosi and their people, with special reference to four Mission Stations in Northern Zululand (1860-1913). MA Thesis. University of Natal.

**Oral Interviews**
Queen Mother MaGwabini – esigodlweni sakwaDlamahlahla, kwaNongoma
Queen Thandekile - esigodlweni sakwaLindizulu, kwaNongoma
Prince Gideon Zulu – kwaMinya, Ondini
Celu Abednigo Shamase – oFasimba, esigodini saseDayingubo
Inyosi Buzetsheni kaSombila Mdletshe – kwaCeza
Induna sayeZibindini Buthelezi – esigodlweni saseZibindini
Prince Reginald KaMagangeni KaDinuzulu – kwaQambushilo, kwaNongoma
Prince Herbert ka KaMagangeni KaDinuzulu – kwaNxangiphilile, kwaNongoma
Dr BV Mthethwa – kwesakaMthethwa
Eric Ngobe – eMsinga
Menzi Jele – eSikhaleni, eMpangeni
Alexander Mbatha – Dube, Soweto
Khosi Mbatha – Dube, Soweto
Reggie Khumalo – eMlaza, eSibululungu

Professor Sihawu Ngubane – eNyuvesi yakwaZulu Natali
Professor Mazisi Kunene – eNyuvesi yakwaZulu Natali
Dr. Thokozani Nene – eLamontville, eSibululungu

**Archival**
Human Rights Update. (1989). *October 1988 – March 1989.* Vol 2. No 1. University of Witwatersrand, Johannesburg.
Ten Proposed Regions for a United South Africa. Discussion document prepared by the ANC Constitution Committee. (1992). Center for Development Studies, University of Western Cape.
KwaZulu Natal Archives, Pietermaritzburg
Government Notice No. 64 of 1852. Report of the Commission, 1852-1853.
NCP 8/1320 Natal Native Commission of 1881 (Pietermaritzburg 1882). Evidence taken before the Commission.
NCP 8/3120 Natal Native Commission of 1881. Evidence taken before the Sub-Commission for Umvoti.
NCP 8/31 Proceedings and Report of the Commission to inquire into the past and present state of the Kafirs, 1852-1853.
South African Native Affairs Commission (SANAC) Vol 3-4. Minutes of evidence (Cape Town, Cape Times, 1905) (University of Zululand – uZulu collection).
The British Parliamentary Papers (BPP) Zululand Affairs
C 2950 No. 69 Kimberley to Bulwer
C 2950 Enclosure (10) Oude Moulen
C 1141 Shepstone to Colenso, March 1874
C 3247 Osborne to Bulwer, March 1882
C 3466 No. 79 Settlement of the Zulu country
C 5331 No. 1 Havelock to Holland
SB Bourquin Collection
The Shepstone Papers
SNA 1/7/1 Native Complaints and Statements
September 1850-Febrnary 1852
SNA 1/7/IA Native Complaints and Statements
February 1852-January 1853
SNA In/2, 1n/3 Reports, Statements, Messages
September 1853 - April 1859
SNA 119/6 Brief Sketch of Zulu History

**Natal Archives, Pietermaritzburg**
Secretary for Native Affairs (Reports, Correspondence and Minutes)
Colonial Secretary's Office (Records, Proceedings and Correspondence, 1/AGO)
Magistrates
Government House
**Periodicals and Newspapers**

Ilanga Lase Natal
Imvo zabantsundu
Natal Advertiser (23 Jul 1888)
Pretoria News (p6, 4 Apr 2012)
Sunday Tribune
The Grahamstown Journal
Mail & Guardian
The Indian Opinion (Jul 1906)
The Mercury (Pictoral Record of the Native Rebellion 1906; Jul 1906; Mar, Apr 1906; June 1907; Jul & Dec 1988)
The Witness
The New Age (p9, Nov 2014)
The Patriot
The Sunday Independent (Life, p9, 27 Apr 2014)
The Times of Natal 1888
The Zululand Observer

**Website Sources**
Ezakwantu Forum website
KZN North Happenings website
Pambuzuka News website
UNESCO website
Wikipedia website
Jcgrimshaw.blogspot.com

**Other Sources**
Killie Campbell Africana Library, Durban
Pictures 231-256 – Courtesy of Killie Campbell Library, Durban
Africana Museum
KwaZulu–Natal Museum Museum Services
Oral History Project Relating to amaZulu People
Robben Island Museum
Mayibuye Archives, University of Western Cape
Defence and Aid Fund Papers – Manuscripts & Archives, University of Western Cape

# GLOSSARY

*abakhongi* – negotiators tasked with asking for the hand of a woman in marriage
*abehla ngesilulu* - those who came down into the land of the Nguni people in a basket
*bahlala phezu kwamahawu* – to be combat ready
*Bayethe, wena weNdlovu* – Hail, your Majesty, great as an elephant
*bexoxa impi* - they discussed war strategy
*abomdabu* – the Zulu people who descended from the reeds
*Coloured* – mixed race person
*Dompas* (pass) - an internal passport for black people they had to carry at all times
*udonga* – steep sided ravine(s)
*ibandla* - the king's council
*ibheshu* - a male leather apron tied around the waist
*idelakufa* – (plural: *amadelakufa*) – a suicide squad
*ibutho* – regiment
*icansi* - (plural: *amacansi*) sleeping mat(s)
*idlozi* - (plural: *amadlozi*) ancestor(s)
*igama* or *ibizo* - first name
*igama lobunsizwa* – name given by peers
*ihlambo* - death cleansing
*inhlendla* – a harpoon-shaped spear
*ihubo* – song
*ihubo lempi* - war song
*ihubo lesizwe* – national anthem
*hlonipha* – respect
*ijadu* - youth matchmaking festivals
*Kaffir* – (plural: *Kaffirs*) an offensive racial term against black South Africans by the Apartheid government
*ukugiya* - to perform a military dance
*ukujutshwa* – granting of permission for a girl to have relationships with boys
*ikhanda* – (plural: *amakhanda*) head(s); military base; also part of the pincer movement military formation
*ukhukhulangoqo* – the national call-up
*ikholwa* – (plural: *amakholwa*) Christian convert(s)
*ukukhehla* – getting ready to be married ceremony
*ukukhunga* - the ceremony of giving a child a birth present
*iklwa* – short stabbing assegai
*ukulobola* - the formalisation of marriage by presenting gifts such as cattle, goods or other property from the man's family to the woman's family or guardian.
*ukuthefula* – a dialect of the amaLala group
*ukuqhobosha* - a slow female sensual rhythmic dance
*ilobolo* - gifts given to the woman's family as part of the formalisation of marriage by the man's family

# Glossary

*amabhinca* – non believers of the Christian faith
*amasi* - curdled sour milk
*Mageba* – totem of the Zulu family
*Mntanami* - my child
*Ndabezitha* – totem of the Mbatha as well as the Zulu family; a legend amongst the enemies
*indwe* – the blue crane bird
*inkatha yezwe* – the Zulu nation's sacred grass coil symbolising unity
*ukusoka* - male circumcision
*ukukhonza* - to apply to become a subject
*ukusoma* - external sex between the thighs
*ukusula izembe* – external sex ritual with the first obliging unmarried woman after a battle
*Laager* – a camp formed with wagons parked in a defensive circle
*umabo* - gifts given to the man's family as part of the formalisation of marriage by the woman's family
*amahlombe* – shoulders; also part of the pincer movement military formation
*imali yamakhanda* - poll tax
*umancintshane* - small calabash
*amaqaba* – non-Christians
*imbizo* – national gathering
*imbongi* - a laudatory praise reciter
*umdlunkulu* - young women living in the king's palace known as flowers of the nation
*umemulo* - coming of age ritual
*imihlalandlini* - permanent palace dwellers
*umhlola* - a bad omen
*imfecane* – internal bloody displacement
*ukukhwabula* – menopause ceremony
*umkhosi* – festival
*umkhosi wokweshwama* - first fruits festival
*umkhosi womhlanga* - reed dance festival
*abamnumzane* - nobility
*imihlalandlini* - permanent palace dwellers
*impi* – war; battle; military member; army; engagement
*impi ebomvu* – total war
*impi kakhandampondo* - poll tax uprising
*ubukhosi* - throne
*ucu* - a string of white enthronement beads
*umuzi* - homestead
*uMvelingqangi* - God
*umyezane* – willow tree
*umdlunkulu* – young maidens living in the king's palaces
*induna* – (plural: izinduna) advisors or officers serving under the king
*ingomane* - a rolling rattle and drumming of a spear shaft beating in rapid succession against a corresponding shield, three times
*inkani* - stubbornness

# Glossary

*inkosi* (*amakhosi*: plural) – king(s)
*inkosi yoselwa* (*amakhosi oselwa*: plural) – rightful king(s)
*insila yenkosi* – the king's body servant
*intelezi* - war herbs
*ontanga yakhe* - peers
*inyosi* - a laudatory praise reciter
*isibhalo* - government tax paid in slave labour
*isibongo* – surname
*isicoco* – maturity head ring for men
*isidwaba* – a female leather skirt
*isifuba* – chest; also part of the pincer movement military formation
*isikhumba* - ox-hide
*ishende* - a married woman's secret lover
*iSilo samabandla onke* - Emperor of kings
*isithembu* - polygamy
*izigxotha* – brass armbands
*Sikhithi* – Mercury, king Shaka's praise name
*utshwala* - a sorghum beer with an alcohol content of less than 5 per cent
*isiphakanyiswa* - an elected chief
*isithakazelo* – one's ancestor's name or family praise name
*isiququmadevu* - (big steaming shell - meaning a ship)
*isiqhwaga* – a bully
*iqhikiza* - an older girl who mentored younger girls
*iqhugwane* - traditional beehive grass hut
*ukungena* (inherit the wife of a deceased brother)
*ukuvusa umuzi* (to carry on the lineage).
*uqhwasha* - home-made firearm
*iviyo* – (plural: *amaviyo*) platoon(s)
*Voortrekkers* - pioneers
*izimbadada* - ox-hide sandals
*izimpondo* – horns, also part of the pincer movement military formation
*ubhaqa* - candle
*udibi* - cadets
*uzwekufa* or *imfecane* - internal bloody displacement
*zinhle izintaba zakwaZulu* - the Zulu mountains are breathtaking

# Glossary

*Shalo Mbatha (author) at the Remembrance Monument of King Dingiswayo Godongwana of the Mthethwa kingdom at oYengweni Palace, in KwaZulu Natal in 2010. She is standing next to the giant granite stone shaped in a Zulu shield.*

*Shalo Mbatha (left) and the owner of the Uitkyk farm in Middleburg, where King Dinuzulu kaCetshwayo was exiled. The farmer shared tales about a legendary treasure secretly buried on the farm by the king. General Louis Botha bought this farm for the Zulu monarch after granting him a pardon as he was found guilty for High Treason in 1910. The king renamed it KwaThengisangaye and lived with his at least seven wives, 37 children (including Crown Prince Maphumuzana), two white nurses from St Helena, cooks, hairdressers, relatives and a full royal retinue. His Majesty died here on the 18th October 1913.*

*Shalo Mbatha, (centre), her daughter Nandi (seated extreme right) and the research team in Middleburg, sharing a good laugh after a long day following a lead on the exact location of the KwaThengisangaye Palace.*

## ABOUT THE AUTHOR

Shalo Mbatha is a royal Zulu historian, journalist and a history lecturer at the University of Zululand, South Africa. She has dedicated 20 years of her life to Zulu history research covering its customs, royal lineage and culture from oral accounts, published and unpublished sources but most important of all, from a Zulu perspective. A body of work that has never been done, let alone from a female historian.

Shalo was born in Soweto to an educated and politically active family. She fled South Africa after the Soweto uprising in 1976, and devoted her life to human rights, black consciousness and Anti-Apartheid resistance in exile. On her return home at the advent of democracy in South Africa, she was burdened by introspection about her Zulu heritage. In her book "Zulu Empire Decolonised" she unfolds the authentic origins and practices of the Zulu nation from pre-colonial times to the 21st century. His Majesty King Zwelithini wrote the Foreword of this book as a seal of authentication and pride.

She is a mother of 2, a grandmother and is currently completing her PhD in Zulu Feminism.

This book is also available in isiZulu.
A signed copy can be ordered from the author, Shalo Mbatha.
WhatsApp: +27 79 260 0149;  Email: info@ilovezuluhistory.com
Website: www.ilovezuluhistory.com

www.ingramcontent.com/pod-product-compliance
Lightning Source LLC
Chambersburg PA
CBHW070334240426
43665CB00045B/1979